THE PLETZL OF PARIS

THE PLETZL OF PARIS

Jewish Immigrant Workers in the Belle Epoque

NANCY L. GREEN

HM
Holmes & Meier
New York   London

First published in the United States of America 1986 by
Holmes & Meier Publishers, Inc.
30 Irving Place
New York, N.Y. 10003

Great Britain:
Holmes & Meier Publishers, Ltd.
Hillview House
One Hallswelle Parade
London NW11 ODL, England

Book design by Ellen Foos

Library of Congress Cataloging in Publication Data

Green, Nancy L.
  The Pletzl of Paris.

  Bibliography: p.
  Includes index.
  1. Jews, East European—France—Paris. 2. Jews—
France—Paris. 3. Jewish trade-unions—France—Paris.
4. Paris (France)—Ethnic relations. I. Title.
DS135.F85P247 1986   305.'.8'924'04436   84-27937
ISBN 0-8419-0995-4

Manufactured in the United States of America

To my parents

Contents

Illustrations

Tables

Acknowledgments

This book would not have been possible without the help and encouragement of Arcadius Kahan and Georges Haupt—two Eastern European Jewish immigrants whose destination points were different (Chicago and Paris) but who both brought with them a cultural cargo of intelligence, critical spirit, and human warmth from which I was grateful to benefit. Their untimely deaths deeply saddened all who knew them.

I would like to thank the directors and personnel of the libraries and archives that proved to be not only places of research but welcome, friendly environments for the immigrant researcher: G. Weill, Y. Levyne, R. Levyne, and A. Doubine of the Alliance Israélite Universelle; K. Vaisbrot of the Bibliothèque Medem; G. Nahon and R. Kohn, formerly of the Consistoire archives; and the late, unforgettable H. Kempinski of the Bund Archives of New York. Without taxing them with any undue responsibility, my sincere thanks also go to Peter Novick, Adam Przeworski, Aristide Zolberg, Arno Mayer, Roger Errera, Alex Derczanski, Claudie Weill, and of course Pierre Bouvier for their critical readings and moral support. I would also like to thank Pearl Kahan, from whom I began to learn Yiddish in Chicago many years ago.

I am also grateful to the George Lurcy Trust, the Memorial Foundation for Jewish Culture, and the National Foundation for Jewish Culture for their financial aid and to all those around the world who lent me word processing equipment through the years. Finally, I would like to thank Max Holmes and Naomi Lipman for their support, editorial advice, and detailed attention in the preparation of this book.

Please note that for the Yiddish transliteration I have followed the YIVO system, modernizing the spelling of words and terms, with the exception of newspaper or book titles, which I have transcribed according to their original spellings. My thanks go to Daniel Soyer for his help in this connection. I take full responsibility for any missing accents in the French.

THE PLETZL OF PARIS

INTRODUCTION

On paraît croire que les juifs sont tous des riches, des banquiers. . . . Et,
pourtant, nous sommes, hélas! le peuple le plus prolétaire du monde.
Letter by Jewish workers, 1898

A specter haunts modern Jewry. It is the specter of the Rothschilds. The
medieval Jewish moneylender has been modernized in anti-Semitic literature
through the Rothschild family's wealth and connections. Yet notions of
Jewish successes in the period since emancipation have not been confined to
anti-Semitic stereotypes alone. Even many quizzical Jewish eyebrows are
raised at the mention of a Jewish proletariat.

It is only in recent years that scholars have turned to the examination of
Jewish workers and of the Jewish labor movements.[1] Prior to that the history
of a people for so long enclosed behind ghetto walls unfortunately often
reflected that isolation. As a minority group, constantly open to attack, the
fact of collective responsibility often implied a united response on behalf of
the entire community. And just as community leaders often minimized internal differences in order to maximize community unity vis-à-vis the non-
Jewish world,[2] an intramural vision of Jewish history, reflecting long
confinement within the ghettos, often obscured the real differentiations—
from court Jews to peddlers—that did exist within those walls and that burst

3

out into the open all the more forcefully with emancipation and the social and economic diversification that followed.

It was the great Jewish historian Simon Dubnow who led the way out of the intramural vision of Jewish history by deemphasizing religious elements and by defining Jewish history as the story of a people held together by a "community of historical fate." (The history itself thus participates in the subject of its inquiry.) Instead of lamenting the Jews' lack of a state, Dubnow exalted the Diaspora, an important first step toward looking more closely at the various conditions pertaining throughout the Diaspora. Jewish history, he wrote, is "most intimately interwoven with world-affairs at every point throughout its whole extent."[3] Salo Baron agreed, noting particularly that the "emancipation era and the integration of the Jewish people into the 'fabric' of the host people" have shown most clearly the interrelation of the Jews to the outer world.[4] He went even further, adding: "An incidental gain of this new approach will be the light which the specific Jewish evolution is able to shed on general history as well . . . from the vantage point of a permanent minority."[5]

Taking Jewish history out of its Jewish historical vacuum has two important effects: the insertion of Jewish diasporic history within the social and economic (and not solely anti-Semitic) history of the host countries; and a closer examination of the social groups making up the Jewish community itself.

Both trends have become apparent in recent years, not only emancipating Jewish history from its own ghetto but shedding light on the different components within the Jewish community.[6] The very definition of Jewish community, as a people sharing a common religious and cultural heritage, has had to give way to an examination of "community" within the context of social and economic factors often objectively dividing that community. That the Jewish people share a common religious and cultural heritage, held together by a "community of historical fate," is undeniable. But that they, as any religiocultural group, do not necessarily share common social, economic, or political identities is also self-evident.

The study herein seeks to further "emancipate" Jewish social history in two ways: by not only examining a specific social group—Jewish immigrant workers—within the social and economic contexts of its place of origin and place of settlement, but by examining the genesis of the Jewish labor movement in Paris as an immigrant labor movement per se. The history of the Jewish immigrant labor movement in Paris is the story of migrant laborers, their particular working conditions, and their response to those conditions. It is not, in my view, primarily a response to the French Jewish community's offerings. While the French Jewish community's attitude toward the immigrant workers has a necessary place in the story of the Jewish immigrant community in Paris, it is rather the social and economic conditions of the workplace that are largely determinant in the development of the immigrant labor movement.

Two trends have generally characterized Jewish migration literature thus far. The first is the study of native-immigrant relationships and the consequences for Jewish community identity that result from the confrontation of assimilated American, English, French, or German Jews with eastern European immigrants.[7] This confrontation has largely been expressed in the struggles over control of community institutions, which reveal as much about the native community in its response to the immigrant challenge as they do about immigrant adaptation. A second characteristic of Jewish migration literature has been the unquestioned acceptance of the specific character of Jewish migrants and particularly the concentration of Jewish migrants in the clothing industries of New York, London, and Paris. The legend of the Jewish tailor, exercising his trade here or there, is thus perpetuated.

I propose a rereading of the modern Jewish migration experience in order to put the immigrant communities and those of them who were in fact tailors, into another perspective. Rather than focusing on the conflict between native and immigrant Jews, I would argue that the Jewish immigrant experience and the Jewish labor movement were instead largely an intra-immigrant affair.[8] My interest is thus in the Jewish immigrants as workers and in their social and economic struggles with their immigrant bosses more than in their political or institutional conflicts with the French Jewish community.

Indeed the studies of the difficult relations between the French Jewish community and the eastern European immigrants have well shown and examined the pitfalls of the very assumption on which they are based: the assumption that the Wandering Jew's first frame of reference is that of the Jewish community in the adopted country. While this first reflex of "Jewish solidarity" cannot be ignored and did shape certain of the parallel institutions created by the immigrants (see chapter 3), the laboring history of the Jewish immigrants was more importantly shaped by the social and economic conditions of late nineteenth-century France.

Jewish migrants were participants in a migration process whose consequences go beyond the Jewish experience. As immigrant workers the Jewish migrants tell us as much about more general aspects of migrant labor as about the particular problems of Jewish migrant laborers. Without denying the specificity of the case under study, which will become clear—and all immigrant groups are by their nature unique—I wish to ask certain general questions concerning immigrant labor in a particular national context.

The eastern European Jewish workers in Paris (like most immigrants) thus stand at a crossroad: a crossroad of Jewish, French, labor, and migration history. The following is a story of Jewish migration; it is the story of a specific case of migration to France, and it is the story of a particular subset of the French labor movement in fin-de-siècle Paris. Within Jewish history, the

Jewish immigrant worker in Paris is perhaps but one more variant on the Wandering Jew. Yet the study of such variants is methodologically important. The image of the Wandering Jew has been the mythological summary of the history of persecutions and migrations of a diasporic people. However, the constant usage of that symbol has too often ignored the particular historical circumstances surrounding those peregrinations. By examining the Jewish migrants more closely, within the social and economic context of sending and receiving countries, the Wandering Jew loses mythological constancy, and a better understanding of particular diasporic conditions is obtained.

Furthermore the Pletzl—the Marais/St. Paul neighborhood of Paris, called "little square" in Yiddish by the Jewish immigrants who lived there—can tell us something about late nineteenth-century French industrialization. The Pletzl was a microcosm of French light industrial development in which certain strengths and weaknesses of the Parisian economy come to light. The Jewish immigrants arrived in Paris at an important moment in the history of French industrialization and at a time when the lack of legal barriers to immigration presaged later explicit immigrant recruitment.[9] Going beyond the facile assumption that Jews are always in the *shmate* (rag or clothing) business, we can see how the actual needs of that industry and the mode of production into which the immigrants would be inserted reflect the nature of the light industrial sector of the Parisian economy and the often uneven development of the French Industrial Revolution.

These conditions would provide the crucial background for the genesis of a Jewish labor movement. In this respect the Jewish immigrants in Paris in many ways synthesized aspects of the strike movements so well described by Ezra Mendelsohn for the Pale of Settlement in Russia and Michelle Perrot for France.[10] The Belle Epoque was clearly not all that "belle" for everyone, and workers would increasingly show their discontent in strike actions and unionization. The Jewish immigrant labor movement thus also provides a case study for that period of labor organizing when there was no such thing as a wildcat strike. Almost all strikes began as spontaneous gestures of grievance, and the growth of trade union sections to channel and strengthen those outbursts is the story of all late nineteenth-century labor organizing.

Finally, this moment in the history of the Jewish Diaspora forms an integral part of migration history in general; ultimately the Jewish migrant must be placed in a more comparative setting from which a theory of labor migration can be constructed. Here too much of the recent migration literature (particularly on the part of sociologists and historians) has examined native-immigrant relations and problems of assimilation and adaptation.[11] Economic studies of labor migration in France and elsewhere have been more revealing of the importance of such migrations for the development of capitalism.[12] Implicit to this study is a belief that the migration of tens and later hundreds of thousands of eastern European Jewish workers to Paris, New

York, London, and Buenos Aires, from the 1880s through the interwar period, forms part and parcel of the history of labor migration in this period. Social and economic conditions in eastern Europe as well as industrial developments in the West form the crucial background for this and other mass movements of peoples. And a study of Jewish workers in the context of the international movement of labor may counterbalance the speculations and castigations to which the international movement of the Rothschilds' capital has been subject!

The story that follows may be broken down into two major parts: those conditions obtaining before migration occurred and the resultant adaptation of the immigrants to Paris. The preexisting structures that must be examined include both those in the old homeland and those in the new. Conditions in eastern Europe, or the forces of emigration or "push" are revealing, particularly with regard to the relationship of economic conditions and anti-Semitism as an important element motivating emigration. The forces of immigration or "pull" are often less explicit, overwhelmed as they are by flight from pogroms. Yet they too are part of the background of migration, constituting the important preexisting conditions in the country of immigration. These forces of immigration can best be studied discretely from the forces of emigration, yet they interact with the latter by providing a feasible destination without which many fewer emigrants would have been likely to embark on such an uncertain journey. Throughout the nineteenth century the most important pull was toward the West and industrial expansion. This was true for France, which also benefited from the favorable image of being the bearer of the Revolution and the first country to have emancipated the Jews.

A negative factor must be added, however. The French Jewish community—that preexisting structure which is assumed to be the primary frame of reference for the immigrants' insertion—was, in fact, due to its own social and economic insertion in France, ill prepared for the arrival of their very foreign coreligionists from the East. The emigration/immigration policy of that community would in many ways aim at discouraging any "pull" rather than encouraging the settlement of the immigrants in Paris.

It is thus within the socioeconomic context rather than the religio-cultural nexus that a more significant pull factor may be identified. The development of French industry and its accompanying labor needs at the end of the nineteenth century, the importance of the light industrial sector in Paris, and the growth of the ready-to-wear industry were all factors helping to provide a destination for the migrants. Increasing foreign competition, the ineradicable seasonal character of the industry, and the putting-out system all encouraged the recruitment of cheaper and more flexible female and immigrant labor. Light industry was thus in many ways an implicit immigration force itself.

Pushed and pulled then, the migrants set out. While Paris was sometimes but a transit point for a further journey westward, approximately thirty-five thousand eastern European immigrants settled in Paris before World War I. With the creation of social and cultural institutions such as religious groups, mutual aid societies, philanthropic, and even political organizations, the immigrants initially adapted to their new environment by a continuity of structures and traditions imported from the old country. An inevitable synthesis of old and new took place, however, and as it did it constituted a response to the lack of corresponding French or French Jewish organizations able to fit the immigrants' needs. The "foreigners'" social structures reveal the specific needs of an immigrant community in what is to them just as "foreign" a new land.

Several sources permit us to sketch a statistical picture of immigrant occupations in Paris that corroborates the implications of the push-pull mechanism. But for the content of that statistical interpretation the artist must focus directly on the workshops themselves. The working conditions under which the immigrants labored, already implicit in the preexisting structure that defined the trades, led to strikes, which revealed the limits of the immigrants' solidarity with their fellow immigrant bosses. Unionization followed, in part due to "imported radicalism" but also due to circumstances arising from Pletzl conditions themselves. Unionization was in turn active in leading new strike actions. The genesis of a Jewish labor movement that resulted took its place as a "national" variant within the French labor movement. The relationship between the Confédération général du travail (C.G.T.) and the Yiddish union sections points to the specific character of the latter and the importance of community in defining the Jewish immigrant workers' movement.

Consequently, within the French labor movement, if not always completely of it, the Jewish immigrants carved out their own trade union structures. Their primary function was to create a solidarity of workers' interests. Additionally, however, another function became apparent: the veritable speaking up—in Yiddish—of the Jewish immigrant workers' community. Strikes, meetings, union sections, and the labor newspaper Der idisher arbayter were all a means of expression for that community that both manifested a certain solidarity and at the same time reinforced it. From the Pale to the Pletzl the path was seldom an easy one. The focus on the Jewish labor movement provides an insight into how some of those immigrants responded forcefully to their condition. Their response was one full of struggle and hope, in a (Yiddish) voice that deserves attention.

One

EMIGRATION AND IMMIGRATION
Push from the East,
Pull from the West

The free movement of peoples across borders—attaining some 43 million people in the nineteenth century, the "century of mass migration"—has been hailed as one of the most basic of human liberties.[1] The "spontaneity" of such movement has been lauded, as has been the audacious and adventuresome spirit of those who undertook the voyage. Yet the image of migration is necessarily a mixed one. The adventuresome explorer or colonizer exists beside the persecuted religious minority or potato-famished farmer. As historians, economists, and sociologists of migration have found, the reality is more complex than those images that have often been elevated to explanatory causes. The migration decision is not a simple one and depends upon interacting factors in both the sending and receiving countries. The "push-pull" mechanism has been largely recognized as an important method for examining the forces of emigration and of immigration comprising any migration movement. Such a double perspective is even more useful when applied not only to political developments encouraging migration but to the social and economic conditions obtaining in both countries as well.

This methodology, successfully employed in so many migration stories, has still met with a certain resistance in the case of migration movements readily explained by one image-cause, e.g., religious persecution. Thus, popular histories of the late-nineteenth century Jewish migration have most often unilaterally linked that migration to one "push" factor: the pogroms in the Russian Empire beginning in the spring of 1881. While the importance of compelling flight in the face of physical violence cannot be questioned, this is only a part of the story, as more recent scholarship has shown.[2] Jewish migration from eastern Europe in the period before World War I must be more closely examined both within the larger sociopolitical and economic context of tsarist Russia and, even more importantly (since it has been considered less), within the social and economic context of the receiving countries. We must necessarily start with the pogroms but go from there to an understanding of what they represented in terms of Russian development. Besides this most forceful "push," the "pull" must be examined as well. Without the availability of certain opportunities in the industrializing West the Jewish migration would have taken on both a different quantitative and qualitative character.

After long months of planning and several previous unsuccessful attempts, the Russian revolutionary group Narodnaya Volya (People's Will) finally hit its mark. On March 1, 1881, Alexander II, Tsar of Russia, was assassinated as he stepped down from his carriage to inspect the damage caused by a first bomb that had not reached its target. The death of the once-"liberal" tsar unleashed a severe repression in Russia that forced the revolutionary groups even farther underground and extended to Russia's Jews, who were blamed as the instigators of the political unrest. In the pogroms that followed, the Jews were made the scapegoats for Russia's political and economic difficulties.

Pogroms spread throughout southern Russia and the Ukraine during the rest of 1881 and into 1882 while the police and troops stood idly by, often accomplices to or even instigators of the destruction. Government and police printing presses were later found to have been the origin of not a few of the incendiary leaflets. While the richer Jews were generally able to bribe their way to police protection, the poor Jewish neighborhoods were the ones most directly afflicted. The government blamed the pogroms on the revolutionaries but also held the Jews responsible for their own fate because of their alleged exploitation of the peasants. While some elements of the Narodnaya Volya at first hailed the pogroms as the beginning of a peasant revolt, the government's role in encouraging this violent anti-Semitism as a distraction from any potential, real revolutionary activity soon became clear.[3]

Physical violence against the Jews continued into the spring of 1882 when the May Laws (Ignatiev's Rules) were enacted. These "legislative pogroms" were issued the same day as a circular against (physical) pogroms and reflected the government's concern over the bad press that had been created worldwide by the violent anti-Semitism in Russia. With the institution of these "dry" pogroms, violence was no longer necessary, for anti-Semitism was now cloaked in legality. Ignatiev's Rules prohibited the Jews from settling "anew" in rural areas, inhibited their purchase of property and merchandise, and forbade their doing business on Sundays or Christian holidays. Approximately five hundred thousand Jews in rural areas within the Pale of Settlement were thus forced to move to the larger towns or cities while the May Laws and their successors further sought to reduce the categories of "privileged" Jews that had been extended under the early reforms of Alexander II. Most notably, secondary education was restricted through a *numerus clausus* (percentage norm) in 1887, and the legal profession and law schools were closed to the Jews in 1889.

From 1884 until the end of the decade overt violence against the Jews abated, only to be renewed in the early 1890s. Over twenty thousand Jews were expelled from Moscow in 1891. By 1893 approximately 1½ million Jews had been uprooted through governmental decrees: from outside the Pale to within it, and from small *shtetlekh* (villages) within the Pale to larger towns and cities.

In 1903 a pogrom occurred in Kishinev, which was not only aided by police and troops but seems to have been instigated with the full knowledge of the lieutenant governor of the province. The Kishinev pogrom touched off similar violence in many other cities. In 1904, with the outbreak of the Russo-Japanese War and Russian defeats at the battlefront, anti-Semitism was stirred up again. Government propaganda depicted the Jews as traitors secretly helping their "kinsmen by race," the Japanese![4] At the same time, mobilized reservists anxious about going off to war set off so-called mobilization pogroms.

Again in 1905, after the October Manifesto, imperial vengeance was vented on the Jews. No longer castigated as "exploiters," the Jews were now decried as dangerous revolutionaries and became the target, along with hundreds of bourgeois liberals, of the government's counterrevolutionary strategy. Then, from 1911 to 1913, Mendel Beilis was brought to trial on trumped-up charges of ritual murder. The worldwide condemnation that this provoked did not, however, prevent the trial from serving as a new pretext for actions against the Jews.

These dates mark only some of the worst and most virulent expressions of anti-Semitism in Russia. From 1881 until the overthrow of the tsarist regime in 1917 Tsars Alexander III and Nicholas II often subsidized and otherwise encouraged anti-Semitic propaganda and pogroms. Russia was not alone in this anti-Semitic policy; similar events occurred in other eastern European countries. In Hungary a ritual-murder trial took place in Tisza Essler in 1882. In Rumania, where many Jews had taken refuge earlier in the century from Nicholas I's conscription policies and later after their expulsion from Odessa, Jews were refused citizenship. Massacres occurred there in 1895 and systematic persecution began in 1899. Long oppressed by other nations, Rumania in turn took vengeance on the Jews.

In the face of these atrocities, the Jewish exodus from eastern Europe at the end of the nineteenth century is not difficult to understand. While from 1800 to 1880 approximately 250,000 Jews left eastern Europe, from 1881 to 1900 approximately 1 million left their homes, and between 1901 and 1914 nearly 2 million emigrated.[5] Jews from the Russian Empire alone accounted for roughly two-thirds of the emigration. By 1925 over 3½ million Jews had left eastern Europe, heading primarily for the United States and Canada (2,650,000 and 112,000), England (210,000), Argentina (150,000), and France (100,000).[6]

The reasons for emigration, the force that motivated such a mass uprooting, seem almost so evident in retrospect as to preclude more discussion. However, the participants in this mass dislocation did not have the advantage of historical hindsight when making their move. In fact only 19.6 percent of the Jews in Rumania, 17.3 percent of those in Russia, and 9.6 percent of the Jewish community in Austria-Hungary emigrated in the years 1881 through 1914.[7]

The factors encouraging emigration, and the particular role of anti-Semitism in the enforced wanderings of the Jews, must be examined more closely in order to penetrate the "push" that caused millions to embark on voyages that meant temporary if not permanent separation from family, friends, and tradition. It is to late nineteenth-century Russian social and economic history that we must turn to better understand the context of that emigration.

The relative tardiness of Russian (and eastern European in general) industrialization and the tensions created through its uneven development go far toward explaining both the anti-Semitism and emigration that were part of their results. The transition of the Russian economy from a feudal to a capitalist basis took a major step forward on February 17, 1861, the date when Alexander II signed the law freeing the serfs. This gesture, symbolic of the tsar's early liberalism and desire for "modernization," was part of a program of belated and incomplete agricultural reforms, which, along with the development of the railroad in the 1860s and 70s, would gradually transform the Russian economy. The railroads enabled the agricultural sector to become more market- and cash-oriented while aiding the mobility of the newly freed peasants. Many of the latter moved toward the cities in search of work (especially during periods of agricultural crises in the 1880s and in 1891), and there they provided the cheap labor needed for the newly developing industries. The emergence of large-scale commercial and industrial centers brought with it the growth of both an indigenous commercial and industrial bourgeoisie and an incipient proletariat.

With the uprising of Congress Poland in 1863, the tsar's liberal facade was quickly dropped in favor of a retreat to reaction. Interpreting the revolt as a consequence of the very Westernization he had attempted to introduce,

Alexander abandoned many of his reforms, while repression, in large part aimed at the Jews, was swift. A very first emigration wave of Jews as well as Poles dates to this period, augmented by the great famine and epidemic in 1868–69.

The continuing strains and tensions caused by the inexorable yet slow-paced and uneven urbanization and industrialization were punctuated by specific years of crises (the Russo-Turkish War of 1878; the economic crisis of the 1880s; crop failures and famine in 1890–91; the Russo-Japanese War of 1904). Poor harvests, famine, and often cholera epidemics exacerbated the difficulties of the still overwhelmingly agricultural economy, and whenever rural crises hit they reverberated to the incipient industrial sector. At the same time a wary landowning and church-based ruling class increasingly feared the full consequences of change to an industrial-based economy.

The growing pains of Russia's clumsy advance toward industrialization, exacerbated by the sometimes capricious whims of her tsar and his advisers, resulted in two strongly negative responses: revolutionary activism and emigration. The former would eventually succeed in assassinating not just one tsar but the regime itself, while the latter, in the meantime, was an outlet for the discontent of many others.

The dislocation of people from the land, pushed by famine and poor harvests, attracted to the cities in hopes of better conditions, or in the case of the Jews, uprooted by governmental decree, jolted many into seeking a further emigration. After the move from the countryside to the city, where expectations were not always fulfilled, the next move, perhaps even transatlantic, was easier to make. In the period from 1871 to 1914, while 1,567,600 Jews emigrated to the United States from tsarist Russia, a greater number of non-Jews, 1,725,300, also did so, while over 3 million Russian peasants migrated to Siberia.[8] Although the Jewish emigration was much greater in relation to its base population than was that of the non-Jewish population (approximately 13.6 percent of the Jewish population left Russia in the years 1899 to 1914 as compared to 4 percent to 5 percent of the Lithuanian, Finnish, German, and Polish populations of Russia), it is nonetheless important to place the Jewish exodus in this context of emigration from Russia as a whole.[9] The disequilibrium of the urbanization and industrialization process, interlaced with selective repression, resulted in the emigration from the empire of not only the Jews but of many other of Russia's minority and starving populations.

This period of economic and social change and unrest is the essential context in which to place the Jewish emigration. The tensions of this transition period, which created the "push" behind that emigration, had two particular effects on the Jews: They gave a particular character to tsarist anti-Semitism, and they affected the economic functions specific to the Jewish community.

TSARIST ANTI-SEMITISM

Anti-Semitism was used by the tsarist regime as both an economic and ideological weapon. Anti-Semitism in Russia had certainly existed before the rise of industrial capitalism. But its renewed virulence and official propaga- tion at the end of the nineteenth century coincided with the tensions occur- ring between the newly developing forces of production and the existing property relations. In the period of social unrest that followed the assassina- tion of Alexander II the Jews were a facile target for three different groups: the declining feudal gentry and the rising commercial bourgeosie, as well as the tsarist regime.

The anti-Semitism of the first was expressed in the May Law provisions, which prohibited the Jews from settling "anew" in rural areas, thus pushing the Jews from the countryside, where they had often functioned as inter- mediaries between peasant and landlord. Somewhat ironically, as the Jews became increasingly urbanized due to the same forces that were leading to the feudal lord's demise, they came to represent more and more the urban ele- ment against which the latter was protesting. At the same time, the exclu- sion of the Jews from the purchase of certain merchandise and property, the prohibition on doing business on Sundays and Christian holidays, along with the numerus clausus, which essentially blocked Jews from professional careers, were all examples of a protectionism in favor of the developing indigenous bourgeoisie.

The economic bases of anti-Semitism were revealed in such legislation and even in the origins of several pogroms (the jealousy of Russian merchants at the start of the Starodub pogrom of 1891; animosities between financiers at the origin of the expulsions from Moscow). Yet this form of hostility against the Jews was neither all-pervading nor impervious to exceptions. The use of anti-Semitism by the tsarist regime revealed an important characteristic of anti-Semitism, one that only further betrays its relation to economic change. That is the arbitrariness that permits the use of "exceptions" as the need arises.

Thus when physiocratic theories were in favor that argued that the Jews could be made more "productive" through agricultural colonization, restric- tions that had kept Jews from the land were lifted. Later, however, under Alexander II's plans for industrialization, "productivity" of the Jews was en- couraged through urbanization and the granting of privileges to certain cate- gories—top-level merchants belonging to the "first guild," skilled artisans, and educated Jews—who were allowed to move into the Russian interior. The Pahlen Commission of 1883–86 (whose report was never published, however) even argued against anti-Semitism on specifically economic grounds, pointing to the Jews' particular role in the economy. Entrepreneurs were given rein to create factories, and prominent Jewish financiers and railroad or sugar tycoons were exempt from all anti-Semitic legislation and allowed to move about freely outside of the Pale. In some areas the May Laws remained unenforced for almost a decade, and it was not until the early 1890s, when poor harvests, famine, and an economic crisis swept the empire, that full and often overzealous implementation of those decrees again took place. Yet then again, as the crisis worsened in 1893, Alexander III halted expulsions of the Jews, recognizing their importance to the rural economy. With the strong upswing in the economy from 1893 on, anti-Semitic outbursts died down and emigration also declined. The use of selective anti-Semitism as linked to the perception of economic utility was thus often a crucial determinant with regard to the status of the Jews.

While arbitrary interpretation of anti-Semitic decrees may have sometimes worked in favor of the Jews, more often than not the Jews became the sacrificial scapegoats for economic and social change. Anti-Semitic arguments led not only to specifically economic forms of restrictive laws, but also to a more pervasive ideology, which provided an outlet for tensions while obfuscating their real causes. It was not difficult to stir up peasant hatred against the Jewish middleman, the most conspicuous symbol of exploitation of the peasant by the landlord in feudal Russia. The tsarist regime thus had a ready diversionary tactic able to deflect potentially dangerous unrest from itself toward a very visible and vulnerable minority. The revolutionary movement was discredited by associating it with the Jews and vice versa. With the adjunction of religious and racial (Slavophilic) motifs, anti-Semitism ensured a ready outlet for discontent on several levels.

The economic and diversionary functions of anti-Semitism were not the only result of the growing pains and strains of tsarist modernization that led to Jewish emigration. Another aspect of late nineteenth-century Russian industrialization that contributed directly to the departure of millions of Russian Jews was the declining economic base of the Jewish community. While the anti-Semitic legislation worsened every aspect of the change, the transition from a feudal to an industrial economy had a specific effect on the traditional bases of the Jewish economy. The consequence was a powerful stimulus to emigration.

ECONOMIC CHANGE WITHIN THE PALE

The most significant factor in the economic history of the Jews in Russia from 1794 on was the Pale of Settlement (see Map 1). In that year Catherine the Great decided to solve the "Jewish problem" (inherited by her in 1772 with the first and then subsequent partitions of Poland and not settled, as it had been hoped, through conversions and assimilation) by confining the Jews to several western provinces.[10] In 1835 Nicholas I constricted and established

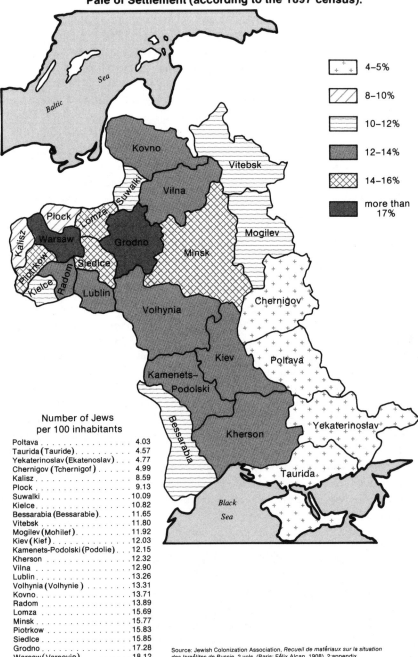

Map 1. Pale of Settlement: Density of Jewish Population in proportion to total population of Poland and the Pale of Settlement (according to the 1897 census).

+ +	4–5%
////	8–10%
≡	10–12%
▦	12–14%
▨	14–16%
■	more than 17%

Baltic Sea

Kovno

Vitebsk

Suwalki

Vilna

Plock

Lomza

Mogilev

Kalisz

Warsaw

Grodno

Minsk

Piotrkow

Siedlce

Radom

Kielce

Lublin

Volhynia

Chernigov

Kiev

Poltava

Kamenets–Podolski

Bessarabia

Yekaterinoslav

Kherson

Taurida

Black Sea

Number of Jews per 100 inhabitants

Poltava	4.03
Taurida (Tauride)	4.57
Yekaterinoslav (Ekatenoslav)	4.77
Chernigov (Tchernigof)	4.99
Kalisz	8.59
Plock	9.13
Suwalki	10.09
Kielce	10.82
Bessarabia (Bessarabie)	11.65
Vitebsk	11.80
Mogilev (Mohilef)	11.92
Kiev (Kief)	12.03
Kamenets-Podolski (Podolie)	12.15
Kherson	12.32
Vilna	12.90
Lublin	13.26
Volhynia (Volhynie)	13.31
Kovno	13.71
Radom	13.89
Lomza	15.69
Minsk	15.77
Piotrkow	15.83
Siedlce	15.85
Grodno	17.28
Warsaw (Varsovie)	18.12

Source: Jewish Colonization Association, *Recueil de matériaux sur la situation des Israélites de Russie*, 2 vols. (Paris: Félix Alcan, 1908), 2:appendix.

16

the definitive boundaries of the Pale. From that time until 1917, the restricted mobility imposed on the Jews in the form of the Pale became a synonym for the deteriorating economic conditions of the Jews in Russia.

The disastrous consequence of the containment of the Jews within the Pale came not only from the overpopulation and lack of suitable markets within a confined area but from the Pale's relation to Russia's late nineteenth-century modernization. The Pale was excluded from the more dynamic centers of economic change just as the need for economic differentiation within the Jewish community became more and more crucial.

The Jewish population of the Pale rose from 1 million at the beginning of the nineteenth century to approximately 5½ million by the end. The situation was described vividly by one commentator in the late 1800s: "The Jews are crowded together more like salted herrings than like human beings."[11] The overpopulation of the Pale was due not to a higher birthrate than the rest of the Russian population but to a lower death rate (especially infant mortality). Furthermore, the various "resettlement" programs of the tsars imported more and more Jews into a smaller and smaller area. While internal Jewish migration toward new centers in the south of the Pale, such as Odessa and Yekaterinoslav, were of some help, this was not sufficient to alleviate the overcrowding, especially of the northwest provinces.

The social and economic function of the Jews in preindustrial Russia was described by Marx as existing in the "interstices" or the "pores of Polish society."[12] The Jews had moved into (had in fact been invited into) those sectors of the feudal economy all over Europe where labor and capital were scarce. They became primarily connected with the sale and, more so in eastern than in western Europe, with the production of consumer goods and services. While restricted from owning land themselves, the Jews in eastern Europe were nevertheless closely bound up with the rural economy, largely supplying the meager needs of the peasant households. As landlords' agents, as itinerant rural merchants for marketable surpluses of agricultural products (grains, wool, etc.), as innkeepers (distilling perishable grain into alcoholic beverages), and as producers of inexpensive clothing for the peasant population, the Jews and their rural clientele were interdependent. The percentage of Jews producing solely for the internal Jewish market (kosher food, religious articles, etc.) has been estimated at only 10 percent.[13]

The effects of industrialization at the end of the nineteenth century therefore affected the Jews in the Pale to the same extent that they affected the agricultural economy as a whole. There were some positive factors. The development of transportation networks linking the fields to a wider, cash, market, helped raise the consumption level of the rural communities. For the Jews, this meant a growing local market, while transportation advances also opened up wider, long-distance markets for their products. If the Jews themselves could not travel outside of the Pale, their goods could. As the standard of living all over Russia and even in the Pale improved with the spread of industrialization, so did that of at least some of the Jews.

In general, however, the agricultural sector was on the decline, and the Pale remained outside the main centers of industrialization and economic opportunity. Urban centers grew in inverse relation to the slow demise of the once economically, socially, and culturally important rural fairs and market towns that had been the hub of the Jews' goods distribution network, and the dependence of the Jews on the rural economy meant that Jewish emigration would be highly correlated with agricultural crises.[14] So, like their peasant clientele, Jews were affected by urbanization, pushed by famine years, and pulled by urban opportunities, with government measures, however, hastening this first emigration for the Jews. By 1898, whereas cities and larger rural towns (*miestechki*) represented 22 percent of the Pale's Russian population, 78 percent of the Jewish population of the Pale was concentrated in them.[15]

The real meaning of urbanization for the Russian Jews was in the changes it portended for the economic stratification of the Jewish community. The distinctive structure of Jewish employment in the Pale at the turn of the century (Table 1a) is noteworthy in several respects: (1) the low number of Jews involved in agriculture; (2) the low number involved in heavy industry; (3) the decline of Jewish merchants in comparison with the beginning of the century; and, by contrast, (4) the increasing number of artisans and their overwhelming concentration in consumer goods, more specifically in the needle trades.

The low number of Jews involved in agricultural pursuits was clearly the most significant factor distinguishing them from the non-Jewish population. While the Jews' dependence on the agricultural economy was great, their direct participation in working the land was very low. (Sixty-three and two-tenths percent of the Russian population was in agriculture as compared to only 2.9 percent of the Jewish population.[16])

Few Jews were involved in the process of industrial concentration and mechanization, either. Of the mere 2.2 percent of the Jews counted as participating in heavy industry, this included the few big railroad financiers, sugar magnates, and other privileged Jews. A good indication of the Pale's existence "beyond the pale" of Russian industrialization is that while the average factory size for all of Russia at the turn of the century was seventy-three persons, in the Pale the average "factory" only employed twenty-eight persons.[17] Whereas 69 percent of the non-Jewish factories in the Polish (Vistula) provinces were mechanized, only 27.3 percent of the Jewish factories were.[18] Thus where "Jewish" industrialization did occur, it was characterized by smaller and more technically backward enterprises.

To the extent that capital and labor concentration did have an impact on the Jewish economy, this occurred primarily within the light industrial sector, where capital investment was less and where Jews had long specialized

TABLE 1

OCCUPATIONS OF JEWS IN EASTERN EUROPE

a - Pale of Settlement, 1897

Agriculture	2.9%[a]	2.5%[b]	1.9%[c]
Mining & Manufacturing (Artisans)	37.9	37.6	38.2
Commerce	32.0	32.1	47.5
Transport	3.3	3.2	
Laborers			7.6
Personal Services	18.8		
Heavy Industry			2.2
Professional Services	5.1	4.9	2.6
Other		19.7	
Total	100.0%	100.0%	100.0%
	(N=1,332,000)	(N=1,477,542)	(N=1,115,000)

b - Rumania, 1913		c - Galicia, 1900	
Agriculture	3.3%[d]	Agriculture	17.6%[e]
Industry & Crafts	38.9	Industry & Crafts	18.7
Trade & Transport	48.1	Trade & Credit	36.4
		Transport	1.9
Services & Liberal Professions	3.3	Services & Liberal Professions	5.4
Servants & Laborers	1.3		
Other & Occupationless	5.1	Other & Occupationless	20.0
Total	100.0%	Total	100.0%
	(N=316,578)		(N=273,129)

[a]Simon Kuznets, "Immigration of Russian Jews to the United States: Background and Structure," Perspectives in American History 10 (1976): 73.

[b]Derived (figures for Russia and Poland combined) from Jacob Lestschinsky, ed., Shriftn far ekonomik un statistik, 2 vols. (Berlin: YIVO, 1928), 1:43.

[c]Elie Eberlin and Georges Delahache, "Juifs Russes," Cahiers de la quinzaine, 6th ser., no. 6, December 1904. Eberlin and Delahache's combined category of "Merchants, intermediaries and persons of indeterminate occupations" has been listed here under "Commerce."

[d]Lestschinsky, 1:36.

[e]Ibid., 1:43.

in consumer goods. The consumer industries in which Jewish factories were most predominant reflected: expansion of the more traditional areas of Jewish activity, such as textiles, ready-to-wear clothes, and especially shoes and tanning; taking advantage of a growing industry, such as bristlemaking; as well as development of new industries where there was little preexisting competition, such as in the tobacco industry, the stocking-knitters' industry, and so forth.[19]

Aside from the cigarette factories, in which Jewish (mostly female) workers were in the majority, the creation of factories by Jewish manufacturers did not assure an increased number of new jobs for Jewish workers. Jewish as well as non-Jewish entrepreneurs discriminated in favor of non-Jewish labor, preferring more skilled German or Polish laborers or the less skilled, but cheaper, Russian peasantry. The explanation most often given by Jewish employers was that gentile laborers were not averse to working on the Jewish Sabbath, and that they were generally less demanding than the Jewish workers, little known for their docility. Some Jewish entrepreneurs did not want to be responsible for Jewish workers working on the Sabbath; others felt that "proper" employer-employee relationships were not possible with their coreligionists as workers![20]

The most significant change that occurred within the occupational structure of the Jewish community in the Pale during the nineteenth century, however, was the decline of commercial activity in favor of manual, artisanal manufacture. Some estimates claim that trade activities occupied as much as 86 percent of the Jewish population in the early nineteenth century before dropping to "only" 32 percent of the working population by 1897.[21] While over 76 percent of all commerce in the Pale was still handled by the Jews at the end of the century, relative to the Jewish community itself, involvement in commerce had dropped remarkably.[22] In any case, apart from the privileged import-exporters or large-scale dealers in agricultural products, commercial activity most often meant the numerous shopkeepers, itinerant salesmen, or even petty smugglers who "devour each other through competition."[23] Artisans, as will be seen below, suffered from the same condition.

Werner Cahnman has described the growth of the Jewish artisanal class as follows:

> Especially where economic conditions deteriorated within the Jewish group while at the same time its numbers were swelling, did a large Jewish artisanal class come into existence. . . . The size of a Jewish artisan class stands in direct proportion to the size of a Jewish community, but in inverse proportion to its prosperity.[24]

In central and eastern Europe, the spread of handicrafts among Jews gained momentum from the middle of the sixteenth century onward. It has been estimated that by the end of the eighteenth century at least one-third of the Jewish working population in eastern Europe was involved in manual trades.[25]

The wide variety of skills represented by the Jewish artisans—from tailors to blacksmiths, from jewelers to joiners—must be emphasized (see Table 2), although this fact is generally overshadowed by the important concentration of clothing workers.[26] Tailors, dressmakers, shoemakers, seamstresses, and hatters accounted for 47 percent of the Jewish artisans. Yet their working conditions were similar to those of the mass of Jewish workers in whatever branch of light industry. Ezra Mendelsohn calls these workers a "Jewish proletariat" (a term also used by contemporary observers at the turn of the century) which was "overwhelmingly a proletariat of artisans," while Salo Baron speaks of the "industrial Jewish proletariat" and the transformation of "independent artisans" into "homeworkers" or "factory laborers."[27] All of these terms reflect the position of the artisanal worker in the transitional period of developing industrialization.

The Jewish Colonization Association, in its report on the economic conditions of the Jews in Russia at the turn of the century, lamented the difficulties facing the Jewish artisans: lack of credit, poor-quality goods, garnering only low prices due to competition among artisans, and a lack of technical training.[28] Finally, the clientele was blamed: The peasant clientele in the countryside or the ready-to-wear market in the cities was seen as creating a demand for cheap clothes and thus low quality.

The poor remuneration for their products and the difficult economic and working conditions under which the mass of Jewish workers labored all resulted in a misery that speaks out forcefully even through the driest of statistics in the Jewish Colonization Association's report. The association concluded that all of the various restrictions on the Jews had led them to "cling on desperately to those métiers condemned to perish."[29] Or, as the Pahlen Commission report stated:

> About ninety per cent of the whole Jewish population form a mass of people that are entirely unprovided for, and come near being a proletariat—a mass that lives from hand to mouth, amidst poverty, and most oppressive sanitary and general conditions.[30]

Thus although economic expansion was occurring outside the Pale, mobility restrictions, exclusion from the newly growing economic sectors (e.g., the civil service, transportation, heavy industry), and increasing pressures to leave their old commercial functions all had serious consequences for the Jewish masses in the Pale. They crowded more and more into the overburdened artisanal trades, and ultimately were affected by Russia's "industrial revolution" more by their exclusion from it and their containment in an area of economic decline than anything else. The consequent push this gave to

TABLE 2

JEWISH ARTISANS IN EASTERN EUROPE

	Pale[a]	Rumania[b]
Clothing & wearing apparel	38.7%	54.7%
Leather goods	17.0	3.3
Food products	11.6	7.7
Wood products	9.9	7.4
Construction and ceramics	6.3	7.3
Crude metals	5.7	9.6
Finer metals	4.1	
Textiles	3.7	5.9
Paper, Cardboard, and Printing	2.3	2.1
Chemicals	0.7	
Other		2.0
Total	100.0%	100.0%
	(N=500,986)[c]	(N=17,505)

Trades Representing 3% or More of Jewish Artisans[d]

Tailors	19.1
Shoemakers	14.4
Dressmakers	6.5
Joiners	6.0
Bakers	4.6
Butchers	4.4
Seamstresses	3.8
Hatters	3.2
Blacksmiths	3.1
(Total	65.1%)

[a]Jewish Colonization Association, Recueil de matériaux sur la situ-ation économique des Israélites de Russie, 2 vols. (Paris: Félix Alcan, 1906-8), 1:241 and 2:Table 41.

[b]Jacob Lestschinsky, ed., Shriftn far ekonomik un statistik, 2 vols. (Berlin: YIVO, 1928), 1:54.

[c]Ibid., A. Menes, "Di yidishe industrye-bafelkerung in Rusland 1897," 1:256, criticized the Jewish Colonization Association report for under-estimating the number of Jews in this category (of "industries and crafts") by about 80-90,000.

[d]Jewish Colonization Association, 1:243.

emigration becomes evident. Similar factors, with some variation, also obtained in Rumania and Galicia, two other areas of important emigration in the pre–World War I period.[31]

In examining the changing socioeconomic structures of late nineteenth-century eastern Europe, the conclusion is therefore apparent that while the physical anti-Semitic manifestations of those changes may clearly account for the peaks of the exodus wave, it was the underlying economic conditions that presupposed and prepared the emigration. "Even without persecutions and restrictions the Jewish minority could hardly have escaped dislocation and economic strain and the inducement to migrate overseas would have existed."[32] As Dubnow said, they were "gasping for breath."

This situation and the particular economic stratification of the Jews in the Pale gave the emigration its particular character.[33] The emigrant population consisted of a higher proportion of males, a lower proportion of females, and a lower proportion of children and the aged than the base population of Jews in Russia.[34] This higher ratio of men to women (contrary to most settled populations) and lower percentage of economically inactive persons conform to the typical pattern of any group having emigrated primarily in search of work.

The occupational structure of the emigrants is even more revealing. As Simon Kuznets has shown in comparing emigrants' occupations to those of the base Jewish population in Russia, it was largely skilled laborers who emigrated.[35] Whereas 37.7 percent of the Jews in the Pale were skilled artisans according to the census of 1897, 64 percent of those who emigrated to the United States between 1899 and 1914 declared themselves in this category. On the other hand, only 5.5 percent of the emigrants were in commerce as compared to the 32 percent of the Jews in Russia discussed above. The two important tendencies already observed with regard to the late nineteenth-century occupational structure of the Pale were therefore accentuated in the emigration process: the declining importance of commercial activity and the rising number of skilled laborers. The high concentration of Jewish workers in the artisanal manufacturing sector of the Pale economy created its own push toward emigration, evident in the overrepresentation of this group within the departing population.

The emigration process encouraged this selectivity. Those with some amount of capital investment were less likely to leave than others whose only assets were an easily transportable skill. The overrepresentation of clothing workers among the emigrants confirms the analysis that outmigration occurred from those trades that were overburdened in the Pale. Fifty-two and two-tenths percent of the skilled emigrants were clothing workers, compared to 37.6 percent of the skilled workers in the Pale.[36] It is thus not just the dates of emigration but its specific socioeconomic character that is important for understanding the emigrants and the "push" that caused their departure. The transformations in Russia's economy and society, skewed and exacerbated within the Pale, would have necessarily created a distinctive pattern to the Jewish emigration. This would, as we will see, find its counterpart in the "pull" of immigration.

Not everyone left, however. Particularly in its first stages, emigration was a journey into the unknown, and, as Simon Dubnow argued at the time, in the long run it was no answer for the vast masses.[37] For growing numbers, however, feelings of insecurity within Russia outweighed their uncertainty over what emigration might bring. And perhaps a certain psychological makeup helped select those who actually made the difficult move. As one immigrants' son described his parents' departure:

> I can write without falsehood that my parents fled from the police repression of 1905. This, however, was only incidental; they fled from their families, from nineteenth-century morality, from fanaticism and bigotry, and to a certain extent, they fled from themselves.[38]

Emigration must therefore also be understood within the context of the already declining religious and secular power of the Jewish community in the East. If industrialization was not allowed to enter the Pale, secular education was. As part of their Westernization policies the tsars encouraged the spread of Jewish Enlightenment ideas within the Pale, but as a result dissatisfaction within the community grew parallel to dissatisfaction with the tsarist regime.[39] Some community members expressed their discontent through emigration, of which many community leaders and orthodox Jews disapproved. For the latter, emigration was considered tantamount to renunciation of the faith, and those who left were discredited as going into "Babylon." ("Young man, I have seen people eating frogs, cats, snails and all sorts of filth" in Paris, complained one religious Jew.[40])

But it was for exactly such reasons that many chose to leave.[41] The decline of community unity on all levels—economic and social as well as religious—helped open up the possibility of departure, and emigration thus became a flight from what was perceived as a parochially and economically confining milieu. Materially, emigration also became easier. Improved and cheaper transportation of the late nineteenth century lessened the real costs of emigration while various immigrant aid organizations that sprang up helped lessen the emotional costs involved. Furthermore, frontiers before World War I were relatively open, and no formidable legal barriers to emigration existed. And as reports on conditions in the West filtered back through letters and articles, the unknown element in the uprooting process was slowly demystified. The emigration movement began to multiply under its own weight. Children even played at emigrating, an important reflection of actions in the adult world.

While the conditions described above were the general background upon which emigration took place, for any individual the determinating incentive may have been a more precise factor. Many simply followed relatives who had already moved. Large numbers of students left Russia when confronted with the numerus clausus limiting their entry into Russian universities.[42] Emigration to avoid the tsar's military service (especially during the Russo-Japanese War of 1904–5) was another very important impetus. And the exile of numerous trade union and political leaders after 1905 would be a significant factor in the makeup of the immigrant community in Paris and elsewhere.

But it was largely as workers that hundreds of thousands of eastern European Jews emigrated. The social and economic history of late nineteenth-century Russia, with its changing socioeconomic substructure, in itself explains the departure of breadwinners and their families. At the same time, anti-Semitism on the part of the tsarist regime on the one hand and the progressive disunity of the Jewish community on the other were both ideological expressions of that changing substructure. All of these factors added their force to the push of emigration, sending workers, students, and revolutionaries alike over the border.

The study of the forces of emigration is important, for one can never dissociate immigrants in a new land from their past. Before they were immigrants they were emigrants, and before that, they were an integral part of a given environment which shaped their actions and thoughts. It is by understanding that environment and by understanding the reasons for emigration that the attitudes and actions once immigrated may be better situated.

Yet understanding the "push" is only half of the migration process. Its complementarity with the "pull," the force of immigration, is crucial for understanding the whole. The Jews were neither the only people to leave Russia nor the only ones to leave Europe. Emigration from Russia and western Europe in the nineteenth century was an integral part of the development of capitalism. The movement from rural areas to urban areas and the exportation of manpower from Europe to the little-populated lands of the Americas, or from eastern to western Europe, was a consequence of the industrial and capitalist revolution of which the Jews were only one part. This congruency of forces of immigration with forces of emigration must be explored.

THE PULL OF THE WEST AND FRANCE'S APPEAL

Immigration is a discrete choice from emigration, although the two merged in the massive flow westward of eastern European Jewish emigrants from the 1880s on. In effect the choice of where to immigrate and the pull that the country of immigration exerts on potential emigrants may itself prompt emigration.[43] With the forces of *emigration* constant, both the qualitative and quantitative aspects of any emigration will vary depending on the forces of immigration involved.

The immigrants came by the hundreds of thousands from eastern Europe. Seeking civic liberty and the right to work, it was not just chance that sent the emigrants to the countries where they settled. There were other areas of the globe where their freedom would not have been fettered. But not everywhere was there work. Those countries to which the emigrants migrated were the industrialized and industrializing countries of the West, whose force of attraction, whose pull on the emigrants, too often overlooked, must be made explicit.

The most direct form of pull on the potential emigrants came from those who had already emigrated. After the first adventurous souls had taken off into the unknown, the paths were then traced for those who followed. Letters, money enclosures, or even prepaid ship or train tickets sent by those already settled in the West were the most direct of all pulls in that direction. Newspapers and the occasional well-dressed returnee who maybe exaggerated just a bit about the benefits of emigration also had their part to play in publicizing the West's virtues. A husband, a sister, the address of a friend, a neighbor, or a cousin of a friend of the butcher, or even rumors that philanthropic agencies would assure passage to America gave the movement its destination, thus encouraging the emigration act itself.

While the individual choice of where to immigrate and the effect this had on the decision to emigrate certainly varied widely from one person to another, it is the aggregate immigration decision that is of interest here insofar as it reflects a general direction—to the West. The socioeconomic underpinnings of that choice and the specific attractions that any particular country, in this case France, had to offer are necessary for understanding the migration act. The migration of the eastern European Jews at the turn of the century was not only a result of a deteriorating economic and political situation pushing them from the East, but must be seen as part of a larger migration pattern that has its roots within the history of the Industrial Revolution of the West.

For the first time since the Diaspora had sent the Jews from the Mediterranean basin northwestward and then eastward, the Jewish migration turned again westward in the nineteenth century. In this the Jews were not alone. Over the nineteenth century 17 million English, 7 million Germans, and 6 million Italians along with 4 million Jews (1830–1925) went westward toward industrial progress, helping balance the labor needs of expanding capitalism.[44] While the forceful push given to the Jews in the form of anti-Semitism caused their emigration to be proportionately much greater with relation to their base population than for any other group, if the emigration had not been accompanied by the continuing economic expansion of the West, the Jewish migration would have never been as great as it was.

"The streets in America are paved with gold." Through this myth the economic strength of the West was expressed, and with each transfer payment of Western "riches," however small, back to the homeland, that myth was sustained. Although the immigrant laborers became quickly aware of the reality of the hard, unglittering pavement that was their new lot, the labor needs of industrial expansion nonetheless offered opportunities that were not available to the Jews in the Pale. Immigration to those centers of dynamic economic activity was such an obvious, almost osmotic, path for the emigrants that its significance has too often been passed over in silence.

The immigrant choices reflected this pull toward economic opportunity. Immigration to Palestine, a return to Zion, was the choice of very few in this period, given the difficult economic conditions in that very pre–milk-and-honey land. But even within the industrializing countries the choice of immigration could depend upon a variety of considerations discouraging or encouraging the potential immigrant. If America was by far the largest major destination of all those headed West, for many the bad press of American materialism ("a huge circus of business dealings and bluffing"[45]) and the well-known severity of the immigration officials led them elsewhere. The growth of anti-Semitism in Germany in the 1880s was an even more significant deterrent. (And one emigrant just felt that Germany was too close to Russia for comfort.[46]) As for England, although it was the second choice in the westward migration, with the passing of the Alien Bill in 1905, immigration was clearly discouraged, if not entirely halted.

Why France for some 100,000 Jews between 1880 and 1925? Above all, that choice was part of the general flow toward economic opportunity in the West. According to Michel Roblin, immigration to France was but a side effect of that exodus to America "leaving behind the sick or more fortunate."[47] Thus, for example, a typhoid epidemic in 1892 (resulting in the temporary closure of American ports) caused the rerouting of hundreds of emigrants through France, where many ultimately remained. But while it is true that much western European immigration was a byproduct of transit stops of the farther westward bound, there were reasons specific to France and French history that attracted many eastern Europeans along with many other immigrants to that country.

France's geographic position was perhaps one factor. Due to its relative proximity to Russia, students who planned to return to Russia after acquiring a university degree, professional revolutionaries who went into exile to wait for a revolution in Russia, or others who retained strong familial and emotional ties could perhaps return home more easily if the situation improved.

It was, however, not just chance, a negative attraction of other countries, or proximity to Russia that caused many emigrants to choose France. French hospitality was renowned, and its reputation as a *terre d'asile* (land of refuge) for political or economic exiles dates to the Napoleonic Wars, when the "liberating" army attracted immigrants from Germany and Italy. By the end of the century, relatively high salaries and worker protection laws served as a further incentive for immigrant workers.

The mystique of France's appeal was embedded in both the embodiment of "civilization" and the enduring aura of the French Revolution. If no longer the language of the court, French was still a mark of prestige and culture in Russia. For the Russified Jewish intelligentsia, "Russification" also included a certain amount of *French* language and literature. French civilization, from its poets and philosophers to its culture and cuisine, had even penetrated the Pale.

The France of the Revolution was above all a France of liberty, equality, and fraternity:

> ah! France. . . .
> When that name was spoken in Rakwomir, faces lit up. Victor Hugo, Voltaire, the Rights of Man, the Revolution, the barricades, liberty-equality-fraternity. . . . The tyrants they had overthrown! The generous causes for which they had become empassioned. Even their national anthem, that noble *Marseillaise* that democrats, nihilists, socialists and revolutionaries sing, as a challenge to the autocrat, under the whip of the Cossacks. . . .[48]

For the Jews, the French Revolution had an additional, particular meaning. France was the first of all western European countries to have emancipated the Jews, in 1791, and served as a model for later countries' legislation. Thus, when in 1898 a group of Jewish workers in Paris wrote to the French Socialist party expressing their disappointment in the French Socialists' weak stance on the Dreyfus affair, their disillusionment was all the stronger

> because we regard you as the true continuators of those who declared the Rights of Man, of those who made the French Revolution and whose strength reached even to us, who exist at the bottom of the ladder of oppressed peoples.[49]

This idealization of the France of the Revolution and trust in the rationality and goodness of French civilization were, however, shaken in the 1890s. The Dreyfus affair, the arrest of a Jewish army officer charged with treason, and the anti-Semitism surrounding the affair brought doubt to the minds of many as to the true possibilities of acceptance of the Jews in the Diaspora. For if in the most civilized country of them all, where the Jews had had equal rights for a century, *"Mort aux Juifs!"* ("Death to the Jews!") could be heard in the streets, where would the Jews ever be safe?

The affair received worldwide attention, and it may be asked to what extent it affected immigration to France in this period. Although it would seem that the affair should have discouraged potential immigrants from choosing France, there is no evidence to support this. While it is true that the kernel of the affair, from Alfred Dreyfus's arrest in 1894 to Zola's *J'accuse!* in 1898, coincided with a lull in *im*migration, this must be attributed more to its falling between two emigration waves—that of 1891–92 and that of 1899–1901—i.e., during a lull in *e*migration, than to the impact of the affair itself. However, the anti-Semitism of late nineteenth-century France, of which the Dreyfus affair was but one significant part, cannot be restricted to these years alone. With the publication of *La France juive* by Edouard Drumont eight years before Dreyfus's arrest, anti-Semitism began in force and continued beyond Dreyfus's revision trials (of 1899 and 1904). Yet throughout this entire period immigration from eastern Europe continued.

French anti-Semitism as a force discouraging immigration was clearly not as strong as the forces encouraging emigration in the same period. Nevertheless, to understand fully its impact on the potential immigrant, French anti-Semitism of the late nineteenth century must be compared to that of Russia, the pertinent frame of reference for the eastern European emigrants. In spite of the polemics of Drumont and his friends, French anti-Semitism was neither as violent, as strongly endorsed officially, nor expressed in the same economic forms as it was in eastern Europe. The whole affair, after all, revolved around a Jewish army officer!—unthinkable in Russia, where no Jew (except a few physicians) could even attain such a rank.

> The Dreyfus Affair, as we know, did not fit into any of the normal categories of the Central European Jewish microcosm. That such an affair could set one-half of France against the other over the issue of a Jewish officer was simply out of the realm of understanding of the hassidic and orthodox milieu. It was rightly incomprehensible, and because of this, the affair never became clear to the Eastern European community. Ah, if it had been a question of a ritual murder accusation or of the desecration of the holy wafer, . . . there one would have been on known territory. But the subtleties of these French, Jews or Christians, were much too hermetic.[50]

The image of France as the land of the Revolution, of Liberty, Equality, and Fraternity stretching out to the downtrodden, was exceedingly difficult to tarnish.

INDUSTRIAL REVOLUTION AND LABOR NEEDS

In terms of immigration forces, France's Industrial Revolution may be seen as a specific case in the general pull of Western industrialization. The economic attraction of France was similar to that of other late nineteenth-century industrializing countries. Yet the rhythm and problems of French economic development provided a particular context for immigrant pull. *Absolute* strides took place, but in comparison to the other industrializing countries demographic and industrial growth were *relatively* slow. As a result much official concern and a renewed push for expansion provided the background welcome for immigrant labor at the end of the century.

France's relative lag with regard to England, Germany, and the United States has been explained by a combination of factors ranging from limited natural resources to the mentality of family-oriented, risk-avoiding entrepreneurs (another sort of natural resource).[51] One factor that especially worried contemporary French leaders was France's declining rate of population growth in the second half of the nineteenth century. While France's rivals continued unhaltingly to expand their labor force and internal consumption power, the rate of French population growth fell from 5.6 percent in the period 1821–41 to 3.4 percent in the next twenty years, then 2.7 percent, and only 1.8 percent by the last two decades of the century.[52]

The relative slowness of France's Industrial Revolution, as compared to the other Western industrializing countries at the end of the nineteenth century, is the significant characteristic of France's economic development emphasized in most histories of the period. However, it is important to remember that in terms of France's own development, and certainly as compared to other much slower industrializers such as Russia, the French Industrial Revolution proceeded apace, expanding not only in terms of heavy industry but, importantly, in terms of light industry as well. This conjuncture of absolute growth with relative lag meant in fact that the effort for expansion was redoubled in order to redress the international (im)balance back to France's favor. Consequently, a double influence may be seen to have occurred with regard to immigrant pull: Immigrants were attracted to France by her absolute growth, while the relative lag and concern with making up for it exerted a parallel pull on immigrants through French industrial and, ultimately, immigrant policy.

Because of concern over the demographic lag, immigration was seen as a possible answer for industrial growth. The maintenance of a sufficient labor force was after all bound up with France's very industrial progress, and therefore national pride.

> If it is proven that the French nation will soon cease to grow by herself, then let us open the frontiers even more so than before, let us attract foreigners instead of repelling them! . . . This time France will have the commercial and industrial interests on her side and the merit of continuing to apply the generous principles of liberal hospitality which have always honored her. [Prolonged applause.][53]

In 1889 a law was passed conferring French citizenship (and hence liability for military service) on immigrants' children. Consequently, from that year to the next, immigrant figures dropped, and the French population grew.

Laws restricting immigration were either nonexistent or little enforced. The only significant legislation in this respect before 1914 was a decree of October 2, 1888, requiring all immigrants to register at the Préfecture de Police in Paris or their local town hall, and a law of August 8, 1893, fining those who did not do so. Neither law was intended to inhibit immigration; they merely required a declaration of one's presence, which the authorities could not refuse to accept. It was not until 1917, when an identity card became mandatory, that officials could refuse an immigrant's request for residence and working papers. These laws of 1888 and 1893, as the police department itself noted, were not at all exceptional and had their counterparts in most European countries. They were, however, difficult to apply and in fact quite often ignored. The Russian immigrants were noted by the police as being especially refractory with regard to registration, but in any case the sanctions were rarely enforced.[54]

Immigration as an answer to French demographic and industrial needs was not unanimously accepted, however. A law of 1899 restricted the percentage of foreign workers that could be hired by state enterprises. Approximately fifty other laws aimed at restricting or taxing immigrants or their employers were proposed between 1883 and 1914.[55] The immigrants were variously castigated as: workers and therefore competitors of French laborers; poor and thus a burden on the economy; disloyal in time of war; criminals; or as having a high number of illegitimate children. However, in spite of such arguments only the regulations of 1888, 1893, and 1899 were passed into law.

The conclusion of the 1899 International Conference on Governmental Intervention with regard to Emigration and Immigration held in Paris was that implicit encouragement of immigration was desirable, although direct government intervention was not.[56] From 1906 to 1913 Polish agricultural workers and then Italian as well as Polish mineworkers were recruited to France. But it was not until after World War I that a conscious policy of foreign labor recruitment began. The Service de la main-d'oeuvre étrangère was created in 1917, and the connection between immigrant labor and industrial growth was made explicit.

By 1911 the immigrant population of France had grown to 2.9 percent of the total population from 1.1 percent in the middle of the nineteenth century.[57] The immigrants' importance to industrial expansion was clear: In 1891, 50 percent of the immigrant workers in France were employed in industry as compared to only 26 percent of the French workers; at the same time 47 percent of the French labor force was active in agriculture, as compared to only 19 percent of the immigrants.[58]

Immigrant figures were even higher for Paris. The foreign population of that city in 1851 was 4.4 percent of the total, as compared to 1.1 percent for all of France. In 1906, 6.3 percent of the Parisian population was immigrant, as compared to 2.5 percent for all of France.[59] The French capital was both the real and symbolic concentration of all of the cultural and political images with which the immigrants viewed France. Paris was (and still is—especially to both Parisians and foreigners) France. But even more importantly, the general attraction of the industrializing West, as embodied in France, was magnified to an even greater extent through the specific appeal of Paris.

The growth of Paris in the century following the French Revolution was largely inspired by Napoleon's centralizing reforms, which gave even more importance to a city already the pole of the *métropole*. Industrialization and urbanization then acted as multiplier effects on Napoleonic centralization, causing the city's population to almost quintuple over the century, from 547,000 in 1800 to 2,714,000 in 1900. While natural increase accounted for some portion of this growth, internal as well as external immigration was the more significant cause. Economic opportunity and Paris's embodiment of French civilization attracted foreigners, provincials, and ex-provincials (from Alsace-Lorraine after 1870) alike. By 1896 only a little more than one-third of the Parisian population had actually been born within the city limits.[60]

The renown of Parisian manufacturing ("distinguished by both the solidity and elegance of its products") and commerce along with high salaries and the periodic attractions of the International Exhibitions all exerted their pull, causing one commentator to extol the cosmopolitan character of the Parisian work force as "one of the most striking examples of human solidarity."[61] *Der idisher arbayter* was more skeptical, noting with tongue in cheek how "our capitalists, naturally big cosmopolitans, have a strong love for men in general. So they take Germans, Italians, Jews, Russians, Poles, . . ."[62]

It is within this context of industrial expansion, demographic weakness, and the need for immigrant labor that the immigration of eastern European Jews must be placed. Eighty percent of all eastern European Jewish immigrants to France at the end of the century chose Paris, and well over half of them found jobs in light industry, which itself accounted for almost one-half of the Parisian labor force (44.2 percent) in 1896.[63] In 1911, 62 percent of the Russian immigrants in France were employed in light industry, as compared to approximately 40 percent of all immigrants in France.[64]

Furthermore, Paris was the heart of the renowned French clothing industry, with approximately 120,000 workers employed in this branch.[65] An examination of the structure of the fashion industry at the turn of the century will more clearly reveal the specific impact of the facts described above. It will also provide the important background of preexisting opportunities that awaited the eastern European Jewish workers.

PARISIAN FASHION INDUSTRY

General labor needs on the part of the receiving country and specific labor needs by various industries at different stages of their growth are important elements that have been insufficiently examined in the history of Jewish as well as other migratory movements. In the case of the clothing industry at the turn of the century its implicit force of attraction—especially in comparison with, and ultimately complementary to, the overcrowding of this industry in eastern Europe—cannot be underestimated. The immigration of Jewish tailors to Paris as to New York and London was not simply fortuitous but corresponded to a need, which must be recognized as an immigration force.

In terms of capitalization, production (machinery usage and concentration in the work place), distribution, and consumption, the history of the garment industry is revealing of the profound changes taking place in the nineteenth-century economy and society. The growth of ready-to-wear (called *confection*; later replaced by the term *prêt-à-porter*) clothing has been described as a result of the democratization of society and thus of style in the nineteenth century. What is clear, however, is that the democratization of style was in fact made possible by a democratization of price, in turn possible through a greater capitalization, standardization, and mechanization of the industry.

Standardization was first achieved in mens' clothing through a more "ample" fashion that "tends to envelop, in [only] several styles, . . . the infinite diversity of the human body."[66] Ready-made clothing for women developed more slowly, but the growth of sportswear (in spite of protests about the "common ugliness" of clothes that minimized the distinctions between the sexes and ignored a November 1800 ordinance forbidding women to wear men's clothes) at the end of the century helped bring womenswear closer to menswear both in style and production (ready-made) methods.[67]

Technological advances furthered the process of relative standardization, capital intensification, and, ultimately, the lowering of prices. The sewing machine, first invented by a Frenchman, Thimonnier, in 1830, later perfected and distributed on a mass scale by Singer ("the Napoleon of the sewing machine"[68]), replaced at least six handworkers by one machine worker. By 1896 it took about one-third to one-half of the time needed to make an individually tailored garment to make a ready-made garment. But production still remained a mixture of isolated homeworkers (*travailleurs à domicile*), small workshops, and "factories" of varying sizes. The ready-to-wear industry was thus a sign of its times. In spite of growing capital concentration in heavy industry, France remained a country of small workshops in which 32.2 percent of the workers in 1906 worked in shops of no more than nine employees. In the clothing industry alone the median-sized shop had only six workers.[69]

Three factors may be identified as particularly important with regard to the industry's labor needs: the marked seasonality of garment manufacture, the organization of the work process through the putting-out system, and the relative market position of the French garment industry. These factors are examined here for the fashion industry in particular but all three obtained in varying degrees in many other branches of light industry in which the Jewish immigrants were employed as well.

Seasonality

One of the objectives of the development of ready-to-wear processes had been the elimination of seasonal fluctuations in production. However, the ready-to-wear industry soon developed the same bad habits of the preceding mode of production, waiting until the last minute to create new styles for the season. The trade thus remained "condemned twice a year to unemployment and twice a year to overproduction."[70] The ups and downs of the clothing seasons were most often blamed on consumer demand, and especially on the whims of the "implacable" female clientele. The *"tyrannie de la mode"* and the *"despotisme capricieux"* of fashion were considered to be the result of "facts and customs which are in the nature of things and over which man [sic] has no control."[71]

The consequent inability to change the seasonal character of the industry meant the need to adapt capital and especially labor resources to the circumstances. This was achieved through a division of labor that permitted the division of tasks in space as well as by function. The putting-out system, which existed alongside increasing concentration of the labor force, was advantageous for the capitalist while exerting a certain attraction for immigrant, and female, labor at the same time.

The Putting-Out System

By tracing the production of a garment from a mere piece of cloth to its finished state, the dual structure of the work process may be seen schematically in Figure 1. The more "industrialized" or concentrated work process is seen on the right, in which the manufacturer organized production in his own workshop or "factory." That manufacturer could be an independent contractor or perhaps a department store. The latter, whose growth at the end of the nineteenth century inspired both awe and fear, not only furthered the concentration of distribution but of the production process as well.[72] Department stores often created their own workshops (or subsidiary companies, such as the Société parisienne de confection of Galeries Lafayette) in order to stock their shelves. Capital concentration and standardization of production had their pitfalls, however. With too heavy an investment in a fixed infrastructure, the off-season could be debilitating. Thus the clothing "capitalists" had frequent if not regular recourse to homeworkers (left side of Figure 1), and it was there that the immigrants came in.

By calling upon homeworkers, even on a regular basis, both overhead

Figure 1. Clothing Manufacture via Home or Workshop

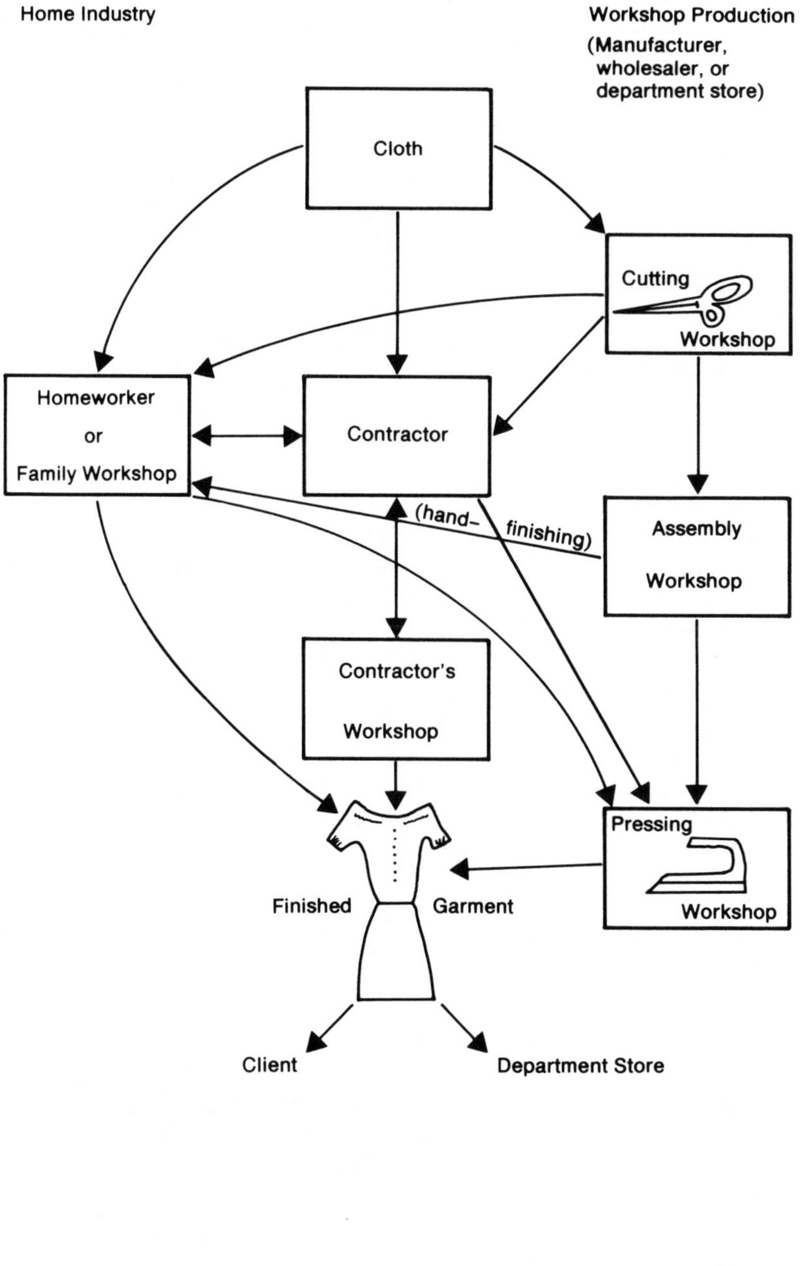

Home Industry

Workshop Production
(Manufacturer,
wholesaler, or
department store)

Cloth

Cutting
Workshop

Homeworker
or
Family Workshop

Contractor

Assembly
Workshop

(hand- finishing)

Contractor's
Workshop

Pressing
Workshop

Finished   Garment

Client   Department Store

35

and wages could be reduced to a minimum for year-long production. Crises of overproduction could be avoided while a reserve labor force was on hand for periods of increased demand. The homeworker had to assume overhead costs and, paid by the piece, bore all the costs of nonproductive time. Furthermore, a homeworker or pieceworker's wage was sometimes as little as one-half that of a workshop worker, and in the slow season it was the homeworker who was the first to go without work.

The contractor (called *entrepreneur* in French) was the intermediary through whom the department stores or manufacturers dealt most often with the homeworkers. He or she collected the often already-cut material from the manufacturer to be distributed to homeworkers for assembly. In some cases contractors organized small workshops in order to avoid the inconvenience of a scattered work force (and thereafter complained of overhead costs), but in any case it was they who imposed deadlines, working conditions, and pay scales on the homeworkers. As a compatriot, generally well informed in the affairs of the immigrant community, the contractor may even have had a part to play in encouraging immigration. Yet as one contemporary observer commented, "whoever says 'entrepreneur' generally says exploiter."[73]

The advantages of this system for the clothing capitalist were numerous. Recourse to homeworkers alongside a process of growing concentration was the employer's method of adjusting supply to demand and of relegating the ravages of the off-season onto the homeworker. Besides the easy mobilization (and demobilization) of a supple and supplementary work force that this implied, this displacement of part of the production process to homeworkers or to small family- or contractor-run workshops also meant that manufacturers could avoid the social legislation that started reaching into factories and workshops at the end of the century. With workshop hours limited to ten or twelve a day (depending on the season), the manufacturer could ignore the eighteen- or twenty-hour days put in by homeworkers and often their families as well.[74] Furthermore, the advantage of maintaining a labor force of isolated individuals was surely not lost on the clothing manufacturers in this period of increasingly vocal workers making demands.

The putting-out system, characterized by this spatially dispersed assembly line stretching from a cutter's workroom to a contractor's workshop or the homeworker's apartment and back again to the pressers' workshop, was both in competition with and complementary to the more modernizing form of capitalism. In certain industries the struggle between these two modes of production had already been fought; in the needle trades it was just getting under full swing in the late nineteenth century. As the noted economist E. Levasseur put it in 1884: "While industrial concentration [*la grande industrie*] was gaining ground, small-scale manufacture [*la petite industrie*] was not expelled; it was displaced. . . ."[75] With the trend toward larger and larger workshops the homeworker did not disappear. (S)he was in some ways more valuable than ever.

Market Competition

The French fashion industry was also a barometer of French industrial strength on the world market at the end of the nineteenth century. Hidden perhaps in a small workshop in the Marais, the Jewish homeworker, just as the important department store Galeries Lafayette, was subject to national and international fluctuations reverberating even to the Pletzl.

As a producer for exportation the fashion industry represented France to a wider market (and still does). By 1889 French clothing exports amounted to 250 million francs, not including the considerable volume of items purchased directly in Paris by foreign buyers; over 60 percent of women's and an even higher percentage of men's ready-to-wear sales went to foreign lands.[76] "Paris is the obligatory center of elegance of the entire world," wrote a French reporter modestly at the time of the 1900 International Exhibition, and the garment industry was described as embellishing life, contributing to its artistic sense, and "spreading French taste and French customs to foreign lands."[77]

This superiority of the Parisian product did not prevent it from foreign competition, however. Beginning in 1869, the growth of protectionism among all of the industrializing countries (including France) began to close markets to French goods while the events of 1870–71, the Franco-Prussian War and the Paris Commune, further hurt French exports. The general industrial stagnation of the next two decades was punctuated by a crisis of overproduction in the clothing industry in the mid-seventies. Not only on the world market but even within France foreign goods were encroaching on French products. From 1877 to 1894 the franc volume of men's ready-to-wear exports fell by over 50 percent, and the French fashion industry's main concern was to defend itself against foreign imports and be competitive on the world market.[78] Imports at least were soon slowed, and by 1900 an upturn was on the way. Nevertheless the French fashion industry needed to remain constantly vigilant.

France's rivals in the clothing market were primarily Germany, England, and the United States along with Austria-Hungary, Belgium, and Switzerland, that is, all of the industrializing countries, which were developing their own ready-to-wear industries. Competition from German goods was, however, that to which industrial reports most often referred. Germany of course was France's most formidable opponent, not only due to the volume of German clothes penetrating the French market but for political reasons as well. Resentment of German products reflected the general political and economic resentment and fear that marked French relations with Germany between the Franco-Prussian War and World War I.

However, the criticisms of German clothes, among others, as "mutilated copies" of French styles, reproduced more cheaply because of less variety, a more mechanized work process, and above all due to a cheaper labor force— are revealing because they indicate self-criticism of the French industry.[79]

The conclusions reached in the extensive reports on the subject were unanimous: It was vital to reorganize the French fashion industry in order to produce goods more cheaply and thus compete more favorably. Alas, elegance was no longer sufficient to ensure adequate sales, although there was never any talk of lowering quality. The two factors most envied when comparing the French to the cheaper foreign goods were the lower price of raw materials (e.g., wool in England, cotton in the United States) and above all lower labor costs (in Germany). Foreign competition was invoked on more than one occasion as setting the limit to salary increases. It may be added that the Parisian garment industry not only had to worry about foreign competition but about provincial French competition as well. There, too, lower labor costs, corresponding to a lower cost of living and a higher degree of mechanization, were noted.[80]

Labor Force

Thus both the position of the French clothing industry on the world market and the organization of its work process worked interdependently to circumscribe the labor needs of the industry. Homework in particular attracted two categories of workers who were (are) particularly vulnerable to exploitation and famine wages: women and immigrants.

All of the factors contributing to the large number of women in the clothing industries are beyond the scope of this study, but it is interesting to note the similar functions that both women and immigrants filled. The clothing industry personnel was in fact 86 percent female in 1896, as compared to an average female labor force of 42 percent in all industries combined.[81] This was explained by the supposedly innate aptitude of women for needlework and the convenience of homework for them. Whenever it was suggested that homework be eliminated because of the awful conditions associated with it, a number of priests, welfare workers, and doctors supported its continuation, arguing that those who did such work had chosen to do so, and to deprive mothers, pregnant women, the infirm, or the elderly of such work would be unfair.[82] But the real advantage for the industry was the lower salary paid to women under the supposed justification that it was only a supplement to the family budget.

Similarly, immigrants were seen as "accept[ing], and even offer[ing] . . . derisive prices [for their work]" due to the immediate needs of the newly arrived and the differential of living costs and standards with the country of emigration.[83] The immigration of some workers already skilled in some aspect of the garment industry also meant a further savings to the employer in terms of training time and costs. But perhaps just as importantly, as concentration to a certain degree of the clothing trade progressed, many older workers, mostly women, moved into the larger workshops and factories, where social legislation aimed at protecting factory and female labor in particular had its first effects. The need for homeworkers and family workshops did not diminish. On the contrary, newly arriving immigrants came propitiously at a time when they could fill these latter functions.

New developments in the clothing trade at the end of the century also provided opportunities for the immigrants. The growth of women's sportswear, for example, was one area in which foreign expertise was particularly appreciated. Womenswear tailors were needed to keep pace with expansion in this field and were gladly received from those countries such as Hungary, Russia, Czechoslovakia, or Germany, where men had always made women's clothes, as opposed to France, where womenswear had been a traditionally female task. It was estimated that 85 percent of the womenswear workers were foreigners as compared to 35 percent in menswear, and womenswear became a specialty among Jewish immigrants.[84] The extension (and democratization) of the usage of furs in France also coincided with the immigration of Russian Jews. Along with Germans, Hungarians, and Swedes, these cold-country immigrants constituted approximately 80 percent of the fur industry's work force, a sector that doubled its franc volume between 1870–71 and 1894–95.[85] Raincoats (previously all imported from England) were another new industry in France at the end of the century in which the eastern European immigrants played a significant role.

Finally, capmaking, which will be described in greater detail below, may be given as an example in which the importance of immigrant labor turned a previously importing sector into an exporting one. The popularization of the bicycle and the automobile at the end of the century was accompanied by their own fashions. As Maurice Lauzel noted in his study of Jewish capmakers in 1912, bourgeois caps as well as workingmen's caps became the rage, the latter, with "all sorts of ornamental additions" having become an object of "common luxury."[86] The cap craze (previously worn only by deliverymen, etc.) continued to grow along with sportswear throughout the early twentieth century, and as the style grew, so did imports. However, largely thanks to the Jewish immigrants who came to dominate the capmaking industry (the Russian-style flat cap was particularly popular), imports leveled off at about 30,000 to 40,000 caps per year, and exports more than doubled from 52,000 in 1892 to 120,000 in 1899.[87]

All of these branches of the clothing industry, ripe for development and expansion, took particular advantage of immigrant labor to do so. Not only was new space available in which the immigrants could find employment but the special needs and structures of those trades (e.g., the high seasonality of raincoats and furs) encouraged the use of immigrant labor as homeworkers.

While the argument that women or immigrants *chose* the conditions of homework ignores the structural circumstances surrounding that "choice," it is clear that there were advantages to such work that complemented the needs of those workers. The possibility of working at home was useful not only for women with children but for immigrants unable to communicate easily in a new language. Homework allowed maintenance of ethnic or religious traditions while the low capital needs (a sewing machine, purchased on credit) and the division of labor, including many skills easy to acquire by those who had never held a needle in their lives, meant a relatively easy access to work for immigrants anxious to begin employment as soon as possible.

It is therefore no surprise that approximately one-quarter of all Parisian clothing workers were foreigners, and that in different specialties, as has been seen, immigrants provided over three-quarters of the work force.[88] The garment industry was described as without doubt the most "cosmopolitan" industry of all.[89]

The structure of the Parisian clothing industry and its particular market needs thus exerted an important, if implicit, force of attraction on the eastern European immigrants. In many ways the mechanism of this pull, as described above for Paris, was a variation on similar conditions in New York, London, Leeds, and Manchester, all of which attracted large numbers of eastern European immigrants to their expanding clothing industries at the turn of the century. Labor needs existed that the immigrants could fill—perhaps even better than most as the eastern European conjuncture sent a high number of skilled workers across the border in search of work.

Any detailed study of the clothing industry in Paris, as one of the largest employers of Jewish immigrant labor in that city, must remain within the context of French industrialization and of Parisian light industry, of which it was representative. The Jews were not the only immigrants in this trade, and clothing was not the only trade in which Jewish immigrants were active. The industry's structure (the putting-out system) and to some extent its particular marketing problems were similar to many other branches of light industry to which the immigrants were attracted. Jewish workers also became cabinet-makers, bookbinders, and shoe finishers; they made small toys, *articles de Paris* (Paris souvenirs), cartons or paper bags, and "all of those thousands of small-scale manufactured items which, even in the twentieth century [1906], remain the lot of the family."[90] Low capital needs, little concentration of the work force, and often a marked seasonality of production all led to easy insertion of immigrant labor in trades searching for lowered production costs as a response to pressures of increasing industrialization and competition. The use of immigrant labor in Paris was by no means a new phenomenon, but the particular *"système bâtard"*[91] of mixed small and big industry in the context of France's relative industrial and demographic lag at the end of the century gave a new urgency to its usage.

While female labor remained by far the major component in the clothing industry's search for a cheap, flexible labor force, the growing number of immigrants in this trade was a constant source of comment in newspaper and police reports. The immigrants could and did fill the same economic functions as women, and in many cases replaced the latter as they moved from homework into workshops. The process of immigrant attraction to these trades was then heightened through the multiplier effect of immigrant concentration within the labor market. Certain specialties, such as womenswear or capmaking, attracted more and more Jewish immigrants by dint of the very fact that they became increasingly "Jewish" trades.

If there had been no jobs, the immigrants would not have come in such large numbers.[92] It was the congruency of immigration with emigration forces that gave the Jewish migration its socioeconomic character. Late nineteenth-century Jewish migration was as much a part of the labor pull of economic development in the West as it was a result of suffocation within the Pale.

Two
ARRIVAL AND RECEPTION
The Pull of French Jewry?

The act of moving, the boats, the trains, the difficulty in finding kosher food, and the clandestine passages are as important as the forces of emigration and immigration in understanding both the determination of the migrants and the shock that their presence created on arrival in the American or western European ports or train stations. The routes taken and the fear and fatigue endured are an important prologue to the immigrants' entrance. That entrance was often dramatic, described as a Tower of Babel by some. The immigrants' arrival in turn set the stage for the reactions of the Jewish and non-Jewish observers that will be seen below.

In the period before World War I, as has been mentioned, western European policy in matters of emigration and immigration was generally that of nonintervention, which meant loose border controls for most countries. In Russia, however, passports were necessary, and the clandestine nature of the emigration process played a large part in leaving for many, especially for draft-dodgers or political or trade union activists. Emigration agencies thus sprouted in certain key cities and even came to be considered "the most fertile branch of Lithuanian commerce."[1] Even if some authorities were just as happy to see the Jews go (not to mention the officials along the route who earned extra cash through bribery), as long as the emigrants were apprehensive, emigration remained a lucrative business for some and a terrifying journey for others.

The routes chosen often reflect in themselves the conscious decisions of destination. The route over the Austrian border to Brody was well traced in the early 1880s, as word spread that passage to America was possible from there. For those who chose France as their goal, the route was partly by foot, sneaking over the Russian-German border, and the path was then direct by train to the Gare du Nord. Students and activists who "chose" Paris sometimes did so after having first tried Zurich, Geneva, or Berlin. Repeated expulsions led to a rather zigzag path back and forth between Russia, Switzerland, Germany, and France.

But for others, immigration "plans" sometimes consisted only in the notion of making one's way to America or Palestine. For these emigrants it was more often the immediate policies of other countries (and their Jewish communities) that influenced their act of movement and decided their route for them, sometimes providing unexpected destinations. In one instance, a boat that set out for Palestine was refused the right to land in the Turkish Empire. Buffeted around the sea like a slow-moving pinball game, after stops at Constantinople, Salonica, and Marseilles, the majority of these hopeful Zionists ended up in Paris or New York.

France served as an important transit point for emigrants going on to the United States or Argentina.[2] There are even stories of families passing through Paris on their way *from* Argentina back to Russia, from Palestine to New York, or others who had gone from Russia to Constantinople to New York and then to Paris. The 120 emigrants who caused a minor scandal in August 1892 because they ended up sleeping three nights at the Gare de Lyon train station in Paris are a vivid example of the trials of the migration move.[3] Expelled from Odessa as foreign Jews (almost all of Rumanian origin) they made their way from there to Constantinople. Unable to find work there and the Constantinople Jewish community no longer able or willing to support them, they were sent on to Marseilles. From there the local Jewish community sent them to Lyon, from where they were sent to Dijon, and so forth to Fontainebleau. There they stayed several nights in the forest until finally continuing on to Paris. The spectacle of this bizarre-looking group of men, women, and barefoot children camping out in the Paris train station was, needless to say, ammunition for the anti-Semitic press and a rude embarrassment to the Parisian Jewish community. But Germany had closed its doors because of cholera in Hamburg; America had likewise halted immigration in fear of typhoid that year. So the Parisian Jews eventually disinfected the emigrants as well as possible and found temporary lodgings until, it was hoped, they could be sent on to Le Havre for a boat to the United States.

A number of statistics from the Société philanthropique de l'Asile israélite de Paris offer some indication of the immigrants' routes toward Paris. For the years 1909 to 1912 the Asile kept track of the most recent whereabouts of the Russians taken in by them (Table 3). In 1909 over one-half of those listed arrived directly from Russia, but a sizable 43 percent had traveled elsewhere

TABLE 3

EN ROUTE

(COUNTRIES FROM WHICH RUSSIAN JEWS ARRIVED IN PARIS)

	1909	1910	1911	1912
Russia	408	217	53[a]	149[a]
France	27	77	366[b]	299[c]
Paris	–	236	–	–
America	85	10	1	4
Argentina	–	–	–	3
Austria	17	11	9	23
Belgium	15	46	28	22
Egypt	–	–	–	1
England	35	35	41	26
Germany	–	47	60	42
Holland	–	3	1	–
Italy	–	–	4	–
Palestine	93	21	1	3
Siberia	–	–	–	7
Spain	–	–	2	1
Switzerland	31	5	11	1
Turkey	2	–	–	17
Homeless	–	–	47	55
Total	713	708	624	653

SOURCE: Société philanthropique de l'Asile israélite de Paris, Rapports des exercices: 1909-12 (Paris: Imprimerie N.L. Danzig, n.d.).

[a] coming directly from train station.

[b] probably having already stopped in a hotel in Paris.

[c] having already stopped in a hotel in Paris.

before coming to Paris. The overall figures show the steadier inflow from the nearby countries of Germany, England, and Belgium. In any case it is clear that the route taken was often far from being the shortest distance between two points.

Zigzag routes were not only a problem at the international level but within countries as well. The major entry points into France were Marseilles, Lille (via Brussels or Antwerp), Belfort, Avricourt, Metz, Verdun, and Nancy (where many stayed). Letters sent to the Alliance Israélite Universelle in Paris complained above all of the lack of coordination with regard to the immigration and the unfair burden falling on those communities situated on the migration route.[4] A letter from Nice in 1905 explained that the Jewish community there often found immigrants returning after having been given train fare to the next town; unable to find funds there to continue on to Paris, they would go back to Nice. Therefore, a coordination of local funds was repeatedly urged in order to provide immigrants with through tickets to their final destination, it was hoped via the most direct way possible. The route from Marseilles to Paris certainly should have not taken a week or more as it had for the Gare de Lyon campers in 1892. Nor should the route from Châlons to Paris pass through Reims or Epernay as had been the case.

Uncertainty and long nights on hard benches were as much a part of the migration move as crossing borders. Whether specifically headed for ·the French capital or out of funds and not "chosen" by the emigration committees to go on to the United States, for better or for worse, many found Paris to be the end of their route. For the emigrants the act of moving itself was symbolic of the process of culture exchange and adaptation that needed to be faced. As Yankel Mykhanowitzki (hero of the novel *Les Eaux mêlées*) later expressed it after ten years in Paris, he would always feel "a foreigner everywhere! I am no longer completely Jewish, yet I am not completely French. Stuck midstream."[5]

NUMBER OF ARRIVALS

It is difficult to estimate the number of eastern European Jews who immigrated to France between 1880 and World War I. Clandestine voyages, the lack of border controls at land frontiers (compared to the shipping statistics and immigrant office statistics available for the United States, for example), and the general disorganization of the migration process transcended organizational attempts at keeping track. As has been seen, of the approximately 3½ million emigrants who left eastern Europe between 1880 and 1925, an estimated one hundred thousand settled in France. However, as for the period before the war, which differs significantly from that after 1919, it may be estimated that the eastern European Jewish community in Paris numbered somewhere between thirty and forty thousand (see Appendix A). This already represented approximately 45 percent of the Parisian Jewish community, which constituted a dramatic shift in the composition of the "French" Jewish community, as will be seen below.[6]

While becoming a larger proportion of the Parisian Jewish community, the eastern European immigrants also became a more important segment of the overall immigrant population in the city. It can be seen in Table 4 that while the proportion of foreigners in Paris from 1881 on was generally two to three times greater than that in France (column 4 : column 1), the concentration of eastern European immigrants in Paris was over ten times greater than their number in France as a whole (column 5 : column 2). By World War I the eastern European immigrants accounted for nearly one-fifth (17.1 percent) of all immigrants in Paris.

While an estimate of 35,000 eastern European Jews in Paris before World War I may be small in comparison to the concurrent emigration to New York, for example, the geographic concentration of the immigrants within Paris (as within other cities) increased the immigrants' relative importance in the neighborhoods in which they settled. Their presence was thus

TABLE 4

EASTERN EUROPEAN IMMIGRANTS COMPARED TO TOTAL IMMIGRANT POPULATION

	FRANCE[a]			PARIS		
	1	2	3	4	5	6
Year	Imm. pop. as % of French pop.	East. Eur. Imms. as % of French pop.	East. Eur. Imms. as % of Foreign pop.	Imm. pop. as % of Paris pop.	East. Eur. Imms. as % of Paris pop.	East. Eur. Imms. as % of Foreign pop.
1851	1.1		2.5	4.4[c]		
1872	2.0[b]			7.4[d]		2.6[d]
1881	2.7	0.029	1.1	7.5[e]		3.9[e]
1883				8.0 (1882)[d]		3.5[e]
1886	3.1[b]		1.2		0.378[f]	4.2[e]
1896	2.7	0.039	1.5	6.4[d]	0.427[f]	
1901	2.7	0.040	1.5	5.9[g]	0.503[f]	8.5[g]
1906	2.5	0.061	2.4	6.3[g]	0.660[g]	10.5[g]
1911	2.9	0.106	3.7			17.1[h]

NOTE: A decrease in the number of immigrants occurred after 1889 (cols. 1 and 4) due to a law of that year that gave immigrant children French citizenship and thence no longer counted them as immigrants. See chapter 2.

[a]Derived from Georges Mauco, Les étrangers en France (Paris: Armand Colin, 1932), p. 38, with the exception of footnote b.

[b]Prince de Cassano, Procès-verbaux sommaires du Congrès international de l'intervention des pouvoirs publics dans l'émigration et l'immigration, tenu à Paris du 12 au 14 août 1889 (Exposition universelle internationale de 1889) (Paris: Imprimerie nationale for the Ministère du commerce, de l'industrie et des colonies, 1890), p. 9.

[c]Résultats statistiques du recensement général de la population (1901), vol. 1: Régions de Paris, du Nord et de l'Est (Paris: Imprimerie nationale, 1904), p. 299.

[d]Louis Chevalier, La formation de la population parisienne au XIXe siècle, Institut national d'études démographiques--Travaux et documents 10 (Paris: Presses universitaires de France, 1950), p. 45.

[e]Annuaire statistique de la ville de Paris (Paris: Imprimerie municipale, year plus 2), for respective years.

[f]Derived from Résultats statistiques, p. 311.

[g]Derived from Annuaire statistique for respective years; cf. De Cassano, p. 10.

[h]Derived from: 35,000 Eastern European Jewish immigrants
204,600 foreigners in the Parisian area (Mauco, p. 285).

practically invisible to those who never came into those areas of the city, yet more strikingly visible to those who did. The response to this immigration by both the Jewish and non-Jewish populations of Paris is interesting not only as to what it tells us about the immigrants but as to what it reveals about the onlookers as well.

ARRIVAL IN FRANCE—PUBLIC OPINION

French response to the potential and actual "influx" of the immigrants can only be understood in the context of the period between the Franco-Prussian War and World War I, in which a heightened nationalism on the one hand and a search for new allies on the other colored foreign and even domestic affairs. Thus even though empathy over the oppression and enforced wanderings of the eastern European Jews was general as news of pogroms and expulsions reached the West, concern over allies and the importance of France's political and economic ties with Russia inevitably mitigated any harsh criticism of the tsarist regime in its treatment of the Jews. Whereas public protest meetings were held in London in 1882 and 1890—and both England and the United States, prodded by some of their more influential Jewish citizens, sent official, albeit very cautious, protests to Russia—France could not afford to do the same as rapprochement with Russia was taking form. After the signing of the Franco-Russian alliance in 1897 the French press became notably silent with regard to political emancipation in Russia.[7]

As for private protest, a short-lived Comité de secours pour les Israélites de Russie (Committee for the Aid of Russian Jews), chaired by Victor Hugo, was created in 1882. In 1903, at the time of worldwide outcry over the Kishinev massacre, Jean Jaurès and Francis de Pressensé, the Ligue française des Droits de l'homme et du citoyen, and the students and professors of the Université de Paris led the only public protests in France.[8] In spite of suggestions that the French republic, in the name of civilized Europe, put some pressure on its ally, the French government remained silent.

As immigrants arrived, the public image of them was in most cases a composite one, different aspects of which—poor, Jewish, foreign, revolutionary, "proletarian"—were stressed, depending upon the viewer. The incident already described at the Gare de Lyon in August 1892 is a good example. At first it was fear of cholera that worried most of the press, accompanied by unflattering descriptions of the unhygienic conditions of the immigrants ("revolting filth," "dressed in sordid rags," "stinking atmosphere").[9] This concern was largely dispelled, however, when it was determined that neither Odessa nor Constantinople, the most recent stopping points on the immigrants' route, had any signs of cholera. After this initial worry most accounts were sympathetic to the immigrants. It was only hoped that measures would be taken to prevent such a spectacle in Paris again—a more or less subtle hint to the city authorities and to the Jewish community.[10]

The anti-Semitic press, however, exaggerated the worst of every aspect of the situation. The very "foreignness" of the immigrants was noted, their clothing and manner frequently described in unflattering detail. No words were minced in describing their filth. The "Dirty Jew" was reified—"The Jewish infection," "yellow with dirt," "dressed in tatters"—and this press was unrelenting in its hue and cry over cholera or other invading microbes ("the children scratch endlessly"; even Rothschild's almoner was described as scratching when he came to hand out aid).[11] It is not surprising that the anti-Semitic newspapers greatly exaggerated the number of immigrants who had arrived in 1892 alone (from ten thousand to over fifty thousand!).[12]

The anti-Semitic response was also couched in terms of defense of the French worker or merchant supposedly displaced by these immigrants. After visiting an immigrant encampment one reporter wrote: "A slow anger came over me as I thought of the thousands of French workers in their own country, in a country which belongs to them, where their fathers lived comfortably before them, who find themselves out of work."[13] This resentment over the Jewish immigrants as competitors for French jobs was heightened by the assumption that the rich Jewish community would take care of its coreligionists (and thus these "future barons" would be successful in a mere ten or twenty years) while French workers had to fend for themselves.[14] The anti-Semitic press was not the only one to take such Jewish solidarity for granted. *Le Figaro* and other papers spoke assuredly of a Rothschild or the Baron de Hirsch coming to the emigrants' aid.

The criticism of the immigrants that best fit into another aspect of French ideology, however—less that of nationalism after the Franco-Prussian War than that marked by the aftermath of the Commune—was the vision of the eastern European immigrants as carriers of revolution. Even while sympathizing with regard to the persecution in Russia, it was occasionally cautioned not to exaggerate the wrongs of that persecution, for the Jews had, after all, played a part in the anarchist movement in Russia. Charles Fegdal wrote, in an article on "Le Ghetto Parisien" in 1915, that "our good Talmudists are ultra-socialists. . . , [the Parisian ghetto being] a refuge of more or less militant international revolutionaries."[15]

The police department, whose job after all was to uncover any such activity, prepared a thirty-nine-page memorandum in 1906 or 1907 devoted to the Russian refugees in Paris, claiming that "all of them must be considered sympathetic to the Russian revolution."[16] Many of the immigrant students were suspected of hiding behind false papers, and the number of draft-dodgers among the immigrants was another factor adding to the "bad elements" (*facteurs mauvais*) that constituted the immigrant community in the eyes of the police. Commenting on the core of organized militants under their watch the police department asserted that they are ready for anything, these are the apostles of an incessant propaganda which is undertaken in a thousand forms among the rather amorphous mass [of immigrants]. . . . The moderation of the immigrant community as a whole is only relative for there is not one of these "moderates" who is not ready to sacrifice everything to help the most criminal maximalist or anarchist.[17]

In one respect, however, the eastern European immigration to Paris had a very positive result: the discovery of the "Jewish proletariat." This term first became widespread in western Europe in 1898 with the publication of a thesis by Léonty Soloweitschik entitled *Un prolétariat méconnu*, which described the conditions of the Jewish proletariat in England, Rumania, Russia, and elsewhere, although not in France.[18] Even before that, however, the existence of the poor Jewish neighborhood had been revealed to the amazement of journalist and reader alike in *Le Figaro* of July 1, 1892:

Public opinion seems content in considering the Jews as having monopolized the most important part of Parisian wealth. The result of my inquiry will well surprise many people. There are relatively more poor among the Jews than among Catholics.

The discovery of the Jewish immigrants came with a tone of astonishment and revelation. One author, in the course of his investigation, was even surprised to learn Talmudic quotations in praise of labor.[19]

The oppression in eastern Europe and the consequent migration of the Jewish "proletariat" to the West raised the Western consciousness with regard to the existence of the Jewish worker both in the East and in the West. In spite of the actual (nonproletarian, i.e., nonfactory) conditions of employment in Paris at the turn of the century, the image of the Jewish "proletariat" would be evoked from 1898 on. For the French Socialists, this was a crucial argument to help unbalance the former anticapitalist equals anti-Jewish equation already being revised through the Dreyfus affair.[20] For the anti-Semites it meant that Jewish capitalists monopolizing the wealth of France were now seconded by Jewish workers taking jobs from French workers. In either case, the eastern European immigration was crucial in the West's reconsideration of the economic role and supposed homogeneity of the Jewish people.

REACTIONS OF THE FRENCH JEWISH COMMUNITY

Ils [les juifs polonais] sont la chair de notre chair et le sang de notre sang; déjà nos frères en humanité, ils le sont plus encore par la croyance, plus encore par le malheur.[21]
[The Polish Jews] are the flesh of our flesh and the blood of our blood; already our brothers in humanity, they are more so by religious belief, and even more so through suffering.

The French Jewish community viewed with horror and anxiety as the situation of the Jews deteriorated in eastern Europe. The suffering of the eastern European Jews was a vivid reminder of the persecution that formed part of the collective memory of the Jews, and reflections on Jewish solidarity were brought again to the fore:

> And in the heart of those Jews most notoriously detached from Judaism, who even turn their back on the synagogue, solidarity resounds with an impera- tive tone when persecution strikes or a catastrophe suddenly befalls a commu- nity, no matter how far away it is.[22]

Appeals for donations for the persecuted Jews in eastern Europe spoke of that "ancient virtue, solidarity," which, if not evident in other domains, at least persisted through charitable works.

The welcome of the eastern European Jews by the French Jewish com- munity can only be understood in the context of the latter's own history. In the last decade several important works have begun to examine modern French Jewish history, particularly Phyllis Albert's comprehensive study of the Consistoire (official body of French Jewry set up by Napoleon) in the nineteenth century and Michael Marrus's skillful examination of the "politics of assimilation" of the French Jewish community at the time of the Dreyfus affair.[23] Paula Hyman and David Weinberg have subsequently explored na- tive and immigrant relations within the French Jewish community and the impact which those relations had on the Jewish community and on Jewish identity as a whole.[24] In essence they were answering the question of how those assimilatory politics (ill)prepared the French Jewish community for the arrival of the emigrants.

For the period from 1881 to 1914 my own purpose is different. The attitude of the native Jewish community toward the immigrants may be examined not only as a reflection of the ideology of the former, but also as an element in the migration process. What part did the assimilatory politics of the native community play with regard to the elaboration of a migration policy? To what extent did the French Jewish community exert a pull, volun- tary or not, on the eastern European immigrants? For Paris was not only the representative of French civilization and an important manufacturing center to which immigrants were drawn. It was also the heart of the French Jewish community. To the Grand Rabbi Zadoc Kahn, it was obvious that for those Jews who suffered "their eyes turn toward Paris, attracted as if by a ray of light and hope."[25] For the French daily newspaper, *Le Figaro*, the attraction was more prosaic: The immigrants turned toward France, where they knew they had rich coreligionists.[26] The prosperity and philanthropy of the French Jew- ish community, especially as incarnated in the Paris-based Alliance israélite universelle, was renowned in eastern Europe, and the image of Jewish solidar- ity undoubtedly had a part to play in immigrant expectations. However, the reality of the native Jewish response, as will be seen, hardly constituted a willing immigration force.

The emancipation of the French Jews in 1791, during the French Revolution, implied a legal equality that was to preface the Jews' economic and social integration. Indeed free to take part in the development of capitalism in the nineteenth century, the Jewish community evolved from the commercial and moneylending roles relegated to it before emancipation into a more diversified petit-bourgeois and bourgeois structure by the second half of the nineteenth century.[27]

The secularization of French society along with its economic expansion favored the cultural as well as economic integration of the Jews. The two major newspapers of the French Jewish community, the more liberal *Archives Israélites* and the consistorial-oriented *L'Univers Israélite,* both pointed proudly to concrete signs of Jewish integration within French society (from appointments to the Legion of Honor to the "Jewish" horses running at the Maisons-Laffitte racetrack). As the radical Jewish journalist Bernard-Lazare sarcastically noted, there were those French Jews "who easily see themselves . . . as having been right there next to Vercingétorix at the battle of Alésia."[28]

As emancipation and integration into French society proceeded apace, the power of the community's institutions diminished. By the end of the nineteenth century the effects of economic integration and the "incomparable seduction of French culture"[29] were manifest in the diminishing cohesiveness of the French Jewish community. On religious matters, *L'Univers Israélite* as well as the *Archives Israélites* frequently complained about poor synagogue attendance. On social questions, mixed marriages were the subject of more than one front-page editorial. Ideologically, the liberal bourgeois ideal of individual responsibility and each for one's own was a recurrent theme, particularly in the pages of the *Archives Israélites.*

Politically, the need to emphasize Jewish patriotism to the state, particularly against the background of the Dreyfus affair, came into conflict with precepts of Jewish solidarity.[30] The attitude of the French Jews with regard to the Franco-Russian alliance is a case in point. The French Jewish community partook in the rejoicing over France's new-found friend, and religious services were held when the alliance and commercial treaties were signed in 1897 and 1906, when the Russian loan of 1909 was negotiated, when Tsar Alexander III died in 1894, and when Nicolas II was crowned. On all of these occasions concern with Russian anti-Semitism took a subordinate position to French patriotic sentiments, although hope was expressed that through the political alliance French civilization would rub off on Russia to the benefit of Russia's Jews. When Tsar Nicolas came to visit France in 1901, the *Archives Israélites* even went so far as to excuse the Tsar for Russian anti-Semitism under the age-old absolution for heads of state: He did not really know what his counselors were doing. In spite of a few arguments of Jewish solidarity that contested this attitude,[31] it was generally felt that it was not the French Jews' place to exert any influence whatsoever in what was essentially the internal affair of another country.

The modern French Jewish community was thus the logical consequence of economic and social integration into French society. The alliance of the French Jews with the French state, economy, and culture was both a voluntary quest for the favors of bourgeois society and a necessary response to the contours and pressures of that society. The homogeneous concept of the French nation made the foreigner unwelcome, and all those with supposedly questionable origins, such as the Jews, were encouraged to assimilate as far as possible.

This "politics of assimilation" was not entirely successful, however, as the Dreyfus affair too clearly showed.[32] The affair revealed the limits of assimilation while bringing to the fore once again accusations of the Jews as foreigners. With the arrest of Dreyfus, whose family had emigrated from Alsace in order to remain French after the loss of that province to Germany in 1870, the fundamental premises of Jewish assimilation were questioned. The importance of the Dreyfus affair for our purposes is not only the challenge it represented to the French Jewish community's integration into French society, but the background of insecurity that was thus created. This insecurity affected the native community's attitude toward the eastern European immigrants and was the background for the elaboration of an emigration and immigration policy in their regard. If Dreyfus's arrest had no directly dissuasive effect on the attraction of France for the immigrants, it would certainly affect that "pull" insofar as the native community's policies toward emigration and immigration were forged in the period of anti-Semitism surrounding the affair.

EMIGRATION/IMMIGRATION POLICY

The conclusions drawn by Theodor Herzl from the Dreyfus affair included a commentary on the effects of Jewish migrations:

> The Jewish question persists wherever Jews live in appreciable numbers. Wherever it does not exist, it is brought together with Jewish immigrants. We are naturally drawn into those places where we are not persecuted, and our appearance there gives rise to persecution. This is the case, and will inevitably be so, everywhere, even in highly civilized countries—see, for instance, France—so long as the Jewish question is not solved on the political level.[33]

This basic pessimism with regard to Jewish existence in the Diaspora may also be taken to describe the fears of the French Jewish community with regard to an influx of immigrants from the East. Anxious to preserve the attainments of a century of emancipation, doubly so in the context of insecurity engendered by the Dreyfus affair, the organized French Jewish community was unable to surmount what has been called a tragic immobility[34] with regard to the condition of Russian Jews and above all with regard to aiding their emigration.

It has been seen that the French Jewish community's support of the Franco-Russian alliance affected its formulation of a position on the condition of Jews in Russia. Although there were occasional individual protests against the community's silence on the matter, the general attitude of the community leaders was little different from that of France as a whole.

Within this context the French Jewish community's emigration and immigration policy was elaborated piecemeal, more often than not outpaced by the events themselves. In the first stage aid for the Jews *in* eastern Europe was emphasized, rather than aiding their emigration. However, as emigration became an undeniable fact, representatives were sent to border towns to coordinate and regulate matters as much as possible in order to distribute the emigrants worldwide. Repatriation was encouraged whenever candidates were (more or less) willing to take that route. Nevertheless, mass immigration in the West ultimately had to be confronted, and efforts then turned to regulating and controlling the dispersion of the immigrants within each country or even within a particular city.

Aid to the Jews in eastern Europe was undertaken by the Alliance israélite universelle as early as twenty years before the era of mass emigration. The Alliance, founded in Paris in 1860, fundamentally reflected the assimilation of the French Jewish community.[35] It aspired to disseminate French civilization and liberty throughout the world, particularly through the French-Jewish schools it set up in the Levant. In the period before 1880, the Alliance intervened on behalf of individual Jews in eastern Europe, attempted negotiations with the Russian government for the Jews' emancipation, and even envisaged, as early as 1866, the possibility of emigration to the United States.

With the massive emigration flow beginning in the 1880s, however, the Alliance policy turned decisively against the idea of emigration as a solution for the eastern European Jews. From 1881 on, subscriptions to help the eastern European Jews were undertaken in France, but the implicit if not explicit purpose of this aid was to prevent potential migrants from becoming actual emigrants. Even aiding the Jews in Russia had to be done with the utmost discretion, however, in worry of provoking further outbursts of anti-Semitism and so as not to be construed as an affront to the tsar, ally of France.

It was argued that encouraging emigration would only be abetting Russia's own plot to rid itself of the Jews, and that it was more important to work for emancipation of the Jews *within* Russia. However, as large-scale emigration became a *fait accompli,* a new plan had to be developed, one that, in its basic extension of the nonemigration policy, would reveal just whom that former policy had been designed to protect. The correspondence between the successive Alliance representatives in Brody (1881–82) and the central headquarters in Paris shows the elaboration of a reluctant immigration policy.

Charles Netter was sent to Brody as the Alliance representative in 1881 in order to find a solution for the thousands of Russian Jews who had fled to that Galician border city in the hopes of making their way to America. Yet the Alliance was afraid of encouraging more emigration if it helped the Brody refugees to do so. So in the first instance only those willing to return to Russia were helped. Train tickets (often to the nearest Russian town) and cash on arrival in Russia (to prevent its misappropriation in Brody for other purposes, such as emigration) were offered. However, not only did few choose this option, but of those who did, it was often only through "constraint" and "the most lively resistance."[36] The failure of the repatriation program quickly became apparent, and urgent telegrams to Paris pressed the Alliance to release money intended for repatriation to alleviate the suffering in Brody itself.[37] Another Alliance representative in Brody, Veneziani, criticized the "striking moral bankruptcy of all of the [branches of the] Alliance and of European Judaism," and when the majority of migrants had finally been dispersed, some back to Russia, he added: "Besides, one must not forget that the Russians, though barbaric, have agreed to accept back these people that we, civilized Europeans, have refused to accept."[38]

Mass, spontaneous emigration was seen as dangerous. The influx of large masses of poor immigrants was feared by the French Jewish community along with the other western European and American Jewish committees, which, from 1881 on, all sought to organize the emigration to whatever extent possible. The results often determined emigrant destinations, as European committees tried to hasten emigrant departures for the United States while the New York committee tried (unsuccessfully) to avoid their clustering on the East Coast.[39] When the United States began to place restrictions on immigration in 1906, the *Archives Israélites* complained that such an action was unjust on the part of such a large and deserted country.[40] Other suggestions for possible destinations ranged from Mexico to Cuba, Venezuela, Brazil, or French Guyana (the latter extolled for its agreeable climate!).[41] The cost of a boat ticket was cheaper than the anticipated burden the emigrants represented.

Unable to stop the outflow of eastern European Jews and repatriation meeting with only limited success, organization and regulation then became the crucial bywords of migration policy. This was not only in order to limit the quantity and ensure an equitable distribution of the emigrants but also in order to assure their quality. Single males who were "young, robust and skilled" were given priority for emigration aid, while those with large families were turned away.[42] The evaluation of one potential emigrant read: "Bern-stein will never be able to earn a living, first of all because he has a large family and secondly because he represents the typical Polish 'type': dirty, smelly and poorly raised. I recommend his being sent back to Russia."[43] Breadwinners were often sent on alone in the hopes that they would later assume the costs for the emigration of their families (even if there was some worry over bigamy "which doesn't frighten the Polish Jews enough; we should be careful not to furnish them the occasion").[44] Behind the organization and regulation of the migratory flow, the Jewish communities' fears were transparent. The migrants represented a financial burden that the receiving communities hoped to minimize or deflect.

From the viewpoint of the French community in particular it was clear that emigration was at all costs to be diverted from France. In 1893 the Marseilles Consistoire suggested, in the case of failure of repatriation, that "the more radical measure would be to prohibit the embarkation and debarkation of the unfortunate migrants."[45] Similarly the Comité de bienfaisance (Jewish Welfare Committee) wrote to the Alliance in 1905 and 1906 asking that it alert its correspondents in Salonica and Cracow to discourage the emigrants from coming to France.[46] In a circular sent to all of the western European Jewish organizations in April 1906 the Comité made a *"pressing appeal to halt all individual or collective exodus to Paris.* . . . The Russian Jewish question cannot be resolved through emigration, and even less so by the overcrowding of Paris."[47]

As the emigrants made their way to France, nevertheless, and headed toward Paris, the Parisian Jewish community cringed before the idea of a too-visible "monstrous grouping" of foreigners that could attract unfavorable opinion if not anti-Semitism: "We must, both in their [the immigrants'] own interests and in the interest of Judaism in general, react against agglomerations which are detrimental from so many points of view."[48] While admitting that ever since ancient times large cities had attracted the Jews, "this tendency to aggregate like molecules" was condemned.[49]

The idea of dispersing the immigrants throughout France was proposed as early as 1882 in order to: (1) avoid the overloading of any one community (Paris); (2) reinforce the provincial Jewish communities; and (3) aid the creation of new Jewish communities in France.[50] In addition to the numerical and religious infusion thus projected for the provincial communities, the Comité de bienfaisance also hoped to ease its own burden with regard to those left in Paris.

There resulted a push and pull of the immigrants between Paris and the periphery in which the Parisian-based assumptions of better (material and other) conditions in the provinces were not always shared or appreciated by the communities concerned. In July 1882 when the Central Committee of the Alliance israélite universelle sent a circular to Jewish communities in the provinces along with a form to complete for accepting immigrant families, the reticence with which most cities responded is notable. Those who declined altogether most often demurred on grounds of limited resources, the small size of their community, the lack of job opportunities, or the fact that they were already hosts to immigrants and suffering the financial difficulties of being located along the migration route.[51]

The cities that did agree to accept immigrant families did so with various stipulations attached:[52]

Sarrebourg (Lorraine)	One family; maximum six people; father must have a trade [*un état*].
Saverne	One family; maximum eight people; family must be "quite suitable" [*très convenable*].
Nancy	Female workers would be accepted; preferably unmarried or with only one or two children; needed for cotton- and wool-weaving industries as well as for book fabrication, locksmithing, tailoring, or tobacco manufacture.
Versailles	Two woodworkers (male), married or not; one tailor, unmarried.
Clermont-Ferrand	Three good tailors; one woodworker.
Lille	Not making an active request but will accept two apt young men with letters of recommendation "that will inspire a little confidence."
Toulouse	Two tailors, unmarried, "of course."
Nîmes	One small family of four to five intelligent people; or better three or four men who are all good workers; but far from a flourishing community here and it will be difficult for them not knowing the language.
Haguenau	One shoemaker knowing how to do rivets, married, two or three children over ten years of age.

In one case a mistake was made, so that later we read: "Here is the menswear tailor . . . in replacement of the womenswear tailor" who had first been sent.[53] The distribution of the immigrants, to whatever extent controllable, was thus largely based upon the labor power they represented. As one participant at an Alliance meeting on the Rumanian emigration summed it up: "It is imperative to control that the majority of emigrants be serious workers."[54] At the same meeting it was proposed that Rumanian Jewish workers be substituted for Italian workers in France, Germany, and elsewhere, a labor substitution that would be beneficial, given the well-known "irascible and combative" character of the latter.[55]

Selective immigration as a means of regulating economic opportunity is certainly nothing new, either within the Jewish community or without.[56] In the case of the French Jewish community of the late nineteenth century, an immigration policy was forged through the desire to protect those attainments that had been obtained from the dominant society. The Dreyfus affair had already threatened those attainments; the French Jewish community hoped to limit any further threat implied by the eastern European immigrants. The resultant migration policy clearly tried to dissuade immigration or stave it off as long as possible. Such an outcome is surprising only insofar as Jewish solidarity is presumed to be stronger than social and economic assimilation to the nation-state. While elements of both may be possible within certain nation-states, such a middle position was untenable in late nineteenth-century France.

As the first immigrants arrived in Paris, they were admired as good skilled workers. Their sad and dirty state on arrival was defended against complaints in Parisian papers, and empathy was expressed for the downward mobility incurred through migration.[57]

The Jewish press, just like the non-Jewish one, thus "discovered" the Jewish "proletariat." Jewish petroleum workers in Galicia and the Jewish proletariat in Russia were now noted along with Russian Jewish tailors in London or diamond workers in Amsterdam, and with each example of Jewish workers the legendary Jewish wealth of the anti-Semitic stereotype was explicitly refuted by the French Jewish press. The Jewish manual worker, a real producer, was the antithesis of the "parasitical" Jewish merchant or financier that the anti-Semites decried. The French Jewish bourgeoisie thus gladly claimed community with the Jewish "proletariat," pointing out proudly that "we" work with our hands. Ironically, this discovery of the Jewish worker was thus used as a shield to protect the attainments, if not the very existence, of the Jewish bourgeoisie.

If the discovery of the Jewish worker was used to deny anti-Semitic stereotypes, it was not the Jewish workers in Paris who were the ones most frequently cited, however. In numerous instances in which the French Jewish press juxtaposed the conditions of Jewish laborers in eastern Europe, the United States, and England with anti-Semitic attitudes—instances in which one might expect at least a sentence or two on the Jewish immigrant workers only a couple of *arrondissements* away—no mention was made of the Paris example. Although referring to the emigrant poor in Paris ever since the first arrivals in the early 1880s, it was not until December 1904 that the Pletzl was used as an example of Jewish workers in the polemic against the anti-Semites.[58]

For example, during a discussion on the Jewish question in the Chamber of Deputies in 1895, Alfred Naquet, a Jewish deputy, took up the attack against the anti-Semites (after prefacing his remarks with the fact that most of his best friends—his wife, in fact—were Catholic). When Jules Guesde interjected at one point that both a rich class and a proletarian class existed among the Jewish "race," Naquet agreed and gave as an example, Amsterdam.[59]

Even leftist intellectuals in the French Jewish community were initially ignorant of the Jewish immigrants in Paris. In this regard Bernard-Lazare's "Jewish journey" is revealing. In 1890 Lazare made the distinction between honest, hard-working *israélites* and dishonest, mean, rich, orthodox *juifs* who were furthermore "voluntary pariahs," adding:

> And what should I care, me, an *israélite* of France, about these Russian usurers, these Galician taverners and moneylenders, these Polish horse-traders . . . [T]hanks to these hordes, with whom we are confounded, it is forgotten that we have lived in France for almost 2,000 years. . . . We should abandon them.[60]

However, five years later in his brochure *Antisémitisme et révolution*, Lazare referred to the poor Jews in Paris, and from 1896 until his early death in 1903 he had numerous contacts with the eastern European immigrants.[61]

In general, what is striking is the paucity of information concerning the immigrants in Paris in the two major newspapers of the French Jewish community. Was this relative silence a simple ignorance or a conscious ignoring of the immigrant presence? Certainly the figurative distance between the immigrant and native communities, reinforced by linguistic, cultural, and economic walls, was much greater than the space of the two or three arrondissements that separated them geographically. Yet a conscious ignoring of the immigrant Jews was also involved. As André Spire wrote: "The French Jews who belong to the bourgeoisie have always proclaimed that to speak of Jews was to provoke anti-Semitism."[62] To speak of poor foreign Jews could only heighten that sensitivity. Perhaps more proud of Jewish workers in the abstract that in the flesh, there was a need to avert the anti-Semitic eye from the direction of the immigrant colony. First hoping to discourage that colony from forming, the French Jewish community then delayed in recognizing its existence. When it did, the view of the of the immigrant community revolved around three images—the immigrants as foreigners, as indigents, or as revolutionaries—all of which expressed the cultural and economic cleavages separating the two communities, and all of which forms the background to the little "pull" that the French Jewish community wanted to exercise.

THE IMMIGRANT AS FOREIGNER, INDIGENT, AND REVOLUTIONARY

Herzl, in the aftermath of the Dreyfus affair, wrote: "The majority decides who the 'alien' is; this and all else, in the relations between peoples, is a matter of power."[63] Indeed the epithet "alien" was especially redoubtable to French society in the period between defeat in the Franco-Prussian War and World War I. However, the French Jews turned the Jew-as-alien prejudice directed toward them against the very un-French immigrants whom they perceived as the real aliens, thus reflecting while protecting their very assimilation (and consequently internalizing a certain amount of French xenophobia). As the immigrant hero of the novel *Les eaux mêlées* complained, "One is always someone else's alien."[64] The eastern European immigrants were almost a symbolic vision of the French Jews' own precarious status as intruders. The very language of the original accusation was sometimes even reproduced in referring to the immigrants, as the anti-Semites had all Jews, as *"éléments parasitaires."*[65] Without roots, the immigrants were the eternal wanderers. As such they had to be distinguished from the settled French Jews.[66]

The foreigners' poverty only magnified their foreignness: "from Russia, from Poland, from one doesn't know where else . . . educationless, shameless, pretentious, dirty and poor—above all poor—they abound. . . . How embarrassing to show these poor relatives."[67] Poverty in and of itself, along with the attendant attributes of filth and disease so often exaggerated by the anti-Semitic press, reinforced the cultural cleavage with an economic one while at the same time representing a financial burden to the native community. The concentration of the immigrants in certain areas of the city was criticized for re-creating the same obstacles for economic development that had existed in the Pale ("in this piling up . . . it is chronic misery to which they are inevitably bound"[68]). The large number of children in eastern European families was seen as another factor contributing to the immigrants' poverty.[69] Poor, dirty, too prolific, overcrowded, underfed—so many qualities often attributed to their foreignness were but in fact manifestations of the immigrants' economic condition.

Finally, the immigrant as revolutionary must be mentioned, although the actual trade union and revolutionary activities of the Russian Jewish immigrants were largely passed over in (fearful?) silence by the French Jewish press. The immigrant nihilist or revolutionary had to be exorcised. When in 1881, after the assassination of Alexander II, the Jewish "race" was accused of nihilism, the May 5 issue of the *Archives Israélites* assured its readers that while *some* Jews may have in fact been nihilists (perhaps even justifiably so considering the conditions in Russia), nonetheless in a country where Jews were emancipated and enjoyed all civil liberties (France), patriotism would clearly preclude any revolutionary activity. Even while later admitting that Moses may have been a revolutionary, the paper emphasized that, particularly given present (emancipated) conditions, "on the whole . . . Israel has hardly the demeanor of an insurgent or rebel."[70]

When it was learned in 1885 that a letter had been sent by the Société des ouvriers russes de Paris to the Guesdist journal *Le Cri du Peuple* in order to express support of the French revolutionary socialists, the *Archives Israélites* was outraged. It denounced this most "crimson" of revolutionary papers and hoped that the letter was but the work of a couple of misled immigrants, outcast by the majority. Furthermore, a protest should be made so that France would know that the Jewish community, in giving aid to the immigrants, was not supporting "enemies of order and public peace."[71] Quite simply, in an 1882 meeting of a Paris committee on immigration, it had been declared that "the rebels must be expelled. An example is necessary."[72] The immigrant as revolutionary was certainly first on the list to be dissuaded from immigrating.

With the immigrant viewed as foreign, poverty-stricken, and/or a real or potential revolutionary, how could the French Jewish community encourage immigration to its "shores"? The cultural, economic, and political cleavages inherent in those images acted as a limit to the counterimage of Jewish solidarity and implied not only objective conditions dividing the native from the immigrant Jews, but also an ideological barrier. That ideological barrier was not only due to the fact that poverty, filth, and large families were anathema to the bourgeois ideal. More importantly, bourgeois individualism and the each-for-one's-own ethic ultimately pitted the established community against the immigrant threat. When the Jews were emancipated in France they had been emancipated as individuals rather than as a nation. This concept was important not only for the Jews' emancipation and integration, but it also became a perfect and well-needed defense against anti-Semitism: Any threats against a Jewish race or a Jewish nation were henceforth contradicted by strident affirmations of individual responsibility. In 1894, for example, one month after Dreyfus was arrested, the involvement of the Jewish community was disclaimed on these grounds:

The Jews—as Jews—thus have nothing to do with this affair; the errors—if there are any—are and must always be considered as individual errors. Neither a nation, nor a creed, nor any profession must bear the punishment for the unlawful acts of one of its members.[73]

Similarly, the contradictions between collective and individual responsibility were best summarized in a first-page editorial entitled "*Solidarité!*" of the *Archives Israélites* of May 1, 1913:

This solidarity, noble waif of that treasury of Jewish virtues which the century has swept away through its steamrace, we reclaim it with rightful pride. . . .

However, it must be recognized that the conditions for the existence of the Jews and their customs have been considerably modified in our modern era. Individualism, for the Jews, as for others, has retrieved all of its rights.

Each man for himself, for better or for worse, such is the principle which must guide us in our understanding of the facts. . . .

This tunic of Nessus which is Jewish solidarity, in the sense in which these "Messieurs" [the anti-Semites who took the crime of one as the crime of all] understand it, has fallen from our shoulders ever since the day when, in right as in equity, collective responsibility ceded its place to individual responsibility.

Such a clear expression of independence from the notion of an externally imposed collective responsibility was only possible after more than a century had elapsed since the Jewish individual's emancipation. As a logical conclusion to its own history, to the pressures and desire to assimilate to French society, and above all to the fear that the hard-won attainments of the century would be destroyed through an indiscriminate (as always) anti-Semitism, this attitude of the French Jewish community necessarily underscored its reception of the eastern European immigrants.

Nevertheless, to ascertain and trace the decline of collective responsibility in the nineteenth century is not however to say that it had disappeared completely. A certain tenacity of cohesiveness persisted, which may be examined in the philanthropic structure through which it remained extant. The contours of Jewish solidarity—as imagined by non-Jews, as expected by certain immigrants, and as expressed somewhat grudgingly by the institutions in question—and its effect as a "pull" factor cannot be completely understood without a look at the philanthropic structure offered the immigrant poor.

PHILANTHROPY

In 1895 the Grand Rabbi Zadoc Kahn lamented that the Jews of France were no longer held together by a "community of suffering" as they had been in the past.[74] Yet, this historical consciousness continued to be expressed through philanthropic expenditures and occasional religious or social events, even if it was a far cry from the morally and structurally tightly woven kahal (community) of the preemancipation period. More importantly for our purposes, the philanthropic structure of the French Jewish community represented an implicit immigration force whether the community intended it or not. Furthermore, it exerted that force in spite of the limited way in which it functioned vis-à-vis the immigrants.

Only a handful of organizations were created in Paris before World War I explicitly in order to deal with the immigrants. The first was the Université populaire juive, founded in 1902 with the purpose of easing the culture shock of immigration by familiarizing the immigrants with the French language and "spirit" and offering information on practical aspects of life in France; Jewish subjects were taught as well.[75] The *Archives Israélites* praised the université for its work toward the "social regeneration of a meritorious class."[76] An employment bureau was opened there in January 1904, and the university's premises also served for literary, scientific, and artistic gatherings. A day school for children operated on Saturdays, and the 1902–3 report expressed the hope of eventually offering medical and legal aid services. A Dispensaire Zadoc Kahn was created there in 1910.[77]

Although its popularity cannot really be measured (one estimate given was five hundred students; a university brochure spoke of two to three hundred people attending the Sunday evening conferences and sixty persons enrolled in French courses), the Université populaire juive was, according to J. Tchernoff, "the first and most efficacious drawing together of Russian Jewish circles, French Judaism and French culture."[78] As expressed by *L'Univers Israélite* the university was to create a Jewish solidarity not only in the sense of a "fraternal collaboration" among all of the "fractions" of the community but in the sense of a melting pot of integration.[79] Assimilation of the immigrants to the Jewish community was to parallel integration of the latter into French society as a whole.

Educational efforts were not enough, however, and various plans were tried in order to help the immigrants find work. The very first of such efforts had been the creation, in November 1882, of three paper workshops, which employed thirteen men and thirty-five women at two francs per day. However, the workers soon complained to the Grand Rabbi about the contemptuous treatment they were receiving, and a delegation also went to see Rothschild. When no satisfaction was reached, twenty of the workers eventually went back to Russia. The workshops only lasted six months.[80]

More successful was the Atelier, founded in 1906 and employing up to sixty-five immigrants in the fabrication of Parisian souvenirs (photo albums, postcards, etc.) and small furniture items. French classes were offered and the Atelier also functioned as a placement bureau for the immigrants. Three to four hundred people per year (about one-fifth of them women) were already being accepted by 1909, and this organization was lauded for utilizing and developing those talents and "treasures of intelligence" that would otherwise be wasted in "exploitative trades and parasitical professions."[81]

Finally, there is also mention of an organization called Soutien aux émigrants which existed from at least 1907 to 1914.[82] However, besides these few works created specifically for the immigrants in the period before World

War I, it was largely to the already-existing philanthropic institutions that the immigrant poor would turn. Generally not eligible for French welfare (limited to French citizens as of 1886; see Appendix B), and expectant with regard to Jewish solidarity, most needy immigrants would first turn to the French Jewish organizations. If 31 percent of those cared for at the Hôpital Rothschild in 1913 were Russians and another 5 percent were Rumanians, the majority of French Jewish charitable institutions were not prepared to adapt to the immigrant influx.[83] One organization, the Oeuvre israélite de travail et de placement, founded in the third arrondissement in February 1881 just before the immigration began, was forced to close its doors only three years later, having been overwhelmed by the increasing numbers of Russian Jews.[84] Le Toit familial, a free employment agency for women founded in 1891, had to appeal to the Alliance israélite universelle for financial help in 1906 because of the increased number of foreigners using its services.[85] The Refuge de Plessis Piquet, an orphanage founded in 1899, agreed to accept five Russian orphans, out of a sentiment of "*haute solidarité religieuse,*" but only "*à titre exceptionnel*"—as an exception.[86]

However, the one organization that came to be the most flexible in responding to the changing needs of the community and that continues this role today for the more recent North African Jewish immigrants in Paris was the Comité de bienfaisance, founded in 1809 by the Consistoire as the Comité consistorial de la Société israélite de secours et d'encouragement.[87] The threefold aim of the Comité, as outlined in 1898, was to take care of orphans and abandoned children, ameliorate the lot of poor workers, and take care of ill, disabled, and aged persons. Various funds were funneled through the Comité, which in turn subsidized different community organizations.

With the first arrivals of immigrants in 1882–83 the Comité arranged for lodging, food, and maintenance for some thirteen hundred Russian refugees (thus preventing "any perturbation which could be troublesome for the community").[88] Three houses were purchased on rue Eugène Sue (Montmartre) and cité Jeanne d'Arc (13th arrondissement) for 154 families coming from Brody, thus integrating these areas with Jews for the first time; later, in 1892–93, the Comité also rented buildings in the 12th arrondissement to house the immigrants on a temporary basis.[89]

The general aid structure of the Comité was divided into two sections similar to the public welfare office's distinction between *indigents*—those receiving annual aid—and *nécessiteux*—those receiving temporary aid. The Comité's category of *pauvres inscrits* (registered poor) included elderly persons, widows, orphans, and all those registered for aid on a regular basis. Admission to this category required a lengthy inquiry into the applicant's circumstances and was thus less flexible in responding to immigration spurts or seasonal fluctuations of immigrant trades. The Comité's second aid category was called *secours immédiats* (immediate aid), distributed both on a bimonthly basis for special appropriations and as *distributions quotidiennes* (daily distributions). The latter consisted of anything from cash to coupons for bread, meat, fuel, or clothing, and these distributions, along with the soup kitchens set up by the Comité, represented the most immediate aid available to the immigrant poor.

A first soup kitchen had been opened in the Pletzl area in 1855, and was seconded by another in 1892 in the Montmartre area (where a special room was set aside for Russian students). The number of portions distributed in these kitchens fluctuated with the weather, and they were closed from April through September. During the events of 1870–71, 185,000 portions were distributed; that figure rose to 208,000 during the harsh winter of 1879–80. With the arrival of the Russian immigrants in 1882–83, 326,000 portions were served. The closing of American and Hamburg ports in 1892 also had its repercussions on the Parisian soup kitchens as emigrants were rerouted through France. In 1905, at the time of the mass exodus, the kitchen in the Pletzl, which usually served 400 to 450 portions per day, served up to 1,800 portions daily.

Aiding the immigrant poor was not without problems. Recidivists at the soup kitchens or at the daily distributions became suspect as professional beggars, and the *Archives Israélites* wrote in 1909 that: "One of the inconveniences of the oppression [in eastern Europe], which drags along so much in its wake, is the creation of a class of parasites."[90] To discourage those professionals who made the rounds of all philanthropic organizations and individuals in Paris, a system of centralized charity was organized through the Comité in 1893, similar to systems that had recently been organized by the town halls of the 4th, 12th, and 19th arrondissements. Donors were requested to give their money to the Comité in exchange for tokens to be given to any beggar who came to their door. It was then up to the Comité, based on its experience in such matters, to decide whether the needy person was sincere or not.

The acumen of the Comité was sometimes brought into question, however. In one incident in 1887 a man came to the office asking for passage money to America. Stopping short of no histrionics, he threatened to commit suicide if his request was not satisfied. The Comité took no heed, believing him to be a professional in such tactics, but then learned that the man had thrown himself into the Seine! Luckily he was rescued, but the moral of the story for the *Archives Israélites* was then: To give, give always—it is better to err in that direction than in the other.[91]

To be sure, a certain amount of outright fraud existed. When deceit was discovered in the annual matzo distribution in 1889, the *Archives Israélites* wrote indignantly about the indigents' taking advantage of the Pesach motto: Let him who is hungry come and eat.[92] To be able to better unmask those *éléments parasitaires* who were taking advantage of French Jewish largesse, a central information office was created by the Comité in 1900. These reorganizational efforts were not accepted unanimously by the community, however. The *Archives Israélites*, while agreeing with the principle of more stringent measures, lamented that foreigners often found the welfare office closed ("*voilà* something which disturbs a little our traditional ideas about the practice of charity") and concluded that resorting to police measures in order to counter dishonesty only ended in wronging the truly needy.[93] Finally it was the *"schnorrer ambulants"* who were blamed for inhibiting the philanthropic process. By abusing the donor's confidence with moving stories, "told to pull the tears from our eyes—and the money from our pockets," it was above all the *vrai pauvre*, the truly poor, who was thus wronged.[94]

The Comité de bienfaisance, consistorial representative of the Jewish solidarity offered the immigrants by the natives, also represented the limits of philanthropic aid. The most important limit of all was a financial one—a concern for the continued welfare of the welfare organization itself. As immigration grew the Comité de bienfaisance had to repeatedly ask the Alliance israélite universelle to increase its contribution (up to 50 percent during the 1905–1906 period) to the Comité's works. The Alliance, already besieged by requests for aid from all sides, answered on at least two occasions by reiterating its international scope and shifting the responsibility back to the Parisian Jewish community itself: "The Alliance cannot do for the rich community in Paris what it cannot do for smaller and less well-off communities."[95] By 1904 the Comité had spent approximately one million francs for either the further transit or the settlement of Russian Jews in Paris. Yet the growing strain on the financial resources of the community was obvious: the refugees "are frightfully expensive" *(nous coûtent les yeux de la tête)*; we must "get rid of" *(se débarrasser)* them.[96]

Finally, however, there was one limit to philanthropic aid that underscored all others: the fear that philanthropy would act as an immigration force. *Le Figaro* of August 25, 1892, had explained that the emigrants who camped out at the Gare de Lyon train station had been pushed by misery, and "some of them had the idea of leaving Constantinople to come to France *where they knew that they had very rich coreligionists*" (emphasis added). During a Chamber of Deputies discussion on the Jewish question three years later, an anti-Semite linked the "infiltration" of Jewish immigrants, among other things, to the fact that they were "greet[ed] with open arms."[97]

The Parisian Jewish community was sensitive to this issue, as became clear in its defensive attitude with regard to such charges. *Le Paris* of August 27, 1892, related that it had been assured by the Alliance israélite universelle that neither it nor the Comité de bienfaisance had ever encouraged the emigrants to come to Paris.[98] Even within the Jewish community such fears were expressed as when the Alliance wrote to the Baron de Hirsch in 1891 criticizing his plan for creating Jewish agricultural colonies in Argentina on the grounds that it would be an incitement to emigration.[99] Worry over philanthropy as an immigrant pull was but an extension of the migration policy described above.

The French Jewish community tried to avoid any actions that could constitute an immigration force attracting eastern European Jews to their country. As in other western European countries and the United States as well, when repatriation failed, organization and distribution became the bywords of immigration policy. Even then, immigration was posited as a temporary phenomenon—for the longest time the refugees were referred to as *emigrants*—and the needy were accepted by the philanthropic organizations as by the provincial Jewish communities only à *titre exceptionnel.* The background of xenophobia and anti-Semitism in late nineteenth-century France could only heighten French Jewish sensitivity in the matter, and the immigration of their foreign coreligionists brought a shudder to the French Jewish community as it subsumed anti-Semitic rhetoric in its own reaction toward the eastern European Jews: dirty, foreign, and poor, if not downright revolutionary.

Nevertheless, expectations of Jewish solidarity did act as an implicit immigration force. The very existence of the important Jewish community and its philanthropic organizations created a sort of magnet whether the organized French Jewish community intended it or not. The addresses of the Alliance israélite universelle and the Comité de bienfaisance often circulated in eastern Europe. If not, they were quickly acquired upon arrival as part of the immigrant information network. Wolf Speiser's *Kalendar*, a guide for the newly arrived, included addresses of French Jewish institutions that could be of aid to the immigrants.[100] Thus, in spite of the community's efforts to circumscribe that "pull" or divert the flow elsewhere, it ultimately could not inhibit growing numbers of immigrants from settling in Paris. Most of all, the Parisian Jewish community could not prevent the attraction of economic opportunities available in France's first and foremost manufacturing center, nor the inertial flow created by the growing immigrant community itself.

If expectations of Jewish solidarity could aid the migration process, they could not prevent disillusionment upon arrival. The unwillingness of the French Jewish community to provide an immigration pull was reflected in the subsequent unwillingness to welcome the immigrants into their community institutions, a struggle well elaborated by Hyman and Weinberg. It is important, however, to reexamine the Jewish immigrant organizations not only as an expression of conflict with the native Jewish community but as resulting from needs relating to the immigrant condition itself. We must therefore now turn to immigrant life and politics in the Pletzl and Montmartre in its Jewish Belle Epoque variant.

Three
LEBN VI GOT IN FRANKRAYKH?*
Settling In

A Paris—la Mecque, pour des milliers de personnes enfermées à l'Est . . .
d'accepter après des années d'illusion une confrontation entre l'imaginaire
et le réel. —*Le Monde*, 1978

Dans le café exigu que tient un immigré, il rejoint ses amis pour dîner d'un
hareng arrosé d'une chope ou d'un verre d' "esprit," jouer aux cartes, discu-
ter sur la politique intérieure de la Russie ou les intérêts de la corporation.
—Maurice Lauzel, 1912

Arrival. Gare du Nord. By following the flow of the crowd to the exit, a first
new word is learned: *sortie* (exit). Ironic greeting, having just arrived. Border
crossings and train station benches behind, the address of a relative or a
friend of a friend found, the settling-in process begins. The settling in of the
Jewish immigrants in Paris, the creation of their own organizations, would
constitute the immigrants' concrete response to the lack of French or French
Jewish institutions capable of meeting their needs. The governmental infrastructure, especially in the period before more organized immigration had
gotten under way, offered little, if only surly bureaucrats, to meet and greet
the newly arrived. The welfare state, with health insurance and retirement
plans, was still a thing of the future; factory legislation and other laws to

*The proverb "To live like God in France" apparently dates to 1693 when King
Maximilian reportedly said: If it were possible that I were God and I had two sons, the
first would succeed me as God and the second would be king of France. The Yiddish
oral tradition adopted the phrase as its own. [André Billy and Moïse Twersky,
L'épopée de Ménaché Foïgel, 3 vols. (Paris: Plon, 1927–28)], 1:243.

protect workers were just beginning to be passed. The attitude of the French Jewish community has been seen.

But above all, immigrant organizations arose from the immigrant condition itself. They were created not only as an answer to the French Jewish community but as a response to the conditions which set the immigrants apart in the first place. Language and culture, geographic and economic concentration, and a precarious material situation all led the immigrants to found their own newspapers and theater, oratories and even a synagogue, mutual aid and philanthropic societies, as well as their own political and trade union organizations.

These organizations, as those of any immigrants, were first characterized by a natural continuation of social and cultural customs from the old country. However, confronted with the legal, economic, and cultural boundaries of the new environment, the Jewish immigrants had to elaborate their own mode of adaptation to French society and its Parisian variant in the Belle Epoque. By examining the organization of immigrant life and the synthesis of cultures and structures that ultimately arose, we can perhaps clarify the strains of adaptation within a nation-state where one belongs to the state but not to the nation.

Ultimately the immigrants were mostly aided by the only people who realized that it was useless to tell them to go home: previous immigrants, *landslayt* (compatriots), relatives, old friends, people who may have written them about freedom yet unemployment, but who had sometimes enclosed a little money that contradicted the latter, and who now took in the newly arrived until they could get settled. The remembrance of one's own apprehensive arrival was in the not-so-distant past, and the strength of any immigrant community lies in the self-help networks which develop out of necessity. A Yiddish calendar-booklet (*Kalendar*) published in 1910 by Wolf Speiser offered information and warnings to the newly arrived: how to get a cab from the train station to the Jewish quarter; consulate addresses for those in transit; addresses of restaurants serving as informal job information offices; warnings against charlatans (a whole page about a firm of imposter-lawyers) who would take the *griner*'s (greenhorn's) money and run. The immigrant network also extended back to emigrant beginnings, that is, to friends and family in eastern Europe. Many in fact arrived with an address in hand, and that address usually led to the Jewish quarter in the Marais—the Pletzl, to which we may now go ourselves.

GEOGRAPHY

The most visible center of eastern European immigrant activity and that which was the usual basis for journalistic accounts of the immigrants' life was

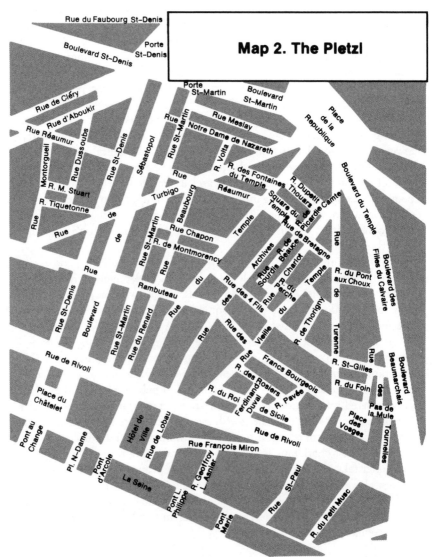

Map 2. The Pletzl

Rue du Faubourg St-Denis

Boulevard St-Denis

Porte St-Denis

Porte St-Martin

Boulevard St-Martin

Place de la République

Rue de Ciéry

Rue d'Aboukir

Rue Réaumur

Montorgueil

Rue Dussoubs

R. M. Stuart

R. Tiquetonne

Rue

Rue

Rue St-Denis

Sébastopol

Rue St-Martin

Rue St-Martin

Notre Dame de Nazareth

Rue Meslay

R. Volta

Rue

Turbigo

Beaubourg

Réaumur

R. des Fontaines du Temple

R. Dupetit Thouars

Square du Temple

Rue de Picardie

Rue de Bretagne

Boulevard du Temple

de

Rue

Rue Chapon

R. de Montmorency

Rue St-Martin

Rue

du

Temple

Archives

Rue Sourdis

R. de Beauce

R. du Perche

R. Charlot

Rue du Temple

R. du Pont aux Choux

Boulevard des Filles du Calvaire

Rue

Rambuteau

Rue du Renard

Rue St-Martin

Rue

des

Rue des 4 Fils

Rue Vieille

R. de Thorigny

de

Turenne

Rue

Boulevard

Rue St-Denis

Rue de Rivoli

Rue

Rue des

Rue

Francs Bourgeois

R. des Rosiers

R. St-Gilles

R. du Foin

Rue

des

Boulevard Beaumarchais

Place du Châtelet

R. du Roi

Ferdinand Duval

R. Pavée

de Sicile

Rue de Rivoli

Pas de la Mule

Place des Vosges

Rue Tournelles

Boulevard Beaumarchais

Pont au Change

Pl. N-Dame

Pont d'Arcole

Hôtel de Ville

Rue de Lobau

Rue François Miron

La Seine

Pont L. Philippe

R. Geoffroy L. Asnier

Pont Marie

Rue St-Paul

R. du Petit Musc

Viviane Issembert-Gannat, *Guide du Judaïsme à Paris* (Paris: Editions de la Pensée Moderne, 1964) the Marais—on the Right Bank in the 3rd and 4th arrondissements. Called the Pletzl (little square) by its inhabitants, it included the rue des Rosiers, rue des Ecouffes, rue Ferdinand Duval, and rue Vieille du Temple, along with rue de Geoffroy l'Asnier and rue de Fourcy on the other side of the rue de Rivoli. Small kosher restaurants, bakeries, and delicatessens gave this neighborhood a far more eastern European than French flavor. With Talmudic or political debates only a café away, with the logistical ease of gathering ten men for a *minyan* (prayer group) and the place des Vosges nearby for *shpatsirn* (taking a stroll), the eastern European immigrants could feel at home in the middle of Paris.

The Marais has a Jewish history dating back (although not continuously) to the thirteenth century. At that time the present rue Ferdinand Duval was first mentioned under its original name, rue des Juifs (Street of the Jews),[1] and the nearby rue des Ecouffes (meaning pawnbrokers) and the rue des Rosiers (perhaps from *ros*, the teeth on a loom) were already known as centers of Ashkenazic Jewry in Paris. More modest Jews lived there, the richer ones—generally of Sephardic origin—preferred the 5th arrondissement on the Left Bank of the Seine. As the historian Sauval described the streets of the Right Bank settlement, they were "narrow, tortuous and obscure" even then.[2]

The reasons why a modern Jewish neighborhood was once again reconstituted in the Marais after the Jews had been expelled from France and from Paris in the Middle Ages are unclear.[3] But by the time the Consistoire was established by Napoleon in 1808, the majority of its 2,736 members lived in that same area, which was known as the Jewish quarter. The census of 1809 showed that almost one-half of the Jewish heads of households in Paris were peddlers, so it is perhaps little wonder that they lived in one of the city's poorer districts.[4] With the social and economic integration of the Jewish community during the nineteenth century, however, those who "arrived" moved out of the poor 3rd and 4th arrondissements, resulting in a more even sociogeographic distribution of the Jewish population in Paris by 1872.[5]

However, the 1872 census also reveals that peddling, if by then only occupying 10 percent of the total active Jewish population in Paris, still represented 19.5 percent in the 4th arrondissement.[6] Fifty-nine percent of the unskilled male Jewish workers and 47 percent of the Jewish artisans in Paris still lived in the Marais, and conversely, artisans (already concentrated in the clothing industry), small-scale merchants, employees, and menial laborers represented the vast majority of Jewish occupations there.[7]

The correlation between housing patterns and socioeconomic realities thus attracted the poor eastern European Jews to this area, but they were not the first nineteenth-century Jewish immigrants to choose this particular poor quarter out of others. An important number of Alsatian Jews had moved there following the Franco-Prussian War, and a much smaller but nonetheless significant number of Polish Jewish immigrants had also moved there in 1863 in the wake of the unsuccessful Polish revolt of that year. While accounting for only 1.4 percent of the Jewish population in 1809, the eastern Europeans already represented approximately 5 percent of the Jewish population of Paris by 1872, but they constituted 17 percent of the Jewish population of the 4th arrondissement alone; conversely this neighborhood was the domicile of over one-half of all of the eastern European Jews in Paris.[8] Thus this corner of Paris, for socioeconomic as well as ethnic reasons, was to be a pole of attraction for the eastern European immigrants from 1881 on. With the relative visibility of the immigrant poor, foreignness and poverty would become synonymous.

After 1881, although the total Jewish population of the 3rd and 4th arrondissements declined (from 46 percent of the Jewish population in Paris in 1872 to 30 percent in 1885–87 to 26 percent in 1895–97 and in 1905–7, reflecting the continued economic and geographic mobility of Jews throughout the city), this tendency was much more marked for French-born than for foreign-born Jews. The immigrant proportion of the Jews in that area increased during the same period (from 16 percent in 1872 to 42 percent in 1885–87 to 45 percent in 1895–97 and to 61 percent in 1905–7) as the majority of eastern European Jews continued to choose the Marais as a place in which to live.[9]

Table 5a and Map 3 show the geographic distribution of Russian and Rumanian immigrants in Paris in 1901, the only year for which such detailed information is available. The attraction of the 4th arrondissement is clear. The immigrants in that district not only represented the largest single concentration of eastern Europeans in Paris, but represented 40 percent of that district's immigrant population in an arrondissement less immigrant-populated than others.

It can be seen in Table 5b, however, that as more immigrants settled in Paris after 1872, a certain movement out of the 3rd and 4th arrondissements began to take place similar to that of the French Jews. Sixty-seven percent of the eastern European immigrants had chosen the Marais in which to live in 1872; but that figure declined somewhat to 58 percent in 1885–87 and to 53 percent in 1895–97. This was still a significant number, but it anticipated the more even housing distribution of the 1901 population (14.8 percent living in Montmartre, the 18th arrondissement, and 10.7 percent in the 11th, contiguous to the 3rd) and the greater dispersal of immigrants that would occur from 1905–1907 on, when only 39 percent chose the Marais.[10]

This relative dispersion of eastern European immigrants during the period from 1881 to World War I was due to several factors, among them a certain differentiation among the immigrants themselves. The study of the forces of emigration and immigration has already evoked the subcommunities that constituted the immigrant Jewish community in Paris: workers, political

TABLE 5

GEOGRAPHIC DISTRIBUTION

a - Russians and Rumanians in Paris, 1901[a]

Arr.	Imm. Pop. (%)	Russians and Rumanians			
		Number	As % of Arr. Pop.	As % of Foreign Pop.	As Distributed among Selves
1	7.9%	212	0.3%	4.3%	1.6%
2	7.3	212	0.3	4.6	1.6
3	5.3	727	0.8	15.4	5.4
4	6.7	2,717	2.7	40.7	20.3
5	4.8	918	0.8	16.3	6.9
6	5.4	400	0.4	7.4	3.0
7	4.5	198	0.2	4.5	1.5
8	10.8	448	0.4	4.1	3.3
9	10.7	1,093	0.9	8.4	8.2
10	6.4	466	0.3	4.7	3.5
11	5.9	1,433	0.6	10.3	10.7
12	4.7	357	0.3	5.9	2.7
13	2.4	329	0.3	10.7	2.5
14	3.6	305	0.2	6.0	2.3
15	3.2	236	0.2	4.9	1.8
16	10.9	579	0.5	4.5	4.3
17	6.7	501	0.3	3.8	3.7
18	5.7	1,985	0.8	14.3	14.8
19	5.3	138	0.1	1.8	1.0
20	4.0	124	0.1	1.9	0.9
Ave. or Total	6.1	13,378	0.5	8.7	100.0

[a]Derived from Annuaire statistique de la ville de Paris, Année 1901 (Paris: Imprimérie municipale, 1903), p. 211 (Serbs and Bulgarians are also included with Rumanians).

b - Jewish Immigrants in Paris--1872, 1901

Arrondissement		1872[a]	1901[b]
Well-to-do:	1-2	3.3%	3.2%
Well-to-do:	5-8, 16	3.8	19.0
Average:	9-11	28.9	22.4
Poor:	3-4	55.7	25.7
Periphery:	12-15, 17-20	8.3	29.7
Total		100.0%	100.0%

[a]Jewish Eastern European immigrants only. Doris Ben-Simon Donath, Socio-démographie des Juifs de France et d'Algérie, 1869-1907, P.O.F.-Etudes (Presses orientalistes de France, 1976), p. 104.

[b]All Eastern European immigrants (Jewish as well as non-Jewish). See Table 5a.

Map 3. Russians and Rumanians in Paris, 1901.

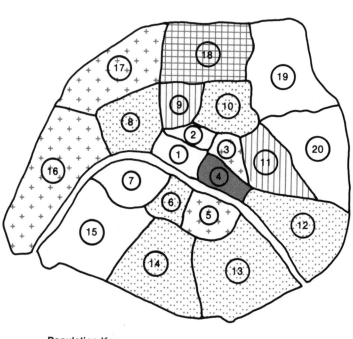

Population Key

- [300–500]
- [501–1000]
- [1001–1500]
- [1501–2000]
- [2001–3000]

Circled numbers indicate *arrondissements.* "Right Bank" denotes those areas north of the Seine (notably the 4th and 18th *arrondissements,* the Pletzl or Marais and Montmartre neighborhoods respectively). "Left Bank" denotes those areas south of the Seine (notably the 5th and 13th *arrondissements,* the Latin Quarter and Gobelins neighborhoods respectively).

activists, and students. Each group sought out those geographical areas best suited for its settlement: Students moved to the Left Bank near the Latin Quarter (5th arrondissement); professional revolutionaries followed political leaders to the 5th and 13th arrondissements (Peter Lavrov had settled in Paris in 1876 on rue St. Jacques); and workers moved to the different areas of the city where their trades were concentrated: capmaking, fur, and leatherworking in the Marais (3rd and 4th arrondissements); tailoring on Montmartre (18th arrondissement); woodworking near the rue du faubourg St. Antoine (11th and 12th arrondissements), where the Marché Trôle provided a well-known outlet for their products; tanning in the Gobelins area (13th arrondissement), etc.

Dispersal also came about due to the overcrowding of the Pletzl. For while seeking to escape from the confinement and limited mobility of the Pale, the immigrants soon became concentrated and cramped in the Marais. Thus a second Jewish workers' community grew up in Montmartre, following the Comité de bienfaisance's initiative at housing immigrant families on rue Eugène Sue. Soon after, several other streets became the center of a new Jewish quarter there—rue Ordener, rue Simart, rue Marcadet, etc.—where, due to the original placing of Odessa-expelled Rumanian Jews, the Montmartre immigrant community also had a more Rumanian character.[11]

The strong if not stifling Jewish character of the Pletzl was at once its charm and its repudiation. The hero of one biographical novel about immigration to Paris in the early 1900s—*L'épopée de Ménaché Foïgel*—called the Montmartre area the "new Jerusalem" in contrast to the more traditional atmosphere of the Marais. As Ménaché became a proud "Parisian" on Montmartre, he even denigrated the Pletzl area:

> This complacency, in the middle of Paris, for oriental negligence was undeserving of French civilization! Was it admissible that in the streets of the City of Lights Jews with *payes* and caftans, just like those which provoked jeers from the urchins in Apukorsovo, could still exist?[12]

Even within the small area of the Pletzl there was (and still is) a marked difference between streets only a couple of blocks apart. The rue des Ecouffes and rue des Rosiers area was dirty, crowded, and slumlike. But a move to the rue des Francs-Bourgeois, the *"faubourg St.-Germain du quartier juif,"* only a few blocks away, was a real sign of upward mobility for Yankel Mykhanowitzki, the hero of another immigrant novel, *Les Eaux mêlées.*[13]

Yankel's and Ménaché's snobbery, which could only be relative given their very modest conditions, points to the differences that existed among the immigrant Jewish workers themselves. Just as the established French Jews deflected anti-Semitic attacks by vaunting their own assimilation and considering all of the eastern European immigrants as *polaks*, the immigrants

TABLE 6

RUSSIAN AND RUMANIAN STUDENTS AT THE UNIVERSITE DE PARIS

Year	Total	Russians	Rumanians	As % of Foreign Students	As % of Total Students
1905-6	1061	841	220	53.0	7.0
1906-7	2064	1801	263	59.5	11.8
1907-8	2444	2142	302	59.0	12.7
1908-9	2656	2377	279	57.8	13.3
1909-10	2858	2505	353	58.5	13.4
1910-11	2690	2367	323	57.6	13.5
1911-12	2731	2362	369	56.5	13.6
1912-13	2649	2219	430	57.4	13.4

SOURCE: Annuaire statistique de la ville de Paris, Années 1905-12 (Paris: Imprimerie municipale, 1907-15).

distinguished among themselves with regard to their insertion in French society. The disgust of the Francs-Bourgeoisiens for those who lived on the rue des Ecouffes, the disdain of the Montmartrois for the Marais inhabitants, the "worldliness" and exasperation of those already settled toward those just arrived (Yankel's readjustment at the arrival of his wife), not to mention the Russian Jew's disdain for the Polish Jew—all of these distinctions are crucial for understanding the immigrant population in Paris.

The immigrant community on the Left Bank also had its subcommunities: A somewhat higher percentage of Rumanians in the 5th arrondissement and of Russians in the 13th seems to bear out the importance of the Latin Quarter (5th) for the many Rumanian foreign students and the importance of the Gobelins area (13th) as a center for Russian revolutionary circles.[14] The eastern European student community deserves to be mentioned apart. It too was the result of both a push from the East, the numerus clausus, and a pull from the West as the Université de Paris encouraged foreign students to matriculate.[15] The number of eastern European students in Paris was estimated at approximately 100 in 1887, double that in 1888 due to the numerus clausus, about 500 in 1894 and double that again by 1904.[16] Then, due to the large exodus after the 1905 Russian Revolution, the Russian students alone more than doubled from that school year to the next, leading the police to comment somewhat disparagingly that they could barely hear a word of French on the rue Flatters (5th arrondissement), where a large number of Russian students lived.

A description that perhaps most clearly depicts the opposite spectrum from the Pletzl is that of J. Tchernoff, by his own account an "entirely Russified Jew," who came to Paris in the early 1890s to pursue a law degree. Tchernoff stressed not only the limited contacts between the French Jews and the Russian immigrants, but he also noted the differences between the immigrants of the Right and Left Banks: the radicals, students, and artists residing on the Left Bank as contrasted to the petit-bourgeois and workers of the Right Bank colony.[17]

Tchernoff's own existence in a series of cheap, tiny apartments in the Latin Quarter, when he was not just trying to make ends meet (the lot of many an impoverished son—and many daughters—of the Russian Jewish bourgeoisie, on their own studying in the West), centered around his studies. Clearly more at home with the Russian intelligentsia, he nonetheless had a certain disdain for them ("the workers . . . less deformed by passion . . . exhibited a candor and purity of soul that you don't find among the intellectuals"), and he too would cross the Seine from time to time, drawn to the Pletzl "by an irresistible nostalgia."[18]

While the differences between the Left and Right Bank immigrant colonies were quite real, they should not be exaggerated nor should the degree of contact between them be minimized. Maxime Rodinson's account of his father's experiences in Paris at the beginning of the century reveals not only the links and flow of many immigrants back and forth across the Seine, but points to a certain mixture of intelligentsia and working class, of political and economic interests that characterized the Jewish immigrant community.[19]

Having left Vitebsk in 1885 in order to avoid military service, Maurice Rodinson left behind the relative comfort of his family's position as well as his studies in Smolensk. He first settled in the Pletzl area, where he was able to find work as a rubber-mantle worker, a trade that he learned in Paris. Similarly, his future wife, who came to France in 1902, worked in rubberizing in the 4th arrondissement. The Rodinsons practiced their trade at home, first in an apartment on the Right Bank (4th arrondissement) and later on the Left Bank (5th arrondissement), two doors down from the Bibliothèque Turgeneff, where Rodinson was librarian.

While an antireligious and nontraditional spirit seems to have encouraged the initial move away from the Pletzl, the Rodinsons' friends on the Left Bank, certainly all of those who came to the house, remained Jews with whom they spoke in either Russian or Yiddish. Furthermore, they kept up their old contacts, going weekly to the Pletzl to see friends and renew discussions. Inescapably aware of their status as foreigners, the Rodinsons, like Tchernoff, nonetheless sought to be French. If asked, they would have defined themselves as French or perhaps Russian, but never Jewish.

These subcommunities that constituted the larger immigrant community are important to recognize so as not to treat the immigrants as an undifferentiated mass—as the French Jewish community and the police department tended to do. Such distinctions are also important for understanding the mobility—however relative—that was possible within a fairly closed environment and that would play a significant role in the economic relationships within the community. Economic, political, and social as well as religious differences would determine each immigrant's identity and dictate the immigrant organizations that he or she would choose to join.

With this in mind we can turn to the immigrant organizations to see how the "flavor" of the Pletzl and Montmartre was created not only through delicatessens, restaurants, and bakeries but through the continuity of language, customs, the organization of religious life, mutual aid societies, the creation of philanthropic organizations, and the reconstitution of political circles. The immigrant structures reveal the immigrants' specific needs, the very first of which has to do with language.

YIDDISH

Language marks the immigrant as a foreigner and is the initial impediment to integration. The hegemonic character of the indigenous language— especially in France, where it is particularly important to speak the language well if one is to speak it at all—reinforces the setting apart of the foreigner, while political considerations can further strengthen that linguistic hegemony. In the period before World War I, anything resembling German was suspect, and the police often mistook Yiddish for German (when spoken) or Hebrew (when written).[20]

The usual description of Yiddish in both the Jewish and non-Jewish press was as a "jargon," and the French Jewish community's disdain for that "jargon" accompanied its politics of assimilation throughout the nineteenth century. Yiddish symbolized preemancipation days. Thus the new impetus given to Yiddish at the end of the century by the eastern European immigrants was hardly received with enthusiasm. At best, *L'Univers Israélite* said to leave it alone, and it would die out of its own accord. As the newspaper concluded, somewhat ambivalently, in 1913: "For social as well as religious reasons, *judéo-allemand* should be neither despised nor detested. Just like those who speak it, if it has no right to our admiration, it merits our sympathy."[21]

But if language is that which sets immigrants apart, it is also that which binds their community together. Yiddish flourished in the immigrant Jewish neighborhoods, and Yiddish theater appeared in Paris during the Bell Epoque. Several touring groups came through as early as 1885, performing plays by Shaikevich and Lateiner in the 4th, 18th, and 5th arrondissements. They were successful but ephemeral. Then a Club dramatique israélite russe was founded in the 18th arrondissement in 1889 with the help of the famous Goldfaden, then living in Paris. The troupe continued performing after Goldfaden's departure, and when *Le Figaro* reviewed one of their plays only to mock it, *L'Univers Israélite* came to the theater's defense and even called Goldfaden a "sort of Molière."[22] In late 1895 another theatrical group was started under the directorship of Leon Gelis, and from 1896 to around 1904 two performances per week were held at the Théâtre des folies Voltaire. A Yidisher literarisher dramatisher fareyn, a Yiddish theater called Théâtre de nouveatés (sic) parisiennes, and even Yiddish vaudeville made their appearance in 1912–14. When Sholem Aleichem passed through Paris, a big literary evening was organized on January 4, 1914, by the immigrants, at which he read from his latest works.[23]

Even on stage, divisions within the immigrant community could be perceived, however. For one thing, certain Jewish labor leaders disliked Goldfaden's Zionist bent and criticized even more harshly other "trash" theater (shund-teater), which they blamed for corrupting good taste and demoralizing the masses.[24] A group led by Berish Unterman, Natan Maltzmacher, and others declared war on this theater and decided to start a Yiddish workers' theater on their own. As early as 1892 a Yiddish play had been produced at the trade union hall on rue Lancry, but in 1902 a more lasting workers' theater was born in a cellar at 50, rue des Francs-Bourgeois (in the Marais), the outgrowth of the Yidishe arbeter bildungs-fareyn (a workers' educational society) located there. The troupe's first performance was an original play about Jewish immigrant life in Paris. In November 1903 Leon Kobrin's Mina was presented by the Zelbst-bildung grupe as an explicit counter to the "old, empty, whimsical" Yiddish theater full of "foolish jokes" typically produced in Paris.[25] Mina portrayed the daily life of a Jewish woman in the ghetto, and the play's proceeds went to a Yiddish library.

As the different groups within the Jewish labor movement saw Yiddish theater as an important cultural adjunct that could draw more workers to their movement, the amateur group started by Unterman split. The anarchists created a group called Frayhayt, members of the small Poalei-Zion group created the Fraye yidishe bine, and the Bundists formed the Fraye yidishe arbeter bine, while a group called the Fraye yidishe folks-bine was closely connected with the Yiddish trade union movement.

From this period until the outbreak of the war, Yiddish theater had an often difficult but stubborn existence in Paris. Plays by Jacob Gordin, Karl Gutzkow, Leon Kobrin, David Pinski, and others were presented. Sholem Ash himself directed a performance of Der landsman in March 1913. Workers' groups organized yearly concerts, balls, and literary evenings that were both cultural, entertaining, and a way to raise money. Most importantly, these other yidishkayt activities reflected a cultural necessity crucially imbedded in the immigrant community.

Several attempts were also made at founding Yiddish newspapers.[26] A Parizer algemeyne yidishe folks-tsaytung existed briefly in 1892; a Zionist Di hoffnung hatikvah appeared in 1897. There is evidence that a paper half in French and half in Yiddish existed before 1905. From 1909 to 1914 several literary, political, and/or general interest Yiddish magazines were created: Di *moderne tsayt, Parizer zhurnal, Dos idishe blat,* and *Der nayer zhurnal,* the latter a weekly literary review by Abraham Reisin, then in Paris.

The leftist Jewish press was also quite active if equally ephemeral. A radical Zionist paper, *Di yudishe tsukunft* (jointly published from Paris and London) appeared in 1904, and a few issues of the anarchist *Der agitator* appeared in 1910. One issue of *Der idisher furyer* appeared in April 1911 and one issue of *Der hitel makher* in June 1912. An issue of *Di ershte boyern-tsaytung in Pariz (sic)* was edited in Paris but printed in London in 1913 for the carpenter's ball in Paris that year. *Der id in Pariz,* a monthly Socialist-Zionist journal, existed at least from 1912 to 1913. *Di idishe tribune* (a Socialist monthly, edited by Isaac Rirachovski, who also founded a short-lived Yidisher Perets-teater) appeared in 1915, the *Rusishe Nakhrikhten* in 1917–1918, and *Der idisher volonter,* half in Yiddish and half in French, in 1919. The most important, however, was *Der idisher arbayter,* a monthly paper of which twenty-five issues (about a thousand copies each, the same number as printed by each of the French Jewish newspapers) were to appear from 1911 until war broke out and halted publication in 1914. The paper is a fund of information about the Jewish labor movement, about working conditions in the immigrant workshops, and about the strikes in which immigrant workers confronted their immigrant bosses. Its important role in the immigrant trade union movement will be described further in chapter 7.

What did the conservative *Le Figaro,* the Socialist *L'Humanité,* and the Jewish *Archives Israélites* all have in common? They were written in French and therefore inaccessible to newly arrived immigrants. Thus the immigrants founded their own papers even with the meager resources at their disposal. But by and large it was the availability of Yiddish newspapers from the larger communities in London, Warsaw, Vilna, or even the United States that kept the immigrants in Paris furnished with plenty of reading material. Reading rooms, restaurants, libraries, and bookstores in the Pletzl, Montmartre, or near the Gobelins area, served as distribution points for these papers. Even more importantly, they became veritable meeting places for the immigrant community, as police surveillance reports often attest. The printed word served as a stimulus and focal point for the spoken word: all in Yiddish. Language was perhaps but a symbol for the cultural uniqueness of the immigrants, but it was an important one and the basis for all of the immigrant organizations that followed.

RELIGIOUS LIFE

Yiddish separated the Jewish immigrant workers from French workers just as it separated them from French Jews. However, one may ask whether in another language, Hebrew, the eastern European and French Jews could find common ground. If there is one area in which native-immigrant Jewish relations are indeed pertinent, it is in the religious domain. Yet as the immigrants set about creating their own oratories and eventually a synagogue, their attempts at religious "independence" only further reflected their particular linguistic, cultural, and even ritual needs.

Although French Jews had ever since emancipation stressed religion (rather than culture) as the main component of their Jewish identity (as "Frenchpersons of the Jewish religion"), even within France the practice of that religion varied widely. The nineteenth century was fraught with often bitter struggles within the Parisian Consistoire over Sephardic or Ashkenazic rituals, the latter winning out by the end of the century. Then, with the immigration of eastern European Jews, further ritual differences came to the fore, this time within the Ashkenazic branch of Judaism alone. Although French Jewry had not undergone a reform movement similar to that in Germany, concessions to "modernization" in the practice of certain rituals (e.g., choirs, organs) had occurred. Consequently, these synagogues, far from providing a meeting place for French and eastern European Jews, became one more example of the distance between the two communities.

The Ashkenazic French Jews' attitudes toward the religious practices of the Ashkenazic foreign Jews were twofold. There were, on the one hand, those more orthodox French Jews who felt that the immigrants could provide a needed support, if not the savior of French Judaism, in the face of increasing secularization and indifference on the part of so many French Jews.[27] On the other hand, many of the more "liberal" members of the French Jewish community could only see the "backwardness" of the immigrants, occasionally complimenting their "ardor" ("which we would do well to imitate") but following such comment by a description of the "crowd, a bit noisy" in the synagogue.[28]

The encounter between Western and Eastern Jews in this period must, however, be seen from another viewpoint. While the disdain of the emancipated Jews for their backward brethren from the East is no longer a new subject, much less has been said about the often similar antipathies felt by the eastern European Jews for the pernicious effects of assimilation. "Babylon!" As such was Paris described. From the viewpoint of eastern Europe, the West and certainly Paris was no place for any self-respecting religious Jew. As old Sarah, a character in *L'épopée de Ménaché Foïgel*, complained, you could not even tell the Jews from the *goyim* in Paris anymore; they dressed like the French, ate like the French (including snails and frogs' legs), and prayed—or didn't—like the French.[29]

It is difficult to measure the "religiosity" of the emigrants in the West. As has been seen, many in fact emigrated because of the attraction of "Babylon." The most extreme expression of this antitraditionalism was the Yom Kippur Balls organized as early as 1900 by immigrant anarchists, which attracted as many as four hundred people.[30] Nonetheless, in comparison to the secularized traditions found in the West, the majority of eastern European Jews transplanted there represented a totally different manner of "Jewishness." The difference between Eastern and Western Jews (often poorly stated in terms of "religiosity," a term mixing faith and practice) was perhaps less one of faith (the ability of a western Jew to identify an eastern European *apikoyres*, heretic, was no better than that of an immigrant to distinguish a *croyant* French Jew) than of ritual practice and traditional styles. As Tchernoff described the differences in the latter:

> When the Jews from Eastern Europe cross the threshold of a temple in Paris, they feel bewildered, out of their element, surprised by the attitude of the worshipers. The manner of these men, wearing top-hats, ceremonious, proper, who speak in whispers of their business affairs during the service, which few of them understand, for whom the enactment of the rituals is part of a certain fashionable snobbery, surprises and shocks the persecuted Jews who, gesticulating wildly, swaying their bodies, put into their prayer the mystic ardor which devours them.[31]

The vivid juxtaposition described by Tchernoff in fact probably rarely occurred within one temple. To see the contrasts described by him one would have had to travel from the 9th to the 4th arrondissement, from the French synagogue on rue de la Victoire to the private eastern European oratories of the Pletzl. For wherever the necessary *minyan* of ten men had been gathered for this purpose, the eastern European Jews created their own places of worship. These minyanim were often ephemeral, and the lack of more religious activity among the immigrants was lamented by some, but insofar as religious life did remain important for a segment of the immigrant community, it was in immigrant oratories, located anywhere from an artist's loft to a shoemaker's workshop, that their faith would be expressed.

Oratories, connected to mutual aid societies, had existed in France throughout the nineteenth century as the bastion of orthodox Jewry. They represented, however, a threat to the Consistoire's authority, and the Consistoire waged a campaign against them in terms of order and morale. Legal measures as well as religious regulations were brought to bear against the oratories, but finally, over the course of the century, they came to be tolerated, as long as they paid dues to the Consistoire. At the end of the century, as immigrant oratories were created by the eastern Europeans, they were generally accepted as a *fait accompli*, and the Consistoire even sometimes helped subsidize a rabbi's salary.[32] But conflicts continued to arise.

Russian and Rumanian oratories appear as early as the first immigration, and by 1900 the *Archives Israélites* counted five immigrant oratories on Montmartre and seven in the Marais–St. Paul area. These small prayer groups sometimes had no other designation than the name of the street on which they were located. Some were designated by the mutual aid society or *talmud-*

torah (religious classes) with which they were associated. Others grouped members of a particular trade (reminiscent of the "tailors' synagogue" in eastern Europe). In any case the officiating *ministres* were usually themselves workers or merchants, the job of spiritual leader for an oratory being hardly a full-time position. By tracing the oratories or their administrators through sporadic appearances in the Consistoire's archives their common characteristics soon emerge: individually ephemeral but collectively persistent. The oratories were small and often underwent several address changes, yet their tenacity was a clear testimony to the particular religious/ritual needs of the immigrant community.

Contact between the immigrant oratories and the French Jewish community did exist. The Grand Rabbi Zadoc Kahn gave them his support, and, although private and independent, the immigrant religious organizations turned to the Consistoire for legal or financial help or even to resolve internal disputes. Furthermore, since places of worship were supposed to be authorized by the Consistoire (before 1905), some complied with this formality, although quite often after the fact. Similarly, as all other associations and societies were supposed to be authorized by the police department, immigrant groups sometimes made themselves known to the Consistoire at that time, requesting the latter's help as intercessor with the French authorities.[33]

One example is the tailors' society Ahavath Reim, which, after fifteen years of existence as an oratory, decided to legally constitute a mutual aid society and drew up statutes for filing with the police on October 15, 1896.[34] Article Twenty-nine of these statutes even provided for a prayer to be said for France and for the president of the Republic during the morning service. However, it seems that having thus drawn itself to the attention of the authorities, the society was closed the following March by the police. It was then that it turned to the Consistoire for help, which in turn commented on how, after having been without authorization for so long, this *"groupement quelconque d'Israélites"* seemed to be showing more responsibility than usual.

While the immigrants began turning to the Consistoire, it, having ignored the oratories for a long time, also began to make efforts to integrate them. In 1904 the Consistoire put Solomon Kohn (former secretary general of the Ahavath Reim) in charge of the merger of three or four Montmartre oratories for which it provided larger premises. In 1907 Mme. Edmond de Rothschild offered still larger and better premises for an immigrant synagogue, but the problem then became what to do with Kohn, who, although by now the undisputed leader of the Montmartre community, did not have the credentials to become a rabbi. Furthermore, he had caused a scandal by illegally marrying the Baron du Gunzburg to Mlle. Brodsky before the necessary civil ceremony had been performed.[35]

In the meantime the separation of the church and state in 1905 altered the legal status of all religious organizations, henceforth to be organized as private religious associations, *associations cultuelles*, beginning with the Consistoire itself. Two of the immigrant oratories, one on rue des Ecouffes and one on rue de l'Hôtel de Ville, were likewise transformed into *associations cultuelles*. The implications of the separation, although by and large supported by the French Jewish community on the side of anticlericalism in the wake of the Dreyfus affair, meant a blow to the Consistoire's hegemony as official spokesperson for the Jewish community. Religious organizations no longer needed consistorial approval to be legal. The Consistoire, however, as a private *association cultuelle*, now "separated" from state subsidies, needed more than ever to be assured of a regular paying membership. It is therefore little wonder that the Consistoire began turning with greater interest toward the growing immigrant community. The Consistoire organized two oratories in the Montmartre area in 1906, one on rue Ste. Isaure (which later became, and still exists, as a temple) and another on rue Nobel. Archival silence with regard to several preexisting immigrant oratories there seems to indicate that these consistorial oratories regrouped or replaced many of the smaller prior ones.

At the same time that the Consistoire attempted to supervise the immigrant oratories more closely,[36] the latter also turned increasingly to the Consistoire. On the one hand the immigrants demanded more representation on consistorial committees.[37] Just as direct appeals were made to the grand rabbi or the Rothschilds because of the spiritual or financial power that they held and even more importantly symbolized, the immigrants looked to the Consistoire because of the institutional, moral, and religious weight it represented. In this sense Jewish solidarity and a certain community behavior pattern were expected.

But on the other hand the immigrants also turned to the Consistoire out of dissatisfaction with their own oratories. This dissatisfaction resulted from the very cultural synthesis they were undergoing and led to two opposite tendencies within the immigrant community: a movement toward a closer relationship with the Consistoire on the one hand and an opposite movement toward complete independence on the other.

In 1913 the president of the temple on rue Ste. Isaure, while petitioning the Consistoire for better and larger quarters (the roof leaked and the toilets backed up), explained how the settling-in process of the immigrant population presaged this dissatisfaction:

> For among this Jewish population on Montmartre, hardworking, serious and frugal, there are many who gradually attain a degree of economic security, and once the needs of their families are assured, their savings go first of all towards religion.[38]

Religion was thus to a certain extent a luxury, but a luxury only insofar as a formal synagogue with its own building implied necessary dues to assure its upkeep. The private oratories, which required only ten men and an apartment or workshop in which to meet, had the clear advantage of being free or requiring only minimal dues and thus initially perfectly suited to the modest needs of a newly established and generally poor community. However, the premises used for worship were often but "makeshift quarters, absolutely unworthy of the usage for which they are destined," as the Consistoire described them.[39] By the 1910s it seems that many immigrants agreed.

A delegation of immigrants from the 4th and 11th arrondissements went to the Consistoire in July 1913 with a request for a temple of their own. A similar request came from the Bastille area (11th arrondissement) in November, and another petition representing the 4th, 11th, and 12th arrondissements was submitted in December. It was argued that "our young people, who have already gone through French schools, refuse to frequent our oratories that are little appropriate to the dignity of a place of worship."[40] It was not only the smallness or insalubrity of the oratories but also tradition itself which was ripe for change as the older generation became sensitive to the more rapid Frenchification of the young (and were themselves not impervious to it). The Consistoire despaired that the immigrants did not even know what they wanted. Earlier that year the Montmartre community, after requesting the installation of a special barrier for the women's section of the rue Ste. Isaure temple (a necessity for the orthodox), had asked the Consistoire to take it down "under the pretext that they were 'in France.' "[41]

To transcend the outgrown oratories, yet to maintain their separateness from the consistorial system, the Agoudath Hakehiloth (called Union des communautés in French, today spelled Agoudas Hakehilos) decided to build its own temple. This group (constituted as an *association cultuelle* with J. Landau as president and J. L. Herzog as rabbi) first appears in the fall of 1911 in a letter to the Consistoire asking that an immigrant be named to the Consistorial Committee for the Supervision of Ritual Practices. The request was granted but a second letter soon followed from another group of immigrants contesting the right of the Agoudath Hakehiloth to speak for the immigrant community. This second group claimed instead that it represented the larger and calmer element of the community in contrast to the few "agitated" followers of Herzog. A report on the situation by a committee called the Société Tipheret Israel described the Agoudath Hakehiloth in the following terms:

> The supposed new rabbi of the Polish *israélites* is but, in reality, a *magid* (preacher), of inferior rank, brought to the fore by a handful of faithless and lawless [*sans foi ni loi*] charlatans, hypocrites and audacious persons who believe they have found a way to raise money.[42]

The Consistoire's Solomon-like decision was to expand its committee in order to permit one member from each immigrant group to be included, but the controversy did not end there. The ensuing struggle for immigrant community control reveals as much about the divisions among the immigrants themselves as about the range of relations possible between the immigrants and the Consistoire. It may be added that this first stage of the controversy in 1911 had the side effect of bringing another group to the Consistoire with a request for help; several immigrant bakers, complaining of demands being made on them by the two antagonistic factions, asked to be put under the Consistoire's protection.

On April 6, 1913, construction on a grand orthodox temple designed by Guimard for the Agoudath Hakehiloth de Paris began at 10, rue Pavée. President Landau provided over seventy thousand francs out of his own pocket for the temple, and additional support came from B. Rapoport, a diamond merchant. In the face of this concrete act, agitation among the immigrant community was heightened. The anti–Agoudath Hakehiloth group wrote to the Consistoire requesting that the existing synagogue on rue des Tournelles be turned over the the immigrant community or that a new (consistorial) synagogue be built. In either case it was stipulated that the ritual of such temple be orthodox, that administration of the temple be given to the delegation making the request (i.e., all immigrants) and that a rabbi from the Ecole rabbinique de France be chosen, but one of Russian-Polish origin.

The next day, however, the Consistoire received yet another letter, from a third party involved: the Alsatian Jews who frequented the rue des Tournelles temple. The author of that letter wrote that as a true *israélite* he was obliged to warn the Consistoire that if the Tournelles temple were given to the immigrants, the Alsatians of the Marais would rise up in a quarrel against the Consistoire.

The issue over the Tournelles temple originated from the very essence of the need for private immigrant oratories in the first place. The Tournelles temple had, among other things, a choir and an organ, which were inimical to the immigrants' traditions. Yet, as has been seen, demographic changes in the Parisian Jewish community had led to the gradual displacement of French (Alsatian) Jews by the eastern European immigrants in the Marais. The result was a consistently declining membership at the Tournelles temple, which the immigrant petitioners argued would be reversed if the temple were put at their disposal.

The Consistoire's position thus had to be forged between the anti–Agoudath Hakehiloth request for the Tournelles temple—at the risk of alienating the Alsatian Jews—and the *fait accompli* of the Agoudath Hakehiloth group. From the Grand Rabbi Dreyfuss's suggestion of conciliation to the extreme attitude of the consistorial delegate sent to investigate the matter, who was outraged by the immigrants' "extreme ingratitude" toward the French community's philanthropy and their insistence on "superannuated customs," consistorial responses ranged from respect for the immigrants' conservative orthodoxy (and a regret that not enough attention had previously been paid to these "exotic elements") to condemnation of the separatists as fanatics.[43]

In the end the Consistoire turned its back on the Agoudath Hakehiloth. In June of 1914 the new Russian-Polish synagogue, 10, rue Pavée, was dedicated, a "modern" temple, with seating for one thousand people, two spacious galleries for the women, special rooms for weddings and meetings, and plans for a talmud-torah for four hundred children. The *Archives Israélites* was very complimentary about the "pious initiative of our immigrant coreligionists" but regretted the absence of the rabbinate and consistoire representatives at the inaugural ceremony. The newspaper chided the community representatives for "pouting" instead of congratulating the immigrants for having done it all on their own, without costing the Parisian Jewish community a sou.[44]

The schism produced within the immigrant community between the Agoudath Hakehiloth and Tournelles factions exhibited the heterogeneity of needs within the immigrant community as it adapted to its new environment. Even the immigrants' religious needs were multidimensional, from freethinkers to "fanatics." Some turned to the established Jewish community as a mode of integration within a subset of French society. Others chose a path of independence representative of irreconcilable ritual and cultural differences. In either case the immigrant oratories that were initially formed represented first of all the particular linguistic and cultural needs of their founders. These needs would be equally apparent in the creation of immigrant mutual aid societies.

MUTUAL AID SOCIETIES

Mutual aid societies, like oratories, ultimately synthesized a French structure with an eastern European tradition in order to create an organization particularly adapted to the needs of the immigrant community. Yet while religious needs could be taken care of immediately (once ten men had gathered), even for the Jew in transit, mutual aid societies represented a more long-term commitment. Just as the Agoudath Hakehiloth temple, an outgrowth from the oratories, represented an investment in settlement in France, the mutual aid societies attested to a desire to create an infrastructure able to care for more long-term needs. In fact many of them were primarily burial societies, called *kegnzaytike hilf* (mutual help) or *sociétés de prévoyance* (societies of foresight). After all, what could be more permanent than a burial plot on *French* soil?

Mutual aid societies (*sociétés de secours mutuel*) in France had been created by the Napoleonic Code in order to replace the pre-Revolutionary confraternities. The societies continued to perform most of the same functions as their predecessors, including health insurance, funeral provisions, and retirement funds, and to act, as William Sewell has described them, as "encompassing communities of friendship, solidarity, and good fellowship."[45] One major difference in the post-Revolutionary societies, however, was that they were now theoretically lay organizations rather than dependent on the church (even though many of them still kept their patron saints), which permitted the development of Jewish mutual aid societies. Such Jewish societies were most often organized specifically for the purpose of purchasing a *caveau*, a group plot, not unlike their non-Jewish counterparts, but in this case in order to assure their members a place in the Jewish corner of the cemetery.

Khevre Kedishes, or burial societies, had also played an important role in assuring a last resting place for their members in eastern Europe. However, it could be argued that, with emigration, concern over a final resting place became even more compelling. Given the poverty of the immigrants' situation and worry about the prospect of a pauper's grave, burial provisions were a key issue that prompted mutual aid. For immigrants, separated from family and the encompassing eastern European community organizations, their isolated lot could be transcended in life as in death through these societies.

Several French Jewish mutual aid burial societies already existed before the immigrants' arrival. But when questioned as to why it was necessary for the immigrants to organize their own societies separately, the secretary of the Société de Chevré Kadischa de Varsovie answered without hesitation: "to have total independence."[46] The entire social, cultural, economic, and ritual gulf between the two communities was expressed in these parallel immigrant organizations. At the same time, the material needs of a poor, laboring population are also evident.

The very first eastern European mutual aid society was the Société de secours mutuel des Israélites polonais de la loi rabbinique founded in 1856.[47] But it was not until the 1880s and again after 1905 that societies were founded in greater numbers. The by-laws of the Société religieuse de secours mutuels des tailleurs russes called "L'Amitié fraternelle" or "Ahavath Reim" (drawn up in 1896) give a good indication of the aims of one such society, which grew out of a tailors' oratory. The stated purpose was threefold: to provide medical, religious, and moral aid for its members.[48] Religious functions were assured by the oratory. "Moral aid" meant that periodic debates would be held. Most important, however, was the medical aid, which consisted of a health insurance plan providing for the payment of doctors' fees and medicine as well as a daily indemnity during a member's illness. Upon a member's death the society would take care of guarding the body (according to religious law) until burial, and the entire membership would accompany the funeral procession (presence being obligatory under penalty of a fine).

Each year thereafter the *kaddish* prayer would be said at the oratory on the anniversary of the death *(yortsayt)*.

Other societies created funds for widows' pensions, philanthropic aid, or small loans. Still others were less interested in mutual financial aid or setting up oratories or talmud-torahs than in simply getting together with fellow immigrants. *Landsmanshaftn* (of which twelve were founded in the period before 1917[49]) were such "amicable" societies *(amicales)*, whose main purpose was simply to reunite people who came from the same area in eastern Europe. Reminiscing or merely making reference to one's past collective experience was something in which neither the French nor the French Jewish community could participate.

Geographic origins and shared religious traditions were important for the founding of mutual aid societies, but so was the common socioeconomic condition that bound the immigrants with similar needs. The poverty of the immigrants made the financial security desired in the burial societies and other mutual aid funds all the more important. It was often as workers that the societies such as the tailors' Ahavath Reim were created. Such societies not only gave mutual support to fellow workers and helped bolster the self-respect of the craftspeople, but they were often precursors to the trade union sections that will be described below (chapter 6).

In this sense another important type of mutual aid came in the form of an employment agency set up as the Bureau russe du travail. As has been seen, the Oeuvre israélite du travail et du placement, opened by the French Jewish community in 1881, had to close its doors three years later because of its inability to keep up with the growing influx of immigrants. Another project for an Office général du travail, proposed by *L'Univers Israélite* in its February 15, 1907, issue, never got off the ground. So, even before 1911, the first year for which Bureau russe du travail records exist, it was through the informal immigrant networks that the informational costs of job-hunting were greatly reduced. The community grapevine served as a fairly efficient employment agency, as did the compatriot contractors who offered the immigrants employment. Speiser's *Kalendar* gave newcomers advice as to which restaurants functioned as informal employment agencies. Razenshtroych's restaurant was a known recruiting center for capmakers, furworkers, and jewelry workers; the furworkers' union section established a more formal placement office at Lander's restaurant.

The most important of such efforts, however, was the Bureau russe du travail, which in 1911 was able to find jobs for 546 immigrants.[50] Serving primarily the Left Bank Russian colony under the leadership of Antonov (pseudonym for the Russian Jewish Social-Democrat Ovseï Josefovitch), this organization, just like those set up by French workers in the late nineteenth century, was more than just an employment bureau.[51] Medical aid and unemployment indemnities were offered to members, language and trade courses were sponsored, and the Bureau served as a legal aid office as well. A fund was created to loan money to the newly arrived, and the Bureau began a sub-sidized workers' restaurant called the Table d'hôte des émigrés, where be-tween two and three hundred people purchased meals daily at three different prices, depending on their resources. (The police called it the daily rendez-vous of the "Russian proletariat of the intellectual world."[52]) The Bureau also supported another, more specialized, placement bureau in the 13th arron-dissement, the Association des travailleurs intellectuels, designed particularly to help "intellectual workers" find employment.

Indeed, for every subset within the immigrant colony a mutual aid group seems to have formed. Student organizations were created, the first being the Association des étudiants de Russie, founded in 1883, which sponsored a range of talks from such people as the immigrant Rabbi Lubetzki to the French Jewish anarchist-journalist Bernard-Lazare at its reading room in the Latin Quarter.[53] The Association later split, to be succeeded by the Zionist-oriented Association des étudiants israélites russes à Paris, while another student organization, the Association des Jeunes Juifs, first appeared in Sep-tember 1900 (also in the Latin Quarter). This latter group was notable for the part it played in helping to organize a meeting on November 20, 1913, to protest the Beilis affair in Russia. The meeting served not only to indicate the importance—and necessity—of immigrants organizing their own meetings to protest issues upon which the French and French Jewish communities dared not touch, but also to explicitly manifest their disapproval of the latter. Just before the final resolution was voted (condemning the Russian government with shouts of "Long live liberty! Liberty for all!") the president of the Association took the opportunity to reproach the French Jews for not being interested in their "race."[54]

In 1913, just as the oratories were joining forces to build a temple, several immigrant mutual aid societies also sought to consolidate. A prelimi-nary meeting took place in October 1912, at which over twenty immigrant societies were represented.[55] The two key founding members of the Fédéra-tion des sociétés juives de Paris were Segall and Marmoreck, both Zionists and both connected with the Université populaire juive, where the Fédéra-tion's offices were first located. The Fédération was based on the principles of "civic duty and social solidarity." It sought to coordinate the social and mutualist Jewish movement in Paris as well as to acclimate Jewish immigrants to French life. Although this organization did not last through the war, it was the precursor of the Fédération des sociétés juives de France (founded in 1926), which would play an important role for the immigrant community in the interwar period and which still exists to this day.[56]

The importance of the Fédération, like the rue Pavée temple, is in the growing strength of the immigrant community to which it attests. The set-tling-in process is a long one, requiring both the mental outlook of permanence in the new country (rather than further transit elsewhere or return) and the material means by which to create more lasting organizations. At the same time, the mutual aid societies attest to a beginning synthesis of eastern European and French cultures. French by-laws were the necessary legal basis to these organizations, and the avowed purpose of the Fédération was to help the immigrants adapt to French life. Informally, society meetings could serve as information exchanges, where the immigrants could learn from each other (in Yiddish) the tricks of adaptation that no (French) language course could teach them.

However, for the most part the self-help character that marked the immigrant societies in the period before World War I implied the maintenance for that much longer of the specific cultural, traditional, and linguistic flavor of the immigrant community. The mutual aid societies were the concrete expression of a more diffuse network of immigrant cooperation, and it was such organizations that gave continuity and solidarity to the lives of the transplanted.

Animated meetings, whether in cafés, apartment, or workshop headquarters, are the image of immigrant societies at work. Even the short appearances of a Russian College and a Russian Clinic (both on the Left Bank) attest to the importance of immigrant self-help. Talking politics, talking shop, planning for an annual ball, celebrating holidays, administering dowries or unemployment funds, visiting sick members, or organizing protests, mutual aid societies were the organizational form through which the immigrants took care of each other in the important matters of life, work, and death.

Finally, the importance of financial aid in a period before social security benefits cannot be underestimated. The immigrants created organizations for material as well as moral support. And as they settled in and were able to slowly establish a prosperity relative to the first days of hardship, "mutual" aid was soon able to be extended to those who did not actually belong to the mutual society itself. With their own, however small, disposable income growing, the immigrants were able to turn to help others by creating philanthropic organizations. The individual efforts of the shoemaker or tailor with an extra mattress to offer the newcomer were thus to be consolidated in institutional form.

IMMIGRANT PHILANTHROPY—THE ASILE

The consolidation of immigrant philanthropy, like immigrant mutual aid, was in no way unique to the Jewish immigrant community. Most immigrant communities in France had their own private philanthropic institutions, and this was but one more sign of the immigrant settling-in process. Immigrant philanthropy represented the memory of the migration process, which did join donors and recipients in a "community of suffering." And sometimes only marginal prosperity differentiated the smallest donors from the recipients.

The first immigrant philanthropic organization was the Société de bienfaisance et d'humanité (Welfare and Humane Society), founded by Léon Novochelski in 1886. This organization, like Novochelski himself (a secondhand clothes dealer), represented a link between the original Polish Jewish immigration to Paris in the mid-1800s and the later immigrations after 1881, because the Société de bienfaisance grew out of the early Société des israélites polonais, which was connected to the oldest immigrant oratory on rue St. Paul (of which Novochelski had also been president). Novochelski described in 1888 how many newly arrived immigrants in need came directly to the St. Paul oratory from the train station.[57]

Another organization, the Prévoyante israélite (Dr. Lazare Klein, president) was founded by immigrant Jews in 1893 with the moral and, through his help, financial aid of the Grand Rabbi Zadoc Kahn. Its dual object was to help immigrants find work as well as to help them learn French. Evening French classes, with 151 students in 1895, represented the largest part of its budget. The Prévoyante israélite did not have its own premises, however, and in 1899 it requested the use of a room in the Tournelles temple. The Consistoire denied the request on grounds that previous night courses there had been unsatisfactory: The doors had had to be kept open all evening; the participants had brought their wives and children; it had been too noisy; there had been eating and drinking on the premises; and there had also been anti-Semitic incidents. Interestingly enough, the Prévoyante israélite, like the French Jewish organizations described above, also saw the necessity of discouraging immigration. In the preamble to the by-laws it announced its determination, in order to "accomplish its task more effectively," "to discourage . . . any poorly thought out emigration movement, especially during periods of economic crisis [presumably in the country of immigration]."[58]

Immigrant philanthropy paralleled French Jewish philanthropy in many respects: handling repatriation, organizing French classes, setting up employment bureaus, etc. Assistance through work took the form of a six-month course at a trade school called Ecole Rachel (on the Left Bank, 14th arrondissement), which specialized in machinery mounting.[59] In each case the very creation of immigrant organizations was a testimony to immigrant cohesiveness while pointing more or less explicitly to the deficiencies of existing structures.

The synthesis of these two factors led to the creation of the most important immigrant philanthropic effort of all, the Société (later Association) philanthropique de l'asile israélite de Paris. As expressed in its annual report for 1905–6:

The Parisian [Jewish] Community, so rich in charitable works, yet lacked that which would have given a provisional hospitality to unfortunate emi-grants, to enable them to become oriented in the labyrinth of the capital. . . . But we have wanted to practice hospitality such as we have seen it practiced in our homeland.[60]

Hospitality rather than welfare was the key to immigrant solidarity. Psalms and Talmudic passages were often quoted in the Asile's reports: "Enlarge the space in your tent"; and during the Passover matzo distribution, "Let him who is hungry come and eat; let him who is needy come and celebrate Pesach." The importance of giving refuge to those who were newcomers or just passing through Paris was felt keenly by those who had gone through the experience themselves.

The Asile was founded, as it said proudly on the cover of each of its annual reports, by the initiative of Russian and Rumanian Jews in 1900. Moïse Fleischer (who was in the hoisery and cotton print business) was the founder and "soul" of the Asile and president until his death in 1905. The immigrant Rabbi Lubetzki also helped in the founding of the Asile, and Solomon Novochelski, son of the founder of the Société de bienfaisance above, became president after Fleischer, from 1905–16. The Asile grew from forty founding members in 1900 to seven hundred in 1909, and in 1910 it moved from the small rented quarters on rue du Figuier (in the Marais) to its own building on 12, rue des Saules (Montmartre). The following year a day-care center was opened, and the name was changed to Société philanthro-pique de l'Asile de nuit et de crèche israélite. In May 1914 an Asile de jour was added at 16, rue des Cloys (Montmartre), although it did little during the war. Afterwards it moved to 16, rue Lamarck, where the combined (in 1923) Asile de nuit, Asile de jour et crèche israélite still exists today.

Starting out with only thirty beds in 1901, expanding to one hundred by 1909, the Asile de nuit sheltered from thirty-four to forty visitors per night; its hospitality represented approximately twelve thousand to fifteen thousand person-nights per year; and the number of nights per person ranged from six to nine. (See Table 7.) Shelter as well as tea, bread, soup, and clothing were offered completely free to those in need, regardless of religion or nationality. Beside the important function this filled for the many emigrants either in transit or about to settle in Paris, the Asile also offered aid to unemployed immigrant or French workers. When necessary, the five- to fifteen-night limit was extended for those who needed to stay longer while looking for work.

While specific in content and purpose, the Asile paralleled other (French or French Jewish) philanthropic organizations in many respects. There were *dames patronnesses,* annual charity balls to earn money and *lits fondations* (the endowment of a bed) inscribed with the donor's name—"you can thus perpetuate the name which is dear to you above all."[61] Even more

TABLE 7

ASILE DE NUIT
POPULATION BY NATIONALITY

Country of Origin	1906	1907	1909	1910	1911	1912	1906-12
FRANCE	5.4%	1.8%	3.0%	5.6%	33.4%[a]	46.4%[a]	19.0%
Alsace	-	-	-	1.2	2.0	3.0	-
Russia	49.9	47.0	43.2	46.3	32.0	26.5	39.3
Rumania	6.6	19.2	12.0	7.3	4.0	2.8	8.0
Austria-Hungary	13.9	15.9	19.6	13.5	10.2	6.0	12.5
(EASTERN EUROPE)	(70.4)	(82.1)	(74.8)	(67.1)	(46.2)	(35.3)	(59.8)
Germany	4.4	4.3	5.1	9.9	5.6	4.5	5.5
Other	19.8	11.8	17.1	16.2	12.8	10.8	15.7
Total	100.0%	100.0%	100.0%	100.0%	100.0%	100.0%	100.0%
N =	1,617	1,523	1,649	1,529	1,952	2,469	10,739

SOURCE: Société philanthropique de l'Asile israélite de Paris, *Rapports des exercices, 1906-12* (Paris: Imprimerie N.L. Danzig, n.d.)

[a]The high number of French visitors to the Asile in 1911 and 1912 was explained as due to the particularly hot summers, which chased many Parisians to oceanside resorts, thereby closing numerous businesses and creating unemployment.

significant than such structural similarities between French and immigrant philanthropy was a similarity of discourse. The annual reports of the Asile echoed many of the same themes: the struggle against begging, the "scourge of pauperism"; the problem of *"faux pauvres"* alongside of *"vrai"* ones (unworthy versus worthy poor); and the importance of work, which "ennobles humanity." Furthermore, praise of France was expressed with a special emphasis on France's hospitality, the most generous in all of Europe. This shows to what extent the more established immigrants already felt at home.

Like the French Jewish community, the Asile spokespersons also found it necessary to reply to certain anti-Semitic accusations. Thus one report emphasized hygiene in order to refute a rumor that the immigrants in the 4th arrondissement had caused a conjunctivitis (eye disease) epidemic. And on several occasions the Asile also had to respond to criticisms concerning the "pull" of philanthropy already echoed in the French Jewish press: that the Asile's philanthropy (renowned even in Russia) was attracting too many emigrants to Paris or that the Asile would become the refuge of professional beggars ("not only do you shelter them, but you feed them; you aid their vices"[62]). The Asile administrators responded by repeating over and again that many of their visitors were merely en route to another country, while the far larger majority who stayed on were "honest workers" looking for work.

Like the oratories and mutual aid societies the Asile also turned expectantly to the Parisian Jewish community for aid. It received the French community's moral and financial backing: *L'Univers Israélite* admired its "discreet and quiet" work while the *Archives Israélites* complimented its efforts as doing honor to the Parisian (Jewish) community; the Grand Rabbis Zadoc Kahn and later J.-H. Dreyfuss gave the Asile their spiritual patronage; and financial support came from the Alliance israélite universelle, the Merzbach family, the Rothschilds, etc.; even the Préfet de police, Lépine, was listed as a benefactor. This unanimous approbation of the immigrant community for taking care of its own and thus easing the burden on both public and Jewish welfare agencies assured the Asile's expansion.

It is nonetheless the mutual aid character of the Asile that is important to emphasize. The Asile's representatives themselves referred to the "collective character" of their philanthropic effort as devolving from the tradition of mutual aid societies. An important source of funding came from a club of immigrant diamond merchants.[63] However, just as significant is the greater number of members who only contributed their twenty francs dues per year; these yearly dues represented one-third of the total revenue in 1905–6. Thus, although it may have been the aid from the Parisian community that permitted the needed expansion of the Asile, the proud founders often repeated how the Asile de nuit had been started with only 150 francs by the immigrants themselves. It seems clear that even on its own the immigrant community would have maintained a poorer, but necessary, Asile.

Immigrant philanthropy, as embodied in the Asile, was the most concrete expression of immigrant solidarity forged through a similar experience of uprootedness and common socioeconomic conditions. Even if the latter was only a recent memory for those who had already begun to benefit from upward mobility, the transfer of funds from those less poor to those who were poorer still is an important testimony to the solidarity of suffering created through the migration experience.

IMMIGRANT POLITICS/PROFESSIONAL REVOLUTIONARIES

No description of the eastern European Jewish community in Paris would be complete without a closer look at the primarily Left Bank activities of the "professional revolutionaries." The Russian political circles that were reconstituted on French soil represented another kind of immigrant organization, if not one, properly speaking, part of the settling-in process. On the contrary, most of these political debates, held in cafés, restaurants, or libraries, manifested a firm hope for return to Russia rather than settling in France. The leaders of those debates—including the more famous Russian émigrés such as Lenin, Trotsky, and Martov—considered themselves exiles or political refugees rather than emigrants. Their focus was on revolution in Russia, and many of them would indeed return there after the revolution in 1917.

Fifty-three percent of the Russian immigrants registered at the Bureau russe du travail declared themselves to be political refugees, an undoubtedly high figure due to the fact that the Bureau largely served the "professional revolutionary" subcolony itself. But this nevertheless indicates the importance of Paris (after Geneva) as a center for Russian exiles in this period, a fact that distinguished the Russian-Jewish colony in Paris from those in London or New York in the same period. The post-1905 emigration brought an even greater number of political militants out of Russia.

The activities of the Russian revolutionaries in Paris are preserved in the police archives and in those of the Ministry of the Interior.[64] The French police had help from the tsar's secret police in Paris, but many of the French informers still had trouble following a debate in Russian or Yiddish or in comprehending the schisms and fusions of the political factions of the Russian colony. If the content of the meetings was not always understood, the animation of the speakers was carefully noted. The noisier the debate and the more excited the participants, the more dangerous the revolutionaries in the eyes of the informant in "this strange milieu where political passions border on madness."[65] In other instances moral considerations had their part to play in assessing an individual's politics; E. G. —— was all the more suspect for the manner in which he abandoned his wife and children to leave for America with nothing but his sewing-machine . . . and his mistress.[66]

Acknowledgment of a Jewish identity among the revolutionary circles varied. According to the police:

> In their meetings, Jews [juifs] and Slavs are intermingled and are friends; in their secret meetings they join their common hatreds, the Jews [israélites] only distinguish themselves because they are the most absolute, the most definitively violent. . . .[67]

According to the Bureau russe du travail, 80 percent of its members were Jews.[68]

As early as 1882, at the beginning of the immigration, a small group of Russian refugees gathered around Peter Lavrov every Thursday at his Left Bank apartment. By the next year there were two groups, one called the Jewish Workers' Society (Evreiskoye Rabochee Obchestvo, set up with mutual aid objectives of helping the unemployed or sick, helping workers find jobs, and developing "moral sentiments") and one called the Russian Workers' Society (Ruskoye Rabochee Obchestvo). On the third anniversary of the Jewish Workers' Society in 1886 Lavrov was elected president and gave a speech in which he praised the socialist potential of the Jewish people.[69] During the same year the two societies merged under the name Russian Workers' Society, probably indicating less a diminution in the actual number of Jewish members than a will toward a more ecumenical identity. Both social-democrats and anarchists attended the weekly meetings at the Café Trésor (in the Marais), which the police kept under surveillance, smug in the discovery of what they considered to be a branch of a vast affiliation of Russian Jewish revolutionary émigrés.[70]

Little by little, from the 1880s on, the Russian revolutionary spectrum was recreated in small cafés or apartments in Paris. The Narodnaya Volya (People's Will) organized a fair in 1892; in 1913 it participated in a protest meeting for the Chicago victims.[71] Socialist-Revolutionaries, successors of the Narodnaya Volya philosophy, numbered seven hundred in Paris in 1907 according to the police department and had at least two libraries, one on Montmartre (Right Bank) and one in the 13th arrondissement (Left Bank) where their activities were centered. The most prominent Socialist-Revolutionary in Paris was Ilya Rubanovich, who directed *La Tribune Russe* from 1904 to 1913 and organized a Russian College in order "to give political instruction to comrades."[72]

The most important political group among the Russian revolutionaries in Paris, however, as in Russia, was the Social-Democrats. From February 1903 to January 1906 a terrorist group (according to the police) with Social-Democratic leanings, called La Russie révolutionnaire, held meetings attended by up to three hundred persons.[73] From 1908 on, the center for Social-Democratic activity in Paris was the Bibliothèque russe, located at 63, rue des Gobelins (where the Bureau russe du travail was located). Eight hundred Mensheviks ("*ultras*" [sic]) and 2,000 Bolsheviks ("*modérés*" [sic]) were living in Paris according to one police estimate.[74] The most famous of the Bolsheviks, Lenin, lived there from 1908 to 1912, doing research at the Bibliothèque Nationale and giving various talks. According to one contemporary, when Lenin was told about the Jewish workers on the Right Bank, he "rushed to bring them the good word" (*s'empressa d'aller leur porter la bonne parole*).[75] He gave several lectures there over a period of two to three months, but finally gave them up due to too many disruptions from anarchists in the audience.

The Russian Social-Democrats in Paris were no more impervious to splits among the ranks than in Russia. In 1907 Boris Kristchewsky and Grisha Baguslovski formed a Russian (but mostly Jewish) revolutionary-syndicalist splinter group in protest that the Russian Social-Democrats were not sufficiently interested in the problems of the workers in Paris.[76] In May 1911 another revolutionary-syndicalist group was founded called Batayovtses, or Friends of the *Bataille Syndicaliste* newspaper. A Russian Workers' Circle, the Cercle ouvrier russe, led by Lunacharsky, also underwent various fusions and schisms, becoming part of the Caisse des émigrés (Emigrants' Fund) and the Bureau russe du travail in 1912 and forming a Cercle ouvrier du culture prolétaire in order to develop intellectual culture among the Russian refugee proletariat abroad. In the meantime, Maslov and Martov left this group with about fifty supporters to form yet another separate organization.[77]

The most important subset of Russian Social-Democracy, for our purposes, is the Bund. The General Jewish Workers' Union in Russia and Poland, by its full name, grew out of a Jewish Social-Democratic group in Vilna in 1897, which felt that the distinctive problems of language and geography (in the Pale) necessitated a separate Jewish organization. It seems that two Bund groups (supported by the Russian Bund) made their appearance in Paris in 1898: an intellectual group made up of students (speaking Russian or Polish) and a workers' group (Yiddish speakers) called Kemfer. The Bund too had its library, which served as reading room and meeting place in the heart of the Pletzl. According to the police department, there were approximately three hundred Bund members in 1907.[78]

The anarchist influence among the immigrants, by many accounts the strongest, is, not uncharacteristically, difficult to chart. The police department counted only 100 "individualist" anarchists and 450 "communist" anarchists in 1907.[79] The Café Trésor, which had at first been a central meeting place for Russian-Jewish militants of all persuasions, became increasingly dominated by anarchists in the late 1880s. Anarchist groups appeared on Montmartre in 1892–94, in the Marais in 1897–98, and a Groupe anarchiste communiste russe was spotted in the heart of the Pletzl in 1907–08.[80] In May 1909 a federation of the Jewish anarchist groups in Paris was undertaken for the purpose of (1) creating a library; (2) making contacts with other (non-Jewish) anarchist groups in Paris; (3) affiliating with the Anarchist International in London; and (4) founding a school of orators to eventually send the best speakers to Russia to reactivate anarchist propaganda there.[81] The federation was short-lived, however, the last archival entry being October of that same year.

Among the individual Russian Jewish anarchists who made a name for themselves were Mécislas Golberg, whose defense of the unemployed and *lumpenproletariat* in his short-lived newspaper, *Sur le trimard*, led at least once to his arrest and expulsion, and, more famous yet, Yankev Lev, who spread his propaganda by the deed rather than the word. Lev, or Jacob Law as he was also known, got fifteen years of hard labor for shooting at some soldiers at the place de la République on May 1, 1907. Born in Russia, a tailor by trade, having come to Paris from America not too long before this incident, Law was described in *Le Figaro* as having "flaming" (*ardent*) red hair and the "look of a nihilist" (*tête de nihiliste*).[82]

In addition to the anarchists, Bundists, Social-Democrats, and Socialist-Revolutionaries, the student associations may be mentioned once again, less for their actual than for their potential politicization. In a report to the Ministry of the Interior in 1910, it was estimated that 95 percent of the Russian students in Paris were *"israélites révolutionnaires."*[83] However, the police didn't seem too worried, apparently ignoring an anonymous letter that denounced the Association des étudiants israélites russes as a group of "vagabonds, bandits, anarchists, revolutionaries, terrorists and thieves" ruining the good Russian reputation. A police report commented that "the regulars [of the Association] all seem to be from good families," most of them, although having socialist opinions, more preoccupied with their studies than with revolutionary action.[84] If J. Tchernoff's case is any example, there was some contact with revolutionary groups (his brother, after all, was Victor Chernov, Russian Socialist-Revolutionary), but those who had emigrated in order to pursue law or medical degrees had little time for anything else.

The political organizations described above are perhaps the extreme example of immigrant societies created by and for the immigrants neither in response to nor for lack of indigenous French or French Jewish institutions.[85] In these political matters the history of the immigrant revolutionary clubs fits more properly into the history of revolutionary exiles from pre-1917 Russia. The "professional revolutionaries" reproduced political debates and schisms occurring in Russia and in other exile centers, with more concern for Beilis than for Dreyfus.[86] For many of the Russian Jewish refugees exile was to be only temporary until the revolution was won, and a large number of Russian revolutionaries did leave Paris in 1917.[87]

These political organizations, while important to the immigrant colony and having many of the same characteristics evident in the immigrant mutual aid groups described above—creating a sense of belonging; providing a focus of solidarity; centering around important immigrant attributes such as language, food, and (revolutionary) culture—nonetheless remained apart from the settling-in process. The Russian focus of their political debates, in Russian cafés, Russian libraries, and Russian restaurants, reinforced their separateness from French social and political life while offering little opportunity for Frenchification. Charles Rappoport, who would turn his energies primarily to the French Socialist party after 1903, was an exception in this period.[88] The "return" perspective by and large meant limited participation in the daily struggles of the immigrant workers who for their part had little intention of leaving France.

Yiddish theater and newspapers, kosher delicatessens and restaurants, private oratories, mutual aid societies, the Asile Israélite, and to a certain extent the political groups are all expressions of the specific needs of any immigrant community.[89] The settling in of the immigrant Jewish community in Paris began with the continuation, as far as possible, of traditions brought with them from eastern Europe. However, just as a new language must be learned, so must previous forms of expression and organization be translated into the new environment, with French by-laws registered with the police, *dames patronnesses à la française,* and annual reports printed in French.

From the oratory to the café (a Parisian institution well adaptable to immigrant life) headquarters of a mutual aid society, the Jewish immigrant organizations constituted an implicit response to a lack of suitable structures emanating from the French or French Jewish community. But they were less a direct challenge to existing institutions than an expression of immigrant needs in the period before World War I. The relative isolation of the Jewish immigrant community, through language, culture, and even economic concentration, as will be seen, only reinforced immigrant cohesion. Immigrant solidarity was thus forged not only as against the majority environment (whether French or the French Jewish subset) but through the collective experience of the migration act itself, a "community of suffering" more concrete than that attributable to a global Jewish solidarity.

The general economic profile of the immigrant community and the labor movement to which we now turn was but another form of immigrant solidarity as foreseen in the forms of organization introduced in this chapter. Under triple jeopardy as immigrants, Jews, and workers, a Jewish immigrant labor movement would be formed that, like the oratories, mutual aid societies, and even restaurants and theaters, would express the specific needs of the immigrant workers.

Four
OCCUPATIONAL STRUCTURE

Manual work is loved by God.

Just as one is obliged to feed one's son, so is one obliged to teach him a
manual trade.

Skin an animal, receive your pay, and do not say: This is too humiliating for
me.   —Talmudic phrases

For all of the *heymish* familiarity of the Pletzl or Montmartre, the eastern
European Jewish neighborhoods in Paris were characterized by overcrowded,
unsanitary facilities, high rents for old and dirty buildings, poor lighting, etc.
The only thing to be said in their favor was that if water was only available on
the landing, it was still better than going outside to a pump. Making such
conditions worse was the fact that, characteristic of the domestic industry
through which most of the immigrants were employed, "housing" as such had
as only *one* of its functions "shelter, lodging; something that covers or pro-
tects." Tiny apartments of one or two rooms often "housed" from six to
twelve people, the main room serving as workshop, dining room, bedroom,
and kitchen. Who had time, especially during the busy season, to enjoy the
luxury of a "living" room?

If linguistically and culturally the immigrant Jewish enclaves in Paris
remained distinctly apart from the French as well as French Jewish surround-

ing communities, in most other respects the Jewish immigrant community resembled any other poor immigrant neighborhood. As one woman whose childhood was marked by this milieu repeated several times during an interview: *"On n'était pas heureux"* (We were not happy). The distance which separated the immigrant from the French Jewish community was in this respect none other than a distinction between working and middle-class living conditions.

It has been seen that with the migration of eastern European Jews to the West the "proletarian Jew" was discovered—discovered to exist in eastern Europe and now reproduced in the West as well. A contemporary observer wrote:

> There exists an immense Jewish proletariat, and the rich, opulent Jews, financiers and speculators are a tiny minority by comparison with this indigent population. This declaration suffices to ruin the anti-Semitic thesis.[1]

In a letter from a Groupe des ouvriers juifs socialistes de Paris to the French Socialist party, the authors stated that the Jews were in fact the most proletarian people in the world.[2] Although strictly speaking there was no real factory Jewish proletariat in Paris either before or after 1881, the working and living conditions of the post-1881 population in Paris led to the use of the term *proletariat* to describe the Jewish immigrants. This Jewish *proletariat*, a term used interchangeably with *immigrant* and *poor*, encompassed wage-earners, secondhand merchants, and peddlers as well as the unemployed, all intermixed in the discovery of the "proletarian Jew."

According to Paul Pottier, in the first in-depth article to appear on the subject and based on Comité de bienfaisance records, there were approximately twenty thousand "proletarian Jews" in Paris in 1899, a figure repeated in other articles even after the 1904–5 immigration added largely to that number.[3] The Comité itself reported that 29,900 poor had been helped in 1900, and in 1907 the *Archives Israélites* reported that a former anti-Semite had "discovered" thirty thousand proletarian Jews in Paris.[4]

An article in *Le Figaro* (Paris) of July 1, 1892, had evaluated the "Misère en Israël," or the poverty in the Parisian Jewish community, at 40 percent, a figure close to that calculated above for the eastern European Jewish immigrants. The exact proportion of immigrant as opposed to "French" (or Alsatian) Jewish poor is impossible to calculate.[5] Immigrants and poor are not only categories well known for their invisibility vis-à-vis officialdom, but there is also a confusion of terms, which makes evaluation quite difficult. The interchangeability of these terms, in an era before minimum-wage laws and the calculation of a "poverty level" made statistics more concrete, often resulted in the use of charity statistics to count "proletarians" or the use of immigrant figures to calculate the poor. The consequent estimates not only

cover a multitude of definitions but seldom take into consideration the working poor who may have had skills and jobs but were underemployed and could
not always make ends meet. It is this problem of chronic underemployment
within the immigrant trades that characterized the working and living conditions of immigrant life in the Marais and which show the poverty of statistics
based upon welfare rolls alone.

DEMOGRAPHIC INDICATORS

The working-class character of the Jewish immigrant community was not
only predetermined by the immigrants' choice of neighborhood but can be
seen in the demographic makeup of the community as well.

> What are the causes of the abominable misery which grips the Jewish pro-
> letariat in Paris? . . . The excessive number of children. . . . We must again
> underline that the overabundance of children is the plague of the Jewish pro-
> letariat.[6]

Thus wrote Paul Pottier in 1899, describing the four- to ten-child immigrant
families in an analysis not far from that of the French community's concern
over the proliferation of the eastern European Jews. For the xenophobic press
this fact took on even more ominous tones, threatening the French race
itself. From the official point of view, even with concern over France's low
birthrate, large immigrant families were not necessarily a blessing, either.
Working-aged, single men were most needed to help France compete with
the other industrializing countries.

Given the paucity of statistics, the continual immigrations and emigrations further West, and the extended period of time over which the reconstitution of families took place, it is difficult to calculate any average size per
immigrant family. Furthermore, to the extent that attempts at organizing the
immigration were successful, figures for those "chosen" immigrants cannot be
an accurate estimate of the immigrant community as a whole. Thus, for
example, the fact that the 504 refugees brought to Paris by the Comité de
bienfaisance in 1882 consisted of 154 families, i.e., 3.27 persons per statistical family, undoubtedly reflects the hand-picked character of this immigrant
group more than any real average family size.[7]

Concern over the large immigrant families in both the Jewish and non-
Jewish press must, however, be brought into perspective by the male-female
ratio of the immigrant community, which more clearly reflects the economic
basis of the migration. Whereas the male-female ratio among the total Parisian population in 1906 was 0.9:1, and the ratio for all foreigners was 1.01:1
(already indicating a larger male and hence working immigrant population),

TABLE 8

MALE-FEMALE RATIO AMONG JEWS IN FRANCE

Birthplace	1872	1885-87	1895-97	1905-07	Average
	male:female	male:female	male:female	male:female	
France	150:165 1:1.1 female=52%	462:574 1:1.2 female=55%	530:685 1:1.3 female=56%	470:662 1:1.4 female=58%	female=55%
Eastern Europe	22:10 2.2:1 male=69%	162:85 1.9:1 male=66%	228:100 2.3:1 male=70%	386:236 1.6:1 male=62%	male=67%

SOURCE: Derived from Doris Ben-Simon Donath, Socio-démographie des Juifs de France et d'Algérie, 1867-1907, P.O.F.-Etudes (Paris: Publications orientalistes de France, 1976), p. 108.

the ratio of males to females among Russian immigrants was even higher, 1.2:1.[8] The incoming Jewish immigrant population, as represented by the Asile de nuit statistics, was overwhelmingly male: 87.5 percent of the arrivals in 1910, 77.1 percent in 1911, and 77.6 percent in 1912.[9] Even as families were reconstituted, the proportions never reached that of the settled French Jewish population—55 percent *female*. Rather, the Jewish immigrant community averaged 67 percent *male* over the period, as seen in Table 8.

The overrepresentation of single males among the eastern European immigrants is corroborated by two sources: the Bureau russe du travail's estimate that only 20 percent of the Russian immigrants were married, and that only 12 percent of the immigrants were children (in 1906); and the Asile's separation of its one hundred beds into a group of eighty for men and twenty for women and children.[10]

The higher number of single young males and thus a lower overall average family size may be attributed to several reasons. For one, the immigration policy itself, as examined above, encouraged the migration of small families or single workers whenever possible. Second, the particular attraction of France for students and political activists increased the proportion of single males (even though both categories included a significant number of females). Third, many emigrants were only en route to the United States or South America, from whence they would send for their families. Or, as in the case of political activists in exile or students finishing their studies, the idea of eventual return to Russia worked against permanent settlement and the establishment of a family. Finally, the higher percentage of single men and lower number of families composing the eastern European immigrant community in France, insofar as this implies a high number of "breadwinners" typical of any immigrant population, also reflects the search for economic opportunities described above.

This characterization, clearly situating the Jewish immigrants within the broader immigrant context, must, however, be tempered by one fact. In France, as in the United States, the Jewish immigrant community, if clearly immigrant in character by its overrepresentation of males, was still more familial in character than other immigrant communities.[11] Political repression and violent anti-Semitism along with the economic forces behind emigration often made the Jewish exodus more permanent (and thus more familial) in character than more purely economic emigrations. Nevertheless, the higher proportion of males on the one hand and the larger families, once constituted, on the other are both common demographic indicators of immigrant and lower-class populations.

The conditions of life and death further attest to the impoverished character of the Jewish immigrant community. The slumlike conditions ("leprous houses, with mephitic odors") in the Marais were reported graphically by the non-Jewish and Jewish press alike:

> . . . in these little rooms where four or five people live enclosed, . . . where never a ray of sunlight enters to brighten it up and where physiological misery oozes from every pore.[12]

> . . . in small, dirty rooms. Seven, eight, ten workers are pressed together in the unbreatheable air. Sometimes a single room acts as workshop and living quarters; they live together like cattle. The adults and the children sleep next to one another on a dirty mattress that sometimes consists of nothing but straw.[13]

The only thing that thrived in such conditions was tuberculosis. The dust-filled air from the cutting of fabric in the tailors' workshops, the cloth-impregnated cauldrons of boiling water into which the capmakers dipped their caps, and the pervasive odor of rubber fumes in the raincoat workers' workshops all contributed to the pollution of air and lungs. Given the home industry in which the immigrants lived and worked, propriety was too often a luxury they could not afford.

In spite of these conditions it is often remarked that the Jewish mortality rate was lower than the non-Jewish one, even as compared to other immigrant workers. Various Jewish customs based on dietary and religious laws may have accounted for this—kosher food specially prepared and inspected; ritual bathing required for women; yearly top-to-bottom cleaning of the home before Passover—even if strict adherence to such rules could hardly have been observed in the immigrants' cramped working and living conditions. The moderate drinking habits of the Jewish workers and a marked lack of physical violence were other factors cited as contributing to their longer life as well as the suggestion that "the cold climate of Poland and Russia . . . has

TABLE 9

JEWISH INFANT MORTALITY
(DEATHS UNDER AGE 20)

	Poor Arrs: 4, 18	Average Arrs: 9, 10	Well-to-do Arrs: 8, 16		
1885-87	62%	35%	3%	= 100%	(N=330)
1895-97	55	36	8	99	(N=208)
1905-07	71	24	4	99	(N=278)

SOURCE: Doris Ben-Simon Donath, Socio-démographie des Juifs de France et d'Algérie, 1867-1907, P.O.F.-Etudes (Paris: Publications orientalistes de France, 1976), p. 306. Comparative data for French infant mortality bears out the relationship between neighborhood and survival rates. E.g., for 1885-87, of all infant deaths in these arrondissements, 58 percent occurred in the 4th and 18th, 29 percent in the 9th and 10th and 13 percent in the 8th and 16th. Annuaire statistique de la Ville de Paris, 1885-87.

conserved the ancient Jewish flesh, flesh of sadness, which, however, never ceases to reproduce itself."[14]

Although the Jewish workers may thus be distinguished from non-Jewish workers in this respect, a nonetheless significantly high death rate remained characteristic of the Jewish immigrant community. Consistorial burial records show that in 1885–87, 49 percent of the Jewish immigrants from eastern Europe died before the age of twenty (largely due to infant mortality) as compared to only 30 percent of the Jews born in France. While this figure remained about constant for the eastern Europeans in 1905–7 (47 percent), the figure for French Jews dropped to 20 percent by that period.[15] A study of mortality by neighborhoods confirms the close correlation between socioeconomic status (as seen in geographic distribution) and rates of survival (see Table 9).

"Hunger" is the title of one story in *Der idisher arbayter* describing the keen disappointment of a man who had always dreamt of going to Paris. When he did and found himself unemployed there, he could only cry in frustration and disbelief, "And *this* in Paris!?"[16] The often desperate extremes of those conditions led at least one Jewish labor leader to commit suicide by jumping off the Liberty Column at the place de la Bastille.[17] His death led to a meeting protesting the immigrants' lot.

The essential demographic characteristics of the immigrant Jewish community are tied to its socioeconomic condition and reflect the economic component of migration: geographically concentrated in working-class neighborhoods; a high birthrate; yet a high death rate; and a predominantly male population. While the eastern European Jewish community may have been more familial than other immigrant communities and had a relatively lower death rate than other working-class populations, nonetheless, its overall demographic profile clearly situates it as working class and immigrant. As one contemporary observer wrote, the indigent Jewish population resembled any other indigent quarter of Paris.[18]

OCCUPATIONAL STRUCTURE

The Jewish as well as the non-Jewish press often remarked—again with a certain surprise at the discovery—upon the variety of manual trades undertaken by the Jewish immigrants. From capmakers to shoemakers, from tinsmiths to goldsmiths, not to mention religious officials, gardeners, the forty-two Russian hairdressers, and two Galician acrobats listed in the Asile statistics, or even pimps, the immigrant Jewish community portrayed a wide range of economic activity. Precise figures on the immigrant trades are as difficult to establish as the number of immigrants themselves. Zosa Szajkowski, in examining the 504 refugees who arrived in 1882, found that almost 40 percent of them were skilled, whereas a much more optimistic Léon Kahn counted over 85 percent of the 200 immigrant heads of households as having "professions." The Bureau russe du travail, which in 1912 handled 578 immigrants looking for work, estimated that about one-half of them had qualified skills, and that the rest were intellectuals (approximately one-fourth of the applicants), servants, etc.[19]

The best extant information on immigrant occupations is found in the records of the Asile de nuit and in Wolf Speiser's *Kalendar*.[20] The Asile collected occupational data on immigrants sheltered there from 1906 to 1912 (see Appendix C), while Speiser drew up an estimate of the overall Jewish immigrant community's occupations in 1910 (Appendix D). The Asile, by its very purpose, undoubtedly reflected the neediest of immigrants (or at least those with no relative or friend to stay with the first nights).[21] Speiser, who estimated the immigrant community at a particularly high 60,000 persons (Appendix A), may have inflated figures. Nonetheless, even with these provisos, the two sources may be used as interesting indicators of immigrant skills on arrival (Asile) and of the actual jobs found by the immigrants once settled (Speiser).

The Asile statistics, broken down by place of origin, may be used as a basis for several useful comparisons. First of all, the immigrants to France may be compared to the occupational profile of the Jewish community in eastern Europe described in chapter 1, the economic need for emigration once again becoming apparent. Second, these entry statistics for Paris may be compared to similar data for the United States in order to distinguish among the emigrants' trades and skill levels as to their points of destination. Third, the

Asile statistics relating to those just arrived may be compared to data relating to occupations of immigrants once settled, as listed in Speiser's *Kalendar*, in order to investigate labor market needs versus imported skills and skill acquisition or downward mobility. Finally, the Jewish immigrants from eastern Europe may be interestingly compared both to other French visitors to the Asile during this period and to other immigrant communities in Paris at the time.

EMIGRANTS VERSUS BASE POPULATION IN EASTERN EUROPE

During the period 1906–12, 4,221 Russian, 1,346 Austro-Hungarian, and 857 Rumanian Jews passed through the Asile (representing 39.3 percent, 12.5 percent, and 8.0 percent of the Asile's visitors respectively, the rest being French), and occupational data were gathered for 2,749 (65.1 percent), 661 (49.1 percent), and 331 (38.6 percent) of these immigrants respectively (see Appendix C for full data).[22] Table 10, which compares the emigration into France (the Asile statistics) with the base population of Jews in Russia and Rumania confirms the emigration forces, which have been described. Among the Russians, a much higher proportion of skilled laborers (76.7 percent compared to 37.9 percent) and especially clothing workers (51.3 compared to 38.7 percent) and a much smaller number of merchants (6.7 compared to 32.0 percent) emigrated from the Pale as compared to the base population. This reflected the overburdened trade situation already noted and the relatively greater mobility of those with skills rather than those with (however small) invested capital—i.e., merchants.

Among the artisanal trades alone (Table 10b; see also Table 11), it is interesting to note that the higher percentage of clothing workers in Rumania (54.7 percent as compared to 38.7 percent in Russia) is accompanied by a smaller percentage of emigrants from this economic branch (40.1 percent) instead of vice versa as is true for the Russians. The greater opportunities for employment in this sector in Rumania lessened the need for emigration out of that economic branch while the contrary was true in the Pale.

It may also be noted that in both Rumania and the Pale the number of food producers—butchers, bakers, etc.—who emigrated is smaller (in Russia, almost by half) than that of the base population. It may be postulated that, even in the context of mass emigration, certain basic services will continue to offer work to part of the population, and such (internal market) economic sectors will therefore never export proportionally more labor than that represented by the base population. For those products geared to an extracommunity market, however, overburdening of those trades and/or insufficiency of

TABLE 10

JEWISH EMIGRANTS TO PARIS
COMPARED TO
BASE POPULATIONS IN THE PALE AND IN RUMANIA

	Russians			Rumanians	
	Paris	Pale		Paris	Rumania

a - All Occupations

	Paris	Pale		Paris	Rumania
Agriculture	0.6%	2.9%	Agriculture	0.0%	3.3%
Mining & Manufacture	76.7	37.9	Industry & Crafts	45.9	38.9
Commerce	6.7	32.0	Trade & Transportation	6.0	48.1
Transportation	0.4	3.3	Servants & Laborers	5.4	1.3
Personal Services	8.9	18.8	Services & Liberal Professions	16.4	3.3
Professional Services	6.7	5.1	Other & No Occupation	26.3	5.1
Total	100.0% (N=2,213)[a]	100.0% (N=1,332,000)[b]	Total	100.0% (N=331)[c]	100.0% (N=316,578)[d]

b - Artisanal Trades

	Paris	Pale	Paris	Rumania
Clothing & Wearing Apparel	51.3%	38.7%	40.1%	54.7%
Leather Goods	7.9	17.0	9.9	3.3
Food Products	6.1	11.6	4.6	7.7
Wood Products	8.3	9.9	6.6	7.4
Construction & Ceramics	4.5	6.3	11.2	7.3
Ordinary Metals	7.8	5.7	7.2 }	9.6
Finer Metals	4.9	4.1	6.6 }	
Textiles		3.7		5.9
Paper, Cardboard, & Printing	2.2	2.3	4.6	2.1
Chemicals		0.7		
Other	7.0		9.2	2.0
Total	100.0% (N=1,699)[e]	100.0% (N=500,986)[f]	100.0% (N=152)[e]	100.0% (N=17,505)[f]

[a] Appendix C: peddling and commerce combined; the personal services category includes all other unskilled workers (minus agriculture, peddling, and transportation) plus white collar workers.

[b] Table 1a (Kuznets).

[c] Appendix C: white collar workers and professionals combined.

[d] Table 1b (Lestschinsky).

[e] Appendix C.

[f] Table 2.

TABLE 11

MOST PREVALENT IMMIGRANT OCCUPATIONS ON ARRIVAL
(IN ORDER OF IMPORTANCE)

	Total N	As % of Active Pop
Tailors	306	10.0
Cobblers/Boot stitchers	199	6.5
Assistants/Clerks	166	5.4
Cabinetmakers/Joiners	142	4.6
Capmakers/Blockers	135	4.4
Furworkers	111	3.6
Metalsmiths	108	3.5
Day laborers	86	2.8
Bakers/Pastry-cooks	82	2.7
Garçons	76	2.5
Housepainters	75	2.4
Upholsterers	67	2.2
Students	63	2.1
Morocco-leather workers	62	2.0
Jewelers	62	2.0
Hatters/Milliners	61	2.0
Sewing machine operators	61	2.0
Printers	60	2.0
Bookbinders	60	2.0
Hairdressers	48	1.6
Tinsmiths	44	1.4
Artists/Photographers	39	1.3
Bookkeepers	35	1.1
(Subtotal)	2,148	70.1
(Total Active Population	3,062	100.0%)

SOURCE: Société philanthropique de l'Asile israélite de Paris, Rapports des exercices, 1906-7, 1909-12 (Paris: Imprimerie N.L. Danzig, n.d.). See appendix C for complete data.

110

markets will inevitably lead to emigration in search of economic opportunities.

EMIGRATION TO FRANCE VERSUS
EMIGRATION TO THE UNITED STATES

"Everybody knew that only the 'dregs' went to the New World."[23] While this comment on the part of an immigrant who chose France may be somewhat of an exaggeration, a comparison of occupational statistics as emigrants became immigrants, that is, as they chose their destination, is revealing. Indeed we may see, by comparing immigrant arrivals in France with those in the United States (Table 12), that a higher percentage of skilled laborers (76.8 percent compared to 64.0 percent) and a lower percentage of laborers and servants (3.4 percent compared to 21.0 percent) chose France. The reasons for this may be threefold. First, it may reflect the French emigration/immigration policy (to whatever extent it was successful), which aimed at deflecting the least desirable candidates from France. Second, this differentiation at the point of immigration may in fact be explicable by a differentiation at the point of emigration. That is, perhaps it was the relatively more prosperous and skilled Lithuanians who emigrated to western Europe, while more southern Russians emigrated to the United States. Unfortunately, existing data do not give precise enough indications of geographic origin in order to prove or disprove this hypothesis. Finally, one contemporary observer of immigrants to Paris commented that immigrants were attracted there because of the prestige of Parisian products and in order to perfect their trade skills.[24] While this is not true for all of the Jewish immigrants, as will be seen below, it may be a partial explanation of the difference between immigration to New York and to Paris.

Even more striking is the higher percentage of "professionals" who emigrated to France rather than the United States (12.6 percent compared to 1.3 percent). While the figure for France includes a large number of white-collar workers (5.9 percent), it also reflects the attraction of France for Russian and Rumanian students, artists, and "professional revolutionaries" (who of course do not appear as such in the statistics) already noted.

Finally, it can be seen that the number of immigrant agricultural workers is proportionately almost four times greater for those entering the United States (2.3 percent) than for those entering France ("outdoor work" = 0.6 percent). This fact, however small the actual numbers involved, is exemplary of the extent to which emigrant expectations of available opportunities prefigure the actual immigration. The wide-open spaces of the United States and various attempts to create immigrant agricultural colonies there are reflected in this small but significant comparison.

TABLE 12

IMMIGRATION TO FRANCE COMPARED TO IMMIGRATION TO THE UNITED STATES

	France 1906-12	United States 1889-1914
a - All Occupations		
Agriculture	0.6%	2.3%
Manufacturing and Mechanical Arts	76.8	64.0
Commerce	6.6	5.5
Laborers and Servants	3.4	21.0
Professionals	12.6	1.3
Others		5.9
Total	100.0%[a]	100.0%[b]
b - Artisanal Trades		
Clothing	36.3%	52.2%
Animal Products	22.8	8.5
Wood Manufacture and Construction	12.8	15.2
Food Industry	6.1	6.2
Metal Industry	12.7	4.6
Others	9.3	13.3
Total	100.0%[c]	100.0%[d]

[a]Appendix C, Russians only, calculated to correspond with Kuznets's categories: gainfully employed only; peddling and commerce combined. Simon Kuznets, "Immigration of Russian Jews to the United States: Background and Structure," *Perspectives in American History* 10 (1976): 101-2.

[b]Kuznets, pp. 101-2.

[c]Appendix C, Russians only, all fur and leather goods combined as animal products.

[d]Kuznets, p. 110.

The differentiation of a seemingly homogeneous emigrating population into relatively specific immigrating populations reflects not only emigrant expectations inherent in the initial decision to leave and the further choice of destination but also corresponds to labor needs in the receiving countries. In the period under study the general industrializing pattern of the West accounted for a basic similarity in immigrant arrival statistics. Different aspects of that pattern, however, corresponding to particular developmental needs of each country, will become even more evident in examining the "settled" immigrant population below.

"SETTLED" IMMIGRANT OCCUPATIONS

The settling in of the immigrants in Paris would necessarily correspond to the actual job opportunities available as distinct from those skills or trades imported from the old country. When the Bureau russe du travail was able to place only 309 immigrants in 1912 although there were 558 available jobs, the reasons given were the immigrants' lack of language or other skills or lack of the proper "certificate." Of those 309 placed, 33.7 percent got skilled jobs, 29.4 percent took unskilled manual jobs, 16.8 percent became domestics, and 20.1 percent of the jobs were for intellectuals.[25] By comparison, in the police department's examination of 14,164 identity cards of Russians registered in Paris in 1918, there were 82.2 percent manual laborers, 9.5 percent bourgeois, 6.2 percent intellectuals, and 2.1 percent *"mondains"* (worldly types).[26]

A more detailed description of the immigrants' occupations in Paris is given by Arthur Ruppin.[27] Out of 16,060 immigrant heads of households in Paris in 1910, he calculated 71.4 percent involved in the clothing industry, 16.8 percent in the metal industry (from plumbers to watchmakers), 6.2 percent in the wood industry, 3.7 percent leatherworkers, and 1.9 percent in other trades. The 11,460 clothing workers were further broken down as approximately 7,000 (60.4 percent) tailors, 2,000 (17.2 percent) hatters, 1,400 (12.1 percent) furworkers, and 1,200 (10.3 percent) cobblers. Ruppin's statistics seem to be based on Speiser's *Kalendar.* However, one important category conspicuously missing from Ruppin's as well as the Bureau russe's and the police department's statistics is that of merchants.

Commerce

It seems that "Jewish" statistics often err on the side of productivity, just as anti-Semitic statistics err on the side of parasitism. While the latter are bent on equating Jews with commerce, the former often ignore commercial activities for which the Jews have so often been criticized. (At the same time, those without professions are also often overlooked.) For example, in an effort to emphasize productive Jewish manual labor, the exhaustive two-volume Jewish Colonization Association report made no mention of Jewish commerce in the Pale. Similarly, not only Ruppin for Paris but other studies for London and Manhattan either ignored merchants completely or subsumed them within the "industry" of the product being sold.[28]

The combining of clothing traders and producers under the sole rubric of the clothing industry, for example, does point to the importance of all aspects of this sector for the Jewish immigrants. Furthermore, it is certainly true that in many cases, due to the complexity of the work process and the marginality of many producers and traders (all poor), it may be difficult to distinguish the worker-artisan (implying production and distribution) from a "pure" salaried producer or "pure" self-employed trader. On the one hand, while working for a contractor a tailor may have also had some clients of his (her) own, not to mention the possibility (necessity?) of peddling secondhand garments during the off-season; on the other hand, the shoe "salesperson" almost certainly also did repair work.[29]

It is nonetheless important to separate commercial from productive activity to whatever extent possible in order to have a clearer conception of the occupational structure of the immigrant community. It may be postulated that a notable characteristic of a settled immigrant community is the reestablishment of a commercial sector. Information on newly arrived, as compared to more settled, immigrants bears out this hypothesis. The occupational statistics on the immigrant community found in Wolf Speiser's *Kalendar* for the year 1910, which may be taken as representative of the "settled" immigrants' economic activity, are revealing (Table 13). Merchants account for 26.6 percent of the immigrants, while secondhand peddlers constitute another 6.1 percent. By contrast, in the "arrivals" statistics of the Asile, merchants were only 6.6 percent and only twelve peddlers were counted in six years. Thus, as the community became more settled, commercial activity was reinstated almost to the levels of importance of eastern Europe (32.0 percent, Table 1a). It may be suggested that a good number of those entering the Asile occupationless later accounted for many of the secondhand traders counted by Speiser.[30]

The virtual "disappearance" in the immigrant arrival statistics of peddling and other commercial activities, only to reappear with the settling in of the immigrant community, corresponds to two factors implicit in the migration process: the difficulty of moving one's capital stock and reestablishing a clientele, and certain expectations or warnings passed along to successive emigrants that productive occupations were more likely to evoke a positive response from immigration officials than would commercial "skills."

However, rather than seeing the reappearance of this economic sector in either instance as a direct carry-over of activities already exercised in eastern

TABLE 13

ARRIVING IMMIGRANTS; SETTLED IMMIGRANTS

	On Arrival[a] (Asile)	Settled Immigrants[b] (Speiser)
a - All Occupations		
Unskilled	4.9%	6.1%
Skilled	73.5	62.1
Merchants	6.6	26.6
"Free" Professions	6.8	4.0
Other	8.2 (white collar)	1.2
Total Active Population	100.0%	100.0%
	(N=3,062)	(N=30,199)
b - Skilled Workers		
Clothing and Apparel	46.5%	60.8%
Tailors, Cutters, Seamstresses, Machine operators, Pressers	19.8	36.8[c]
Capmakers/Blockers	6.0	10.1[d]
Hatters/Milliners	2.7	0.3
Furworkers	4.9	7.5
Cobblers/Boot stitchers	8.9	6.1
Other	4.2	
Leatherworkers	8.0	3.2
Woodworkers	7.6	15.4
Construction	5.6	0.5
Ordinary Metalworkers	8.3	8.0
Precious Metals/Precision Work	6.4	7.5
Other	17.6	4.6
Total	100.0%	100.0%
	(N=2,251)	(N=18,769)

[a]Asile statistics, total active eastern Europeans, see Appendix C.

[b]Wolf Speiser, Kalendar (Paris: n.p., 1910). For complete data, see Appendix D. Note that "Unskilled" are all peddlers, and that "Other" includes barbers, wigmakers, bristle workers, store clerks, lemonade makers, and waiters, all combined by Speiser. The figures for "settled" skilled workers and merchants compare closely with those found by Hyman for the occupations of fathers of immigrant children enrolled in Jewish primary schools, 1907-9. Paula Hyman, From Dreyfus to Vichy (New York: Columbia University Press, 1979), Appendix A.

[c]including non-specialized clothing workers.

[d]including non-specialized capmakers.

Europe, peddling or dealing in secondhand wares may be seen as particularly propitious *immigrant* activities. The sale of secondhand or refurbished goods, through which a large number of immigrants got their start, meets two essential criteria necessary for any immigrant: a minimal amount of initial capital necessary and the possibility of almost immediate (however small) earnings. Whether selling secondhand clothing, bric-a-brac, oranges, pickles, toys, ribbons, shoelaces, or confetti, or peddling a service such as knife-grinding, repair work, etc., these *marchands de paniers* (basket merchants) could begin making two francs a day without any apprenticeship or much investment practically from the first day of arrival.[31]

The use of peddling (goods or services) as a short-term venture before finding something more stable or even as an interim recourse to avoid unemployment during the off-season became a fundamental characteristic of the immigrant communities in New York, London, and Paris.[32] Nonetheless the importance of peddling in terms of an overall appreciation of immigrant occupations and of commerce remains problematic. Should the peddler's few possessions be seen as a stepping-stone toward capital accumulation and later commercial success, as the founding stories of some department stores and successful retailers would have us believe (Galeries Lafayette, Sools, Levitan)? Certainly, peddling may have been an initial phase toward self-employment, the aspirations to which played a large part in the immigrants' choice of employment. However, more often than not contemporaries grouped the peddler under the encompassing word "proletariat," seeing the peddler's meager goods and poverty as symptoms of a wandering, nonpossessing class.[33] Dispossessed psychologically and often materially by the migration process itself, petty commerce was often the only recourse short of the welfare office.

Skill Continuity and Skill Acquisition

Peddling and commercial activities may have been a more visible immigrant occupation, but it was nonetheless the backroom production that constituted the bulk of immigrant occupations. About those with trade skills the question then is: To what extent did migration represent a continuity of skills from one labor market to another or did the immigrants have to become trained or retrained in order to fit into the French labor market? Although those who attempted to organize the migration and the emigrants themselves, insofar as they were self-selected with a view toward future job opportunities, tried to ensure the emigration/immigration of needed skills, advance expectations were not always perfectly matched with available opportunities. Thus a former skill could be rendered superfluous and a skilled laborer could become *relatively* unskilled if job expectations and opportunities did not coincide. The different labor needs of the sending and receiving countries (or the pertinent regions involved—in this case the Pale and Paris) and especially the needs of specific economic sectors formed the essential background of skill usability and ultimate employment of the immigrants.

Cigarette workers may be taken as one example. Only six cigarette workers appeared at the Asile in the period 1906–12 and none are listed by Speiser. Reference to only one new cigarette and cigarette-holder "factory," which employed recently arrived Russian Jewish immigrants, has been found.[34] This occupation, which was a large employer of Jewish labor in Russia at the end of the nineteenth century, was undoubtedly little represented in Paris both because it continued to offer significant employment in the Pale and because the industry was little developed in France.

By comparing once again the entering (immigrat*ing*) population with the more settled (immigrat*ed*) one (Table 13a), indications of skill acquisition or skill continuity may be seen. The decrease in skilled workers from 73.5 percent of the entering immigrants to 62.1 percent of those settled must be explained in part by the increase in commercial activity that occurs through settling, as already noted. But it also reflects a certain incompatability of labor needs.

The breakdown among the skilled trades (Table 13b) points to specific examples of skill acquisition on the one hand and cases of skill superfluity on the other, both corresponding to economic opportunities in Paris. The increase in garment workers (up 14.3 percent from the Asile to Speiser's statistics) and particularly that of tailors, et al. (up 17.0 percent), woodworkers (up 7.8 percent), and furworkers (up 2.6 percent) indicates the vitality of the ready-to-wear industry, the expansion of the fur industry, and the importance of the faubourg St.-Antoine woodwork industry for the immigrant jobseekers and thus the inducement to skill acquisition in these trades. However, the need for leatherworkers (down 4.8 percent) seems to indicate that conditions in Paris were less than what many skilled workers in this field might have hoped.

Other adaptations had to take place. Saddlers, for whom there was no need in Paris, could perhaps become *maroquinier* leather workers. The rubber coat industry, new to France in the early 1900s, provided opportunities for many Jewish immigrants who learned this trade in Paris. (Not one immigrant rubberworker appears in the Asile lists.) And more generally, the large decline in the category of "other" skills (down 13.0 percent), which may in part be due to enumeration techniques (Speiser only lists forty-one different categories, whereas the Asile lists over two hundred), undoubtedly also represents skill transfers or acquisitions of new trades induced through adaptation to a new labor market.

The capmaking industry on the other hand is perhaps the best example of both skill continuity and skill acquisition. This industry was essentially imported to France or at least greatly expanded by the eastern European Jews, as has been seen. Already in 1872 over one-third of the eastern European Jews living in the 4th arrondissement were involved in this industry, and the number of capmakers grew from approximately 70 that year to 1,500 by 1912.[35] (The number of capmakers increased from 6 percent to 10.1 percent from the Asile's to Speiser's figures.) Capmaking was relatively easy to learn, and the expansion of this industry offered plenty of opportunities for newcomers. Although Speiser suggests that a saturation point was eventually reached as competition among capmakers grew and as more of the newcomers brought with them a greater diversity of skills,[36] this trade remained almost exclusively "Jewish" and of particular importance for the Jewish labor movement, as will be seen below.

The acquisition or adaptation of skills in tune with economic opportunities in the country of adoption is important. Tailoring was not an immutable condition of the Jewish immigrant. Many picked up a needle for the first time in their lives because of the opportunities to do so in Paris (as in New York or London). Yet for many clothing workers and capmakers skill continuity was a valuable tool in a ripe economic environment. The importance of the skills imported by any particular immigrant group is best seen by comparison to the occupational profile of the indigenous labor population and by comparison to other immigrant populations.

IMMIGRANT JEWISH WORKERS; FRENCH WORKERS

The importance of skill importation can best be seen by comparing the incoming immigrant visitors at the Asile with the poor French workers who also availed themselves of the shelter's services (Table 14). The greater number of skilled immigrants (60.2 percent) compared to the French (35.5 percent) is striking. And the concentration of the immigrants in the clothing trade (although a high number of female seamstresses among the French workers also corresponds to the description of the clothing industry's labor force seen above), their high numbers in leatherwork (and shoemaking/repair), and the precision metal and stone trades all indicate areas in which the immigrants were able to import skills less prevalent among the French workers.

However, it may be unfair to compare a just-arrived population, in which preselection by skill has been part of the migration process, with native poor who have had recourse to a welfare hostel. Such a comparison of newly arrived poor with a perhaps more deep-rooted indigence on the part of the indigenous poor may perhaps only point to a temporary condition on the part of the former as distinct from a permanent condition of the latter. It is therefore necessary to take the settled immigrant population statistics (Speiser) for comparison with the (presumably settled) French poor having

TABLE 14

ARRIVING IMMIGRANTS; FRENCH POOR
(ASILE)

	Eastern European Arrivals (1906-12)	French Poor (1911-12)
a - All Occupations		
Unskilled	4.0%	46.4%
Skilled	60.2	35.5
Merchants	5.4	1.6
White collar workers	6.7	7.3
"Free" Professions	5.5	3.6
No Occupation	18.2	5.6
Total	100.0%	100.0%
	(N=3,741)	(N=1,753)
b - Skilled Workers		
Clothing and Apparel	46.5%	33.2%
Tailors, Cutters, Seamstresses, Machine Operators, Pressers	19.8	17.7
Capmakers/Blockers	6.0 ⎫	1.2
Hatters/Milliners	2.7 ⎭	
Furworkers	4.9	0.2
Cobblers/Boot stitchers	8.9	2.8
Other	4.2	11.3
Leatherworkers	8.0	3.2
Woodworkers	7.6	7.4
Construction	5.6	14.8
Ordinary Metalworkers	8.3	14.1
Precious Metals/Precision Work	6.4	2.9
Printing	2.7	5.1
Food	6.4	11.4
Other	8.5	7.9
Total	100.0%	100.0%
	(N=2,251)	(N=622)

SOURCE: Appendix C.

recourse to the Asile; and both can be compared to the overall structure of gainfully employed persons in France (Table 15).

Once again, the correlation of commerce with "settledness" suggested above is corroborated. The commercial activity on the part of the settled immigrants (26.6 percent) contrasts sharply with the more skill-poor and capital-poor indigent French (1.7 percent merchants). It is much closer, however, to the percentage of commercial activity of the overall French community (20.9 percent). And insofar as the settled immigrants even surpass the French in this category, the not uncommon pattern of immigrant social mobility through shopkeeping can be seen.

There were both more skilled and less unskilled workers among the settled immigrants as compared to the French poor and the overall French population. This points once again to the self- (as well as induced) selection character of the migration process, with value placed on having above all else a skill among one's baggage. The importation to France of useful skills, corresponding to labor needs in the clothing, leather, and woodwork trades is also again apparent.

JEWISH IMMIGRANTS; OTHER IMMIGRANTS

Just as interesting is a comparison of the Jewish immigrants with other immigrants in Paris at the turn of the century (Table 16). If various elements of economic or industrial development can explain overall labor migration patterns, it remains nonetheless true that migrant workers cluster in different sectors. Language and cultural affinities and the facility of intracommunity labor force recruitment all led to a tendency of the different immigrant groups in Paris to occupy different if never entirely discrete economic sectors.

Among the Belgians there were a larger number of clothing workers as well as leatherworkers, furworkers, woodworkers, and metalworkers. German immigrants were in large numbers employed as domestics, while the Italians in Paris undertook many of the most laborious tasks of hard labor, transportation, and construction. The latters' culinary abilities were also praised, and they indeed showed slightly higher activity as restaurant owners in the food category. Finally, the Swiss living in Paris were both in large numbers domestics as well as active in commerce.

Compared to these immigrants, the high percentage of Jewish skilled workers is still notable (62.1 percent) although not unique (59.8 percent of the Italians and 53.6 percent of the Belgians). The high number of Jewish clothing workers (29.3 percent) was well seconded by Belgians in this trade (22.0 percent), although the Jewish immigrants did stand out with 10.4 percent in the leather and fur trades. The Jewish immigrants were surpassed by the Swiss in commercial activities and by all of the other groups in

TABLE 15

SETTLED IMMIGRANTS COMPARED TO
FRENCH POOR AND OVERALL FRENCH OCCUPATIONS

	1 French Poor (1911-12)[a]		2 Settled Immigrants (1910)[b]	3 French Occupations (1896)[c]	
AGRICULTURE		1.5%	0.0%		0.3%
UNSKILLED		47.7	6.1		19.7
Domestic	14.6			14.4	
Labor and Transport	29.5			5.3	
Other	3.6		6.1 (peddlers)		
SKILLED		37.7	62.1		44.2
Clothing	10.4		29.3	16.9	
Leather	3.3		10.4	2.9	
Wood	2.8		9.6	4.2	
Construction	5.6		0.3	4.7	
Ordinary Metals	5.3		5.0 ⎫	7.6	
Precious Metals	1.1		4.6 ⎭		
Printing	1.9		0.1	2.1	
Food	4.3		0.3	2.2	
Other	3.0		2.5	3.6	
MERCHANTS		1.7	26.6		20.9
WHITE COLLAR WORKERS		7.7	1.2		0.0
"FREE" PROFESSIONS		3.7	4.0		9.0
State Functions				4.7	
Other				4.3	
OTHER					5.4
UNKNOWN					0.5
Total Active Population		100.0% (N=1,654)	100.0% (N=30,199)		100.0% (N=1,466,911)

[a]Appendix C (Asile): Shoe and furworkers have been included under leather goods rather than clothing to correspond to census data.

[b]Appendix D (Speiser): Shoe and furworkers have been included under leather goods rather than clothing to correspond to census data.

[c]Résultats statistiques du recensement des industries et professions (1896), vol. 1: Région de Paris, au Nord et à l'Est (Paris, Imprimerie nationale for the Office du travail, 1899), pp. 204-5.

121

TABLE 16

IMMIGRANT OCCUPATIONS IN PARIS

	Jews[a] (1910)		Belgians[b] (1901)	Germans[b] (1901)	Italians[b] (1901)	Swiss[b] (1901)	French[c] (1896)
AGRICULTURE	0.0%		0.1%	0.1%	0.1%	0.3%	0.3%
UNSKILLED	6.1		22.0	45.7	18.5	30.1	19.7
Peddlers		6.1					
Domestic Services			15.8	42.4	8.8	26.6	14.4
Hard Labor, Transport			6.2	3.3	9.7	3.5	5.3
SKILLED	62.1		53.6	26.1	59.8	35.6	44.2
Clothing		29.3	22.0	10.0	12.5	9.8	16.9
Leather and Furs		10.4	4.8	2.5	4.4	2.0	2.9
Wood		9.6	8.0	4.1	7.2	3.5	4.2
Construction		0.3	5.7	1.4	19.2	9.5	4.7
Ordinary Metals		5.0	7.2	3.3	8.5	5.4	7.6
Fine Metals		4.6	1.3	0.5	1.1	0.7	2.2
Food		0.3	0.8	2.5	3.5	2.6	5.7
Other		2.6	3.8	1.8	3.4	2.1	
MERCHANTS	26.6		19.8	22.3	15.2	29.2	20.9
WHITE COLLAR WORKERS	1.2		4.5	5.8	6.4	4.8	
"FREE" PROFESSIONS	4.0						9.0
State		0.0	0.6	1.4	0.4	0.7	4.7
Other		4.0	3.9	4.4	6.0	4.1	4.3
OTHER							5.4
UNKOWN							0.5
Total	100.0% (N=30,199)		100.0% (N=19,175)	100.0% (N=18,866)	100.0% (N=15,082)	100.0% (N=14,522)	100.0% (N=1,466,911)

[a] Table 15, column 2.

[b] Mlle. Schirmacher, La spécialisation du travail—Par nationalités, à Paris (Paris: Arthur Rousseau, 1908), pp. 171-74.

[c] Table 15, column 3.

unskilled workers. The latter were particularly made up of (German and Swiss) domestic labor, in which the Jewish immigrants took virtually no part.

In addition to these aspects of labor market segmentation, each community also had its own internal labor market for both goods and services. Special groceries, bakeries, ethnic restaurants, butchers, and delicatessens (whether for religious needs or merely out of habit) catered to the immigrant communities' specific customs and perhaps nostalgia. Jews skilled in traditional or religiously based trades could continue to ply them, while bookbinding and candlemaking, for example, could also be expanded into nonreligious markets. Some Jewish immigrants became part of the synagogue "proletariat," so described by the Consistoire archivist; i.e., those janitors and other workers whose poverty is revealed in the Consistoire reports on the administrative workings of the synagogues.[37]

Services internal to the community included translations, correspondence, or even teaching French, which those already more proficient in the new language—many students—could handle for their "better off [but] more ignorant compatriots."[38] There was also a lucrative trade in the fabrication of necessary documents such as diplomas or birth certificates, particularly when the latter barely existed in Russia or when births had gone unregistered in order to avoid military obligations.[39] Then there was also the colorful Baruch, described in *L'épopée de Ménaché Foïgel,* who was a one-man employment agency, real estate agent (helping the Foïgels find an apartment), and storehouse of useful information. He even kept file cards on the preferences of Parisian philanthropists, information available for sale to the needy so that they would know to whom and how they should best apply for aid.[40]

The fact of producing goods or services for the community itself did not, however, shelter the immigrants from external fluctuations. When the off-season came to the clothing industry it came to neighborhood restaurants and cafés as well. Nor were the community workers sheltered from poor working conditions or patterns of exploitation by virtue of working for a community clientele: the case of the bakers will be seen below; the translation business was described by Tchernoff as a sweating system.[41]

Beyond specific internal immigrant markets or immigrant clustering in certain economic sectors, several factors were characteristic of all of the immigrants in Paris at the turn of the century. Over one-half of the Belgians, Italians, and Jews who settled in Paris found employment in the growing light industrial sector, while the Swiss and Germans filled domestic functions as the indigenous population moved toward industrial occupations. Also, as the immigrant communities settled in, all of them moved into commercial activities, which employed from 15 to 30 percent of each community. The Germans, the Jews, and especially the Swiss even surpassed the average French participation in this area, although the franc value of French and perhaps Swiss commerce (banking falling within this category) was undoubtedly much greater than that of the simple shops that represented a meager measure of upward mobility for many immigrants.

Therefore, market needs helped determine immigrant occupational distribution, and notably the high number of skilled workers who came to Paris in this period. Yet the question may still be asked, what type of skill? The level involved was clearly not always that of the renowned Parisian specialty goods. The Jewish immigrants' "specialties," for example, were often the cheaper models (rabbit fur, "fantasy" furniture—imitations of Louis XV style, etc.) or inferior products. This also attests to an important aspect of the role of immigrants in the labor market.

As indicated earlier, the structural development of light industry provided easy insertion for immigrants, a "pull" to which the Jewish immigrants along with many others were susceptible. Thus, although skill continuity, especially in the clothing industry, seems to be a notable feature of the occupational structure of the Jewish immigrant community, this tendency was reinforced by factors that made Jewish concentration in light industry an "immigrant" just as much as a "Jewish" phenomenon. The Jewish immigrants thus imported certain skills which the Parisian ready-to-wear and other light industries were only too glad to put to use. A Yiddish phrase well describes the process: the skilled worker was described as having a skill *in hant*. The image is one of easy mobility rather than being tied down to fixed assets. And as has been seen, the exportation of skilled laborers was largely a result of an asphyxiation of economic opportunities in these sectors in the Pale.

However, at the same time many Jewish immigrants also acquired new skills or transferred like skills according to job opportunities in Paris. If the forces of emigration explain certain imported skills, the conditions of immigration explain the skill acquisition and adaptation to new markets, which were necessary. Finally, immigration networks favored sectoral concentration. As paths toward the West were traced for emigration as a whole, paths toward certain industries also became well trod.

We will now turn to those sectors of light industry in which the Jewish immigrants found employment. The statistics as to their numbers are silent as to their working conditions. It is to police reports, a Yiddish labor newspaper, and a variety of extant leaflets that we may now turn in order to examine the condition of the immigrant worker in the workshop itself.

Five
AT WORK, ON STRIKE

Jewish subcontractors waited at the Paris train stations, as in New York they waited at the docks, to offer work and lodging to newly arrived immigrants. Such a welcome from a Yiddish-speaking sympathizer was impossible to resist. As one author dramatically described the result:

> Confused and alarmed [in their new environment] they accepted the mediation of these soul-sellers who dealt in men's flesh, who offered them the prospect of daily bread under the guise of manna from heaven. He [the poor immigrant] is imprisoned, and the cord of misery soon closes fast around his neck.[1]

The putting-out system already described had certain advantages for the immigrants that paralleled the interest manufacturers had in this system. Little capital was needed and often little skill as well. Easy access to the trades was facilitated through informal communication networks within the immigrant neighborhood. And the familial character of the plethora of small workshops meant that transition to a foreign language and culture was much less brutal (if in some cases almost nonexistent). Religious or traditional customs could be maintained and children could be cared for, and put to work.

But perhaps even more importantly, homework also meant a certain independence and a sense of self-employment for many. Homework implied a

flexibility which contrasted with the constraints of a factory, many immigrants working for several different manufacturers, arranging their hours to
their own convenience. And there was the possibility of becoming truly self-
employed, an essential attraction of light industry for those who aspired to
save the little capital necessary to buy a sewing machine, hire another worker
or two, or make the transition to small-scale commerce.

This sense of independence was, however, largely illusory and not far
from the "cord of misery" described above. Flexibility of hours meant that a
few hours a day in the slow season became sixteen or twenty hours a day when
the busy season arrived. Exigent deadlines further degraded the "independence" of the homeworker's schedule. Total dependence on one or more
contractors meant time wasted waiting for work to be delivered or waiting
around at the contractor's workshop, only to be told in the off-season: "Sorry,
no work today; come back tomorrow." "Independence" equaled insecurity in
the face of the ups and downs of seasonal demand.

The material disadvantages of the immigrants' "independence" were
even more blatant. Time was lost in transportation as the easily recognizable
pieceworker went back and forth in the métro carrying the large black cloth
(*toilette*) containing pieces to be assembled for a finished garment. The overhead that the manufacturer avoided by farming out work meant that heating,
lighting, and tool maintenance all devolved upon the family workshop. The
thread, needles, and sometimes even buttons had to be supplied by the
worker. Workshop workers too had to bring their own needles and scissors
and furnish their own sewing machines (bought on credit) as well as the oil to
keep them greased. Rubber-mantle workers had to supply the benzine used to
join the pieces together. Upholsterers had to provide glue, varnish, and
sandpaper. As for diamond workers, the small diamond fragments (bort) used
as an abrasive that they had to furnish took up approximately one-third of
their weekly salary.[2]

Finally, the "independence" of the homeworker or even small-time boss
also meant isolation, an isolation reinforced by manufacturers and contractors who negotiated separately with each worker who was "free" to accept or
reject any offer as he or she pleased. With the slack season just around the
corner, that "free" choice was sorely circumscribed. The illusion of independence only reinforced the immigrant worker's isolation, while the small hidden workshops escaped the work inspector's and legislation's scope.

It is the overcoming of this isolation and the articulation of grievances
against many of these conditions to which we now turn. The strikes undertaken by the Jewish immigrant workers are especially important in three
respects. First, they are strident testimony to workshop conditions, which, I
would argue, were sufficient in and of themselves to lead to strike actions.
(The issue of revolutionary leadership or French union participation in the
Jewish immigrant strikes will be examined in the following chapter.) Second,

the strikes also reveal the larger structure of domestic work—piecework, seasonality, workers' competition—which determined the terrain of struggle. Finally, as springboards to union organizing, these strikes are an important indicator of the growing consciousness of the Jewish immigrants in Paris. That consciousness would culminate in a Jewish labor movement in Paris, which, if not renowned for its size or strength, provides an important case study of immigrant labor organizing.

THE CLOTHING TRADES

And it was said in Paris: "Aha! So you too want to marry a tailor?" just like it was said in Russia: "Aha, so you want to marry a doctor?"[3]

Be it cloth, fur, leather, or rubber (for raincoats), outer garments, inner garments, or accessories (shoes, hats, belts, purses), the variety of articles that needed needle and thread to piece them together provided an important source of employment for Jewish and other immigrant workers in Paris. Of the Belgians, Germans, Austrians, Hungarians, Russians, and Rumanians involved in these trades, it was said that the Jews were the most exploited of all.[4]

The division of labor characteristic of the clothing industry created a labor hierarchy by salary and status corresponding both to the difficulty of the item (e.g., jackets are harder than pants) and the specific task involved. At the top of the task hierarchy were the (almost always French) designers (*modélistes*) who conceived the season's styles. In the actual production of garments, where immigrants played an important role, the cutters reigned supreme (once a cutter "he is altogether a gentleman" ["*il est tout à fait un monsieur*"[5]]) and often became workshop foremen. They used sabers or ribbon-saw machines to cut the piece goods, which were then distributed for assembly.

The assemblers who pieced the garment sections together were called machine operators (*mécaniciens*), machine-pickers (*piqueurs à la machine*), or pieceworkers (*apiéceurs*) and accounted for approximately two-thirds of all workers in the garment industry. Almost all of them worked at home or in small family or contractor-run workshops. While running a sewing machine was not difficult to learn (and the quality of ready-to-wear goods was not expected to be that of *haute couture*), it was hazardous to the health. Bent over the machine, foot pressed against the heavy pedal day after day, the sewer's position caused digestive problems, headaches, eyeaches, dizziness, and even metritis (inflammation of the uterus), which could lead to birth defects or infant mortality.

The most common work-related disease, though, was the endemic tuberculosis resulting from poor ventilation of the cloth-dust–filled work-places. In the case of leather or fur articles the chemicals—arsenic, among others—used to treat the skins added to the foulness of the air. Rubber-workers pieced together raincoats with gasoline, which also impregnated their lungs.

After assembly a garment would go to any number of finishers who would put in the lining (the *apprêteurs* who cut the lining material were not particularly skilled, since the material used was inexpensive), finish seams, sew on buttons, etc. Many of these tasks were done particularly by women, although the male contractor might even lend a hand when an order was rushed. Finally, the product would go to a *pompier* (literally, pumper), a skilled worker, for its final touches before the last stage of all, and the lowest in the needle hierarchy, the presser's iron.

The real functioning of this division of labor and the consequences of the working conditions that this schematic description hides are best revealed in the strike actions that were undertaken by the tailors and seamstresses in Paris. And whenever a strike arose, it seems a police informer was there to report on it and to gather information, from the leaflets passed out or posted on the workshop doors to the strike committee and trade union meetings at which strategies were elaborated.

The most important of the early tailors' strikes occurred in February 1901 and involved over seven hundred out of eight hundred workers em-ployed in fifty-five womenswear workshops in Paris.[6] The strike even caught the attention of the *Archives Israélites*, which noted the large number of coreligionists involved on both sides of the strike: that approximately one-third of the establishments were Jewish-owned, that a large number of the workers involved were "our own" (*des nôtres*) and that even the clientele was also probably in large part *"nos élégantes."* The "quasi-religious" nature of the conflict was thus seen as "overabundantly prov[ing] that Jewish solidarity is a vain word."[7]

The first strike meeting took place at the Bourse du travail on January 31, 1901—just before the beginning of the export season—and the initial demands called for a wage increase, an equalization of wages among the various establishments involved, and the abolition of piecework. At the very outset the vice-president of the employers' union expressed his confidence that the strike would fail. After all, he said, the strikers were all foreigners, earning more in France than they ever earned in their homelands, a fact that the risk of expulsion would bring home to them. The large number of foreign-ers among the strikers was repeatedly noted by all of the press and caused the anti-Semitic *La Libre Parole* to exclaim over the veritable Tower of Babel at each Bourse du travail meeting; this same paper was nevertheless surprised to note that Jewish workers did indeed exist.[8]

From the very beginning the strikers appealed to the solidarity of all immigrants and women so that the workshop owners could not turn to homeworkers to fill their orders. At one of the first meetings at the Bourse du travail a Jewish tailor made a special appeal to his coreligionists for their solidarity, and soon a group of Jewish tailors in Montmartre joined the strike. In the discussions concerning their particular exploitation at the hands of Jewish contractors, one of the basic divisions within the trade and consequently one of the weakest links in the efforts to organize the needleworkers in Paris came to light: the division of work between workshop and home. Whereas the strike that began in the "Center" of Paris aimed at abolishing piecework in order to prohibit the bosses from turning to homeworkers to undercut workshop workers, the Jewish tailors on Montmartre sought to abolish piecework not only because of its competitive nature (vis-à-vis workshop workers) but because of its inherently exploitative properties at the hands of their coreligionist contractors. While in the Center the strike lined up mostly French workshop workers against their French bosses on the one hand and against largely female and immigrant pieceworkers on the other, the struggle on Montmartre took place almost entirely among Jewish immigrants. Jewish workers struck out against compatriot contractors and against the piecework system itself.

Three to four hundred strikers attended the meetings organized at the Maison du peuple on Montmartre, and it was on February 13 that the Jewish tailors voted solidarity with the strikers of the Center. The strike was not a matter of nationality or politics, they declared, but strictly a trade issue demanding the unity of all. On February 16 the feminist paper *La Fronde* (which gave excellent coverage of the strike and was instrumental in getting 140 female pieceworkers to join it) described the entrance of the Montmartre tailors at the Bourse du travail: Singing the "International," they entered to the acclamation of the entire meeting hall.

Letters of support and some financial aid arrived from abroad. Tailors in London and Manchester (where there were also large numbers of immigrant Jewish workers) as well as Belgium assured the Parisian workers that they would not accept work from Parisian manufacturers trying to break the strike. Nonetheless, the Parisian bosses found a way to carry on, and at the strike meetings homeworkers who were continuing to take work were castigated.

By March 6 the French union began to complain of diminishing funds and discouraged the idea of extending the strike to other establishments. The union spokesmen pressed for a compromise on wage demands and urged that the call for the elimination of piecework be dropped altogether. When these issues came to a vote, the weary strikers all supported the union's suggestions, with the exception of five Montmartre tailors. The latter protested that the union did not really understand the catastrophic nature of piecework and the problems of being at the contractors' mercy, and that if the union were abandoning the struggle against piecework in order to appease those pieceworkers of the Center, the Montmartre tailors could no longer follow the union either in this regard or with regard to lowering the wage demands. It would be better to obtain nothing than to give in on the most essential demand: Down with piecework!

Over one month and 21,210 person-working days later, the strikers followed the union's directive to return to work. Conditions remained unchanged, the only positive result of the strike being the increase in the number of union members. The union grew from 1,500 members before the strike to 4,000 afterward and boasted of the "school of solidarity" that the strike had been. On the other hand, 150 immigrant tailors went back to their home countries after the strike's end, another 200 remained out of work, and over 30 were arrested. As the ministerial report on the trade summed it up, the "happy result" of the strike was the partial replacement of foreign workers by female Parisian seamstresses.[9]

Many of the issues involved in this early showdown between garment workers and their employers were typical of the other forty-five strikes in this trade (for which we have information) in which Jewish immigrants took part between 1889 and 1916.[10] The strike demands form a microcosm of workshop conditions and particularly of those conditions that the workers were no longer willing to accept.

From the large workshops of the Center to the small contractors' workshops on Montmartre or in the Pletzl, the basic conditions were the same and resulted in the same strike demands over and over again. Higher wages or refusals to accept a wage cut were the principal issues (in thirty strikes) that began almost every list of demands. They were often accompanied by complaints about the rising cost of living and the necessity of a decent living wage. (The various wage ranges for different trades can be seen in Figure 2, although daily wage rates, hiding variable hours and the months of unemployment in the off-season, can only give a relative idea of the different trades' earning powers.)

But it was not merely higher wages that were at issue. Related economic issues also affected the workers' take-home pay. Haggling over piece rates (which varied depending on the item) was decried, and in several instances there were demands to create a joint committee of workers or union delegates and the employer in order to set uniform rates. The wide variation in wages from one workshop to another (even if working for the same contractor), from one specialty to the next, from workshop workers to homeworkers, and from male to female workers was another source of dissatisfaction. Demands for the establishment of uniform wage schedules accompanied criticism of such variations.

In addition, workers struck over who should pay for what. On several occasions the strike issues included demands that employers provide thread

Figure 2. Daily Wages

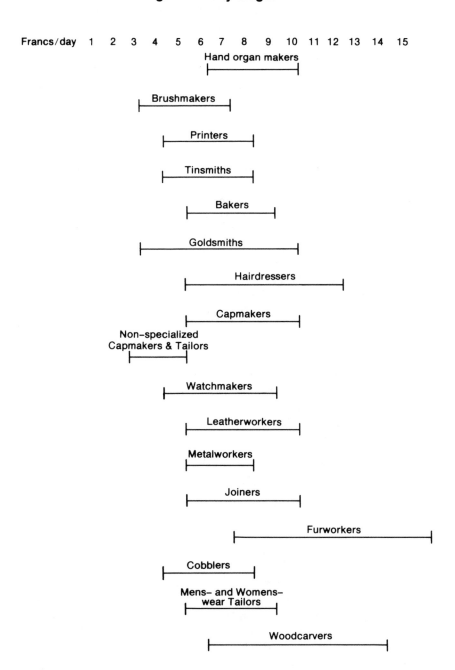

Francs/day   1   2   3   4   5   6   7   8   9   10   11   12   13   14   15

Hand organ makers

Brushmakers

Printers

Tinsmiths

Bakers

Goldsmiths

Hairdressers

Capmakers

Non–specialized
Capmakers & Tailors

Watchmakers

Leatherworkers

Metalworkers

Joiners

Furworkers

Cobblers

Mens– and Womens–
wear Tailors

Woodcarvers

Derived from Wolf Speiser, *Kalendar* (Paris: n.p., 1910), pp. 78–80.

and needles, that they reimburse transportation costs and delivery of rushed jobs, that they share the costs of accidents, burns, or spots on the clothes, etc. In one case, a group of furworkers struck over the imposition of arbitrary fines and a system whereby a franc per day was withheld from the worker's salary as a guarantee against poor workmanship; fines for spots on the fur, burns, etc. were deducted from the worker's pay at the employer's discretion and entirely lost if the worker was fired without notice.

Other demands relating to wages included: the right not to have to wait around to be paid; insistence on being paid on Saturday (as was the general custom) instead of on Monday—by which the employer "in his workers' best interest" saved them from squandering all of their savings over the weekend but also ensured the return of his work force promptly at the beginning of the next work week; and demands that wages be equalized on an hourly or weekly basis, i.e., down with piece wages. An unsuccessful attempt at one shop to replace piece wages by an hourly salary resulted in a strike when the piece-work wages were reinstituted.[11]

If economic issues often set off a strike, other matters linked to overall conditions were soon added to the demands. Complaints over long hours and demands for a shorter workday head the list. One Yiddish leaflet complained of fifteen- to sixteen-hour workdays imposed on the tailors. In another strike eighteen-hour workdays were at issue. Leatherworkers, for example, often worked ten hours in the shop and then another eight hours at home. Demands for a ten-hour day and occasionally even the eight-hour day appeared. In one tailors' strike in 1911 a change in the working hours rather than the number of hours itself was at the origin of the conflict: When several workers protested the change from a 7:00 A.M.–6:00 P.M. to an 8:00 A.M.–7:00 P.M. schedule (the manufacturer-retailer wanted to align the production crew's hours with those of his retail store), and one of them was fired for such dissent, 31 out of the 100 workers went on strike. In a similar conflict in a leatherworkers' shop the employer said he couldn't get there at 6:00 A.M., as the workers preferred. The workers responded by mocking the boss's 7:00 A.M.–8:00 P.M. proposal with a counteroffer of an unheard-of 8:00 A.M.–6:00 P.M. schedule.[12]

Beyond wage or hour issues, complaints arose relating to specific working conditions. Machine operators refused to do any handwork; cap assemblers refused to do any cutting. In the first case the operators complained that hand finishing work was beneath them; in the second case, the assemblers said, if they were not paid cutters' wages, why should they do cutters' work? Other demands included more hygienic working conditions. As one furworker warned: "Our health is the only thing which gives us a value in the eyes of the boss. Workers, watch your health! Because that is your only possession."[13] Dissatisfaction with internal workshop regulations, or with having to wait around too long while work was being controlled, joined demands for longer lunch hours or the elimination of basement workshops. In the worst cases workshop discipline was described as "draconian" or even prisonlike.

But above all it was the very dignity of the workers that was at stake. "Humane" working conditions and proper respect for the workers (*onshtendike mentshlekhe batsiungen*—proper human relations) were among the strike demands. The insolent and arrogant attitude of the bosses was severely criticized, from the Galeries Lafayette director to the smaller workshop owners, where a more paternalistic attitude was expected. In the latter case disappointment over unfair treatment seems to have hurt the most. Animosity frequently crystallized against the workshop overseers—a function often filled by the cutters, those "zealous servants of the bosses"—who were criticized for abusing their hiring, firing, and work distribution powers. The twelve machine operators who struck at Braunstein's shop in 1904 did so in protest over one worker's having been accused by the foreman (head cutter) of stealing; fabric had been found in his pocket at quitting time. The strikers argued that this was not sufficient grounds for accusation of theft, but they also complained more generally about the head cutter's arrogant attitude toward the workers and his practice of searching them at the door. (The strike ended by Braunstein's replacing the strikers.)[14]

In a rubberworker's strike in 1907 the workers insisted that the workshop foreman be fired and that verification of work be done, not by the foreman or owner, but by a union delegate. In another instance workers struck in solidarity with a Russian tailor, Esch, who had been fired after getting into a fight with the head cutter, Heidt. The latter was criticized for his "excessive severity," and the ensuing demands included the rehiring of Esch, the firing of Heidt, and a raise in wages. The conflict was only resolved when Heidt quit.[15]

Insistence on more "urbanity" between the overseer and the workers and more respect for the workers' "dignity" thus joined more material demands for higher wages and lower hours. In a microcosm of the strikes detailed by Michelle Perrot in her masterful *Les ouvriers en grève*,[16] the Jewish immigrant clothing workers struck not only for more money but for better conditions and a say in those conditions. Or, as Ezra Mendelsohn described the situation in Russia: "In its broadest and most general sense, the Jewish strike movement was directed squarely against the anarchical, chaotic conditions that prevailed in the Jewish shops and factories."[17] The organization of the work process in France and the transitional stage of industrialization in which the putting-out system continued to flourish created similarly anarchic conditions that affected the workers through the arbitrary control of each individual employer. In protest the workers cried out not only for bread-and-butter issues but also with definite ideas as to how that bread should be (alas, so meagerly) buttered.

CAPMAKERS

Capmakers' conditions were similar to those of other clothing workers, and strike demands were similar too. Yet the capmakers may be examined separately for two interrelated reasons. For one, because the capmakers played an important role in the Jewish labor movement in Paris, as will be seen. But the capmakers also merit separate consideration because of the particularly high concentration of Jews in this trade. Although both Jewish capmakers and Jewish tailors were producing for the French as well as export market, the Jewish tailors worked in an industrial branch that was in the hands of French capitalists, and their strikes took place within the context of a solidly implanted national industry including both French workers and other immigrant workers as well. The capmaking industry, however, was, from top to bottom, essentially Jewish. There was not the same presence of French department store owners, numerous French workers, or other immigrant workers to complicate the sides taken. The effect of this homogeneity of participants would become clear in the creation of the separate Jewish capmakers' union.

Capmaking was divided into four basic tasks performed by: cutters, paid by the year (thus effectively never laid off) for cutting six to eight layers of cloth at a time; machine operators (*mécaniciens*), paid by the piece (approximately eight to ten of them for every cutter); *bichonneurs* (literally, curlers) who blocked the caps by attaching them around a form and dipping them into the top steam section of a giant double boiler (one blocker for ten assemblers); and garnishers (mostly women, sometimes French, sometimes daughters of the other workers) who sewed on the visors by hand and attached buttons or other accessories to the caps. Auxiliary functions included cutting the lining and opening seams with an iron.

From inexpensive caps made out of secondhand clothing material to the more elegant cloth needed for the bourgeois cyclist or automobile owner, from peasants' caps to yachtsmen's caps, all of the varieties of this new fashion were created almost exclusively by the Russian Jewish immigrants.[18] (Of the 10 percent or 15 percent French workers in the trade, most of them were women.[19]) If capmaking was sometimes considered a luxury industry, certainly booming at the end of the century, that did not mean that luxury conditions obtained for the capmakers. Expected to produce a cap every ten minutes, the operators suffered from all of the usual sewing-machine–related maladies. Even the cutters, at the top of the workers' hierarchy, suffered from hand cramps and swelling from the constant manipulation of four- to five-pound scissors. But worst of all was the mixture of cloth dust and steam exhaled by the *bichonneur*'s cauldron and unavoidably inhaled by the worker. The increasing division of labor and mechanization of the trade led Yankel

Mykhanowitzki, for one, to miss the state of his art as he had exercised it in Rakwomir:

> Sometimes he surprised himself, fairly naively, at being bored in the workshop. Only yesterday wasn't the least gesture of his trade a constantly renewed source of pleasure? To appreciate from afar a fresh piece of material, to appreciate in advance the suppleness of the cloth, its texture, with a squint in order to carefully judge the color. A cluck of the tongue, a knowing nod of the head, the look of a connoisseur: "Hmm! It would be a jewel, I tell you!" . . .
> No: that was in the old days, in the Rakwomirian days. Now Yankel's work was mechanized. He no longer jokes, he no longer smiles at jokes. . . .[20]

Between 1886 and 1919, when the first collective agreement was signed, sixty-two capmakers' strikes occurred for which we have information. The first of these took place in February 1886, when the workers at Herse and Weidenbach's shop struck in protest over a wage decrease, which they blamed on the foreman (who was beaten up during the course of hostilities). The employers insisted that there was nothing that could be done, given the onset of the slack season, and the police reporters concurred, editorializing that the pay cut was justified because Herse and Weidenbach had not fired any of their workers. There was some talk of hiring other immigrant workers to replace the strikers, but given the general lack of work this never became necessary. Only one-half of the strikers were finally taken back, at the same conditions as before. Herse and Weidenbach had no trouble replacing the others.[21]

In September 1901, seven months after the large tailors' strike, four hundred out of twelve hundred capmakers walked off the job in fifty different workshops for almost a month. Cutters, machine operators, and blockers joined together in the movement for higher wages and fewer hours. In January 1906 a strike against the introduction of machines operated by women began at Rotshteyn-Levinski's workshop and spread to four others in the months that followed. Of the original twelve strikers all of them were eventually replaced (presumably by women), and the entire workshop was "suppressed" (presumably by machines?).[22]

The most important strike action of all occurred in 1912.[23] Beginning in April, in the midst of the good season, a movement for a uniform wage schedule originated with three-day strikes at Oberstein's and Sarezinsky-Kourland's. In signing the wage agreement that ended those strikes, Oberstein and Sarezinsky-Kourland insisted that the other manufacturers sign similar agreements. Four others did so after three- or four-day strikes occurred in their shops. However, on April 25 another employer, Finkelstein, refused to sign. This set off a wave of resistance among the workshop owners; Talkovsky refused to sign, and Spieguel tore up his already-signed agreement. At the end of May nine employers sent a letter to the capmakers' union threatening a lockout if the strikers from Spieguel's and Talkovsky's workshops did not return to work immediately. Twelve hundred capmakers met and decided to respond with an ultimatum of their own. If Spieguel and Talkovsky did not sign the wage agreement within forty-eight hours, a general strike would be called. On June 14 the workers in seventeen shops walked off their jobs. Nine of the seventeen bosses signed a wage agreement immediately, but eight others resisted, leading to a conflict that was to last through the end of the year.

The strike demands formulated by the capmakers' union included not only the uniform wage schedule, to go into effect for a period of one year, but the promise that other manufacturers would hire Spieguel's, Talkovsky's, and Finkelstein's workers while refusing to fill any orders for those manufacturers. A one-thousand-franc fine to be paid to the union would be imposed if those conditions were not met. In the end, all but 40 of the 275 strikers were rehired (it is uncertain under what conditions) either in their former shops or elsewhere, including several new workshops and a workers' cooperative, which had been born during the long strike.

The success of the capmakers' strikes and the more organized and relatively unified character of their actions was due to the double specificity mentioned above: the capmakers' union and the high percentage of Jews in this trade. The union was able to give direction to the 1912 strike movement. But it was the relatively homogeneous work force that not only reinforced strike unity with community unity but avoided one of the characteristics of the immigrant trades which usually inhibited concerted action, namely workers' competition, which will be explored below.

BAKERS

If the capmaking trade was more "Jewish" than tailoring by both work force and employer composition, baking was even more "Jewish" still; employers, employees, and clientele all belonged to the same ethnic community. When Jewish bakers, like Jewish waiters,[24] went on strike, they epitomized an intracommunity struggle that affected producers and consumers. Nonetheless, this community context could not shelter the Jewish bakers from conditions similar to those of all bakers, particularly impossible hours and night work. They complained bitterly of the latter as the "tragedy of our life," for it kept them, like French bakers, away from their families.[25] Here, too, several strikes are revealing of the difficult conditions under which the Jewish bakers baked bread.

The division of labor among bakers consisted only of the head baker (called the *brigadier*), who earned from fifty to fifty-three francs per week and their *aides*, who earned from thirty-nine to forty-two francs per week, for producing four ovens of regular bread and three ovens of challah per day. The typical bakery had only two to four workers in all.

In January 1908 all thirty workers in twelve bakeries struck for thirty-seven days for the hiring of additional workers. They argued for an augmented work force in order to decrease the number of hours worked as well as to decrease unemployment in the field as a whole. In the end ten strikers were fired, fifteen went back to work at the old conditions, and five workers stayed on at a bakers' cooperative created during the strike. (It employed over thirty workers, and its clientele, according to the police, was principally those Jewish restaurants frequented by Socialists.) In the summer of 1909, twenty-five of the thirty employees in (the same?) twelve bakeries went on strike for a salary increase and an end to challah production. They argued that this special braided bread required too much work, but the strike against this Jewish bakery staple was a failure.[26]

At the end of February 1913 all twenty workers at nine Jewish bakeries went on strike for higher wages and an increased work force (an additional aide, thus two per brigadier). The strike began at Patatzki's, who was considered the leader of the bakery owners and criticized for his "impossible" (*ummeglekhe*) exploitation. After four weeks of the strike and just as Passover was coming up, Patatzki joined with four other bakeries in a show of force that only led to the spread of the strike. A boycott was called of the bakeries involved as well as a boycott of any restaurants buying their bread. The striking bakers even sent a circular to this effect to a meeting of striking garment workers.

As the strike progressed other issues were added to the initial demands, including: higher wages for special pastries and the insistence that any agreements concluded be signed, for "we've had enough of simply taking the bosses' word."[27] Another leaflet cried out against technological change in the form of recently acquired electric machines:

We will not forget our years of sweat by which you earned the money to buy [these] machines. Upon us lies the dirt of your ovens in the dark cellars in which we have spent our best years. Now you will bake bread not only with men's sweat but with their blood.[28] [A worker had recently lost a finger in a machine.]

The supposedly kosher cleanliness of the machines was also brought into question: "You say your matzo is kosher—that is not our affair—but how can it be if leavened meal has been used in the machines?"

As Passover approached (April 10) the workers only reaffirmed their demands in the hopes that the holiday season would exert pressure on the owners. They were right. The strike was ended by the hiring of second aides and a wage increase of three francs more per week (although two francs less than had been demanded).

Whether sewing a shirt, cutting a cap, or baking bread, there came a time when the workers put down their tools. When they did so the workshop conditions—from the dust in the air and workers' lungs to the number of hours it had to be inhaled—stood accused. The strike actions, in their most immediate demands, pointed above all to two basic aspects of the immigrant workers' struggle for existence: long hours for low wages. Even more fundamentally, however, the work organization process of the Parisian light industrial sector was brought into question. The combination of long hours and low wages represented more than an efficacious method of exploitation. It represented homework, piecework, and the off-season that was endemic to this industrial structure and that would determine the limits of the workers' struggle.

THE PUTTING-OUT SYSTEM STANDS ACCUSED

In addition to the tailors' strike of 1901, five other clothing workers' strikes (and one of the four woodworkers' strikes) explicitly called for the elimination of piecework, while a sixth complained that the manufacturer gave work to his hourly wage workers to the detriment of the pieceworkers, thus forcing the latter to be idle when there was not enough work to go around.

In the fourth issue of the Jewish workers' paper *Der idisher arbayter*, three banes of domestic industry were attacked: piecework, long hours, and homework.[29] Piecework was called the "workers' bribe" (*shokhed hapoalim*) and a "sly swindle" (*khitre dreydl*) and was seen as the fundamental cause of long hours. Only exhausting "overtime" (and never paid as such) and often the whole family's help allowed the pieceworker to earn a passable sum from the low piece wage paid. Knowing that the off-season was always just around the corner, the pieceworker could rarely refuse extra work. But those added hours to finish yet another piece, if adding to the worker's total wage sum, only drove the per-hour remuneration down while eating into the workers' strength and health.

Homework usually implied both piecework and long hours. As Alexander Losovsky wrote in an article entitled "Down with Homework" in *L'Ouvrier chapelier* of February 1, 1912: "It is the sword of Damocles that hangs over the union worker's head." When a law was proposed in Parliament in 1914 aimed at regulating homework in order to rid it of its most obvious evils—hygienic, etc.—the Jewish tailors' section registered its disagreement with such a proposal. Homework should not be strengthened through amelioration, they said; it must be abolished altogether.[30] An echo of the five dissenting Montmartrois tailors of the 1901 strike can be heard.

Of course the criticism of the putting-out system was not the province of the Jewish workers alone. The French garment workers', hatmakers', and leatherworkers' federations all voted resolutions for the abolition of piecework from the 1890s on. The hatmakers described it as a system leading to industrial ruin, the leatherworkers called it the "system of sweat," and the garment workers said it was a "plague" on the industry.[31]

But perhaps worst of all were the good and bad seasons that underlay and supported this entire structure. Called the *morte-saison* (literally, death-season) in French and borrowed in Parisian Yiddish, the slack season was also sometimes just called *la morte*, death. All of the light industrial trades were affected at one time or another during the year, causing woodworkers to turn to repair work or upholstering, or a well-qualified machine operator to lie about his skill in order to find work as a mere presser. Even ragpickers had their off season when the summer exodus from Paris occurred. But in other cases, when the morte-saison struck, skilled workers had to turn to the welfare office to tide them over. Thus long, demanding hours in the good season were intertwined with the off season and often seen less as an exploitation derived from the industrial structure than as an investment against la morte.

In some cases the workers formulated explicit complaints against the ravages of seasonality, demanding that no worker be let go during the morte-saison and that a more equal distribution of the (decreased amount of) work be made instead. La morte was explicitly or implicitly criticized in eight of the garment workers' strikes, including five in which the workers refused to sign an agreement allowing firing without notice, the employer's most immediate response to a slack in orders. If few envisaged the possibility of eliminating the morte-saison altogether, many hoped to reduce its impact. In a rubberworkers' strike of 1907 a contract guaranteeing an annual salary, to shelter workers from seasonal fluctuations, was demanded. In preparation for a 1913 mass meeting organized by the Jewish section of the leatherworkers' union, just before the "golden time" of the full season got under way, a Yiddish leaflet castigated this "unnatural condition" of the constant ups and downs of the production season and asked:

> Are we going to go on as before, accepting the off season and then the exploitation of overwork, and so on? No! No! . . . If we cannot totally destroy this binding death-season which exists more or less in all trades and which is a product of the evil bourgeois order, at least we can . . . attenuate it. . . . We want to work a normal workday all year long.[32]

Even when employers agreed to strike demands their acquiescence often only lasted as long as the season. As work slacked off, so did their goodwill. If the bakery bosses were conciliatory before Passover, once the matzo season was over they often went back on their concessions. Lack of work alone could kill a strike, as a strike at Kemler's menswear workshop in February 1905 showed. When the contractor Kemler (in the Marais) had almost one-quarter of his work taken away from him (to be given to homeworkers) by his main client, his thirty-two workers at first agreed to a wage cut. However, when yet a further cut appeared in a later week's pay, the workers declared a strike. Kemler, with less work to do anyway, was just as happy to be without anyone to pay. He and his family set to work on the orders that remained, and the strike ended ignominiously on March 6, with only six of the original workers rehired.[33]

Strikes could therefore be defeated by la morte itself. More fundamentally, however, it was the putting-out system as a whole that limited the success of workers' actions. For when the workload had not diminished, strikes were defeated by simply replacing the workers with other homeworkers, perhaps by newly arrived immigrants anxious for work at any price or by women. Domestic industry, based on homework, paid by the piece and subject to important fluctuations of demand, structured the limits of workers' actions. An important byproduct of that system, workers' competition, further undermined much of the activity of the Jewish labor movement.

WORKERS' COMPETITION

As Engels wrote with regard to the working class in England:

> Competition . . . a battle for life, for existence, . . . is fought not between the different classes of society only, but also between the individual members of these classes. . . . But this competition of the workers among themselves is . . . the sharpest weapon against the proletariat in the hands of the bourgeoisie.[34]

Paul Gemähling, writing on homework in France at the turn of the century, described the division between homework and workshop work as "that invisible fissure" that inhibited all efforts at reducing unemployment or regulating production.[35] Even Pierre du Maroussem, reporting for the labor ministry's Office du travail, wrote in his study of the Parisian woodworkers: "The most painful spectacle which can present itself to a social study is certainly that of the hatred and jealousy at the heart of each class which follows from the hostility declared between the classes themselves."[36] As Der idisher arbayter wrote on March 8, 1913, "We well know that the worst competition is hungry workers."

The coexistence of factory workshops, contractors' workshops, and isolated homeworkers, of those working by the piece and those paid by the hour or the week, created a situation whereby individual workers' interests would often be very different when it came to formulating strike demands. If immigrant and female labor together represented a reserve army of labor in relation to the French male labor force, the structure of work opportunities within that reserve army created still another form of workers' competition. The already precarious position of the immigrant worker was only sharpened through a situation in which he or she was placed in constant competition with fellow immigrants or other reservists (women).

Thus workers' divisions were manifold and overlapping. Divisions by workplace (shop or home), sex and/or nationality, or by payment method and task performed all remained the weak link in efforts to unify and organize clothing workers. The garmentworkers', hatworkers', and leatherworkers' national unions all criticized workers' competition as one more evil resulting from the piecework system. Antagonisms were created even within workshops between hourly workers and pieceworkers when there was not enough work to keep everyone occupied. When the former were given the available work to do, the pieceworkers during a leatherworkers' strike in 1912 complained bitterly: So the hourly workers have to eat and we don't?[37] At the same time the division of labor by task function proved another source of problems for certain strikes, for production was able to continue if only machine operators or hand finishers went on strike. If there were times in which a "general strike" joined operators and finishers in a unified front, more often than not the division of labor *within* the workplace was but a variant of divisions of labor *among* workplaces and among sexes and nationalities.

The differing interests of workshop workers and homeworkers was seen in the 1901 tailors' strike. Things had not improved fifteen years later when, right in the middle of the war, a strike broke out at Galeries Lafayette only a couple of weeks before a promotional sale for which special goods were needed.[38] This strike is a classic example of employer manipulation of the putting-out system and inherent workers' competition at its best. In an effort to lessen dependence on homeworkers (who after all were "free" to work for other manufacturers or retailers as well) Galeries Lafayette had created the Société Parisienne de Confection in 1912. The S.P.C. was a group of workshops constituted separately from the department store but producing exclusively for it. When the machine operators at one S.P.C. workshop went on strike in 1916 (because the director refused to meet with a workers' delegation headed by a union leader), Bauer, the general director, felt confident that he could hold out by transferring most of the work from the striking Montmartre workshop—directed by a Mr. Leibovici and comprised mostly of Jewish immigrant workers—to the rue de Provence workshop—of mostly French and mostly female workers. Five days into the strike, however, some of the rue de Provence workers joined the strike movement, and the strikers kept up an *équipe de débauchage*—walking nonstrikers and retail clerks to and from work to try to convince them to join the strike—throughout the month-long strike; the Jewish strikers were relayed by non-Jewish ones during the

High Holidays. Eventually over 360 machine operators and female skirtmakers joined the strike (out of 1,500 workers employed in the S.P.C.'s workshops).

The initial strike demands included the range of issues discussed above: an increase in wages; a joint workers-employer commission to set wages; a more efficient organization of the work distribution and reentering process so as to avoid wasted (and unremunerated) time; no firing without prior notice; and the abolition of a new rule penalizing workers who were five minutes late by preventing them from working for a half day. (It was demanded that the late period be reduced to half an hour, as before, adding that the new rule was particularly dangerous for women who, stuck out on the street for half a day, would be open to temptations!) And finally, the strikers insisted that all meetings with the S.P.C.'s directors be held in the presence of a union representative.

On October 8, one day after Yom Kippur, a concert was held at the Confédération générale du travail headquarters in order to collect money for the strike fund. Approximately twenty-five hundred people attended; French songs, Yiddish songs, and a Russian orchestra provided entertainment; Henri Guérin spoke on anarchism; and sixteen hundred francs were earned for the strikers' benefit.

However, the union and the strikers could not hold out much longer. Bauer had simply closed the refractory Montmartre workshop, transferring its operations to rue de Provence, and Galeries Lafayette was able to bypass its own production company altogether by turning to outside homeworkers and contractors' workshops to furnish its needs. Ultimately the strikers saw the full season going by without their being able to take advantage of it. Negotiations, without union representation, finally led to a slight increase in wages, certain assurances that an eight-day notice would be given before any layoffs, and that efforts would be made to reduce the work control period, etc.

In the face of a dispersed work process workers found themselves implicitly in competition with one another as the putting-out system allowed a relatively easy shift of orders from one place to another, from manufacturers' inside shops to contractors' or family workshops. Furthermore this meant that the department store owner or wholesaler was able to distribute work through contractors or in this case the S.P.C., without coming into direct contact with the production crew. Mr. Bader, president of the Galeries Lafayette, effectively chose to hide behind that layered and indirect work distribution in 1916. When asked to comment on the S.P.C. strike he refused to even discuss the issue, saying that the S.P.C. workers were not, strictly speaking, part of his personnel.

In certain instances workers overcame these divisions during strike actions. When a strike broke out in the womenswear workshop of the Printemps department store in March 1916, the thirty Russian, Rumanian,

Armenian, Czech, Italian, and Swiss strikers made a special appeal to the Jewish homeworkers on Montmartre (leaflets were printed in Yiddish) not to accept orders that would undercut the strike movement.[39] At a meeting held at the Club des émigrants israélites on Montmartre, seventy persons (including thirty women) voted their solidarity with the Center, and the striking machine operators also succeeded in getting five out of seventeen female skirtmakers to join their movement.

Too often, however, foreign workers, who frequently went on strike first, lamented the fact that the French women workers did not join them. In several instances locational divisions of labor were overlaid by nationality and sex divisions. Foreign male machine operators who walked off the job complained that French female shirtwaistmakers or seamstresses did not join them.[40] In a 1913 strike at Galeries Lafayette only 15 to 20 Frenchwomen joined the 280 striking foreign machine operators,[41] while during the 1916 S.P.C. strike, 3 French skirtmakers from the rue de Provence shop walked out of a strike meeting in protest that they could not understand the speeches in Russian. A strike at Maurice (Maladeski)'s shop in 1916 that united ten Russian male tailors with five French female shirtmakers was the exception.[42]

If men and women, immigrant and French workers found themselves objectively opposed during certain strike actions, it was not by accident. The hiring of women was used as a threat by Wormser and Boulanger against their three French, four Russian, two Greek, one Italian, and one Belgian all-male workforce in 1916, as it was used by Galeries Lafayette on other occasions.[43] Alexander Losovsky addressed women capworkers in L'Ouvrier chapelier of November 21–December 20, 1911, as follows: "You, doubly exploited workers. . . . The emancipation of the workers will only be the work of the male and female workers [travailleurs et travailleuses] themselves" (and the capmakers' union even lowered dues for female workers in order to attract them).[44]

However, besides playing on divisions between workshop- and homeworkers, or threatening to replace male immigrant tailors with French seamstresses, the employers often found another source of workers' competition within the immigrant community itself: the grine. The grine, or greenhorns, were the newly arrived immigrants whose position relative to the more established immigrants mirrored that of the immigrants relative to the indigenous working population as a whole. Anxious to start work immediately, often unaware of the labor conflicts involved, and initially impressed by the higher wages compared to eastern Europe, the grine often became gele ("yellows" or scabs) as train stations became recruiting grounds for unwitting strikebreakers. In the 1913 bakers' conflict the workers accused the bakery owners of importing strikebreakers directly from eastern Europe.[45]

Whether out of desperation, ignorance, or lack of "consciousness" as attributed to them by the Jewish labor press, the grine represented one of the weakest links in immigrant labor organizing. Even when two articles in Der *idisher arbayter* of July 5, 1913, addressed the griner problem with a more sympathetic interpretation of those potential strikebreakers, the successive arrivals of grine maintained a continual pressure on the labor market and on strike activity. On the one hand, the newspaper called them newcomers instead of "grine" (purposefully placing grine in quotation marks), suggested the creation of a committee to take care of them and explain conditions in Paris to them, and argued that the blame was not on the grine, but on themselves: We need to include the newcomers in our struggle "un fun unzer 'grine' faynd—royte fraynd tsu makhn"—to make of our "green" enemy a red friend. Elsewhere *Der idisher arbayter* described the problem as that "murderly, fraternal war" (*bruder merderishe milkhome*) that rips apart the proletarian organization.[46]

Finally, an even more fundamental source of "immigrant competition" that inhibited labor organizing and combined several of the divisions described above was the *façonnat*. The work process that has been described created not only structural divisions among workers but also an ideological ambiguity of the lines to be drawn between employer and employee. In fact, the definition of *façonnier* is at times hard to discern. In some contexts façonniers were equated with small-time bosses; in other instances they were described as independent homeworkers taking work on their own account.[47] The reason for this equivocal definition is quite simply that both sorts of façonniers existed, representing in that term the ebb and flow between homeworkers and small-time bosses characteristic of the light industrial sector. After all, one of the major attractions of light industry was the possibility of going into business for oneself in order to

> escape the *salariat* [wage-earning class] by becoming a modest boss, first a façonnier, then a small-time manufacturer—a dream which charms almost all of the capmakers, and which parcels up into individual aspirations the push towards a better existence.[48]

The façonnier's lot may have been as insecure as that of a mere worker— Lauzel remarked that for forty new capmaker façonniers who appeared at the beginning of each season only two or three were left by its end—but the possibility or dream of working on one's own led many to try.

In this regard homework itself was faulted for providing conditions that led toward the formation of small-time bosses, façonniers, and the like. The façonniers were harshly attacked in the Jewish labor press as strikebreakers, thieves, parasites, the "most dangerous of our competitors," and the "worst enemy of the daily struggle"; they were even accused of waiting for each pogrom in order to get cheap workers.[49] Nor were former union members immune. Talkovsky, one of the targets of the 1912 capmakers' strike movement, had been a union leader himself only two or three years previously. At the point at which he left being a worker to become a manufacturer, "in this

moment his interests stand in sharp contrast to those of the workers," wrote
Der idisher arbayter.[50]

The manufacturers had one last classic weapon with which to combat workers' demands that is not specific to the putting-out system but must be mentioned nonetheless. The police intervened in fourteen of the forty-six
clothing workers' strikes and in the sole rubberworkers' strike for which we
have details. They were often called in when violence occurred between
workers and foremen or between strikers and nonstrikers. But they were also
called in to arrest strikers for picketing (*refus de circuler,* refusal to circulate)
or for discouraging nonstrikers and strikebreakers from working (*entrave de la
liberté du travail,* impeding the right to work). It is probably through the
ensuing arrests that the police department even became aware of so many of
the small strikes involving but ten to twenty employees.

Police intervention as a means of protecting strikebreakers or ending a
strike was criticized as an *alt mitl* (old, well-known means) in the Yiddish
leaflets, and it shows to what extent the immigrant bosses considered themselves a class apart from their workers by turning to the French administration
for aid. During the bakers' strike of 1913 the strikers complained bitterly of
the employers' "arresting our best comrades right off the street."[51] The brutal-
ity and insolence of the police was documented in a *La Bataille Syndicaliste*
article (March 5) on the Galeries Lafayette strike of that same year: Cries of
"*sales youpins*" (dirty kikes) and "*sales étrangers*" (dirty foreigners) marked
police intervention in that strike. Needless to say, police involvement was
particularly redoubtable for immigrants whose legal status could be easily
jeopardized. The fact that the terms "anarchist" or "nihilist" were often used
by the bosses to describe the strikers didn't help matters.

The miserable working conditions expressed in the strike demands were thus
the effect of a work organization and labor recruitment process that the
manufacturers both symbolized and implemented. Division of labor between
men and women, immigrants and natives, homeworkers and workshop employees, and settled and newly arrived immigrants created a situation of
workers' competition within an already complex work structure. All of these
factors are necessary for understanding the situation of the Jewish immigrant
worker in Paris. But a study of strikes would be incomplete if the most
obvious aspect of their manifestation were lost from view: a growing consciousness, which led first to strikes and then to labor organization.

GROWING CONSCIOUSNESS

If these strikes are forceful testimony of workshop conditions and the larger
trade structure, they are also expressive evidence of growing consciousness.

As Michelle Perrot has said, strikes constitute the speaking up (prise de parole) of the workers, important not only for certain demands but also as a form of expression in and of itself.[52] The very language employed in the Yiddish strike leaflets expressed a sense of right and wrong leading to a consciousness of the need for unity to defend those rights. This growing consciousness developed through several stages. At first the workers expressed a perception of their own worth and demanded that such be recognized within the working relations. This led to an increasing sense of explicit and often hostile differentiation of the workers from their bosses that also turned against coworkers who did not join in that solidarity, i.e., strikebreakers. Finally the growing perception of class interest led to manifestations of worker solidarity expressed in the development of the strikes themselves. The next step, that of union organizing, will be discussed in the next chapter.

As we have seen, more than one strike demand included a call for more humane relations within the working environment. "Humane and rightful demands" (mentshlekhe gerekhte foderungen) or "humane treatment" (mentshlekhe bahandlung) were seen as the workers' due in contrast to the "lowly treatment" (niderike handlung) or "inhumane exploitation" (um-mentshlekhe eksploytatsie) from which they suffered. Bakers complained that they wanted to be mentshn and to assert their "right to life," a right that had been robbed from them by their bosses. The workers insisted on being treated like men, not as slaves, nor as machines![53]

The insult of such treatment was felt all the more keenly due to expectations within the paternalistic immigrant workshop. Thus the further pay cut at Kemler's workshop was seen as particularly unjust since the workers had manifested their loyalty by accepting a first wage decrease. Disappointment in the working relations was the first step to an alignment of the workers against their bosses. The latter became identified not merely as "breadgivers" (the irony of this function being underlined in the bakery workers' tracts against their bosses) but as "oppressors." Even more vehemently they were described as "robbers" if not "leeches" (piavkes) and in one case as a despot and barbarian (for hitting a worker).[54]

These attacks on the boss as the enemy were rivaled only by the energy expended in castigating those renegades of the working class: the strikebreakers. Called "renegades and traitors" in the French half of one leaflet, the Yiddish half was even more forceful: "vile and dirty" (nidertrekhtike un shmutsike) traitors. At times they were referred to as "ugly lumpen," "hooligans," or as "lowly creatures" (niderike bashefenishn); in one instance they were described as "vile, creeping vermine" (krikhende shrotsim nidertrekhtike).[55] Strikes were started in protest over the hiring of well-known strikebreakers. An article in L'Ouvrier chapelier of August 1, 1912, described them as bandits and thieves and even tried warning the bosses that they were becoming enslaved by those very elements to whom they turned for help: "They insult you, are insolent, demanding, but you sacrifice your dignity for your profits. These scabs that you have bought are but felons. We suggest you put up a sign in your shops saying 'Beware of pickpockets.' "

From a violence of tone to a violence of action the step was not far. One striker was arrested for threatening to kill his boss. In some cases hostility was aimed against the employers' workshop representative, the overseer or head cutter, whose determinant role in the distribution of work and accompanying airs were especially resented. In other instances it was the nonstrikers or freshly hired scabs on whom the wrath of the strikers fell, in attempts to convince them, at first verbally, but many times physically, of the error of their ways.[56] Thus the growing consciousness of workers' solidarity was necessarily preceded by a demarcation from their employers on the one hand and from those employed by the latter to exert their control on the other.

At the same time, strikes were not only expressions of demarcation from boss-leeches or "yellow" or "green" strikebreakers, but they were also moments of explicit solidarity among workers. At least ten strikes were begun or extended in anger over firings of fellow workers. In one case an employee had been fired for a poorly stitched collar, but in other cases the origin of the dismissal was shop-floor agitation (or for having the *chutzpah* to protest, as *Der idisher arbayter* reported[57]). Actions not only moved from defending an individual to wider workshop solidarity and demands, but they also spread from one workshop to another. Strikes begun in one shop were picked up in others, both in protest of the same working conditions and so as not to function as strikebreakers if orders were diverted to those shops. In other instances workers not affected by a strike pledged 10 percent to 20 percent of their salaries to the strike fund in what was known as a solidarity tax. Finally, this growing consciousness had two wider implications. Strike activity developed alongside the formation of union sections, the interrelationship of which will be discussed in the next chapter; and unity also spread beyond the work environment. In the final chapter we will examine the relationship of the Jewish labor movement with the community from which it emerged.

In the workshop and out of it, at work and on strike, the Jewish immigrant workers portray the putting-out system of the late nineteenth century Parisian light industrial sector at its best and at its worst. At its best the work organization process benefited the employers' labor needs and the immigrants' employment needs alike. At its worst the exploitation of the latter revealed all too clearly the illusory nature of the "independence" of homework and the debilitating effects of la morte.

The number of strikers ranged from four, out of a five-man workshop (with the fifth worker beaten up for not striking), to over three hundred when a general strike spread to several shops. But more important than the numbers involved were the demands articulated through the strikes, which offer a strident description of the working conditions of the putting-out system. Both the immediate conditions under which the immigrant workers labored and the larger industrial structure of which those conditions were a part are revealed in even the smallest of shop strikes.

Yet at times resentment against these twelve- to eighteen-hour days exploded. If the morte-saison or piecework did not always stand immediately accused, it was because the more visible source of animosity was the boss or overseer who implemented—often arbitrarily—the rules of that work process. The demarcation of the workers' from their bosses' interests and the growing perception of the latter as an enemy accompanied an increasing solidarity among the workers themselves. To give it a lasting power and a more concrete strength, was the next obvious step.

In February 1912 a union worker at Rosenthal's shop on the place de la République was fired under the pretext of poor workmanship.[58] A strike ensued in solidarity with the fired union member. Such a move was but one step before demanding the right to organize itself. Already in August 1905 the right to unionize had been one of the demands at a strike at Braunstein's womenswear shop, and during a one-month general strike in the spring of 1909 the striking workers decided that no workshop should negotiate with the employer without a strike committee delegate present.[59] At issue in a 1911 capmakers' strike was union recognition, and in the Société Parisienne de Confection strike of 1916 union representation at the negotiations became an essential demand of the strikers and just as intransigent a refusal on the part of the S.P.C.'s director.[60]

This, then, leads to the Jewish labor movement itself. From shop conditions to grievances to strikes to wider solidarity, the Jewish labor movement was born. Its relation to the French labor movement, its specific needs and characteristics, and its importance for the immigrant community from which it sprang all need to be examined more closely. The unionization of eastern European immigrants in Paris before World War I, to which we now turn, provides an interesting case study in immigrant labor organization.

Six
IMMIGRANT UNIONIZATION
IN PROCESS

The immigrant strikes were manifestations of discontent which on one level revealed labor conditions and the constraints of the light industrial structure. On another level the strikes represented a growing consciousness of workers' interests that necessitated unity to overcome the workers' competition inherent in that industrial structure. We can now explore the form that workers' unity took—Jewish immigrant union sections—and examine the union sections' relationship to the strike movement just described and to imported leadership from abroad.

I have argued that workshop conditions alone were sufficient to set off strikes. However, we still must ask what other factors could and did influence the immigrant strikes and, more generally, the development of a Jewish labor movement. What was the relationship between strike activity and the immigrant union sections? To what extent were the Jewish strikes and trade union movement imported along with the immigrants from eastern Europe?

IMMIGRANT UNION SECTIONS

Which came first, the strikes or the union sections? The relationship between strike movement and trade union organization is a complex one. Peter Stearns, for one, stridently rejects most descriptions of worker adherence to union leadership in this period. His aim, however, is not to argue for worker "spontaneity" but rather to support the thesis that revolutionary syndicalism, as propounded by the C.G.T., had no real support.[1] Charles Tilly and Edward Shorter counter that interpretation by stressing the importance of union participation in accounting for strike duration in the period before World War I.[2] No union influence versus determinant union influence; such a polarization of the issue seems unnecessary. Michelle Perrot's description of the "*syndicalisation de la grève*"[3] seems preferable. Strikes often proved to be the spark of unionization. Yet it is less a question of determining a precise cause and effect than of seeing both the strikes and developing unionization as manifestations of a growing consciousness on the part of the late nineteenth-century workers. This is apparent in the development of the Jewish labor movement in Paris and its relationship to the strikes just examined.

Jewish immigrants began to organize fairly shortly after their arrival in France, and that organization first took the form of mutual aid societies. As has been seen, mutual aid societies were primarily concerned with burial problems, but their by-laws also reveal a more general need for collective financial and moral insurance against death and disease. The funds collected for mutual aid were not always destined for doctors and funeral plots, however. In some cases they were turned into strike funds. Thus several of these societies became the breeding ground for trade union sections, if not fronts for union organizations, as the police saw it.[4]

The capmakers, the first of whom had emigrated from Poland in the post-1863 period, created a mutual aid society as early as 1879 and another in 1887. About one hundred Jewish rubberworkers formed a short-lived society in 1887; the furworkers first attempted to organize in the 1890s, and in 1890 the tailors created the Moderne Shnayder society. In 1898 a mutual aid society of Russian woodworkers in Paris was formed and its by-laws sent, as required, to the Ministry of the Interior; the Ministry of Interior forwarded them to the Ministry of Foreign Affairs, only to have the society dissolved by ministerial decree in 1905.[5]

These mutual aid societies, based on trade interests rather than burial intentions or affinity by town of origin, reflected the often paternalistic family-workshop nature of the crafts, with employees and their small-time bosses joined together in an attempt at mutual support. However, such mutual aid societies soon gave way to purely workers' organizations, which most often took the form of union sections attached to the pertinent French C.G.T. union.[6]

In 1900 the Russian woodworkers constituted their own union section in the 11th arrondissement, the center of the woodworking trade. This initial section did not last more than a couple of years, but another attempt was made in 1905. In May 1906 the section was sixty members strong when the eastern European immigrant woodworkers took part in the general strike of the furniture trade that year, demanding, along with their French counterparts, the eight-hour day. (In the course of their strike surveillance, the police noted some Russian men and women of "mysterious allure" who met regularly in a house where a red flag had been spotted, leading them to believe that foreign revolutionaries, even anarchists, were connected with the strike.[7]) But again the woodworkers' section did not last, apparently due to the financial strain of a restaurant that was opened to sustain Jewish and non-Jewish strikers. Attempts were made again in 1909, in 1911, and in 1913, at which time the Jewish woodworkers formally joined the C.G.T. Chambre syndicale des ouvriers ébénistes du département de la Seine (Woodworkers' Trade Union Committee of the Seine Department).[8]

Although as early as 1882 and again in 1896 the idea of a separate Jewish furworkers' organization had been suggested, it was not until after the 1904–6 inflow of immigrants to Paris that the furworkers had enough strength to organize. The only existing furworkers' union in 1906 was a German section, which a group of Jewish workers decided to join at the end of that year. Within a year, however, it was further decided that a separate Jewish section was needed. One was organized in November in the Marais, which attracted some 150 paying members.[9]

This separation from the German furworkers resulted as much from an emulation of the latter as from any differences that might have existed between the two groups. The fact that the German workers had forged the way in creating a separate immigrant labor organization only strengthened the Jewish workers' resolve. Furthermore, the separate Jewish furworkers' section that existed from 1907 to 1913 corresponded to the growing number of Jewish workers who were to a certain extent displacing German workers within the trade. Yet one other factor was important in the affirmation of Jewish specificity: a strong Bundist influence in the trade. The Bundist ideology of Jewish cultural autonomy within a socialist framework translated into the need for separate Jewish union sections within the labor movement. Its effect on the furworkers lasted until January 1913, when forces were once again joined with the German furworkers.

In the same year that the furworkers began to organize, the Jewish bakers also attempted to unite during the general bakers' strike of 1906. The resultant bakers' section did not last long, but another was formed in January of 1909 and later consolidated in the spring of that year. The organization of Jewish bakery workers was considered all the more eventful in that although the bakery owners were the symbol of wealth within the community, the bakery workers were mostly renowned for their card-playing, drinking, and horse-betting![10]

It was also 1909 when the Jewish leatherworkers joined forces. Several spontaneous strikes by the immigrant workers, which were supported by the French union, spurred the Jewish workers into creating a section of their own. Within a short time there were 145 members, although, according to a later labor leader, the "petit-bourgeois" leadership of the section led to only poorly thought-out strikes, preventing "the normal development" of this section.[11]

As for the tailors, the idea that the Jewish tailors form a union section appears in 1904 during a strike at Braunstein's, but here too the example of the German tailors may have been decisive. During a strike at Doucet's womenswear shop in February 1900 a German tailor named Locker had announced that, while having great esteem for the French people and believing in international entente among workers, the German womenswear tailors had decided to organize their own "international" section of foreigners only.[12] (The French, he added, were in any case but a minority of the womenswear workers in Paris.) It was in September 1910 that a Jewish tailors' section became a reality. In part the tailors were urged to organize by the capmakers who feared the tailors could be hired as replacements during strikes. Even then, due to a severe morte-saison in the winter of 1910–11, the tailors' section did not really gather strength until February of 1912. At that time the Montmartre tailors (three to four hundred strong) joined the previously Center-dominated section, bringing a new vitality to the organization and thereby giving it a good *klap* (jolt) as *Der idisher arbayter* described it.[13]

Organization among the Jewish immigrant workers thus gained momentum in the years before World War I. Approximately sixty Jewish tinsmiths joined the French union in this period, while there were various attempts to form their own separate section. An immigrant metalworkers' section was founded in the Marais in 1907. A group of Russian (in name, although almost all Jewish in membership) typographers became affiliated with the French Fédération du Livre in 1912 and started a placement service at the Bureau russe du travail in December of that year. On at least two occasions the Russian printers were cited for the strength of their organization, and their participation in the one-day C.G.T. general anti-militarist strike (December 16, 1912) against the already foreshadowed war, was lauded in contrast to the poor showings of many other Jewish union sections.[14]

The important year for the development of the Jewish workers' organizations in Paris was 1913. As has already been seen, this was the year in which religious oratories and mutual aid societies sought to consolidate their forces through the building of a synagogue and the creation of the Fédération des sociétés juives de Paris. During 1913 Jewish barbers, cobblers, locksmiths, metalworkers, and upholsterers all created separate union sections while the woodworkers, as just seen, finally stabilized their organization with the

C.G.T. as well.[15] The waiters' section founded that year was said explicitly to prove that they were not *luftmentshn* or *poshete shnorers* (simple beggars) as often criticized. Even though many of these sections began with no more than a handful of members, they often constituted a significant proportion of the category of workers involved (e.g., thirty-five out of forty or forty-five barbers).

Not only were individual trade union sections created, but so was an umbrella organization called the Intersektsionen Byuro (precursor to the C.G.T.U. Yiddish Intersyndical Commission created in 1923) and a Jewish labor newspaper called *Der idisher arbayter*.[16] The Intersektsionen Byuro, representing the capmakers' union and all of the Yiddish-speaking union sections affiliated with the C.G.T., was founded on December 18, 1910, at a meeting of 109 Jewish immigrant labor leaders.[17] A year later, on October 9, 1911, a form letter announcing the existence of the Intersektsionen byuro and the creation of *Der idisher arbayter* was sent to the eastern European Jewish immigrants in Paris along with the first issue of the newspaper.[18]

The Intersektsionen Byuro acted as the formal link between the Jewish labor movement and the French labor movement, while labor leaders such as Losovsky (who represented the Jewish capmakers within the Fédération des syndicats ouvriers de la chapellerie française—Hatters' Federation—and was a frequent contributor to *L'Ouvrier chapelier* on capmakers' issues) served as informal links. In December 1912 it was decided that the Intersektsionen Byuro alone would represent the Jewish workers to the French labor movement in negotiations with the C.G.T. Union de la Seine over the possibility of receiving financial aid from the latter for the Jewish labor movement.

Not only could the Intersektsionen Byuro and *Der idisher arbayter* henceforth speak on behalf of a more organized Jewish labor movement, but through their efforts new union sections (such as the shoeworkers' and barbers') would be constituted. The Byuro reflected as it consolidated the growing strength of the Jewish labor movement in Paris: "We have brought together in one stream the small forces which have been born and which have spread in all of the trades."[19]

The union sections thus emanated from the internal dynamic of the Jewish immigrant trades, but how did they in turn affect the strikes in question? The self-assigned role of the Intersektsionen Byuro was to raise the consciousness of the immigrant workers and encourage the formation of union sections. In this context, several organizational meetings were held between 1911 and 1914. Two meetings in February 1912, for example, one attracting three hundred people on Montmartre and one attended by two hundred people in the Bastille/Marais neighborhood, sought to revive the tailors' section and were successful; spokesmen included the Bundist Mark Liber, Charles Rappoport, and a French union leader.[20] A conference on the state of the Jewish workers' movement in Paris was held in December of that year, and its tone was self-congratulatory.[21]

However, a heated debate as to the role of the Intersektsionen Byuro and its relative autonomy with respect to the sections took place in *Der idisher arbayter* in the March, April, and May issues of 1913. The question was raised as to whether the decisions adopted at the December 1912 conference were binding on all of the sections, or whether, as the (more anarchistic) tailors' section argued, the final decisions should rest with the individual trades. The Intersektsionen Byuro was criticized as being autocratic, but its defenders argued against measures that would only turn the Byuro into a purely mechanical organization for rubber-stamping members' decisions.

It is at the level of the union section itself that the interfacing with the strike movement is most interesting. Strikes led to the formation of union sections just as union sections encouraged calls to strikes. In the case of the Russian woodworkers in 1905, the bakers in 1906, and the leatherworkers in 1909, strikes gave birth to union sections. Similarly, a tinsmith's strike in 1913, successful after twenty days in its demand to have a hated foreman fired, led all of the strikers to join the (French) union and call for the formation of a separate Yiddish section.[22]

Successful strikes were also noted as strengthening existing union sections. But what is somewhat harder to identify is union influence on strike actions. Union presence is one thing; union leadership is another. As has been seen, several tailors' strikes included demands concerning the right to unionize, the right to have a union delegation oversee work control or firing procedures, be present at negotiations, etc. In two of the solidarity strikes undertaken on behalf of unjustly fired fellow workers, those workers were union members fired for strike agitation. Such examples denote a union presence, if in formation. There is only one case in which a strike action was clearly led by the union section, a woodworkers' strike of 1913.[23] However, the more diffuse effect of an in-workshop union member or other activist who could have led a strike movement or encouraged dissent is more probable, if more difficult to measure.

Ultimately union presence and encouragement of strike activities seems to be located less at the origin of the largely spontaneous strikes themselves nor as part of the initial strike demands, but rather as a force, where present, turned to for support once a strike was undertaken. Strikers turned to existing institutions for help, such as in 1902 when a group of striking diamond workers asked the French union for aid (and also got support from the Syndicat ouvrier israélite et catholique des diamantaires d'Anvers).[24]

There is one case, however, in which union leadership was decisive, in that which was the best organized of the Jewish immigrant trades: capmaking. The capmakers' organization was the avant-garde of the Jewish trade union movement in Paris in this period and is an important indicator of both its strengths and limitations.

CHAMBRE SYNDICALE DES OUVRIERS CASQUETTIERS HEADQUARTERS: BOURSE DU TRAVAIL (C.G.T.)

On July 20, 1896, ten years after the first strike in the trade at Herse and Weidenbach's, a capmakers' union was founded. As distinct from the above trades, which constituted union sections or subsections within a preexisting union, the capmakers formed a union of their own, which in June 1902 became affiliated with the Fédération des syndicats ouvriers de la chapellerie française of the C.G.T. Pottier counted 250 members in 1899; the Bonneffs estimated 500 to 600 in 1908; there were 380 members in 1909, according to the labor ministry; and by 1912, according to its secretary, Alexander Losovsky, one-half of the 1,500 capmakers in Paris belonged to the union.[25]

The hatters had been among the earliest crafts to organize in France, with mutual aid societies founded at the beginning of the nineteenth century and the first nationwide union created in 1879 at 3, rue de Rivoli in the Marais. Jewish capmakers, as has been seen, began to immigrate to Paris after the unsuccessful Polish revolt of 1863, settling for the most part in the Marais. The growing demand for this product at the turn of the century and the relatively simple skill which could be easily learned then attracted successive waves of Jewish immigrants to the Marais and that métier.

The transformation of the mutual aid society into a union in 1896 was the result of a series of conflicts that had plagued the capmakers' societies since the first one was formed in 1879. The uneasy coexistence of workers and their bosses within one organization was finally resolved in 1896 with the exclusion of the bosses and the formation of a workers-only union. Article Twelve of the union's constitutive by-laws clearly stated that if any member became a boss, contractor, or merchant, that person would automatically be excluded from the union.[26]

Class lines could not be drawn so clearly by a sole statutory article, however, and continual conflicts as to membership eligibility reflected the often fine line between those who took work from others, those who gave it to others, or those who did both. Thus some of the older society members disputed the advantages of a workers-only union, and heated debates were held as to whether or not employers should be admitted. Although an employers' union was formed six months after the workers' union, some employers still remained within the workers' union, even calling in the police to denounce the workers-only protagonists as dangerous anarchists.[27]

As Albert Matline, longtime secretary of the capmakers' union, explained years later, the 1896 union could not easily shirk off its mutual aid society character. Small-time bosses remained within the union while older union members controlled admission to it much as guilds had once regulated corporate membership. (To enter the union, a capmaker had to be sponsored by two union members.) Not until the immigration of more politicized immigrants of the post-1905 emigration and especially the leadership of Alexander Losovsky did the capmakers' union became a purely workers' union.[28]

It was in 1911 that a group of capmakers turned to Losovsky to become their secretary. At that time the resignation of the former secretary had brought to the surface a quarrel between the older and younger union members. The latter, part of the post-1905 emigration, were feared by the former as "anarchists." The most recent emigrants indeed had more revolutionary ideas with regard to the union and hoped to find a strong leader in Losovsky, whose speech at a metalworkers' meeting had impressed them.[29]

Alexander Losovsky (pseudonym for Solomon Dridzo, born in March 1878), whose father was a *melamed* (teacher) and whose mother sold notions at the market, himself sold matches, tobacco, lemons, and other miscellaneous items at the local fairs and marketplaces near his native Danilovka (Yekaterinoslav Province, Russia) from the age of eight.[30] At eleven he worked as a butcher's aide, at age twelve and a half as a grocery clerk, at fourteen he was apprenticed to a blacksmith, and at seventeen became a blacksmith himself. Sent to a *kheder* (Jewish primary school) as a youngster, it was not until the age of twenty that he was able to embark on more serious studies.

Around 1900 Losovsky became a Social-Democrat and began organizing workers' circles among the railwaymen in Russia. His political activities led to his arrest and exile in the aftermath of the 1905 Revolution, but on his way to Siberia he escaped, fleeing first to Geneva and then reaching Paris in January of 1909. In Paris Losovsky worked in different small factories as a blacksmith and metal-turner, administered some adult classes in electric assembly (1911), managed an automobile garage (rue de Grenelle, 1914) for several months, and went to a chauffeurs' school for a short period. He was also for a time secretary of the Bureau russe du travail.

Losovsky was one of the leaders of the Bolshevik group in Paris although aligned with the Bolshevik conciliators who were opposed to Lenin. In 1912, while secretary of the capmakers' union and in closer contact with the French revolutionary-syndicalists, notably Monatte and Rosmer, he broke with the Bolsheviks. Later, however, after his return to Russia in 1917, he became general secretary of the Profintern (Red International of Trade Unions) from 1921 to 1937 and vice-minister of foreign affairs from 1939 to 1946. Largely due to his activities as head of the Jewish anti-Fascist committee during World War II, Losovsky was purged by Stalin in 1949 and deported to a camp, where he died in 1952.

Losovsky's activities among the Jewish capmakers in Paris may be seen as a logical confluence of three aspects of his political development: a turning away from the political quarrels among the various fractions of the Russian Social-Democratic émigrés in Paris; his belief in the importance of union activity, which would be determinant during his years as secretary of the Profintern and which, during his Paris years, was influenced by the French revolutionary-syndicalists; and, what was rare for even those Russian Social-Democrats of Jewish origin, an understanding of the Yiddish-speaking workers and an appreciation of the possibilities of working with them.

Losovsky was one of the few Russian-Jewish Social-Democrats to bridge the Seine. Living among the Russian (political) refugee colony on the Left Bank, Losovsky was also at home among the Yiddish-speaking immigrants in the Marais. Whether he spoke in his native Russian as at his first capmakers' meeting (at which he was elected) or in the "strange" Yiddish he had acquired, his oratorical abilities were impressive, and he commanded the respect even of the employers with whom he dealt. Losovsky's dedication to the workers' interests was described as with "life and love," and his activities among the Jewish capmakers in France in this early period were undoubtedly important for his later theories with regard to union activity and its role in the revolutionary movement.[31]

If the Jewish workers of Paris were to be organized, the obvious place to start was among the capmakers. Conversely, if the capmakers were to be organized it was obvious that it would be as a distinct Yiddish-speaking union. Both the fact that the industry was 85 to 90 percent composed of Jewish immigrants and that it was a new specialty, hitherto unorganized, meant that when organization came, it was logical that it be distinct—as immigrants, Jews, and capmakers.

It is within the capmaking trade that the effect of union leadership on strike activity may best be seen. Within the other trades plied by the Jewish immigrants, union section activity was less strong, less directive, and the interplay between union direction and spontaneous strikes fluctuated; a strike action precipitated a movement toward organization, which organizing in turn attempted to promote strike activity; more often than not, however, early efforts only collapsed when confronted with a particularly severe morte-saison, only to start the cycle over again in short order.

The greater organization and stronger leadership behind the capmakers in Paris reflected while it enhanced a unity based on the uniqueness of the trade, as described above. That is, stronger organization grew out of a more solidly unified trade basis, but organization in turn further strengthened the unity of the capmakers. Both the strategies elaborated and the demands that were at the origin of many of the capmakers' strikes give evidence of their greater cohesiveness and stronger resolve.

The use of solidarity strikes in support of fired coworkers figured in thirteen of the forty-three capmakers' strikes for which we have information. Furthermore, whole shops would often follow a first once a strike action had been declared. This tactic was institutionalized through the union's use of the *index,* calling for a boycott against employers who would not comply with strike demands. Articles in *Der idisher arbayter* and *L'Ouvrier chapelier* announced the *mise à l'index* of recalcitrant employers or shops, a strategy feared by the manufacturers in the relatively small community within which capmaking took place. In at least one case the employers fought back by spreading the rumor that the blacklist had been lifted in order to fool the workers back to work, since the busy season was getting under way. The union responded with a leaflet (in Yiddish) unmasking the bosses' lie.[32]

Two important demands articulated by the capmakers' union in the 1910s reflected the greater strength of their organization. They were the demands for a uniform wage scale and for a collective bargaining agreement. The uniform wage scale *(tarif général)* was a needed corrective to the often arbitrary, if not anarchic, conditions that reigned in the capmaking trade just as in so many other small workshop and home-based light manufacturing industries at the end of the nineteenth century. Each manufacturer or contractor paid whatever wages he or she could get away with, often pointing in justification to another who paid less. The isolating nature of the putting-out system facilitated this practice, while even within workshops employers maintained competitive secretiveness about salaries, assuring each employee that he or she was earning a privileged sum not to be disclosed to the others.

The idea of a general wage scale was put forth as early as 1897 in the strike at Fraenkel's cap shop.[33] But it was not until 1912, when the union (under Losovsky's leadership) launched a trade-wide strike movement for a tarif général, that any gains were made. From April to November of that year the union led strike after strike in order to force the discussion of wages *"au vu et au su"* (in sight and with the knowledge) of everyone. The idea of such above-board bargaining was as dreaded by the employers as the wage increases that accompanied most of the demands.

The several agreements that ended many of the 1912 strikes not only assured the payment of a union wage scale but further manifested the growing strength of union intervention in the hiring, firing, and work process. Employers agreed to hire only union members and not to accept work from other shops on strike (under penalty of a one-thousand-franc fine payable to the capmakers' union in damages). In some agreements it was also added that any employer-employee conflict be handled through the union, and that no strikes be called until a union delegation had investigated the conflict and decided that a strike was necessary.[34]

These gains and most particularly the principle of closed shops and recognition of the union as the bargaining representative for the workers were consolidated after the war. A collective bargaining agreement (*convention collective*) for the capmakers' trade was signed on June 11, 1919 (by Goldfein for the manufacturers and Perivier for the capmakers), after a six-week strike involving twenty-five hundred workers.[35] In addition to most of the terms granted in the 1912 settlements, the 1919 agreement also stipulated that the "English week" (Saturday afternoons off) go into effect, that the union's placement office become the official labor exchange, that a hygiene committee be allowed to inspect shop premises once a month, that no work could be given to homeworkers to the detriment of shopworkers, and that workers who were paid by the week (all but the assemblers) would be entitled to paid vacations.

Loss of manpower due to the war undoubtedly had its part to play in the wave of collective bargaining agreements signed in 1919. But the prewar strike demands and the 1912 agreements set the stage for eliminating some of the worst arbitrary conditions in the trade. In this respect the capmakers' union led the way in establishing agreed-upon rules for determining wages, hiring and firing practices, work distribution, and even sanitary conditions. Union control over the work process began to be institutionalized.

It must be noted that the union's power was not only thus exerted vis-à-vis the employers but over spontaneous strike actions as well. Although spontaneous strikes had initially worked to promote union formation, once the union was formed it offered control over non–union-approved activities as a bargaining issue in return for employers' agreement to other measures. (The capmakers' union thus tried to ignore a wildcat strike at Veisman's shop in May 1914 and would not support it.[36]) The last two elements listed from the 1912 agreements, that all conflicts be handled through the union and that only a union delegation could call a strike, were strengthened in the 1919 collective agreement. All problems were now to be referred to a mixed (employer-union) committee, which would have eight days to settle them, during which time the workers were enjoined from striking.

Finally, these agreements also exhibited the union's expansion into other than strictly wage-related domains. For one, the very accession to the trade was to be placed under union control. Even before its official recognition by the employers in 1919, the union's placement office (*bureau de placement*) was envisaged by the union as a way of destroying the employers' power over the labor market through "free" contracts. *Der idisher arbayter* described a union placement office as a "*bafrayungs-mitl,*" a means of liberation from the bosses' oppression.[37] By channeling all hiring through such an agency, information with regard to job opportunities could be centralized and labor contracts better controlled in line with union wages and working conditions. Besides regulating the supply and demand of labor in this manner a placement office was also a method of encouraging closed shops and union solidarity. The union could thus help striking or fired members find other work, just as it could prevent known strikebreakers from getting work. Union members were urged to let the union know as soon as jobs became available; they were expected to impede the hiring of workers who did not have a letter from the union's secretary general; and if a union member helped a nonunion member get a job, this would be considered an *atteinte grave* (serious attack) against the union itself, for which the member would receive a severe reprimand the first time and be excluded from the union if it occurred more than once.

A bureau de placement along these lines was created by the capmakers' union in June 1912.[38] The furworkers' section also created a placement office, in late 1912, with the express hope of preventing the employers from recruiting grine and strikebreakers in the neighborhood restaurants and cafés. A shoemakers' placement office appeared in October 1913, and a month later the "Yidishe komisyon baym frantseyzishn sindikat" (the Intersektsionen Byuro?) announced the opening of two general (not craft-specific) placement offices—one in the Pletzl, the other on Montmartre.[39]

Efforts to increase workers' or union control over wages, working conditions, and the hiring process also spread to the production process, with the creation of cooperatives. Once again the capmaker's union, under Losovsky's leadership, led the way with a cooperative created during the 1912 strike movement.[40] "L'Union," as it was called (located at 5, rue des Guillemites in the 4th arrondissement), was one of only two such cooperatives under the auspices of the Hatters' Federation, which had voted a resolution in favor of cooperatives at its 1912 congress. The capmakers' union gave one thousand francs toward the cooperative's initial capital of twenty-five hundred francs, and the rest came from the issuance of sixty shares at twenty-five francs each. "Thanks to comrades" and help from the Hatters' Federation, the cooperative was able to function on an additional two hundred to three hundred francs a week. Two cutters, two bichonneurs, and two (women) garnishers (all paid by the week); and sixteen (of which two were women) machine operators (paid by the piece), one bookkeeper, and two *piqueurs de tête* (literally, head-stitchers) were employed by the cooperative, which, within three months of its opening, already had to expand into an additional apartment. Orders were coming in from all over France. Of the 10 percent to 12 percent clear profits that were realized: 50 percent was reinvested; 18 percent was set aside for "social works," i.e., for strikes, unemployment, or illness; 15 percent was distributed among the personnel; 10 percent went into a legal reserve fund; and 7 percent was set aside for a health insurance program (*caisse de maladie*). Both with regard to wages (as to rate and equal pay for men and women) and working conditions, the cooperative hoped to set the pace for industry-wide practices. The cooperative was to be not only an element of union strategy in time of strikes, but an ongoing exemplar of an ideal production workshop.

In July 1913, in the fourth month of their strike, the bakers set up a cooperative called Brudershaft (brotherhood), which soon had several distribution outlets in the various Jewish neighborhoods of Paris (the Pletzl, Montmartre, faubourg St.-Antoine, and the Russian quarter on the Left Bank). A small printers' cooperative, also called Union, appeared in January 1914, and that same month there was talk of the woodworkers' and the tailors' sections setting up their own cooperatives.[41] Finally, a consumer's cooperative called Solidaritet announced its opening in the faubourg St.-Antoine area in January 1914, proclaiming itself better than the other cooperatives, which only sought to increase their earnings and to divide the profits among themselves. Solidaritet aimed rather at the general spiritual *(gaystike)* development of the working class and would use its profits to support *Der idisher arbayter,* to aid workers' libraries, and to create a mutual aid fund.[42]

The creation of cooperatives, beginning with that of the capmakers', set off a sharp debate in the pages of *Der idisher arbayter* similar to the larger debate over the role of cooperatives in relation to syndicalism in France.[43] Losovsky (who also seems to have been instrumental in the setting up of the Brudershaft cooperative) began his defense of the capmakers' cooperative in anticipation of criticisms of reformism. He emphasized that cooperatives did not let workers escape from capitalism, nor would they bring about the creation of an ideal future society.[44] In an October 1, 1912, article in *L'Ouvrier chapelier* he elaborated his position, writing that cooperatives

> can and must play a subordinate role in the labor movement, that cooperation does not suffice in and of itself. . . . It is not a matter of making the social revolution through cooperatives; it is simply a matter of creating favorable conditions for the struggle towards social transformation. . . .

Yet others weakened Losovsky's defense by writing about cooperatives as a form of the future society, provoking a vigorous denunciation of such reformism by the editorial board of *Der idisher arbayter.* Cooperatives cannot escape the laws of capitalism, the editors wrote, commenting by the title of one article that "the big mountain of pessimism has built a small molehill."[45]

This debate over workers' strategies with regard to the transition toward social change was not confined to cooperatives alone. Various self-help and mutual aid funds started by the union sections came under attack for similar reasons. In addition to a strike fund put into effect as early as 1901 (over twenty-seven thousand francs were spent during the important year of 1912), an unemployment fund (for "involuntary unemployment," i.e., the mortesaison, as distinct from "voluntary unemployment," i.e., strikes) was set up by the capmakers' union in April of 1912.[46] Losovsky wrote in *L'Ouvrier chapelier* of November 21–December 20, 1911, that such a fund could not make unemployment, which resulted from the anarchy of capitalist society, disappear, but that through the unemployment fund (Caisse d'assurance contre le chômage) the morte-saison could be attenuated. If unemployed capmakers were aided, they would not weigh on the labor market (thus driving down wages) and would therefore have a greater independence with respect to employers, no longer forced to take the first job offered. At the same time the fund would heighten union solidarity, since it would be in the members' interest to keep up their dues in order to benefit from it. Finally, the fund would also be able to provide statistics on unemployment with which the union could better study the effects of the labor market.

The tailors' union section had a mutual aid fund, the woodworkers' section sought to create a medical plan, and even the small group of unionized barbers decided to organize an unemployment fund.[47] When an unemployment plan was suggested in the twelfth issue of *Der idisher arbayter*, it was defended, like the capmakers' cooperative, against the potential double (and contradictory) criticism of pretending to be a model for a future society or of being little better than a reformist strategy. Its defenders argued that the fund was necessary to better conditions in the present (rather than the future), and that it would help keep workers from having to knock on the "hated Rothschild and Company's" door for alms. The fund was *not* to be seen as a mere savings plan but rather as a model for proletarian ideas and an important means to attract more workers to the movement.[48]

On February 9, 1913, approximately one hundred people gathered to create an Arbeter ring on the model of the Bundist-inspired organizations of the same name in the United States and London.[49] Through the debate concerning the Arbeter ring, the issue of mutual aid benefits came clearly to the fore. The Arbeter ring proposed "platonic help"—financial aid, sickness funds, and cultural works—as a method of fostering workers' solidarity free from any political slant. On the one hand this was argued as a necessary corrective to the political squabbles dividing the other workers' organizations. On the other hand the Arbeter ring's mutual aid benefits were to be open to all workers, regardless of religious beliefs. This distinguished it from the traditional mutual aid societies, most often linked to oratories, as seen above, from which "freethinkers" had benefited very little. Medical aid was to be of prime importance for the Arbeter ring, especially for people suffering from long-term diseases such as tuberculosis. Its medical fund was envisaged as an alternative to going to the hospital and being surrounded by sick people and strangers or from just giving oneself up to fate.

Yet such mutual aid benefits, whether offered by the Arbeter ring or by the individual union sections, were harshly criticized in *Der idisher arbayter* as fostering petit-bourgeois attitudes and deviating from a purely economic workers' struggle.[50] The issue led to a heated debate and even a split within the leatherworkers' section (with a "reformist" group splitting off to create its own medical fund.)[51] Arguments as to whether strikebreakers or ex-union members who had become employers could subsequently draw from these funds also divided many a union meeting.

Losovsky took a characteristically balanced stand, welcoming the Arbeter ring as an adjunct to the workers' movement but warning of possible contradictions.[52] He argued that mutual aid funds were an important means of attracting more workers to the labor movement—especially in the face of disgust by many over recurrent political squabbles—and that through such attraction "unconscious" workers could be taught the basics of economic struggle. He warned, however, of the "illusory principle" expounded by the Arbeter ring of welcoming all progressive elements to its ranks, including nonworkers. Such a policy could only lead to the internecine quarrels that the Arbeter ring wanted to avoid.

In fact, the old mutual aid function had never been exorcised, and with reason, given the material needs of the immigrant community. The capmakers' union, under Losovsky's leadership, led the way in an ecumenical interpretation of a trade union movement. From strike actions to mutual aid funds, from the establishment of a soup kitchen during the war to organizing a collection on behalf of a needy comrade, the capmakers' union was especially vigorous in representing the workers' interests through a variety of ways. The strength of that union and the solidarity of its membership was not without fissures, however, that went beyond the issue of mutual aid funds.

A recurrent problem, important both in its material and moral consequences, was that of irregular dues payments. The capmakers' union (under Lozovsky's signature for the most part) struck out publicly in the pages of *L'Ouvrier chapelier* and *Der idisher arbayter* against recalcitrant members who had not paid their two francs monthly dues. In 1912, the same year in which Losovsky reported to the Hatters' Federation convention in Bort that one-half of the fifteen hundred capmakers in Paris were unionized, Lauzel, in his study on the capmakers, stated that barely three hundred of them paid their dues regularly.[53] Especially after dues were increased as of January 1, 1911, in order to pay membership fees to the federation, the number of refractory members increased. At the September 12 general meeting of that year, eighty members were excluded who had not paid their dues for the last four or five years (and their shops were alerted that they were no longer union members). At the same meeting a member who had fallen sick but was not up to date in his dues payments was refused health benefits. This measure seems to have met with more resistance than the previous one, but Losovsky and Karpel, the treasurer, insisted that the rules had to be respected.[54] Similarly, the Bureau du Placement and strike funds were closed to those who had not met their dues obligations.

A draft article or leaflet written by Losovsky in 1911 complained of the "indifference of the unconscious masses," a complaint echoed by almost all of the trades in the "Fakh korespondentsyies" section of *Der idisher arbayter*. The criticism was aimed not only at nonunionized workers but at union members themselves. The latters' "passivity" was deplored along with the fact that defaulting on dues payments and lack of attendance at meetings characterized those periods when union activity was calm. But, the article continued, once a strike was launched or a member fell sick, those same members came running to the union for their benefits, attending all meetings, and giving long speeches on solidarity. Then, once again, the strike over, "these good activists return to the shadows and all of their solidarity melts like snow under the sun's rays. What is to be done?"[55]

Passivity, bordering on fraud—e.g., workers showing their union cards in order to be hired when in fact their payments were long overdue—called for stern measures. Tight control over hiring procedures became necessary. Thus, in conjunction with the establishment of the Bureau du placement, union members were encouraged to request that job candidates get a letter from the secretary general (in addition to a union card) attesting to the regularity of their dues payments.

Divisions also existed between the older (less political, more mutual-aid–oriented) and newer (more militant) immigrants within the capmakers' union. As in other trades, the newer immigrants called the older immigrants reactionary and the latter saw the former as dangerous revolutionaries and anarchists.[56] And the division of labor within the trade also created strains within the organization. Both the cutters, the aristocrats of the trade, and the pressers, pariahs of the production hierarchy, tried to organize separately. Only a bichonneurs' section was actually set up (ca. 1911–12), however. The bichonneurs felt that their particular working conditions, wages, hiring procedures, and other corporative issues needed to be represented separately before the union's Commission du travail. However, the section had no independent funds and was ultimately bound by the entire capmakers' union's decisions.[57]

Internal factions, recalcitrant dues payments, and the necessity for assuring a certain amount of tight control are problems common to the internal operations of most institutions. They reflect the structural limits to which even workers' associations are bound. With the growing strength of the capmakers' union, its very functioning as a viable organization created new problems no longer strictly related to employer-employee relations. Dues payments and membership activity became important issues alongside strike strategies. While the need for ensuring continuing institutional viability shaped the labor leaders' response on certain questions, these organizational constraints were, ironically, also testimony to the growth of the union itself.

The capmaker's union led the way in the unionization of Jewish workers in Paris before World War I. Losovsky's leadership was clearly an important factor in the capmakers' successes, but so was the largely homogeneous (Jewish immigrant) nature of the trade itself. This brings us to the question of imported leadership. Losovsky is by far the best example of a determined revolutionary émigré putting his theories into practice in the country of immigration. But we must ask whether he was representative and whether the political exiles' organizations in Paris as a whole were active in the development of Jewish strikes and union sections. More generally, was there a tendency to strike imported by the Jewish workers?

IMPORTED RADICALISM?

The emergence of a Jewish trade union movement, like other manifestations of the immigrant community, arose from a combination of factors both imported by the immigrants from eastern Europe and specific to their living and working conditions in Paris. Although I have argued that conditions in the workshops of Paris were sufficient to create a strike movement and provide the basis for the first Yiddish trade union sections, the question must be asked to what extent class consciousness or a propensity to strike was imported from eastern Europe.

The reconstitution of Russian political groups among the more Russified Jewish émigrés on the Left Bank has already been noted. The immigrant political groups did take an active interest in the trade union movement as the Bund Archive's "Kemfer" files attest. Bundists and anarchists both influenced the Jewish workers' movement, sometimes directly as in the furworkers' or tailors' sections respectively, or more diffusely, by setting the climate in which the trade union movement was able to take root. Even the Russian Social-Democrats put out leaflets in Yiddish aimed at the Pletzl population, and the formation of a Union intersyndicale russe, connected to the Cercle ouvrier russe, was announced in 1913.[58]

However, three things inhibited the professional revolutionaries from having a greater impact on the labor movement; first of all, their "return" perspective described above. Workers, students, and revolutionaries had different ideals with regard to emigration and immigration, the revolutionary groups reconstituted in Paris focusing on political concerns *in Russia* and possible return there in the event of revolution, the immigrant workers concentrating on settling in and adapting *in France*. As has been seen, two Russian revolutionary-syndicalist splinter groups explicitly criticized the Left Bank revolutionaries for not being sufficiently interested in the immigrant workers in the Pletzl.[59]

These different perspectives on locus of action and prospects for return or settlement became explicit in the course of a meeting of the Comité officiel du rapatriement des émigrés politiques russes en France (Official Committee for the Repatriation of Russian Political Emigrés in France) in 1917 at which a split occurred over the issue of return to revolutionary Russia. Those political refugees who planned on going back to Russia no longer had much in common with those workers who had left Russia in order to escape military service and seek better opportunities for making a living.[60] The assumption, underlined by the police commentator, was that these latter by and large had no intention of leaving France. As a *Der idisher arbayter* article described the political parties' activities in Paris, their purpose was "to help their parties in Russia both morally and materially, but for the working masses in Paris they do *gornit* [nothing]."[61]

Even more debilitating perhaps were the political differences, which only divided the already tiny movement and dispersed energy through internal struggles. In spite of the united front which *Der idisher arbayter* hoped to represent by stressing trade organizing instead of politics, political differences sometimes emerged.

The Bundists, for example, criticized the Intersektsionen byuro and *Der idisher arbayter* as not "Jewish" enough, while the anarchists felt they were too "Jewish." Within a year from the founding of *Der idisher arbayter* the Bund's criticism of the insufficient autonomy of the Jewish workers' sections was aired in the paper. Sviranski, a furworker, argued that language, special forms of exploitation, and the concentration of the Jews in certain trades necessitated separate organizational structures.[62] For the Bund it was essential that the Jewish workers not become submerged into the French labor movement but that they express the particular conditions of their trades and their community through clearly distinct organizations.

But the Bundist argument for Jewish cultural and trade union autonomy could only make the pro-C.G.T. faction cringe in fear of criticisms of Jewish separatism. Sviranski's article in *Der idisher arbayter* was harshly attacked by the editorial board on the front page of the next issue, less for itself than for the logical conclusions of nationalism and chauvinistic tendencies that could be drawn from Sviranski's arguments.[63] Sviranski's project was qualified as "scandalous," and his use of the term *eyn gantsen kerper* to describe how he felt the Jewish workers should be drawn together into one body was seized upon and vehemently criticized (in a manner reminiscent of the French Revolutionary attacks on prerevolutionary *corps*).

The anarcho-syndicalists disapproved of what they called the "reformist" and "even Bundist" socialism of *Der idisher arbayter*, and those within the tailors' section put forth a motion for the newspaper to drop the name "idisher" from its title. They disagreed with the paper's ties with the C.G.T. and even boycotted a ball it was sponsoring over this issue. Other Russian anarchists wrote in to *Der idisher arbayter* to criticize the union movement altogether, arguing, from the standpoint of conspirators, against its mass character. As far as *Der idisher arbayter* was concerned, these anarchists were troublemakers who not only bred dissension but also discouraged the French trade union from giving money to the Jewish workers' cause.[64]

Finally, a third factor, in addition to the "return" mentality and political squabbling, which rendered difficult any effective "imported" leadership by the revolutionary refugee groups, was the *embourgeoisement* of ex-radicals in the West.[65] Defection from the revolutionary movement by those who had been active in eastern Europe proved a disappointment to Jewish labor leaders in Paris. "More French Socialists answer our requests for articles than do those immigrants who were in the forefront of our movement in eastern Europe," complained one issue of *Der idisher arbayter;* "you who fought *in der heym* (in the old country) are guilty of indifference, and it is because of you that our movement is weak," accused another article.[66] "Intoxicated" with the new life of the West, "influenced by modern decadence," some of these old fighters went so far as to criticize *Der idisher arbayter* in the bourgeois press. Others, pessimistic over failures in eastern Europe, where they had worked for such a sublime cause, apparently could not be made interested in the Jewish labor movement in Paris.[67]

Thus this difficult relationship between immigrant political groups and trade union sections, the limited aid of the former to the latter, and the suspicion of the latter (especially the tailors) for the former, all sapped the energy of the Jewish labor movement. In this respect Losovsky, preparing for his role in the Red Syndicalist movement in Russia between the wars, was the exception. Other names, notably those of the Bundist Mark Liber and Charles Rappoport, also appear at occasional union organizational meetings. But by and large the political refugee community seems to have been primarily concerned with political events in Russia and the possibility of revolution there.

However, the question is less one of individual leaders and revolutionary activity versus trade union organizing than one of a more diffuse influence of "imported" radicalism. If we have little proof of direct "skill transfer" in the domain of strike organizing, we can nonetheless look to three interrelated factors of the eastern European experience that undoubtedly had an impact on the development of the Jewish trade union movement in Paris: the strike movement in the Pale from the 1870s to 1890s, the emigration "wave" of 1905, and Bundist ideology.

The strike movements of the 1870s to 1890s in the Pale have been well documented by Ezra Mendelsohn in his *Class Struggle in the Pale.*[68] As social and economic conditions deteriorated within the Pale, social differentiation and dissension within the Jewish community increased. By the 1880s, the corporate solidarity between masters and journeymen that had characterized the Jewish guilds and mutual aid societies ever since their inception in the sixteenth century broke down. If some Jewish factory owners and their workers still said their morning prayers together before work, more often the collaboration between employer and employee was coming to an end. In one case the purchase of their own Torah (religious scroll) by a group of journeymen tablemakers was symbolic of their split from their masters' guild.[69]

Secular-oriented workers' *kassy* (originally, self-help funds connected with workers' educational circles) arose parallel to the more tradition-bound guilds, and these *kassy* were eventually used as strike funds. As conditions transformed the independent artisan into a wage laborer, and as the journeyman saw his chances of becoming a master artisan diminish, the former paternalistic structure began to collapse.

Spontaneous and locally led strikes in the 1870s and 1880s revealed the cleavages beneath the surface of the Jewish community. But it was in the 1890s that the strike movement really took off, spreading to the important manufacturing cities of Bialystok, Lodz, Warsaw, etc. Ber Borokhov counted 2,276 Jewish strikes between 1895 and 1904 (a strike every one and a half days.).[70] The majority of these strikes—especially numerous among the tanners and bristle workers—were unplanned, small shop strikes occurring without the help of any "outside agitators."

The rank-and-file character of the majority of strike actions reflected the fragmented mode of production in the Pale already described, the plethora of small workshops, and the changing nature of the artisanal manufacturing process. As had happened earlier in the century in western Europe, the consciousness of the artisanal workers was raised not through their objective proletarianization but rather first in resistance to the threat posed by a transitional, industrializing economy. Thus, these workers struck in order to demand higher wages, shorter hours (a twelve-hour day), and most importantly, the stabilization of relations between employer and employee.

In the struggle between "the poverty-stricken and the indigent,"[71] the Jewish workers' movement in the Pale never really succeeded in securing significant and lasting gains for the workers. Promises extracted from poor Jewish employers by their poorer employees were often quickly reneged upon. However, the strike movement reflected a new perception on the part of the workers, no longer seeing themselves as temporary employees on the way to becoming self-employed. As Martov noted, the "proletarianization" and raised consciousness of the Vilna carpenters occurred when they no longer "regard[ed] themselves as future employers; they have become permanently hired laborers."[72] Social differentiation became class dissension, and Jewish community unity, always greater in theory than in reality, increasingly broke down within the context of late nineteenth-century socioeconomic change.

It was this propensity to change, this perception of a disintegrating community structure and of increasing social tensions, that was imported with the flow of eastern European Jewish emigrants to the West. That flow increased quantitatively and qualitatively with the emigration wave of 1905.

In 1905 revolution broke out in Russia and did not subside until the tsar promised the Duma and other reforms in his October Manifesto. The results for the Jews, as Jews, were disastrous. Once again they became the scapegoats of social and political unrest, and pogroms added to the emigration wave. For those Jews who were trade union or political activists, emigration became an even more compelling necessity, as they were pursued along with Russians for revolutionary activity against the regime. Recurrent mention is made of the "radicalization" of the labor movement in Paris after 1905. Indeed, the increase of immigrant activists must in part explain the increase in Jewish immigrant strikes in the 1905–14 period.[73]

Finally, what was imported with the immigrants was not only a familiarity with strikes from the 1890s and a radicalization after 1905, but a Bundist ideology, which, without being clearly predominant in the pre-1914 Parisian situation, nonetheless clearly left its mark on the Jewish immigrants' polemic with the C.G.T. The Bund, founded in 1897 in Vilna, developed largely as a result of disillusionment on the part of many "professional revolutionaries" of Jewish origin who had begun their careers as assimilated Russian radicals. With the pogroms beginning in 1881, they turned their attention from the Narodnaya Volya theories of "going to the people," i.e., the peasants, to the conditions of the Jewish masses, helping to organize the workers' educational circles in the late 1880s and early 1890s. While the Russian-assimilated origins of the activists prevailed in the first stage of the Bund's activity, Arkady Kremer's pamphlet "On Agitation" marked a turning point for the Vilna movement. In accordance with Kremer's call to action among the masses, Russian was soon forsaken in favor of Yiddish, the language of the vast majority of the Jews, and the Bund went on to defend Jewish nationalism even in the face of Bolshevik opposition.[74]

The strike movement of the 1890s at first caught the revolutionary leaders unprepared. However, the Bundists soon became especially active in some of the larger strikes and among the more "backward" workers. Bundist leaders militated among the often illiterate cigarette and match factory workers, who constituted the only real Jewish factory proletariat—largely female—in northwest Russia, and among the bakers, whose working conditions, when not self-employment, were highly paternalistic. The Bund's organization of Jewish self-defense during the 1905 pogroms was another important contribution toward a more self-assertive attitude of the mass of Jewish workers in the Pale.

However, it is the Bund's polemic over the "national question" that is of most interest here. In eastern Europe the Bund's dispute with the Russian Social-Democratic Workers' Party (RSDWP), of which it was a founding member, revolved around this very national problem, leading to a temporary break between the two from 1903 to 1905. In France the problem would revolve around the Jewish union and union sections' relation to the C.G.T.

It cannot be argued that the Bundists played a decisive role in the trade union movement in Paris. Their voice was only a minority one (if strongest among the furworkers), and, like the other Russian revolutionary groups in Paris, the Bund there was primarily concerned with strategic questions relating to events in Russia and to its relationship with the RSDWP. However,

Bundist writers do appear in the pages of the Jewish labor press in Paris, and they stressed there, as in Russia, the importance of Jewish workers' autonomy as a fundamental and vital element of the Jewish labor movement. Not satisfied with the Yiddish-language union sections, the Bund urged separate unions altogether, along the lines of the capmakers'. And although the Bund initially greeted the creation of a Jewish workers' paper warmly, it soon became dissatisfied with *Der idisher arbayter*'s emphasis on the necessity of working within the French union structure.

The implications of this debate will be explored more fully in the next chapter. What is important here is to understand the more general role of refugee leaders in shaping the labor movement in Paris. As for the Bund it may be argued that its ideology had a diffuse rather than a direct impact on the Jewish trade union movement in Paris. While it represented perhaps the most strident demand for a separate Jewish labor movement, aspects of that demand would eventually be acknowledged even among those who argued for close cooperation with the C.G.T., as will be seen below.

More generally, however, such political debates weakened the Jewish immigrant trade union movement in Paris, as certain leaders complained. Political quarrels, along with the *embourgeoisement* of some and the "return" perspective of others were all criticized as elements that inhibited the effectiveness of the trade union movement. Or, more correctly, the latter two sapped its potential while the first actually caused dissension among the ranks. The global influence of political refugee movements on the trade union movement was thus limited and so, one could therefore argue, was "imported radicalism."

Nonetheless, important precedents were imported by the immigrants: strike activity of the 1880s and 1890s in the Pale, radicalization of 1905, and a Bundist ideology whose emphasis on the "idisher" in *Der idisher arbayter* was not entirely ignored. Most strikingly, the effect of skillful leadership such as that of Losovsky is a good case in point of how "imported" leadership could have a decisive effect.

However, having taken note of all of these factors, the shopfloor character of the Jewish labor movement's activities must not be lost from view. Losovsky's actions were effective because of the particularly homogeneous and concentrated character of Jewish capmakers in Paris. And, with the exception of the capmakers, strikes led more often to the creation of union sections than vice versa. The *syndicalisation de la grève* was an important impetus to the creation of *Der idisher arbayter* and the Intersektsionen byuro in the first place. Whatever strike leadership or more diffuse tendency toward radicalism was imported from eastern Europe, it was clearly activated by conditions in the Pletzl.

If a Jewish labor movement was thus positively constructed as a result of imported tendencies and concrete conditions in the Pletzl, it was in many ways negatively constructed with regard to the French labor movement. International solidarity collided with workers' protectionism as the presence of immigrant laborers grew in the late nineteenth and early twentieth centuries. Both French and immigrant labor leaders espoused international solidarity, but both labor movements were subject to criticisms of chauvinism or protectionism. The resultant ambiguities within the French labor movement and tensions between French and immigrants erupted from union meetings to shopfloors. These tensions, to be sure, were underlaid by the very divisions inherent in the industrial work structure itself.

This brings us to the question of class and community. How can an immigrant labor movement define itself within a national context? How were the Jewish trade union sections perceived by the French labor movement, and to what extent did the French trade union movement represent an option for insertion for the immigrant workers? In other words, what were the possibilities and problems of a Franco-immigrant alliance on the shopfloor or picket lines? It is time to turn to the community network that set the Jewish immigrants apart from their French comrades and gave the Jewish labor movement its specific character.

Seven

CLASS AND COMMUNITY
The Jewish Immigrant Labor
Movement

In early September 1899, at the height of the Dreyfus affair, a number of Jewish workers gathered and decided to constitute a group called Le Pro-létariat Juif de France.[1] The group's aim was to provide a forum for the Jewish workers outside of the trade union structure and to combat the errors of anti-Semitism by proving that Jews worked in factories and workshops, suffering the same conditions as their "companions in misery," i.e., the French workers.

On September 16, a public meeting was held in the Maison du peuple on Montmartre at which several hundred Jews and non-Jews spoke out against anti-Semitism. Clericalism and religion itself were attacked ("all are the same exploitation of belief") as was the confusion propagated by the anti-Semites in subsuming all Jews under the "princes of finance." Anti-Semitism as a form of clericalism and as the socialism of fools was denounced, and the slogan "Liberty, equality, fraternity[2] peace to all men and to all races" was adopted unanimously. The following resolution was passed at the close of the meeting:

> The citizens[3] gathered the sixteenth of September at the Maison du peu-
> ple, rue Ramey, declare that for all men of heart and good sense there can be no
> war between the races; that anti-Semitism is a disgraceful trap[4] held out to the

proletariat in order to make them forget their ideas of social freedom and to put them at the mercy of their cruellest enemies.

They [the citizens] hereby stigmatize the *misérables* who have hatched this plot and declare the international brotherhood of all human beings regardless of race.

The Jewish workers thus agreed with the (Marxist) interpretation of anti-Semitism as being a diversionary tactic—"disgraceful trap"—aimed at dividing the working class. Internationalism was seen as the correct interpretation of "brotherhood." And underlying the Jewish workers' appeal was the faith that reason and the French revolutionary ideals would triumph on the side of justice. It was this synthesis of (a qualified) Marxism, French revolutionary tradition, and an ideal of international brotherhood that would characterize the Jewish immigrant labor movement.

These September 1899 meetings attest to a refusal of silence with regard to the Dreyfus affair that contrasts sharply with the French Jewish community's reaction. The September 16 meeting was reported only briefly in the *Archives Israélites* under "Miscellaneous News" and only with regard to the anti–anti-Semitic aspect, i.e., not the more general socialistic tone, of the meeting. *L'Univers Israélite*, which had, however, given more attention to the earlier preparatory (totally Jewish) meeting, did not report the September 16 meeting at all.

That the only public Jewish protest meeting held with regard to the Dreyfus affair was held under the aegis of a self-proclaimed group of "Jewish proletarians" is significant. The double oppression or double onus on these immigrants, as workers and as Jews, led to an explicit action of protest that the French Jews did not dare express or did not even feel necessary. The cleavage between those two communities was thus revealed in yet one more aspect in September 1899. Cultural, social, and economic differences were now accompanied by an explicitly political difference.

However, it is not the French Jewish bourgeoisie but the French labor movement that is the more pertinent frame of reference for understanding the development of the Jewish immigrant labor movement in Paris. In this context the *Lettre des ouvriers juifs de Paris au Parti socialiste français*, published during the Dreyfus affair in 1898, remains important in its critique of the French Socialists. For in this first manifestation of a "Groupe des ouvriers juifs socialistes de Paris" it was not only or even primarily as distinct from a Jewish bourgeoisie that the Jewish workers' presence was made known. (The attitude of the bourgeois French Jewish community was perhaps disappointing but not unexpected and certainly did not call for a direct appeal to that community to come to the Jewish workers' aid.) Rather, it was as separate from the French labor movement that the Jewish workers wrote their *Lettre*, expressing their keen disappointment with the French Socialists' weak stance on the Affair, all the keener because of the high hopes they had placed in the French revolutionaries of the land of liberty, fraternity, and equality. A particularly pointed criticism seemed to be aimed at Jules Guesde (who led the more intransigent stand against Socialist participation in the Affair): "We find our anger cannot be exhausted through the reasoned revolt of Marx and his disciples. They exert their anger in too narrow a sphere, that of the class struggle; but our anger cannot stop there."[5] The struggle of the Jewish immigrant workers would have to go beyond a strict bourgeois/proletariat analysis and address the issues of small-time employers and exploitation *within* the immigrant community. In any case the Jewish workers ended their *Lettre* with the hope and appeal that the French Socialists would come to their aid.

These high hopes, often tinged with disappointment, would characterize the relationship between the Jewish and French labor movements in Paris. The often difficult integration of immigrant labor within a national labor movement was problematic. Ideological unity sometimes confronted labor protectionism in the workshop, if not in ambiguous newspaper articles or congress resolutions. The "national question" came to the fore within a single country as a microcosm of the problem of national groupings within an international unity: Immigrant groupings within the nation-state framework of labor organizing created contradictions often difficult to resolve. When Marx wrote "Working men of all countries, unite!" he did not know how pertinent that phrase would become as the increased migration of labor brought working persons of all countries together within one land.

THE FRENCH LABOR MOVEMENT AND IMMIGRANT WORKERS

From the middle of the nineteenth century and particularly from the late 1860s on, the growth of *chambres syndicales ouvrières* (trade union committees) in France defied the Le Chapelier law of 1791 that forbade the constitution of workers' (or employers') organizations. By 1870 approximately sixty to seventy thousand workers—particularly in the skilled trades—in Paris belonged to the by now tolerated *chambres syndicales ouvrières*, and in 1884, a law legalized this *fait accompli* by recognizing the right of freedom of association.[6] Two years later a meeting in Lyons initiated by the Guesdist faction of French Socialists created the Fédération nationale des syndicats. That same year the first Bourse du travail was set up in Paris as a combination labor exchange, workers' club, and cultural center, and six years later thirteen such *bourses* became federated under the leadership of Fernand Pelloutier; by 1912 there were 153 bourses.[7]

The Fédération nationale des syndicats lasted only two years, to be succeeded in 1895 by the Confédération générale du travail (C.G.T.). The

Bourses du travail and the C.G.T. existed side by side until 1902, when their fusion led to the "heroic period of the C.G.T., when it firmed up its structure, extended its organization, and defied employers and government with the gospel of revolutionary syndicalism."[8] Direct action and the general strike were the strategies propounded. Economic pressure was to take precedence over any political or parliamentary maneuvers, and a policy statement against union involvement in party politics concluded the Charter of Amiens, voted by the C.G.T. in 1906.

The needle trades, like the majority of other skilled trades, had begun the century organized in *compagnonnages* (types of trade guilds) and mutual aid societies. In 1868 the first Parisian tailors' *chambre syndicale* was formed, followed a year later by that of the hatters. The latter moved quickly toward a national union in 1870 (the first in any trade, although still called a *chambre syndicale*: the Chambre syndicale des ouvriers chapeliers de France), while the national clothing workers' union (the Fédération nationale des travailleurs de l'habillement, eventually including tailors, seamstresses, shirtmakers, collarmakers, corsetmakers, and glove workers as well as furworkers, featherworkers, and artificial flower workers) did not take shape until 1893, the same year as the constitution of the national leather- and furworkers' union (Fédération nationale des cuirs et peaux).

The French unions' relationship to the Jewish immigrant labor movement is complex. On an ideological level, unity of the immigrant workers' cause with that of French workers was repeatedly underscored. In practice, however, certain tensions developed which would ultimately help lead the way toward separate immigrant organizations.

The fundamental importance of unity among all workers and the necessity of organizing to effectuate that unity were repeated by the C.G.T. leadership each time there was a strike in which immigrants were involved. Solidarity between workshop workers and homeworkers and between female and male workers was stressed as was the importance of unity regardless of nationality or religion. A Conseillers prud'hommes (labor court) meeting in 1899 stated that:

> All workers, no matter what nationality, race or religion, are brothers and have the same rights to work and to life. The Congress takes this occasion to salute the entrance of the Jewish workers' organizations into the struggle for the emancipation of the proletariat.[9]

Elsewhere Jewish workers were often defended and even praised in the French labor press. An article in *La Bataille syndicaliste* of April 10, 1913, pointed to the example of the Jewish bakers' strike as a lesson for all French bakers. Racamond, secretary of the French bakers' union, wrote to *Der idisher arbayter* of February 8, 1913, with praise for the solidarity of immigrant and French workers in a recent strike. "For us, union workers, there exist no nations . . . there exists only one nation—that of the exploited class."

An important protest meeting was organized by the French garment workers' union on July 2, 1914, on behalf of two Russian ready-to-wear tailors who had been deported. As reported in *L'Humanité* and *La Bataille syndicaliste*, the Russian tailors (brothers), who had taken off work on May 1, were greeted the next day by their employer with the comment: "You're not at the Bourse du travail here." The next Sunday the two brothers were "surrounded by a band of 'apaches' who terrorize the Jewish workers of Montmartre" and beaten up, apparently at the instigation or even with the participation of the boss Bocalter (also referred to as Buchlalter and Brocader) and his son. The brothers were subsequently arrested and expelled. At the protest meeting, which attracted over twelve hundred people, the Socialist deputy Marcel Sembat declared that it was inadmissible that foreign workers be punished merely for striking. The meeting ended with "Vive l'Internationale."[10]

Concrete support of immigrant strikes often took the form of providing premises, paying for leaflets, or giving financial aid. The Bourse du travail headquarters in Paris was a common meeting place; publicity leaflets with the C.G.T. stamp attest to its help for that important communication medium; and the French union occasionally helped out with strike funds enabling the strikers to hold out that much longer.[11] Beyond this, moral support from the French unions was also important.

All such manifestations of solidarity reflected the basic ideological premise of workers' unity. Yet various tensions arose that threatened that ideological unity. Institutional constraints of the French union structure, the disparity between the French leadership and the immigrant rank and file, disagreement over political involvement, and dissensions between French and immigrant coworkers all created concrete obstacles to theoretical unity. Finally, strains of anti-Semitism reveal the most basic contradiction of all, the issue of labor protectionism.

Institutional constraints sometimes created tensions, if not outright conflicts, between the union organization and the desires of the strikers. If during the August 1905 strike at Braunstein's negotiations bogged down because union intervention had led to intransigence on certain demands, in most cases it was the contrary. A strike became too long and "onerous" for the union and particularly for its strike fund. This was seen in the tailors' strike of 1901. It was also true during the 1916 S.P.C. strike. Nine days after the beginning of the strike (which was to last over a month), the union suggested going into negotiations in order to arrive at a settlement, and eventually it even urged the strikers to negotiate without it although union representation had been one of the initial demands. The strike committee, led by a Jewish immigrant named Gorodetsky, refused and was criticized by certain strikers and union leaders for thus prolonging the strike. However, when a secret vote was held on the union's suggestion of coming to a quick settlement, the majority held out for continuing the strike until the director of the S.P.C. agreed to meet with union representatives.[12] While often profiting from strikes as a platform for membership drives, the unions, like any institution, also had to take care to maintain their own existence. The point at which strike funds dropped too low became the moment at which strike demands had to be reevaluated. It was also the moment when union leaders sometimes came into conflict with the rank and file.

Tensions over tactics between union leaders and strikers were overlaid by the fact that the union leadership was French and the workers with which we are dealing were immigrants. In 1901 it was the five Jewish immigrant tailors from Montmartre who refused the union's back-to-work directive. In 1916 it was the strike committee led by Gorodetsky that was at odds with the union leadership and a part of the striking workers. For the police this immigrant activity was no secret. On numerous occasions they commented on what they saw as foreign troublemakers, the immigrant strike leaders being known for their "advanced ideas."

This relative "advancement" of the immigrant leaders could only make the French union uncomfortable. Leaders such as Gorodetsky threatened the union's hegemony in strike matters. Perhaps it was due to the imported radicalism discussed above, or perhaps it was simply due to the double oppression on worker and immigrant that led to a greater exasperation on the part of certain immigrant workers. In either case, the immigrant workers, less circumscribed by an established union structure, could at times be more combative or more intransigent than the French workers or their representative institution.

This difference of attitude spilled over into the political realm as well. The immigrants' own experience and their continued ties with the home country resulted in a political consciousness and a willingness to express those ideas that conflicted with the French union's ideal of trade union activity. The C.G.T.'s Amiens Charter of 1906 officially proscribed the involvement of the union in party politics, a position with which Pierre Dumas, president of the garment workers' union, agreed. He emphasized that the union's role should be purely economic rather than political, that it should be kept out of Socialist hands, and that it should be organized around a strictly corporative basis.[13] The Intersketsionen Byuro and *Der idisher arbayter* were both criticized for not adhering to this injunction, and dissensions within the ranks broke out over this issue. The Jewish tailors' section, defending, like Dumas, a revolutionary syndical strategy to the exclusion of political issues, published an open protest against the Intersektsionen Byuro in the March 8, 1913, issue of *Der idisher arbayter*. The tailors protested a meeting that had been organized by the Byuro at which a certain Moishe Katz had lectured on the latest

events in Russia. This, the tailors argued, had nothing to do with the French
or general labor movement. However, this protest was in turn harshly
criticized in the same issue by "B.S." (B. Sobol, later treasurer of the paper),
who argued that, on the contrary, the Jewish workers' movement should not
be reduced to a *groshn-kamf*, or bread-and-butter struggle.

Indeed, the pages of *Der idisher arbayter* exhibit the wide variety of issues
raised, from the "Alveltlekhe khronik" (international news column) to the
coming war. And the Jewish workers organized meetings to protest the Dreyfus affair, the tsar's visit to France in 1901, and the Russian Beilis affair. As
World War I approached, the militant pacifism of a large number of the
Jewish immigrants would be one more political bone of contention between
them and the French revolutionary syndicalists.[14] These different perceptions
of the political role of the trade union structure (and an insistence on a
pacifist stand even after the French socialists had voted war credits) were one
more element separating the Jewish immigrants from the French labor movement.

However, the discomfort the French unions could feel with regard to
immigrant workers went much deeper than institutional constraints or
French-immigrant leadership struggles over tactics and strategies. The premise of ideological unity was threatened by the division of labor already described, which would bring immigrant workers into conflict with their fellow
workers. More generally it was threatened by the ambiguous position of the
immigrant in French society. This latter, in the case of Jewish immigrants,
often translated as anti-Semitism.

Anti-Semitism in the period under study, while largely the domain of
the petite-bourgeoisie, nevertheless flared from time to time among the workers.[15] Demonstrations incited by the anti-Dreyfusards at the time of the Affair
brought the sounds of *"Mort aux Juifs!"* to the streets in the fall of 1898.
Stephen Wilson's study of the subscribers to the Henry Monument (in memory of the forger of the documents which incriminated Dreyfus, who com-
mitted suicide in his prison cell) points to a significant number of workers and
artisans who thus manifested their hatred or resentment of the Jews.[16] The
July 1899 Conseillers Prud'homme meeting cited above felt the need to
protest "energetically against certain workers who, under the pretext of nationality or religion, systematically shut out Jewish workers who come to
their shops looking for work."[17] However, the Affair itself remained largely a
struggle between different factions of the ruling class, and in the following
period leading up to World War I references to anti-Semitic incidents among
workers are sporadic.

The position of the organized French labor movement with regard to
anti-Semitism is a complicated one that cannot be dealt with in detail here.[18]
The Conseillers Prud'homme resolution was at least a symbolic attempt to
rout anti-Semitism. However, at the same time the group of Jewish workers
already mentioned wrote their open *Lettre* to the French Socialists criticizing

their weak stance with regard to the Dreyfus affair. The Socialists were accused of ignoring the "immense, eternal and universal proletariat" that was the Jewish proletariat and of regarding anti-Semitism as a "profitable ill" onto which socialism could later easily be grafted.[19] The Jewish workers concluded:

> In the name of this fraternity of misery, . . .
> In the name of the entire people which is the Jewish proletariat, which from all the corners of the globe turns its eyes toward you, and looks to you as its defenders,
> We ask your aid and support![20]

It was, however, largely through the Affair, especially after the turning point of Zola's *J'accuse* letter of 1898, that the French Socialists began a rethinking of the Jewish question. While anti-Semitism among socialists throughout the nineteenth century had often been expressed as an equation between anti-capitalism and anti-Semitism, aiming at the attainments of the assimilated Jewish bourgeoisie, the Dreyfus affair revealed the reactionary, antirepublican uses to which anti-Semitism could be put and thus led to its eventual denunciation by the Socialists. While the Guesdists continued to insist that the Dreyfus affair was an internal quarrel among the bourgeoisie that need not concern the working class, Jaurès led the way in condemning anti-Semitism and also bringing attention to the oppressed conditions of the Jews in Algeria.[21] At the same time articles in *La Revue socialiste* began to take note of the Jewish proletariat in Rumania and elsewhere. As a result of the Affair as well as in response to the oppression and emigration of eastern European Jews, the crucial distinction between a Jewish bourgeoisie and a Jewish proletariat came to be recognized, and the latter defended by the French Socialists.

The purging of leftist anti-Semitism through the experience of the Dreyfus affair did not occur without relapses, however. In October 1910 an important railroad strike took place against the Chemin de Fer du Nord, the shares of which were mostly owned by the Rothschild family. On April 3, 1911, at a meeting of the electric workers' union where Emile Janvion was speaking on "Free-masonry and the Working Class," Emile Pataud, secretary of the union, used the word "Jew" as synonymous with foe of the working class. Although no record of the meeting itself is extant, the anti-Semitic character of Pataud's remarks became infamous in the outrage that followed the meeting. Articles in *L'Humanité* and *La Guerre sociale* sharply attacked Pataud, and nearly two thousand Jewish workers showed up at a protest meeting organized by the capmakers', furworkers', and leatherworkers' unions and the Bund, held at the Bourse du Travail on April 6. Anti-Semitism was denounced as a sin, and the motto of the International was recalled: to organize all workers without distinction of sex, race, or religion. Alongside the Bundist Mark Liber there was the French Socialist Jean Longuet, who began his speech with "The French Socialist Party is with you, Jewish workers!"[22] When Pataud tried to defend himself, saying that he had only meant to attack the big Jewish financiers as capitalists, he was booed in disbelief, and a resolution was passed "desolidarizing" those present with the citizen Pataud. A week later the anarchists held a similar meeting (organized by Sébastien Faure) at the Bourse du travail and called for yet another meeting two weeks later under the auspices of the clothing workers' union. Two years later, *Der idisher arbayter* described the Pataud-Janvion affair as second only to the Dreyfus affair in helping purge the French left of anti-Semitism.[23]

Only eight months after the Pataud affair, however, a tailor wrote in to *La Guerre sociale* (the socialist-revolutionary paper edited by Gustave Hervé) complaining that the competition of Jewish tailors had caused him to lose his job, and that if there were an anti-Semitic movement he would join it.[24] One of the fundamental bases to this form of anti-Semitism can thus be seen: anti-Semitism as protectionism. As Bernard-Lazare wrote in his work on anti-Semitism, it was not always the Jew but often the immigrant worker who was the butt of anti-Semitic attacks.[25] In effect, it was the job competition discussed above, between indigenous and foreign labor, which largely characterized whatever rank-and-file animosity existed toward the Jewish immigrants.

Faced with this situation of workers' competition, the French union more often than not supported the "protection of national work," i.e., protection of French labor. It was this protectionism that lay at the crux of the contradictions that affected relations between the French labor movement and the Jewish as well as all other immigrant workers in Paris. If on the one hand the unity of all workers, regardless of sex, race, nationality, or religion, was idealized, on the other hand the protection of French workers' interests first and foremost sometimes led to ambivalent, if not sometimes hostile, opinions with regard to immigrant labor.

Theoretically, the problem of immigrant labor was situated within international economic developments, as Gaetan Pirou pointed out in an article in *La Revue socialiste* of May 15, 1912. That is, with the growing encouragement of "external" migration to fill industrial labor needs, which were no longer adequately met through "internal" migration, this "external" migration brought with it the "immigrant problem" to which the labor movement, in its concern for both French workers and the international proletariat, had to respond. If for the Ministry of Labor the cause was clear—it was the immigrants who "come to Paris to compete with French laborers and *provoke* a considerable lowering of salaries"[26]—for the French Socialists the blame of provocation lay elsewhere. As Jaurès said before the Chamber of Deputies on February 17, 1894:

We protest against the invasion of foreign workers who come here to work for cheap wages [*travailleurs au rabais*]. And here there must be no misunderstanding; we do not intend, we who are internationalists, to arouse animosities of jealous chauvinism among manual workers from different countries, no; but what we do not want is that international capital seek out labor on the market where it is the most debased, humiliated, depreciated, to cast it onto the French market without control and without regulation, and to bring salaries everywhere in the world to their lowest level.[27]

Yet misunderstandings were not always easy to avoid. Emile Pouget, a well-known revolutionary syndicalist, responded to the complaining tailor in *La Guerre sociale* by writing that "Jewish infiltration is one aspect of the issue of foreign competition," and that the Jews' solidarity leads to their "insinuation" into a workshop once one of their members has "penetrated" it.[28] Needless to say, this answer provoked several letters of criticism, to which Pouget was compelled to respond two issues later. The title of his second article, "La question des étrangers—Le péril antisémite," marked a significant change of tone from the first, "La question des étrangers—L'invasion." Although Pouget began this apology in rather suspect terms, saying that he did not want the "sensitive skins" of "our Jewish comrades" to "shudder" any longer and that blind philo-Semitism was no better than blind anti-Semitism, he went on to commend the Jewish militants who had written in. He reiterated that the essential battle to be fought was that against the bosses, while the double peril of anti-Semitism and nationalism had to be exorcised.[29]

This still equivocal response hardly settled the issue. A hatters' convention in 1912 lamented the influx of foreigners that led to overproduction and the lowering of wages. Parisian woodworkers blamed foreign workers for driving down prices with inferior goods, which drove down wages as well.[30] At the International Congress of Needle Workers held in Vienna July 15–19, 1913, the French Clothing Workers' Federation asked the International to halt immigration to Paris for one year. Pierre Dumas, secretary of the French federation, defended this position before the Jewish workers in the July 5, 1913, issue of *Der idisher arbayter*, by arguing that the function of the federation within France had often been a regulatory one—warning tailors not to move to a certain community if a strike was in progress or if unemployment was high there. It followed, according to Dumas, that the same principles should be applied on an international scale, given that the overabundance of clothing workers in Paris, largely due to foreigners, was driving wages down.[31]

The protectionist issue was thus twofold: affecting both jobs per se and, more frequently, wages. Pottier, who wrote favorably of the Jewish immigrants, dismissed both aspects of the argument by stating that since immigrant wages were so low French workers lost nothing by being displaced from those jobs anyway.[32] However, the xenophobic response was (and is to this day) to inhibit immigration and thereby safeguard national jobs. This the labor movement could not countenance. Thus, while speaking of the "invasion" (a term used by xenophobes, Socialists, the Jewish bourgeoisie, and "displaced" workers alike) of immigrants, the third national corporative congress of the Syndicats ouvriers de France in Bordeaux in 1888 passed a resolution against the expulsion or limitation of foreign labor.[33] In general, the French Socialists voted against all measures aimed at restricting immigration, at imposing taxes on the immigrants or their employers, etc.

However, rather than tackle the job side of the issue, at least one Socialist came up with a proposal to solve the wage-depression issue instead with a minimum wage law.[34] Legislation for a minimum wage was proposed in 1906 and again in 1910 by the Socialist deputy Jules Coutant, who argued that a legal minimum wage was the only way to ensure equal wages regardless of the workers' nationality, religion, or sex. By thus wanting to regulate the employers' wage offers, Coutant clearly pointed out who was doing the "provoking" of lowered wages.

No such law was ever passed in the period before World War I, however, and the French labor movement's defense of immigrant laborers remained in the realm of ideology more than practice. International solidarity continued to be the theoretical ideal, repeated throughout all strike actions along with the imperative of workers' unity and organization. Yet in the face of contradictions arising from labor protectionism, in the face of the realities of the division of labor within the workshop, and perhaps in response to a certain "atavistic racial rancor" as described by Gemähling and fed by the structured competition among the workers, when it came to organizing, the immigrants felt the need to do so separately.[35]

The implications of that separate organizing were multiple. On the one hand it reflected perhaps the diffuse, imported Bundist ideology discussed in the last chapter. On the other hand, the separate union sections derived from a double set of conditions in Paris: the at times ambiguous position of the French Left with regard to immigrant labor, and the particular conditions in the Pletzl, which only the Jewish immigrants themselves could interpret and mobilize against. Thus the Jewish labor movement in Paris was constructed both negatively vis-à-vis the French labor movement and positively as an outgrowth of the immigrant community. What resulted was a dual language similar to that of the French left, with precepts of theoretical unity coming into conflict with the reality of separate organizational forms. The "national question" as seen from the Pletzl meant that this duality between theory and practice had to be bridged. More importantly, it meant that the reality of the separate Yiddish sections had to be rationalized and explained to the C.G.T.

THE "NATIONAL QUESTION" IN THE PLETZL

The expression of the Jewish labor movement's community identity is seen most clearly in *Der idisher arbayter*, the Jewish labor paper whose repeated theme was unity with French workers and with their most representative organization, the C.G.T. *Der idisher arbayter's* polemic with the C.G.T. and its recognition of the contradictions between theoretical workers' unity and the practicality of separate Jewish union sections reveal the "identity problem" of class and community that the Jewish union sections represented. Proclamations of class unity and the reality of community specificity were synthesized in the paper's columns while *Der idisher arbayter* implicitly addressed the problematic issue raised in the *Lettre des ouvriers juifs* over a decade earlier. The class struggle alone could not suffice for the Jewish immigrant workers; the issues of exploitation *within* the community had to be addressed.

The tenth issue of the paper set out the following goals for a workers' paper: (1) to mirror the life of the workers; (2) to spread news about the worldwide proletariat; (3) to address the burning issues of the day, particularly as they affected proletarian life; and (4) to develop class consciousness. The first three would further the last and most important of the paper's goals.

The first of these aims was well attended in the paper's "Fakh korespondentsye" column, which occupied at least one-quarter of the space in each issue of the large-format, four-page paper (there were some complaints that this was still not enough space for trade news, however). This column gave members of the different trades an opportunity to write in about their particular working conditions, about strikes under way, etc., and such correspondence was often signed merely *"an alter arbeter"* (an old worker), *"ekhod mehapoalim"* (one of the workers), or "Abraham *der Mashiner*" (Abraham the machine operator).

The Yiddish paper also served to disseminate information about the worldwide proletariat and about the French labor movement in particular. An international workers' news column reported on strikes and workers' activities in various countries; there were reports on international Socialist and labor congresses, on affairs in eastern Europe (especially instances of repression, the Beilis affair, etc.), and, as the war approached, growing concern over its likelihood.

Even more importance was given, however, to the "life and struggles" of the French proletariat. *Der idisher arbayter* served as an important communication medium to explain the "burning" issues of the French labor movement to the Jewish immigrants. As Losovsky stated in the first editorial: "Before coming here we knew of the blood that had been shed during the French Revolution and the Commune for the freedom of the working class, but now we must come to understand contemporary conditions in France."[36] The first two issues of the paper contained lengthy articles explaining the organizational structure of the C.G.T. and the value of its revolutionary-syndicalist ideology. A series of articles by the Polish socialist Sofia Posner examined French syndicalism, while French labor leaders such as Léon Jouhaux, A. Roux, Georges Yvetot, and A. Savoie contributed articles to the paper explaining various aspects of the French labor movement's struggles.[37] *Der idisher arbayter* carried reports of the C.G.T. congresses, and it supported the C.G.T.'s demand for the eight-hour day and the English work week. It urged participation in French May Day celebrations and supported the C.G.T.'s call to a one-day general strike on December 16, 1912, to protest the oncoming war. *Der idisher arbayter* (run by many who themselves had undoubtedly fled the tsar's military service) also published the C.G.T. manifesto and several articles against the 1913 law increasing military service to three years. Articles on proposed workers' legislation also provided an important information service to the Jewish immigrants while such proposals were interpreted along revolutionary-syndicalist lines, arguing that the only real betterment of the workers' condition would come through the efforts of the workers' themselves and the downfall of capitalism.

Der idisher arbayter's concern for French affairs certainly derived in large part from its close alliance with the C.G.T. and its clear interest in those aspects of life relating to the day-to-day struggle of the immigrants in France. However, it should be noted that this French-oriented stance distinguished the Yiddish trade union movement both from the nonpolitical Yiddish papers and from the majority of Russian-Jewish Social-Democrats, who looked mainly to events in Russia for inspiration. *Der idisher arbayter* recognized the permanence of the immigrants' position in France and addressed itself to the concrete problems of existence within that context.

The most important of the paper's goals, the development of class consciousness among the Jewish immigrant workers in Paris, was urged on every page with calls to unity and organization. In the very first editorial of October 9, 1911, Losovsky wrote:

> Jewish workers in Paris!!! . . . [to those] men and women who have been torn from their homes, and who are exploited in Parisian workshops. . . . [In the] struggle for a better life [and] for freedom from the capitalist yoke, the union of workers from all workshops, from all trades and from all lands [is necessary].

Virtually every article in the three years of the paper's existence was an appeal to the benefits of solidarity and the strength in unity through which the Jewish workers could better their condition.

The organization so urged was to be within the C.G.T. On the masthead of *Der idisher arbayter*, alongside the motto "Workers have nothing to lose but their chains" was the maxim "In unity is there strength." The underlying theme of the paper was "hant bay hant mit unzere frantseyzishe khaveyrim . . . zeyer tsore iz unzer tsore"; "zayn kamf iz unzer kamf; zayn tsukunft iz unzer tsukunft" (hand in hand with our French brothers . . . their misery is our misery; [the French movement's] struggle is our struggle; its future is our future).[38]

The importance of immigrant solidarity with French workers was stressed from the first editorial in which Losovsky continued that the greatest goal for the Jewish workers was to join their Jewish union sections with the general workers' movement. In the second issue Losovsky stressed the commonality of the Jewish workers' and French workers' oppression: Jewish workers are exploited like their French comrades [*khaveyrim*]; to stand aside is a sin. The rising cost of living hits the Jewish workers just as the French, doesn't it? Are Jewish wages higher? No! Some say, why should I protest? I am not French. No, but you are a worker. You are not a French citizen, but you are exploited by French capital. "A klas kegn a klas!" (Class against class!) We must struggle hand in hand with our French comrades.[39]

The purpose of organizing the Jewish workers was thus a double one: to raise the consciousness and consolidate the unity of the Jewish workers as workers in opposition to their Jewish bosses but also to prove the immigrants' solidarity with French workers and with the French labor movement. It was this latter function that was the more problematic, as revealed through the sense of malaise that often comes through *Der idisher arbayter*'s proclamations. Insistence on workers' unity, in fact, sometimes rings of "protesting too much." The paper reflected while it addressed two sorts of criticisms formulated against the Jewish immigrant workers: criticism of their not being class conscious and criticism, if class conscious, of organizing separately.

With regard to the former, on more than one occasion the Jewish workers were specifically exhorted to organize in order to counter accusations coming from the French movement. One immigrant, for example, urged his compatriots to organize because the French workers see you as *"opgeshtanene finstere"* (backward, obscurantist) creatures.[40] In the second issue of *Der idisher arbayter* (November 17, 1911) the secretary of the French woodworkers' union, Toussaint, wrote to urge Jewish woodworkers to unionize, for he warned them that the Parisian woodworkers saw the Jewish workers as using strikes in the trade to their own advantage: to get more orders for themselves or to be hired as strikebreakers. The Jewish woodworkers responded in the next issue (the first one in which their section appears on the paper's masthead) by declaring, "We are not strikebreakers; the Jewish woodworkers must be seen as a special category; and in fact we are 'shamefully misunderstood.'" Then, addressing the Jewish woodworkers themselves, the latter were urged to join the Jewish section and thus defend themselves against any future accusations.

Organization of the Jewish workers and solidarity with the French labor movement were thus often explicitly recommended not only as valuable in themselves but in order to defend the Jewish workers from the common array of complaints against immigrant workers (as competing with indigenous labor, taking away jobs, lowering wages, etc.). The very existence of the Intersektsionen Byuro and *Der idisher arbayter* was given as proof of workers' unity and that the immigrants were not all strikebreakers without any consciousness. Although it can hardly be argued that an all-Yiddish paper was directly addressing a non–Yiddish-reading audience, this defensive function of the paper was nonetheless an important one. And that proof addressed to the French labor movement of the Jewish workers' solidarity was an important function of the Jewish labor movement itself.

The creation of the Intersektsionen Byuro and *Der idisher arbayter* was hailed enthusiastically by French labor leaders. In the very first issue of the paper "brotherly greetings" were addressed to the "Jewish comrades" by A. Roux of the Hatters' Federation. The garment workers' union voted 100 francs to its Jewish section in 1912 to help launch the Yiddish paper, and Pierre Dumas, the union's secretary, sent a letter of congratulations on the paper's twenty-fifth issue.[41] (Greetings were also sent from the German immigrants in Paris by Paul Riebke of the Deutschen Arbeiter Kartel.)

However, regardless of the will to unity repeated in the pages of *Der idisher arbayter*, the actual organization of the immigrants took place within foreign-language sections of the C.G.T., described variously as the Yiddish section "by" *(baym)* the French union; the Yiddish section "under the direction" *(unter der laytung)* of the French union; or merely "the Jewish section" (either *section israélite* or *section juive*). For in spite of fervent and impassioned appeals to class unity and workers' brotherhood regardless of race, religion, or nationality (as the Jews were variously defined), and in spite of the paper's role as primary vehicle for organizing the Jewish sections *within* the C.G.T. in order to concretize that unity, concrete solidarity took the form of Yiddish-speaking union sections. Declarations of workers' unity thus often seem to be attempts to minimize the ideological contradictions represented in these "by" or "under the direction" formulations.

If it was well and good that immigrant workers should begin to organize, should they do so separately? Did that not reinforce their separateness rather than integrating them fully into the national proletariat? This problem was not a new one for the Jewish labor movement, as has been seen, and all of *Der idisher arbayter*'s proclamations of workers' unity in general and of unity between the French and Jewish immigrant workers in particular still did not shield the immigrant workers from criticisms of separatism. For May Day 1914 the C.G.T. had to ask the Jewish immigrants not to march separately but to join the French paraders as one.[42]

Even when criticisms concerning the consciousness of the Jewish immigrant workers were answered by the existence of a growing Jewish labor movement, the fact that such consciousness was expressed separately, in the Yiddish-speaking sections, raised problems. The contradictions inherent in the very medium—Yiddish—by which this solidarity was expressed underlay the often defensive posture of *Der idisher arbayter*. Consequently, the reasons for that separation had to be addressed, and they ranged from language to working conditions to the community character of the Jewish labor conflict itself.

Language

The most obvious justification for separate immigrant organizations—and for the Jewish workers this was no exception—is language. Language represents the most basic level of immigrant difference from native workers while it also symbolizes the immigrant culture as a whole. Language was not only a barrier to a more complete understanding of workers' issues and to full participation in the French labor movement, but it was a factor isolating the Jewish worker. However, it was also a factor that could only be overcome through its own means. When the suggestion of a separate Jewish tailors' section was first raised, it was argued that the very exploitation of the immigrant workers came from their ignorance of Parisian wages due to the language barrier and the immigrants' newness to the city. The furworkers explained elsewhere that they had not taken part in the 1901 strike in their trade because they had not understood the issues involved. The language barrier was given as the basic reason behind separate leatherworkers' and bakers' union sections. In the latter case, opposition from the French bakers' union led to an explicit understanding that the separate organization of the Jewish bakers was due to language alone and was only justifiable for propaganda purposes, to which it would be confined.[43]

In fact, the primary role of the (separate) Jewish labor movement, of the Intersektsionen byuro and of the Yiddish sections within the C.G.T., was said to be that of *agitatsye un propagande,* of which *Der idisher arbayter,* along with numerous Yiddish leaflets, was the crucial expression. Although learning French was surely desirable, it could not be learned from one day to the next, and in fact, wrote one Jewish worker, we are too exploited to have the time to learn it.[44] Consequently, since French leaflets would be useless and the C.G.T. clearly could not write Yiddish ones itself, it was up to the Jewish workers' sections to handle their own Yiddish media. In this context, *agitatsye un propagande* were seen to be *Der idisher arbayter*'s and the sections' very *raison d'être.*

Working Conditions

Justification of separateness based on language problems alone did not completely explain the immigrant situation, however. The Jewish workers did indeed need their own "propaganda" arm, but not only for the form—Yiddish—of their grievances. Yiddish union sections were also necessary to explain the particular content of the Jewish immigrants' struggles. The argument, which attempted theoretically to separate strictly propaganda from other union activities, was incomplete. It was not merely language that necessitated distinct organizational forms but also the specific conditions resulting from the immigrants' role in the economy.

The "specific exploitation" of the Jewish worker, different from the conditions that obtained between French workers and their compatriot employers, was referred to on several occasions in *Der idisher arbayter*. This specificity was in fact so apparent to the readers that it was rarely defined. When defined, these conditions were none other than those of the putting-out system that have already been described: homework, piece wages, exigent demands of overtime, and low pay.[45] For not only language but the putting-out system also isolated the immigrant worker and created unique conditions necessitating particular means of labor organizing. As Parisian workers in light industry gravitated toward larger and larger workshops and small factories, immigrant laborers were attracted to the transitional economic form of home industry and the putting-out system, and they needed a particular forum by which to express that economic role. Furthermore, concentration not only isolated the immigrants from their French counterparts but also created specific issues that were not always those of the latter.

As has been seen, during the large tailors' strike against piecework in 1901 the issue at hand was clearly not the same for the workers in the center of Paris as for the Jewish tailors of Montmartre. In the first case piecework represented the undercutting of (French, largely female) workshop workers by (immigrant and female) homeworkers working for lower piece wages. But for the Jewish tailors on Montmartre the piecework issue represented above all the exploitation of the Jewish immigrant homeworker by Jewish immigrant contractors.[46]

Thus not only the concentration of immigrants in a certain economic sector but the specific conditions of work pertaining to immigrant workers—homeworkers often in a more precarious position than their French counterparts—necessitated specially immigrant forms of expression and organization, to which *Der idisher arbayter* often attested.

Jew vs. Jew

Finally, one other factor impelling the separate Jewish labor organizations was revealed with astonishment by Paul Pottier in his exploration of the misery of the Marais. *"Où est-elle la solidarité juive?"* (Where is this Jewish solidarity?) he cried.[47] The exploitation of the Jewish worker by the Jewish employer was an element of surprise to any observer, Jewish or not, ingrained with notions of Jewish solidarity or unaware of the patterns of immigrant labor recruitment leading to the congregation of immigrant bosses and workers in certain trades.

The labor recruitment advantages of intracommunity hiring have already been examined. Both employer and employee benefited from the lower costs of information facilitating hiring within the immigrant group. However, the community character of the work context could not be allowed to mislead, warned the Bonneffs in examining the capmakers: "Even though the workers and bosses are of the same origin and belong to the same race, the social conflicts are just as bitter, just as violent in this industry as in the others."[48]

For Yankel Mykhanowitzki, hero of *Les eaux mêlées,* the realization of the hypocrisy behind the boss's paternalistic offer of a cup of tea before asking him to come in to work on Saturday was a harsh disappointment:

> These Jewish bosses that he sought out in the belief that they would be more humane, more fraternal toward a compatriot, but they were the worst of the exploiters! They took advantage of the misery and ignorance of the poor immigrants in order to impose famine wages upon them. . . . A boss who was a compatriot and philanthropic, who spoke Yiddish and treated you as a comrade, offered you cups of tea and exploited you.[49]

In their strike of 1913 the Jewish bakers accused their (Jewish) bosses of exercising the "privilege" of treating their workers so badly and with such awful working conditions that they would bring a "shudder even to . . . a French boss."[50] "The question of race is a mystification," said one worker after a 1902 strike in the Marais. He continued:

> Everything gives way before interest. One would have to be a journalist, that is, someone unfamiliar with the problems of work [a dig at his interlocutor?], in order to assume that an employer takes into consideration the religion of his employee or worker. . . . [Even the bosses are fighting among themselves.] A pretty farce is this Jewish solidarity. Everyone must look out for himself, and that's that.[51]

The *bavustzinike* (literally conscious) workers thus expressed their class consciousness by rejecting the paternalism of the small, neighborhood workshops. Strikes within the Jewish immigrant workshops were expressions of class, and this expression of a class interest as against a religious one was crystallized in the May Day slogans of the Jewish immigrant paraders: "*veyniker zmires un mer lokshn, veyniker arbet un mer loyn*" (fewer hymns and more noodles, less work and more pay).[52]

However, while thus explicitly expressing the class character of the struggle, the intracommunity nature of the immigrant conflicts was also clearly revealed. The Jewish labor movement was formed as a class response to the community-based solidarity proffered by the bosses, but it was nonetheless a class movement defined with reference to the immigrant community. Those *bavustzinike* workers who did organize against their Jewish immigrant bosses were rejecting not an ethnic or religious identity per se but rather the paternalistic model of workplace solidarity encouraged in the immigrant milieu. The paternalist strategy had to be combatted with another interpretation of community-based solidarity, that of the workers' alone. Thus the cleavage between immigrant boss and immigrant worker, which became apparent with every strike, was a cleavage that took place within the immigrant community framework. Although a bond based on the "community of suffering" had been burst between immigrant boss and worker, the eruption still did not go beyond the community framework, and it was within that framework that it had to be resolved. The intracommunity nature of the immigrant conflicts largely defined the character of the Jewish labor movement. And it is for this reason that a separate labor organization, within the C.G.T. but not entirely of it, was necessary. For means of expression as well as for the content of that expression, the Jewish labor movement represented a variation on workers' unity that is important to the immigrant context.

Class and Community

Finally, the community parameter of the Jewish labor movement was due not only to the internal nature of the conflicts involved but to the movement's interrelationship with immigrant culture as well. Not only could the immigrant workers emphasize their class interest vis-à-vis their immigrant bosses without rejecting their immigrant culture, but they could and did use that culture as an important component of the Jewish labor movement itself.

The community context of the Jewish labor movement may be described as ethnic, geographic, and psychological. It included the cultural, and to a certain extent, religious, uniqueness of the Jewish workers. It was circumscribed within the small space of the immigrant neighborhoods, and it drew upon the collective memory of the migration experience. This community identity had an important effect on the actual waging of struggles within the Jewish immigrant context, for community ties could and did help reinforce class solidarity.

The importance of community was for too long ignored in studies of class interest, the former being considered inimical to the latter. Yet recent studies have begun to illuminate the cultural or social context of labor movements, following the path-breaking work of E. P. Thompson. For France, Michelle Perrot has described the strike as a *"fête"* because it serves to assemble people; strike meetings and demonstrations form a part of the collective life of strikers which in some (textile and mining) communities easily turn into family gatherings.[53] Michael Hanagan has pointed to residential concentration and neighborhood cafés as favoring artisanal solidarity, while historians of womens' struggles have also stressed the importance of community networks in those movements.[54]

Strike meetings in the Jewish immigrant community, as elsewhere, were events that called upon popular participation in a way that no official political process could. Attendance at strike meetings was often many times that of the number of strikers involved. Entire families (who were themselves often part of the extended work process) as well as sympathetic nonstrikers came to find out the particulars and to show their support.[55]

Specific incidents also proved the close links possible between community solidarity and the immigrant labor movement. For example, at the time of the death of a worker named Birnbaum in October 1905, the more than five hundred Jewish immigrants who came to pay their last respects at Birnbaum's funeral turned their grief into a protest demonstration against their bosses.[56] Similarly two years later, when the American Yiddish radical poet Morris Rozenfeld was involved in an accident, a committee was formed to collect material and moral support for the renowned poet. This committee joined together all of the often quarreling leftist political factions of the Jewish immigrant community in a unity that presaged the later formation of the Intersektsionen byuro.[57]

Solidarity among trades was also facilitated by the community context and information network within which the labor movement was inserted. When waiters in the Marais were affected by the bakers' strike of 1913 (due to a boycott of restaurants serving scab bread) the latter helped the former to organize and demand better working conditions.[58] During the same strike the bakers sent a communiqué to a meeting of the striking tailors asking for their support, while in another instance the bakers' cooperative turned to the woodworkers' section for its furniture needs.[59] Interimmigrant solidarity was also effected through subscription lists that circulated throughout the immigrant community via *Der idisher arbayter*, during meetings, or at balls in order to raise money to support strikes. One such list on behalf of the striking bakers (in 1913) showed that money had been collected from several Jewish union sections as well as from two Galeries Lafayette workshops, from the German metalworkers, and from the Russian workers' club.[60]

Beyond mutual support among the immigrants as producers, the community context of the labor movement also facilitated solidarity between producers and consumers. Appeals were often made to the community members, as consumers, to support a strike. The barbers asked the workers to be shaved in union shops only. Workers were asked to boycott Ribby's shop (specializing in cheap workers' clothing) in 1913 until he acceded to the strikers' demands. Bakers appealed to consumers to support their strike effort in 1913 just as waiters appealed to potential clients through the pages of *Der idisher arbayter* to stay away from Lander's and Kowarsky's restaurants during conflicts in those two establishments a year later.[61] Two articles in *Der idisher arbayter* also warned against Berezniak's print shop, the source of many a strike leaflet (and the early printer for *Der idisher arbayter* itself), revealing that, contrary to Berezniak's pretensions, his was *not* a union shop; the union sections were urged to take their leaflets elsewhere.[62] Similarly, producers' cooperatives looked first and foremost to the community as the clientele for their bread, caps, etc.

Just as community ties could thus be called upon to strengthen the unity of the labor movement, so could they be called upon to exclude strikebreakers. During strike actions *Der idisher arbayter* or posters were used to discourage strikebreakers by naming them publicly and accusing them of betraying their fellow workers. There were calls to boycott strikebreakers, their families, and even the cafés they frequented.[63] Such appeals could only be expected to have an effect within the context of the small community in which the immigrant workers' actions were situated, for social ostracism was the obverse of community cohesion. Class ties could thus be strengthened through shame of community betrayal. Such community pressure was indeed proven effective on at least two occasions when public apologies were printed in *Der idisher arbayter*. In one case a leatherworker apologized for having gone to work in a boycotted workshop; in another instance someone admitted to having unjustly testified against a union member.[64] While the separate immigrant labor movement thus emanated from the specific conditions of the immigrant community and drew upon the latter to strengthen itself, in turn the movement also reinforced the community from which it evolved. As Ezra Mendelsohn has written with regard to the Jews in the Pale of Settlement in Russia:

> Indeed, the struggle itself, irrespective of the results was vitally important. . . .
> A raise of two kopeks a week or a reduction in the workday from fourteen to twelve hours, might be won today and lost tomorrow, but the feeling of pride and exhilaration derived from the struggle was a permanent gain.[65]

In Paris, too, the immigrant community's labor organization served another purpose besides that which was its ostensible goal. The movement functioned not only for the future material betterment of the workers but offered an immediate cultural and social role to the community, which was invaluable.

Articles in *Der idisher arbayter* explicitly aimed at the "moral development" of the Jewish workers.[66] The paper urged the founding of a workers' library and stressed the importance of cultural actions alongside the day-to-day struggle, crying out that men are not just machines that have to be fed and housed, but are higher beings—*kultur-mentshn*—with consequently special needs. The furworkers' section talked of organizing cultural circles, while the woodworkers' section held occasional meetings on such topics as health problems and set up drawing classes.[67] Even the prizes offered in the newspaper's lottery seemed to have an educational purpose: three-month subscriptions to a variety of newspapers including Russian or Yiddish papers from St.

Petersburg, Warsaw, Vilna, New York, and London, as well as *L'Humanité* and the *Bataille syndicaliste*; copies of plays by playwrights including Peretz, Asch, Mendele Mokher Sforim, and Ibsen; as well as the memoirs of Kropotkin and the Erfurt Program printed by the Bund.[68]

In addition to the newspaper itself and the thousands of leaflets that are mentioned in the paper's budgets (which must have represented an important means of communication within the relatively limited geographic area of the Pletzl), numerous balls, fairs, concerts, and literary evenings were sponsored by the Intersektsionen byuro and the trade union sections. The labor movement's involvement in Yiddish theater has been described in chapter 3 above. Furthermore, groups such as the Yiddish "Friends of the *Bataille syndicaliste*" (the French anarchosyndicalist newspaper) or "Friends of *Der idisher arbayter*" sponsored balls or plays as fund-raisers. The Socialist-Zionist Workers' Organization in Paris held yearly May balls, and the Bundist cultural group "Kemfer" organized an annual Purim ball, while the Russian Social-Democrats as well as the Bundists in Paris held anniversary parties for the founding of their respective parties in Russia.

These gatherings were both fund-raising events and meeting places for the immigrant community. If mutual aid benefits were contested as a strategy for workers' unity, concerts, balls, and plays were not. The cultural production of the Jewish immigrant community, as expressed in these plays, libraries, newspapers, and even leaflets was encouraged by the Jewish labor movement and became an integral part of it. *Der idisher arbayter* not only served as a forum for advertising cultural events within the immigrant workers' community while pursuing its own explicitly "cultural politics," but it too was a cultural product of the movement.

The immigrant labor movement thus both emanated from and was a reflection of three factors: language, working conditions in the trades in which the immigrants were concentrated, and the intramigrant nature of most struggles. These factors necessitated specific forms of labor organization for means of expression as well as for the content of that expression. The Jewish labor press that promoted unity with the C.G.T. nonetheless also attested on every page to the importance of the community network for the immigrant worker and the immigrant labor movement.

The Jewish labor movement looked to the Jewish immigrant workers' community for support and drew from that community the specificity that distinguished it both from the immigrant bosses and from the French labor movement. Pride is evident in the pages of *Der idisher arbayter*, pride not only that the Jewish workers had begun to organize, but also in the growing strength of the community of Jewish workers in Paris, in all of its economic and cultural manifestations. Labor movements, among other things, provide an opportunity for the *prise de parole* (speaking up) of workers.[69] The Jewish labor movement was the *prise de parole* of a hitherto silent immigrant community, and *Der idisher arbayter* was its voice.

CONCLUSION

On December 22 and 25, 1912, the second conference of the Jewish labor movement in Paris took place (the first one having been that which organized the Intersektsionen Byuro and launched *Der idisher arbayter* over a year before). The tenth issue of *Der idisher arbayter*, reporting this conference, was exultant: *"Di kinder-yorn zaynen farbay"*; the infancy of the Jewish workers' movement was now over. Moving speeches, beaming faces, trembling voices, and a *royter fodem* (red thread) ran through the conference meetings, which attracted 150 to 200 people in addition to the 30 delegates.

However, the scope and success of the Jewish labor movement in Paris must not be exaggerated. While two thousand copies were printed for the first issue of *Der idisher arbayter*, subsequent issues ran only one thousand copies. A mere fifteen hundred of the thirty-five thousand Jewish immigrants in Paris in 1912 belonged to the capmakers' union and union sections combined.[1] The last issue of *Der idisher arbayter* (just before the war) was a triumphant one in which French and even foreign labor leaders congratulated the paper, as it did itself, for its efforts at organizing immigrant workers. Yet at the same time the editors complained that the paper's existence had been a difficult one and that wide support among the masses was lacking.

The fight against indifference among union workers was perhaps as great as the fight to raise the consciousness of those who had never joined. Com-

plaints of unpaid dues, lack of interest, and poor attendance at union meetings were repeated in *Der idisher arbayter's* pages. The Intersektsionen Byuro
even reproached each of the union sections by name (in hopes of embarrassing them into action?), e.g., Shoemakers and leatherworkers, why haven't
you paid your dues? Capmakers, why haven't your delegates come to our
meetings? (Interestingly enough, by 1914 even the capmakers' union was
accused of disaffection and egotism, i.e., of leading a corporatist struggle to
the detriment of the more general Jewish workers' movement, a falling-out
that seems to correspond to Losovsky's retirement from the capmakers' union
in 1913.[2])

The paper's financial difficulties had been evident throughout the
twenty-five issues, although the editors were nonetheless hopeful that the
paper's influence would grow. Then came World War I. Over ten thousand
Jewish immigrants, including many former draft-dodgers from the tsar's military service, went off to war.[3] The Intersektsionen Byuro was dissolved
shortly after the war's outbreak, and *Der idisher arbayter's* twenty-fifth anniversary issue of July 4, 1914, was its last.

Political quarrels and the uneasy relationship with the French labor
movement may have partly accounted for the weakness of the Jewish labor
movement in this period. But the more fundamental cause is both structural
and economic. It lies in the working conditions of the light industrial sector
in which the eastern European Jews labored and in the economic role as
immigrant workers that they were called upon to fulfill. As much as this study
reveals about the conditions of the Jewish immigrant workers in Paris from
1881 to 1914 it is also an important case study in the difficulties of organizing
immigrant labor in general.

The material conditions of the Jewish immigrant workers' lot in Paris
have been described both from the general context of the French light industrial sector and as revealed in the immigrant strikes. To a large extent the
indifference to union organizing on the part of many workers that was often
criticized in *Der idisher arbayter* must be attributed to the very struggle for
survival, which was the immigrant's major preoccupation. For many the first
task at hand was to save enough to bring over family members from eastern
Europe. "Fight for the union of the proletariat? Yes: but first for the union,
the reunion of one's own, dislocated family."[4]

To the extent that the initial movement of migration was by and large
for the purpose of bettering one's material condition, the relative social
mobility that could be represented by a move from the rue des Ecouffes to the
rue des Francs-Bourgeois or from the Pletzl to Montmartre was important. It
also meant a different mentality with regard to potential labor movement
activity. Migration to the West in and of itself represented a relative betterment of condition, and discontent in the absolute nature of those conditions
would have to be relative to conditions in France.

The struggle for economic survival also had undertones of legal survival. For immigrants, the fear of police intervention in strikes or other protest activity was always implicit.[5] Deportation was the most extreme legal representation of the basic precariousness of the immigrant situation, and it did occur. More importantly the threat of its possibility undoubtedly had a diffuse inhibiting effect on labor organizing. In the period after World War I the possible illegality of the immigrants' situation would become greater as residency and work permit requirements became more stringent.

For the most part, however, the greater insecurity of the immigrants' lot derived from the working conditions themselves. The structural conditions of the trades in which the immigrants found work were powerfully dissuasive factors to labor organization: the seasonality of most of the trades, the debilitating morte-saison and the long hours of the good season, which were the corollary to homework and piecework. Working-class consciousness or educating the immigrant workers as to their "true" interests was no easy task when the worker's most immediately perceived interest was one more cap or cabinet to finish in order to make it through the next morte.

Paternalism, façonniers, and constant arrivals of grine further impeded the efforts of labor leaders. An article in Der idisher arbayter of June 29, 1912, warned against any false illusions as to the boss's paternalism, but on the one hand, hope that the paternalistic aura of the small workshop would translate into material aid if needed kept many workers loyal to their bosses. The other side of paternalism, however, was a fear that by joining a union and therefore explicitly breaking the supposedly familial character of the working conditions, employer retribution—from the hurt father—would be swift. The image of the boss as a khaver (comrade), brother, or father not only implied these hopes and fears of a paternalistic work order but revealed aspirations of upward mobility as well.

The light industrial structure suited the immigrants' needs in several ways. Homework or small compatriot workshops eased the transition to French society. Low skill requirements meant that rapid employment, facilitated by the immigrant network and compatriot contractors, was possible. But furthermore, low capital requirements meant that the possibility of self-employment was also relatively great. The rise and sometimes demise of the façonniers is a case in point, and one that also points to the continual movement of the migration process. Movement does not end once the frontier has been crossed; geographic as well as social mobility was possible even for the first generation. For the façonniers, light industry meant the possibility of movement out of the workers' condition via the path of upward mobility.[6]

The successive arrivals of grine also symbolize the dynamic element of migration. The movement of eastern European Jews westward was a continuous process stretching from the 1880s to 1914 (and recommencing with renewed vigor after World War I). As the grine entered from the East other workers and even labor leaders moved off toward greener pastures in the West. France was often but a stopping point on the westward trail, and the eastern European immigrants, if not seasonal laborers such as the Germans, Italians, or other frontier migrants, nonetheless had their own brand of transiency. It was necessary to perceive France as a long-term (if not permanent) destination and to fight for betterment *sur place*—on the spot—before a labor movement could be effectively organized. If the ultimate goal was only to move on, or, as for many political exiles, to return to Russia, activity with regard to conditions in France would remain difficult to mobilize.

In this dynamic of the immigrant workers' community, Montmartre- or Francs-Bourgeois– (upward) bound workers, disillusioned or *embourgeoisés* revolutionaries, and structural constraints of the work process all competed with the labor movement for the immigrants' attention. Workers' competition, present in any capitalist labor market yet exacerbated by the constant inflow of immigrant labor (grine) and outflow of petit-bourgeois aspirations (façonniers), all troubled the Jewish labor movement in Paris. Paris was but a transit point for many and as such represented an even higher degree of movement, flux, and insecurity than that which generally characterize immigrant workers' communities.

Nonetheless, the slow consolidation of a small Jewish labor movement took place in Paris in the years preceding World War I, and it attests to the consolidation of the community itself. The settling-in process, as evident in the federating of mutual aid societies and the merging of small oratories for the building of a real synagogue, came with the growing numbers of immigrants after 1905 and perhaps with a lessening of any hopes that conditions might in fact ameliorate in Russia. More significantly, the post-1905 immigration was important not only quantitatively but qualitatively. To a greater extent than before political émigrés and trade union leaders formed an important component of the emigration, and if there were those leaders to whom the struggles in France were insignificant, others, such as Losovsky, took an active part in seeking to better conditions wherever the immigrant landed.

The class struggle in the Pletzl was not that of an immigrant Jewish proletariat pitted against a French Jewish bourgeoisie. Examination of the economic relations informing the immigrants' lives reveals a complex web set in the background of developing French industrialization. The French demographic problem, worries over the world market position of the Parisian fashion industry, and the structure of the light industrial sector all created a background conducive to the hiring of immigrant workers. The eastern European emigrants' search for better economic opportunities thus coincided with actual labor needs in the West. However, the terrain on which the subsequent struggles would be waged was that of the Jewish immigrant community itself, from which world markets and French demographics were far removed. This study has aimed at examining the nature of that community and the conflicts that were generated within it. The larger social and economic structures in which Jewish immigrant labor was inserted were the fundamental causes of those conflicts, but it was through the immediate immigrant community that those larger structures would be (literally and figuratively) translated.

Within this context the struggle between the bourgeoisie and the proletariat was displaced. The immediate terrain of struggle was reduced to one between immigrant workers and small-time immigrant bosses as well as among the immigrant workers themselves for job opportunities. The complex work and distribution process joined cutters, sewers, finishers, pressers, contractors, and wholesalers as so many pieces stitched together to form a mini-economy. Yet the multitude of layers—as from a lowly lining to a sumptuous silk—were but so many folds separating labor and capital.

The genesis of a Jewish immigrant labor movement arose directly out of these conditions. But it was also a product of the migration process itself. The push of emigration selected out the more daring, those more willing to break with existing conditions in search for something better. Then, the very hopes raised and implicit in migration were too often frustrated. The search for something better was thus not ended, and for many it took on new forms through workers' organizations.

Thirty-five thousand immigrant Jews was a substantial number, indicating a viable community capable of its own support structures, its own internal conflicts, and its own resolutions. From reading to praying, from celebrating holidays to holding funerals, the immigrants continued their eastern European traditions with only slow and minimal adaptations necessary to the French context. Yiddish newspapers, oratories, and mutual aid and burial societies represented this uneven synthesis of cultures that occurs in the first stage of immigration and, as Ménaché Foïgel complained, reminded him of the *peyes* and caftans of Apukorsova. Yet these organizations created subsets of solidarity important for the immigrant condition. After all, the immigrants might have been foreigners to the French, but for them it was the new country, the French, and the French Jews who were the alien element.

These immigrant societies were also the first step in creating a consciousness that led toward the Jewish labor movement. Oratories, mutual aid societies, political circles, or trade union sections all expressed the immigrants' discontent while offering a positive solution toward changing those conditions. The trade unions consciously aimed at self-determination in the economic sphere just as the oratories and Agoudath Hakehiloth synagogue aimed at self-determination in the religious sphere. In response to the triple handicap—as Jews, as immigrants, and as workers—under which they labored, the Jewish immigrant workers would need their own organizations, surely separate from the French Jewish bourgeoisie but also distinct from if nonetheless within the C.G.T.

The strikes that took place in the Pletzl pitted Jewish workers against their Jewish bosses within the immigrant microcosm. Even if they were the larger economic structures which ultimately organized the labor needs and exploitation of the light industrial sector, it was the immediate "oppressors" and "leeches" against whom the workers turned in protest about their working and—given the sixteen- to eighteen-hour days—living conditions. The workshop bosses or contractors were the "bread-givers," i.e., the "work-givers," and in the instability of seasonal fluctuations it was that function more than any other that represented their power over those they employed. When the class struggle in the Pletzl erupted it was over issues such as hours, wages, workshop conditions, the bosses' "inhumanity" toward the workers, etc. But it was fundamentally a general expression of frustration over the immigrant workers' lot. Those immigrants were Jewish and their strike leaflets were in Yiddish, but Chinese, Turkish, or Yugoslav laborers today would find much in common with their content.

The immigrant labor movement is the dissolution of certain community ties before class ones. Yet, and importantly so, it remains an expression of, and is solidly rooted in, a community network. The Yiddish union sections in Paris at the turn of the century, tiny as some of them may have been, stand proudly at the crossroads of Jewish, French, labor, and migration history. That crossroads reflects the matrix of experience within which the Jewish immigrant laborer must be situated. As workers, as immigrants, as Jews, the population under study had a triple identity that fused in the Jewish labor movement. And, as for any immigrant labor movement, while the basic grievances were class-derived, their consequent manifestations were expressed ethnically. The Jewish immigrants' leaflets were printed in Yiddish, and Hebrew expressions sprinkled the condemnations of their bosses. *Lebn vi got in Frankraykh* (live like God in France)? Not if (s)he had been an immigrant worker in the Pletzl!

Epilogue

Most of the shops [contracting shops, consisting of twenty to forty sewing machines] sew and finish goods that have been cut by the manufacturer. . . . [Sewing machine operators] are paid by the piece, and because they work primarily on low cost garments, they have to churn out a comparatively large amount of work per hour in order to earn an acceptable hourly wage. . . . On the whole, the shops are not well ventilated. . . . New immigrants may feel it is better to accept less than the minimum wage, while gaining experience, than to be out of a job altogether.[8]

The time—the present.
The place—Chinatown, in New York City.
As for France:

> Right now [March 1977] in the Sentier, the garment district of Paris, the battle for the pleated skirt is being waged. . . . For the buyer, it's heaven; he gets the latest fashions just as they hit. . . . For the Sentier, it's cyclical hysteria: periods of devastating lulls alternating with weeks of frenzied activity in which lightning-speed designing and miracles of manufacture are accomplished. *"C'est un métier de fous."* [It's a trade for madmen.][8]

The "miracles of manufacturing," now as at the turn of the century, are most often implemented by immigrants. "There are rumors that the extra help brought in (mostly Yugoslav immigrants) often sleep and work in alternate shifts in the workshops."[9] More recently, one thousand illegal Turkish ready-to-wear workers used the upcoming yearly fashion show (Salon de Prêt-à-Porter) to press for "regularization" of their status.[10]

Whether in the land of the melting pot or in Western Europe today, legal or illegal immigrant labor often functions as the *"volant du travail"*—that loose, movable element of the labor force that is always welcome in the search for lower labor costs, until an economic crisis hits and unemployment grows.[11] The finger of blame is then pointed at the foreigner, and those who have been invited to take part in the industrialization process are asked, bribed, or forced to leave when their usefulness is no longer compatible with economic developments.

Yet the garment industry, still labor-intensive, still vulnerable to seasons and fads, and now worried about foreign competition from cheaper ready-to-wear goods manufactured in the Far East, has retained an economic profile particularly suitable to and desirous of immigrant labor. The garment industry, as a subset of the light industrial sector, offers a fascinating microcosm for the study of migrant labor over time. From the turn of the century, in Paris, in New York, and in London, to the present, immigrants have often been behind the labels marked "Fabriqué en France," "Made in the U.S.A.," etc.

Most migration studies, like the present one, have concentrated on particular migrant populations, highlighting those factors important to each group. Our attentions now may turn in another direction, toward studies of individual industries, and particularly light industry, heretofore little studied, as employers of migrants. Through a comparative social history of the garment industry over time, for example, and as the above quotes show, we should be able to find out just how the structure of an industry continues to shape its labor needs and in what ways they may correspond to immigrant needs. Clearly, those needs are not Jewish-tailor–specific. The legendary Jewish tailor was above all an immigrant worker, since replaced by later generations of immigrants. It is within this context that the foregoing study must now be placed.

APPENDIX A
Immigrant Jews in Paris, 1881–1914

The difficulties in estimating the number of immigrant Jews in Paris date to 1872, when the French Jewish community's assimilation into French citizenry advanced one step farther. In that year the Third Republic decided that religious affiliation was a private matter (a full thirty-four years before the actual separation of church and state) and that consequently it should no longer be asked on the government census. Frenchpersons of the Jewish religion thus became assimilated to all Frenchpersons for statistical purposes—the liberals' gain but the historians' loss. Enumerations of the Jewish population in France since the 1872 census have therefore relied basically on two sources, consistorial records and burial records, both of which underestimate Jews in general (e.g., those not belonging to an official Jewish organization) and poor Jews in particular (e.g., those unable to pay for an official ceremony). * The immigrant flows that brought thousands to Paris, more or less legally and for varying lengths of stay, also account for the difficulty in

*The major work on the demography of Jews in France is Doris Ben-Simon Donath, *Socio-démographie des Juifs de France et d'Algérie, 1867–1907*, P.O.F.-Etudes (Paris: Presses orientalistes de France, 1976). See also Michel Roblin, *Les Juifs de Paris: Démographie, économie, culture* (Paris: A. et J. Picard et Cie., 1952) and Zosa Szajkowski, *Poverty and Social Welfare among French Jews, 1800–80* (New York: Editions historiques franco-juives, 1954).

establishing accurate numbers for the Parisian Jewish community as a whole from 1881 on.

As for the immigrants themselves, their minimal insertion into the French Jewish community's institutions leaves as somewhat suspect the un-doubtedly low estimates of the latter as to the immigrants' numbers. Yet the figures of the French Jewish community were sometimes caught in a contra-diction. On the one hand, there was a tendency to exaggerate the number of immigrants, partly out of fear and ignorance of them and partly in support of appeals for philanthropic donations (see footnotes [1] and [s] below). On the other hand, in order to counterbalance anti-Semitic or even Jewish-based exaggerations, there was also a tendency to deny or diminish the presence of the foreigners.[1]

An enumeration of Jewish immigrants must therefore look to non-Jewish sources as well. Given the official policy of nonintervention on the part of the French government with regard to migration and the little-heeded and little-enforced laws of 1888 and 1893, no complete immigrant rosters exist for the period under consideration. Government censuses and police estimates of immigrants by nationality do exist; however, such sources gener-ally require a certain manipulation in order to determine what percentage of the Russians, Poles, etc., were Jews. While the census reports and police estimates may at least reflect many immigrants not visible in the Jewish archives, the immigrants' suspicions (especially on the part of draft-dodgers and political exiles) of any official registration procedure may obviate that advantage. On the whole, however, the poor registration rate of Russian immigrants, remarked upon by the police, may be counterbalanced by the latter's tendency to exaggerate categories of the population they considered dangerous! These precautions do not eliminate any possibility of arriving at a numerical estimate of the population under study, but the pros and cons of each data source and the audience for which the statistics are destined must be kept in mind.

In the following table, the asterisked figures (rounded to the nearest hundred) have been derived according to the following assumptions:

Seventy-five percent of the Russian immigrants were Jews (averaged from Roblin [⅔], police department [¾], and Bureau russe du travail [⅘] estimates; see notes [e] and (f) below and report, February 23, 1912, BA1708: Russo-juifs à Paris, File "Bureau Russe du Travail," Préfecture de Police Archives, Paris);

Eighty percent of the eastern European immigrants to France chose Paris (Arthur Ruppin, *Les Juifs dans le monde moderne*, trans. M. Chevalley [Paris: Payot, 1934], p. 67); and

One hundred percent of the Rumanian immigrants were Jews (Roblin, see note [e] below). Thus, for example, when only figures for Russian immi-grants in France have been found, 80 percent of that figure is taken to represent those who went to Paris and 75 percent of that derived figure may be estimated as Jews. Where not asterisked, number and/or derivation is directly attributable to the source listed.

Source	Date	Number	Derivation
Census[a]	1881	7,000*	=75% of 80% of 10,489 Russians +100% of 80% of 857 Rumanians in France
De Cassano[b]	1886	7,200*	=75% of 80% of 11,980 Russians in France
Lefebvre[c]	1891	8,600*	=75% of 80% of 14,357 Russians in France
Census[d]	1896	8,400*	=75% of 9,200 Russians +100% of 1,531 Rumanians in Paris
Roblin[e]	1880–1901	8,200	=4,000 Russian Jews (2/3 of Russian immigrants) +1,200 Galician Jews (1/2 of Galician immigrants) +3,000 Rumanian Jews (1/1 of Rumanian immigrants) in Paris
Police Department[f]	1901	8,200*	=75% of 10,925 Russians in Paris
Census[d]	1901	10,900*	=75% of 9,846 Russians +100% of 3,532 Rumanians in Paris
Université populaire juive[g]	1904	20,000	
Archives Israélites[h]	1880–1905	24-32,000*	=80% of 30-40,000 Eastern European immigrants in France
Immigrant leaders[i]	1906	10-12,000	
Didion[j]	1906	12,800*	=75% of 80% of 21,261 Russians, Rumanians, Serbs, and Bulgarians in France
Census[k]	1906	13,400*	=75% of 17,923 Russians in Paris
Comité de bienfaisance[l]	1906	60,000	
Russian colony[f]	1907	30,000*	=75% of 40,000 Russians in Paris
Police Department[f]	1893–1907	26,300*	=75% of 35,000 Russians who registered at the police department in this period.
Leaflet[m]	1908	100,000	
Speiser[n]	1910	60,000	

Source	Date	Number	Derivation
Census[a]	1911	27,500*	=75% of 80% of 35,016 Russians +100% of 80% of 8,080 Rumanians in France
Losovsky[o]	1911	40,000	
Der idisher arbayter[p]	1912	20-25,000	
Consistoire[q]	1912	24-32,000*	=80% of 30-40,000 eastern European immigrants in France
Presse nouvelle hebdomadaire[r]	1912	40,000	
Roblin[e]	1901-1914 (1880-1914)	13,000 (21,200)	=10,000 Russian Jews (2/3 of Russian immigrants) +3,000 Rumanian Jews (1/1 of Rumanian immigrants) in Paris
Oeuvre française pour l'éducation morale de la jeunesse juive immigrée[s]	1914	50,000	
Szajkowski[t]	1914	100,000	

---

[a]Georges Mauco, Les étrangers en France (Paris: Armand Colin, 1932), p. 38.

[b]Prince de Cassano, Procès-verbaux sommaires du Congrès international de l'intervention des pouvoirs publics dans l'émigration et l'immigration, tenu à Paris du 12 au 14 août 1889 (Exposition universelle internationale de 1889) (Paris: Imprimerie nationale for the Ministère du Commerce, de l'Industrie et des Colonies, 1890), p. 9.

[c]Yves Le Febvre, L'ouvrier étranger et la protection du travail national (Paris: C. Jacques et Cie., 1901), p. 16. (Based on 1891 census.)

[d]Résultats statistiques du recensement des industries et professions (1896), vol. 1: Région de Paris, au Nord et à l'Est (Paris: Imprimerie nationale for the Office du travail, 1899), p. 311.

[e]Michel Roblin, Les Juifs de Paris: Démographie, économie, culture (Paris: A. et J. Picard et Cie., 1952), pp. 66-67, 70. Roblin's estimates, which are relatively low both as compared to police department and census figures and as compared to certain immigrant sources (the Russian colony, Der idisher arbayter), may be seen as an expression of the French Jewish community's very desire to assimilate and to minimize the poor and foreign elements within its midst. Thus, in addressing a wide and not necessarily all-Jewish audience in his book, Roblin hoped to show the Parisian Jewish community at its assimilated best. In this regard, his estimates may also be compared to the much higher Comité de bienfaisance estimate (footnote (1) below), which aimed at a different audience.

[f]Police report entitled "Les réfugiés révolutionnaires russes à Paris," pp. 15-16, F 12894, Archives nationales, Paris.

[g]Université populaire juive, Compte rendu et statuts, 1902-3 (Paris: Imprimerie N. L. Danzig, 1904), p. 5.

[h]Archives israélites (Paris), January 19, 1905. This article served explicitly to refute a German Jewish newspaper's estimate that 150,000 eastern European Jews had immigrated to Paris since 1881.

[i]Letter signed by ten immigrant leaders representing different Russian-Polish and Rumanian societies in Paris to Consistoire, June 5, 1906, B78, File "Associations cultuelles," Association consistoriale israélite de Paris Archives. This particularly low figure must also be interpreted with regard to the audience for which it was written. The immigrant leaders' estimate appeared in a petition/letter requesting that a representative of the immigrant community be appointed to the newly organized Consistoire. This (low) figure was cited to support this request, adding that they didn't think they were being modest in asking for ⟨only?⟩ one representative. The low figure may reflect a hesitancy on the part of the immigrants of being too visible and hence frightening off the French Jewish community.

[j]Maurice Didion, Les salariés étrangers en France (Paris: V. Giard et E. Brière, 1911), pp. 11-12.

[k]Annuaire statistique de la ville de Paris, Année 1909 (Paris: Imprimerie municipale, 1911), p. 678.

[l]L'Univers israélite (Paris), April 6, 1906. This high estimate was cited in a brochure sent to the French and other western European Jewish communities with an appeal to halt immigration to Paris. The Comité clearly wished to impress upon its readers the strain already caused by the increasing number of immigrants in that city.

[m]Leaflet, n.d. (ca., September 1908), announcing the publication of a new Yiddish newspaper called Di moderne tsayt and explaining the need for such a paper due to the number of Jewish immigrants in Paris. ("Laugh not. Some may think we are narenkop ⟨fools⟩ for putting money into this, but we are certain to succeed.") New York, Bund Archives, Pariz: Bundisher fareyn "Kemfer" afishn File.

[n]Wolf Speiser, Kalendar (Paris: n.p., 1910), p. 45.

[o]Zosa Szajkowski, Etyudn tsu der geshikhte fun ayngevandertn yidishn yishev in Frankraykh (Paris: Fridman, 1936), p. 22.

[p]Speaking of immigrant workers in an article by Sviranski, Der idisher arbayter, September 7, 1912.

[q]Report by Monsieur le Substitut Piedelièvre, n.d., Letter received, B92 (1912), File "Affaire Sloutsky," Association consistoriale israélite de Paris Archives; cf. Archives israélites figure above for 1880-1905 as well as André Spire, Les Juifs et la Guerre (Paris: Payot, 1917), p. 24, who also estimated at 30,000-40,000 the number of eastern European Jews in France before World War I. It may thus be noted that this Consistorial figure for 1912 (as well as Spire's) seems to merely repeat earlier estimates without taking into consideration the important post-1905 immigration.

^{r}La Presse nouvelle hebdomadaire (Paris), November 18, 1977.

^{s}Archives israélites, July 9, 1914. A relatively high figure, constituting part of an appeal for funds.

^{t}Szajkowski, Etyudn, p. 24.

In general, in evaluating the number of immigrants in Paris on the eve of World War I, we can see that there are three sorts of estimates:

(1) census figures of Russians only (footnotes [a] and [f] from which we may extrapolate the presence of 26,000–30,000 Jews, but which does not include Rumanian or Galician Jews.

(2) estimates on the part of the French Jewish community ranging from Roblin's low figure of 21,200 (footnote [e] to the high figures of 50,000–60,000 by the Comité de bienfaisance and the Oeuvre française as explained above (footnotes [l] and[s]). The figure of 24,000–32,000, derived from the *Archives israélites'* effort to refute an exaggerated estimate in 1905 (footnote [h]), seems to be the figure most repeated afterward (footnote [q]).

(3) immigrant figures which, with the exception of the 1906 petition (footnote [i]) and the 1912 *Der idisher arbayter* article (footnote [p]), are generally higher, ranging from 40,000 to 100,000 (footnotes [o], [r], [n], [m], and [t]). Given these varying estimates with all of their attached qualifications, I believe it is not unreasonable to suggest an immigrant population of around 35,000 in Paris before 1914, a number higher than that suggested by the *Archives israélites,* closer to that estimated by the immigrants themselves, but less than those figures that seem particularly inflated, for one reason or another.

APPENDIX B:
Public Aid to "Indigents" Russians, Poles, Rumanians

Year	Heads of Households Receiving Public Aid[a]		Refuges de nuit[b]
	Paris	4th arr. only	
1886	92	53	
1889	5	0	38
1890			17
1891			41
1892	8	0	31
1893	10	3	34
1894	8	1	39
1895	11	5	36
1896	9	3	36
1897	8	3	18
1898	11	2	30
1899	15	2	5
1900	4	2	18
1901	12	3	24
1902	6	3	19
1903	6	3	15
1904	15	5	36
1905	20	6	8
1906	22	7	12
1907			14
1908			18
1909			17
1910			48
1911			28
1912			20
1913			14
1914			14

SOURCE: Annuaire statistique de la ville de Paris, Années 1886-1914 (Paris: Imprimerie municipale, 1888-1916).

[a] Russians and Poles only.

[b] Russians, Poles, and Rumanians. Combined figures for:
  Refuge du Château des Rentiers (1889-1902, called the Refuge Nicolas-Flamel from 1903 on)
  Refuge Benoît Mâlon du Quai de Valmy (1889-1903)

APPENDIX C:
Occupations Registered at the Agile, 1906–12

	Russians	Austro-Hungarians	Rumanians	Total Eastern Europeans	French
Transportation and Hard Labor					
Movers/Deliverymen		2		2	33
Chauffeurs/Coachmen	8	2		10	26
Unskilled laborers	3			3	17
Diggers/Paviors		1		1	14
Day laborers	49	22	15	86	397
Domestic service					
Maids	2		1	3	165
Governesses/Companions	1			1	4
Housekeepers	6		1	7	71
Butlers		1		1	1
Agricultural work					
Gardeners	11	2		13	21
Farmers	3			3	4
Grooms					5
Peddlers or Hawkers	4	8		12	29
Other					
Billposters					2
Cardboard-makers	2	1	1	4	6
Distributers					1
Packers	3	1		4	8
Dishwashers		1		1	9
UNSKILLED	92	41	18	151	813
Cloth goods					
Tailors	261	28	17	306	29
Cloth preparers					1
Cutters	14			14	4
Seamstresses	28	2	1	31	41
Pinkers					1
Machine operators	45	10	6	61	33
Pressers	31	3	1	35	5
Capmakers	101	13	11	125	2
Blockers	9	1		10	
Hatters	52	5	3	60	3
Milliners	1			1	4
Launderers	2			2	20
Buttonmakers	5			5	
Embroiderers	10	1	1	12	
Rubber-workers					1
Necktie-makers	1			1	
Breeches-makers					2

	Russians	Austro-Hungarians	Rumanians	Total Eastern Europeans	French
Designers	11			11	4
Artificial flower makers	1			1	7
Linen-workers		1		1	2
Lacemakers	18	4		22	3
Darners					2
Dyers	6	2	2	10	7
Weavers	21	1		22	3
Leather and fur apparel					
Cobblers	127	18	2	147	17
Boot leg stitchers	51		1	52	
Furworkers	71	24	16	111	1
Glovemakers	3			3	1
Feather dressers	1			1	15
Beltmakers	1			1	
Apparel Industry	871	113	61	1,045	208
Morocco-leather workers	56	5	1	62	5
Bookbinders	28	19	13	60	8
Riveters					1
Saddlers	13		1	14	2
Tanners	36	7		43	1
Harness-makers					3
Trunk-makers	1			1	
Leather Industry	134	31	15	180	20
Joiners	76	17	5	98	33
Cabinet-makers	39	3	2	44	6
Woodcarvers	13	1		14	
Chair-caners	8			8	
Chair makers			1	1	
Wheelwrights	1			1	1
Picture framers			1	1	
Parquet floor-layers					4
Coopers	4		1	5	2
Wood Products	141	21	10	172	46
Housepainters	48	14	13	75	18
Electricians	15	6		21	4
Glass-makers/Glaziers	9	6	2	17	5
Masons	3	8	1	12	25
Carpenters			1	1	13
Cement-makers					2
Roofers					12
Chimney repairers	1			1	11
Stonecarvers/stone-cleaners					2
Floor polishers					2
Construction	76	34	17	127	94
Metalsmiths	83	22	3	108	34
Tinsmiths	31	5	8	44	1
Blacksmiths	13	5		18	17
Gunsmiths		3		3	1
Coppersmiths	2	6		8	3

	Russians	Austro-Hungarians	Rumanians	Total Eastern Europeans	French
Cutlers					1
Smelters	2	2		4	1
Ovenmakers					1
Strikers					6
Plumbers	1			1	17
Welders					2
Sheet-iron makers					2
Wire-drawers					1
Ordinary Metals	132	43	11	186	87
Jewelers	41	19	2	62	4
Watchmakers	22	11	2	35	6
Goldsmiths	8	8		16	
Silversmiths			1	1	
Bronze workers	6	1		7	
Diamond cutters		2		2	
Gilders	4			4	3
Enamellers					1
Engravers		4	5	9	
Opticians	3	2		5	
Polishers		2		2	4
Glass cutters		1		1	
Precious Metals/ Precision Work	84	50	10	144	18
Stereotypers					1
Printers	4			4	19
Lithographers		1		1	
Typographers	34	14	7	55	12
Printing	38	15	7	60	32
Bakers	52	8	4	64	11
Butchers	32	5	2	39	7
Ritual slaughterers	1			1	
Cooks	5	1	1	7	47
Pastry-cooks	1	17		18	3
Brewers		3		3	3
Cigarette makers	6			6	
Confectioners	7			7	
Food Products	104	34	7	145	71
Upholsterers	33	27	7	67	7
Hairdressers	42	3	3	48	5
Brushmakers	17	11		28	2
Turners	21	4	3	28	3
Fitters	1			1	13
Land-surveyors	1			1	
Quarriers	1			1	
Yard foremen					1
Jockeys		1		1	
Lampmakers or lamplighters	1	3		4	
Marblecutters		1		1	
Mattressmakers					4
Miners		1		1	5
Molders					4

	Russians	Austro-Hungarians	Rumanians	Total Eastern Europeans	French
Parchment-workers		1		1	
Umbrella makers	2		1	3	
Borers					1
Sawyers					1
Basketmakers		7		7	
Other Skilled Trades	119	59	14	192	46
SKILLED	1,699	400	152	2,251	622
Food and drink					
Milkmen		1		1	3
Grocers	1			1	1
Café-keepers		1	1	2	1
Merchants	129	32	18	179	3
(Traveling) Salesmen	8	3	1	12	15
Drug sellers	2	1		3	
Booksellers					1
Stationers	1			1	3
Perfumers	2			2	
Market stand lessors	—	—	—	—	1
MERCHANTS	143	38	20	201	28
Assistants/Clerks	86	52	28	166	87
Office-boys or waiters (garçons)	38	35	3	76	34
Insurance salesmen					1
Lawyer's clerks					1
Postmen					2
Sailors	7	1	1	9	2
Secretaries	—	—	1	1	1
(WHITE COLLAR) EMPLOYEES	131	88	33	252	128
Students	50	9	4	63	
Bookkeepers	20	4	11	35	31
Journalists	15	4	3	22	1
Lawyers					1
Correspondents		4		4	
Writers		1		1	2
Engineers					1
Schoolteachers	4	2	1	7	6
Interpreters	2	2		4	
Professors	5	1	1	7	2
Chemists		1		1	
Dentists	6			6	
Nurses		1		1	1
Pharmacists	5	2		7	2
Artists	25	2	1	28	14
Photographers	10	1		11	1
Rabbis	1			1	
Officers		1		1	

	Russians	Austro-Hungarians	Rumanians	Total Eastern Europeans	French
Acrobats		2		2	
Actors	3			3	
Singers	1			1	
Musicians	1			1	
Pianists		1		1	1
"FREE" PROFESSIONS	148	38	21	207	63
NO OCCUPATION	536	56	87	679	99
TOTAL	2,749	661	331	3,741	1,753

SOURCE: Société philanthropique de l'Asile israélite de Paris, Rapports des exercises, 1906-7, 1909-12.

APPENDIX D:
Immigrant Occupations, 1910 (Speiser's Kalendar)

Peddlers	1,850
TOTAL UNSKILLED	1,850
natmakers	60
Capmakers	1,400
Non-specialized capmakers	500
Menswear tailors.	3,500
Womenswear tailors	2,800
Non-specialized clothing workers	600
Cobblers	1,150
Furworkers	1,400
Apparel Industry	11,410
Leather Goods	600
Joiners	2,500
Woodcarvers	400
Wood Products	2,900
Construction (House painters)	90
Tinsmiths	300
Automobile mechanics and metalworkers	1,200
Ordinary Metals	1,500
Goldsmiths	1,200
Watchmakers	200
Precious Metals/Precision Work	1,400
Printing	45
Bakers	82
Butchers	12
Ritual slaughterers	5
Food Products	99
Hand organ makers	200
Brushmakers	65
Turners	400
Hairdressers	60
Other	725
TOTAL SKILLED	18,769

Precious Stones	4,000
Auctions	480
Parisian Articles	120
Market traders	3,000
Pawnbrokers	350
Grocers	80
	——
MERCHANTS	8,030

Photographers, Dental Assistants, Drugstore Clerks	200
Doctors, Dentists, Lawyers, Pharmacists	1,000
	——
"FREE" PROFESSIONS	1,200
OTHER	350
	——
Total	30,199

Summary

Unskilled	1,850	6.1%
Skilled	18,769	62.1
Merchants	8,030	26.6
"Free" Professions	1,200	4.0
Other	350	1.2
	——	——
Total	30,199	100.0%

SOURCE: Wolf Speiser, _Kalendar_ (Paris: n.p., 1910), pp. 78-80.

NOTE: "OTHER" includes barbers, wig-makers, bristle workers, store clerks, lemonade makers, and waiters, all combined by Speiser.

NOTES

INTRODUCTION

1. With regard to the 1880–1914 period, see notably Ezra Mendelsohn, *Class Struggle in the Pale: The Formative Years of the Jewish Workers' Movement in Tsarist Russia* (Cambridge: Cambridge University Press, 1970); and Ezra Mendelsohn, ed., "Essays on the American Jewish Labor Movement," *YIVO Annual of Jewish Social Science* 16 (1976); Melech Epstein, *Jewish Labor in the U.S.A.* (New York: KTAV, 1969); Ronald Sanders, *The Downtown Jews* (New York: Signet, New American Library, 1976); and Irving Howe, *The World of Our Fathers* (New York: Simon and Schuster, 1976). For England, see William J. Fishman, *East End Jewish Radicals, 1875–1914* (London: Duckworth, 1975); and Jerry White, *Rothschild Buildings: Life in an East End Tenement Block, 1887–1920* (London: Routledge and Kegan Paul, 1980). And for France, I gladly give due credit to Michael Marrus's by now classic description of the "bourgeois" French Jewish community in his *The Politics of Assimilation: A Study of the French Jewish Community at the Time of the Dreyfus Affair* (Oxford: Oxford University Press, 1971), in which I read the first intriguing references to the Jewish proletariat in Paris.

Since then two fine studies have dealt with immigrant Jews in Paris from 1906 through 1939: David H. Weinberg, *A Community on Trial: The Jews of Paris in the 1930s* (Chicago: University of Chicago Press, 1977), and Paula Hyman, *From Dreyfus to Vichy: The Transformation of French Jewry, 1906–1939* (New York: Columbia University Press, 1979). See also the works in Yiddish by Zosa Szajkowski, particularly *Etyudn tsu der geshikhte fun ayngevandertn yidishn yishev in Frankraykh* (Paris: Fridman,

1936); and *Di profesyonele bavegung tsvishn di yidishe arbeter in Frankraykh* (Paris: Fridman, 1937); and Charlotte Roland, *Du Ghetto à l'occident, Deux générations yiddiches en France* (Paris: Les Editions de Minuit, 1962).

2. Only recently, Guy de Rothschild, president of the Fonds Social Juif Unifié in France, stated: "Diversity is a richness of our community. . . . Diversity, yes, but not divisions." *Le Monde* (Paris), November 5, 1977.

3. Simon Dubnow, *Nationalism and History, Essays on Old and New Jerusalem,* ed. Koppel S. Pinson (New York: Atheneum, 1970), pp. 263–64.

4. Salo W. Baron, *History and Jewish Historians, Essays and Addresses* (Philadelphia: Jewish Publication Society of America, 1964), p. 25.

5. Ibid., p. 102.

6. See also Raphael Mahler, *A History of Modern Jewry 1780–1815* (New York: Schocken Books, 1971); Jacob Katz, *Out of the Ghetto: The Social Background of Jewish Emancipation, 1770–1870* (Cambridge: Harvard University Press, 1973); and the uneven but interesting *Economic History of the Jews* by Salo Baron, Arcadius Kahan, and others, Nachum Gross, ed. (New York: Schocken Books, 1975).

7. In addition to the works cited in footnote 1, see Nathan Glazer, *American Judaism* (Chicago: University of Chicago Press, 1957); Lloyd Gartner, *The Jewish Immigrant in England, 1870–1914* (London: Simon Publications, 1973); Michel Rudnianski and Patrick Girard, "Les relations entre Israélites français et Juifs russes," 2 vols. (maîtrise, U.E.R. d'Histoire, Université de Paris I, 1971–72); Steven Aschheim, *Brothers and Strangers: The Eastern European Jew in German and German Jewish Consciousness, 1800–1923* (Madison: University of Wisconsin Press, 1982); and Jack Wertheimer, "'The Unwanted Element': East European Jews in Imperial Germany," *Leo Baeck Institute Yearbook* 26 (1981): 23–46.

8. Cf. Hyman, who has described the Jewish labor movement as "crystalliz[ing] the conflict between native and immigrant Jews," pp. 114, 89. Surely it reflected the different socioeconomic realities of the two communities, but the Jewish immigrant labor movement did not represent a direct conflict over class between them.

9. Nancy L. Green, "The Politics of Migration: Migration to France before World War I," presented at the American Historical Association Meeting, December 28, 1981.

10. Mendelsohn, *Class Struggle in the Pale;* Michelle Perrot, *Les ouvriers en grève, France 1871–90,* 2 vols. (Paris: Mouton and Ecole Pratique des Hautes Etudes, 1974).

11. See the interesting article by Dominique Schnapper, "Centralisme et fédéralisme culturels: Les émigrés italiens en France et aux Etats-Unis," *Annales E.S.C.* 29 (September-October 1974): 1141–59; Michel Oriol, *Bilan des études sur les aspects culturels et humains des migrations internationales en Europe occidentale, 1918–1979* (Strasbourg: Fondation Européenne de la Science, 1981); and *Les Migrations internationales de la fin du XVIIIe siècle à nos jours* (Paris: Centre National de la Recherche Scientifique, 1980).

12. See, e.g., Michael Piore, *Birds of Passage* (Cambridge: Cambridge University Press, 1979); Stephen Castles and Godula Kosack, *Immigrant Workers and Class Structure in Western Europe* (London: Oxford University Press, 1973); Georges Tapinos, *L'économie des migrations internationales* (Paris: Armand Colin and Fondation Nationale des Sciences Politiques, 1974).

CHAPTER 1: EMIGRATION AND IMMIGRATION

1. Hilde Wander, *The Importance of Emigration for the Solution of Population Problems in Western Europe* (The Hague: Martinus Nijhoff, 1951), p. 5; Julius Isaac,

Economics of Migration (New York: Oxford University Press, 1947), pp. 1–40; Jean Randon, *De l'émigration et de l'immigration au point de vue du droit international* (Paris: Imprimerie Henri Jouve, 1909), pp. 1–7. See Paul Ladame, *Le rôle des migrations dans le monde libre* (Geneva and Paris: Librairie E. Droz and Librairie Minard, 1958) for an extreme libertarian vision of population movements.

2. Anti-Semitism and persecution have, unfortunately, had to be constants in the history of the Jewish people. Léon Poliakov, *Histoire de l'antisémitisme*, 4 vols. (Paris: Calmann-Lévy, 1955–1977). However, without denying the importance of anti-Semitism, I do not believe that Jewish history need be written as an extension of Sartre's famous precept that without anti-Semitism there would be no Jews . . . or Jewish history? It is important to go beyond these constants, not only to understand the context of anti-Semitism itself but to examine other social and economic factors that have shaped the destinies of the Jews. On scholarship pointing to the "pull" as well as the "push" in Jewish migrations, see, e.g., Simon Kuznets, "Immigration of Russian Jews to the United States: Background and Structure," *Perspectives in American History* 10 (1976): 35–124.

3. Claudio S. Ingerflom, "Idéologie révolutionnaire et mentalité antisémite: Les socialistes russes face aux pogroms de 1881–1883," *Annales: Economies, Sociétés, Civilisations* 37 (May–June 1982): 434–451. The best comprehensive history of the eastern European Jews remains Simon Dubnow, *History of the Jews in Russia and Poland*, trans. I. Friedlaender, 3 vols. (New York: KTAV, 1975).

4. Dubnow, 3:94–95.

5. Arthur Ruppin, *Les Juifs dans le monde moderne*, trans. M. Chevalley (Paris: Payot, 1934), p. 52. Cf. Jacob Lestschinsky, "Jewish Migrations, 1840–1946," *The Jews*, ed. Louis Finkelstein, 2 vols. (New York: Harper and Row, 1955), 2:1218.

6. Jacob Lestschinsky, *Di yidishe vanderung far di letste 25 yor* (Berlin: HIAS Emigdirekt, 1927), p. 6.

7. Liebman Hersch, "Jewish Migrations during the Last 100 Years," *The Jewish People, Past and Present*, 3 vols. (New York: Jewish Encyclopedic Handbook, Inc., 1955), 1:410. Cf. Kuznets, p. 50, who estimates that an even smaller number—only 12 percent—of the Russian Jewish population emigrated.

8. Kuznets, p. 43; Salo Baron, *The Russian Jew under Tsars and Soviets* (New York: The Macmillan Co., 1964), p. 83.

9. Kuznets, p. 51. The Poles were the second largest group of emigrants from the Russian empire, representing from 21.4 percent in 1906 to 38.6 percent in 1913 of the total emigration. The Jews averaged 40.8 percent of the emigration from 1900 to 1914. Lestschinsky, *Di yidishe vanderung*, pp. 56, 60.

10. Thus the term *Russian Jew* as used herein actually refers to those Polish-Russian Jews who lived within the Pale.

11. E. B. Lanin, *Les Juifs de Russie*, cited in *Les Juifs de Russie: Recueil d'articles et d'études sur leur situation légale, sociale et économique* (Paris: Léopold Cerf, 1891), p. 64.

12. Karl Marx, *Capital*, 3 vols. (Moscow: Progress Publishers, 1967–71), 1:83.

13. Arcadius Kahan, "The Early Modern Period," *Economic History of the Jews*, ed. Nachum Gross (New York: Schocken Paperbacks, 1976), p. 67.

14. Liebman Hersch, *Le Juif errant d'aujourd'hui* (Paris: M. Giard et E. Brière, 1913), pp. 222–23.

15. Kuznets, pp. 70–71. See also Ruppin, pp. 70–72; Jacob Lestschinsky, *Dos idishe folk in Tsifern* (Berlin: Klal-Verlag, 1922), pp. 45, 69, 98, 141.

16. Kuznets, p. 73.

17. Jacob Lestschinsky, *Der idisher arbayter (in Rusland)* (Vilna: Vilna-Tsukunft, 1906), Table X.A.

18. Georges Gliksman, *L'aspect économique de la question juive en Pologne* (Paris:

Editions Rieder, 1929), p. 57. As the Jewish Colonization Association reporters commented: "The more we visit Jewish factories, the more we are struck by the insufficient tools, technological backwardness, dirtiness, disorder, irrationally-constructed buildings, deplorable hygienic conditions in the workshops, *voilà* the distinctive characteristics of the Jewish factories." Jewish Colonization Association, *Recueil de matériaux sur la situation économique des Israélites de Russie*, 2 vols. (Paris: Félix Alcan, 1908), 2:175.

19. See Ezra Mendelsohn, *Class Struggle in the Pale, The Formative Years of the Jewish Workers' Movement in Tsarist Russia* (Cambridge: Cambridge University Press, 1970), chapter 1; Lestschinsky, *Der idisher arbayter (in Rusland)*; and Kahan, "The Modern Period," in Gross, part I, chapter 10.

20. Jewish Colonization Association, 2:162–65.

21. This 32 percent figure may be compared to 1.4 percent commercial activity among non-Jews. Kuznets, p. 73. For commercial activity of the Jews in 1897 see Table 1a. For figures for the early nineteenth century, see: Abraham Léon, *La Conception matérialiste de la question juive* (Paris: Etudes et Documentations Internationales, 1968), p. 121; and Jacob Lestschinsky, ed., *Shriftn far ekonomik un statistik*, 2 vols. (Berlin, YIVO, 1928), 1:55–57. Salo Baron sharply contests this high estimate of commercial activities of the Jews at the beginning of the nineteenth century. Baron, p. 97.

22. Kuznets, p. 73.

23. Leonty Soloweitschik, *Un prolétariat méconnu* (Brussels: Henri Lamertin, 1898), p. 90.

24. Werner Cahnman, "Role and Significance of the Jewish Artisanal Class," *Jewish Journal of Sociology* 7 (December 1965): 210.

25. Mark Wischnitzer, *A History of Jewish Crafts and Guilds* (New York: Jonathan David Publishers, 1965), p. 216.

26. Clothing is taken to be the general term including dresswear *and* accessories: hats, shoes, coats, etc. Garment is the narrower term, for dresswear only.

27. Mendelsohn, p. 157; Baron, pp. 99, 116. Cf. Jewish Colonization Association, 1:262, which described the "artisan" who worked for an "entrepreneur-capitalist" as part of a "stage towards those modes of production which remove the professional personality from the artisan."

28. See Jewish Colonization Association, particularly 1:256–70, 327–28, 376–77.

29. Ibid., 2:199.

30. Dubnow, 2:366–67.

31. On the history of Jews in Rumania, see Carol Iancu, *Les Juifs en Roumanie (1866–1919): De l'exclusion à l'émancipation*, Etudes Historiques 4 (Aix-en-Provence: Editions de l'Université de Provence, 1978). On Galicia see Raphael Mahler, "The Economic Background of Jewish Emigration from Galicia to the United States," *YIVO Annual of Jewish Social Science* 8 (1952): 255–67.

32. Kuznets, p. 88.

33. Hersch, *Le juif errant*, pp. 276–77, 320.

34. Kuznets, p. 96. It must be noted, however, that while the demographic profile of the Jewish emigrants, as compared to the base Jewish population in Russia, corresponds to an "emigrant" population profile, as compared to *other* emigrant groups the Jewish emigrants are characteristically more familial. See Hersch, *Le Juif errant*, pp. 66–67, 72–73, 102–3; and Kuznets, pp. 94–100.

35. Kuznets, pp. 101–2.

36. Ibid., p. 110.

37. Dubnow, *Nationalism and History, Essays on Old and New Jerusalem*, ed. Koppel S. Pinson (New York: Atheneum, 1970), pp. 198–99, 233–35.

38. Lionel Rocheman, *Devenir Cécile* (Paris: Editions Ramsay, 1977). p. 150.

39. E.g., see Chaim Weizmann in Lucy S. Dawidowicz, ed., *The Golden Tradition: Jewish Life and Thought in Eastern Europe* (Boston: Beacon, 1967), p. 377. For the origins of this problem in the eighteenth century see Chimen Abramsky, "The Crisis of Authority within European Jewry in the 18th Century," Siegfried Stein and Raphael Lowe, eds., *Studies in Jewish Religious and Intellectual History Presented to Alexander Altmann on the Occasion of his Seventieth Birthday* (Alabama: The University of Alabama Press and the Institute of Jewish Studies [London], 1979), pp. 13–28; and for the early nineteenth century, see Michael Stanislawski, *Tsar Nicholas I and the Jews: The Transformation of Jewish Society in Russia, 1825–1855* (Philadelphia: Jewish Publication Society, 1983).

40. André Billy and Moïse Twersky, *L'épopée de Ménaché Foïgel*, 3 vols. (Paris: Plon, 1927), 1:168; see also Dubnow, *History . . . in Russia and Poland*, 2:304–8, on the rejection of emigration at an April 1882 St. Petersburg conference of forty Jewish notables.

41. Nancy L. Green, "L'émigration comme émancipation," *Pluriel*, no. 27 (1981): 51–59.

42. J. Tchernoff, *Dans le creuset des civilisations*, 4 vols. (Paris: Editions Rieder, 1937), 1:77. This was true not only of Jewish students. See Claudie Weill, "Les étudiants russe en Allemagne, 1910–1914," *Cahiers du monde russe et soviétique* 20 (April–June 1979): 203–25.

43. Michael J. Piore, *Birds of Passage: Migrant Labor and Industrial Societies* (New York: Cambridge University Press, 1980); Georges P. Tapinos, *L'économie des migrations internationales* (Paris: Armand Colin and Fondation Nationale des Sciences Politiques, 1974); and Harry Jerome, *Migration and Business Cycles* (New York: National Bureau of Economic Research Inc., 1926).

44. Lestschinsky, *Di yidishe vanderung*, p. 2.

45. Editorial by Abraham Cahan in 1911, cited in Ronald Sanders, *The Downtown Jews* (New York: Signet, New American Library, 1976), pp. 344–45.

46. See Yankel Mykhanowitzki's debate with himself as to where to immigrate in Roger Ikor, *Les fils d'Avrom: Les eaux mêlées* (Paris: Albin Michel, 1955), pp. 88–95.

47. Michel Roblin, *Les Juifs de Paris: Démographie, économie, culture* (Paris: A. et J. Picard et Cie., 1952), p. 65.

48. Ikor, pp. 93–94.

49. Karpel and Dinner for the Groupe des ouvriers juifs socialistes de Paris, *Le prolétariat juif: Lettre des ouvriers juifs de Paris au Parti socialiste français* (Paris: Imprimerie typographique J. Allemane, 1898), p. 17.

50. Rocheman, p. 172.

51. David Landes, *The Unbound Prometheus: Technological Change and Industrial Development in Western Europe from 1750 to the Present* (Cambridge: Cambridge University Press, 1969); Jesse R. Pitts, "Continuity and Change in Bourgeois France," in Stanley Hoffmann, ed., *In Search of France* (New York: Harper & Row, 1963), pp. 235–304.

52. Georges Mauco, *Les étrangers en France* (Paris: Armand Colin, 1932), p. 18; E. Levasseur, *Questions ouvrières et industrielles en France sous la Troisième République*, (Paris: Arthur Rousseau, 1907), pp. 280–92.

53. Prince de Cassano, *Procès-verbaux sommaires du Congrès international de l'intervention des pouvoirs publics dans l'émigration et l'immigration, tenu à Paris du 12 au 14 août 1889* (*Exposition universelle internationale de 1889*) (Paris: Imprimerie nationale for

the Ministère du commerce, de l'industrie et des colonies, 1890), p. 11.

54. Police report entitled "Les réfugiés révolutionnaires russes à Paris," pp. 12–15, F⁷ 12894, Archives nationales, Paris.

55. Mauco, p. 58; Yves Le Febvre, *L'ouvrier étranger et la protection du travail national* (Paris: C. Jacques et Cie., 1901), pp. 28–29; Jean-Charles Bonnet, *Les Pouvoirs publics et l'immigration dans l'entre-deux guerres*, Centre d'Histoire Economique et Sociale de la Région Lyonnaise 7 (Lyon: Université de Lyon II, 1976), p. ii. See also the excellent recent study by Gary Cross, *Immigrant Workers in Industrial France: The Making of a New Labor Class* (Philadelphia: Temple University Press, 1983).

56. Nancy L. Green, "The Politics of Migration: Migration to France before World War I," presented at the American Historical Association Meeting, December 28, 1981.

57. Mauco, p. 38; De Cassano, p. 9.

58. Mauco, p. 48. Cf. Eveille, *L'assistance aux étrangers en France* (Paris: Jouve et Boyer, 1899), p. 8, and Le Febvre, p. 18.

59. See Table 4 below.

60. Louis Chevalier, *La formation de la population parisienne au XIXe siècle*, Institut national d'études démographiques—Travaux et documents 10 (Paris: Presses universitaires de France, 1950), p. 46.

61. Mlle. Schirmacher, *La spécialisation du travail—Par nationalités, à Paris* (Paris: Arthur Rousseau, 1908), pp. 32 and 167. With regard to the International Exhibitions see Madeleine Rebérioux, "Approches de l'histoire des expositions universelles à Paris du Second Empire à 1900," *Bulletin du Centre d'Histoire Économique et Sociale de la Région Lyonnaise*, no. 1 (1979): 1–20.

62. *Der idisher arbayter* (Paris), July 4, 1914.

63. Ruppin, p. 66; *Résultats statistiques du recensement des industries et professions (1896)*, vol. 1: *Région de Paris, au Nord et à l'Est* (Paris: Imprimerie nationale for the Office du travail, 1899) (hereafter cited as *Industries et Professions: Paris*), pp. 204–5.

64. Derived from Mauco, p. 562.

65. March 22, 1914, F⁷ 13740: Habillement, File "Notes 1914," Archives nationales, Paris.

66. Pierre du Maroussem, *La petite industrie (salaires et durée du travail)*, vol. 2: *Le vêtement à Paris* (Paris: Imprimerie nationale for the Office du travail, 1896), p. 210.

67. *Exposition universelle internationale de 1900 à Paris: Rapports du jury international*, Groupe XIII: *Fils, tissus, vêtements, 2ème partie, Classes 85 et 86*, by Léon Storch (Classe 85), Julien Hayem and A. Mortier (Classe 86) (Paris: Imprimerie nationale for the Ministère du commerce, de l'industrie, des postes et des télégraphes, 1902), p. 90.

68. Jacques Sylvère, "Le 'Sweating System,' Naissance de la machine à coudre," *Presse Nouvelle Hebdomadaire* (Paris), June 16, 1978.

69. Fernand Braudel and Ernest Labrousse, gen. eds., *Histoire économique et sociale de la France*, tome 4, vol. 1 (Paris: Presses universitaires de France, 1979), p. 259.

70. Alfred Picard, gen. ed., *Exposition universelle internationale de 1889 à Paris: Rapports du jury international*, Classe 36: *Habillement des deux sexes*, by Albert Leduc (Paris: Imprimerie nationale for the Ministère du commerce, de l'industrie et des colonies, 1891), p. 58; Du Maroussem, p. 306. On the importance of variability of demand in general with regard to immigrant labor, see Piore, pp. 35–43.

71. Leduc, pp. 92, 59–60; Du Maroussem, p. 135.

72. See Zola's masterful *Au Bonheur des Dames* and Michael B. Miller's recent work, *The Bon Marché: Bourgeois Culture and the Department Store, 1869–1920* (Princeton: Princeton University Press, 1981).

73. Schirmacher, p. 70.

74. Albert Aftalion, *Le développement de la fabrique et le travail à domicile dans les industries de l'habillement* (Paris: J-B Sirey and Journal du Palais, 1906), p. 142.

75. Cited in Georges Mény, *La lutte contre le sweating system* (Paris: Librairie des Sciences politiques et sociales and Marcel Rivière et Cie., 1910), p. 27.

76. Leduc, pp. 29, 65; Gaston Worth, *La couture et la confection des vêtements de femme* (Paris: Imprimerie Chaix, 1895), p. 74.

77. Storch, Hayem, and Mortier, p. 39; Worth, p. xv.

78. Du Maroussem, p. 294.

79. "En ce qui concerne l'Allemagne, affirmons une fois de plus, sans crainte d'être taxé d'aveuglement, de vanité ou de chauvinisme (qualités que nos voisins se plaisent à nous reconnaître), que l'industrie de la confection dans ce pays y est, à l'exemple de tant d'autres, basée sur le principe de la reproduction, de la copie tronquée et à des prix inférieurs, de nos articles." Worth, p. 95.

80. Those branches of the clothing industry that were more highly mechanized, e.g., shoemaking, were in fact leaving Paris. *Industries et Professions: Paris*, p. 207; L. Delpon de Vissec, "De la distribution du travail à domicile dans l'industrie de la confection parisienne," *Memoirs et documents du Musée social* (March 1908), p. 87; Aftalion, pp. 69–83.

81. *Industries et Professions: Paris*, pp. 207, 232–33.

82. De Vissec, p. 93.

83. *Rapports sur l'application pendant l'année 1907 des lois réglementant le travail* (Paris: Imprimerie nationale, 1908), p. 3.

84. *L'Humanité* (Paris), July 22, 1913. Cf. *Der idisher arbayter* (Paris), July 5, 1913.

85. Du Maroussem, p. 702.

86. Maurice Lauzel, *Ouvriers juifs de Paris: Les casquettiers* (Paris: Edouard Cornély et Cie., 1912), p. 23.

87. Storch, Hayem, and Mortier, pp. 204–5; see also Henri Dagan, *De la condition du peuple au XXe siècle* (Paris: V. Giard et E. Brière, 1904), pp. 364–65.

88. Du Maroussem, p. 20.

89. Schirmacher, p. 60.

90. Cited in Mény, p. 21.

91. Pierre du Maroussem, *La question ouvrière*, vol. 2: *Ebénistes du faubourg St. Antoine* (Paris: Arthur Rousseau, 1892), p. 191.

92. Cf. Arcadius Kahan, "Economic Opportunities and Some Pilgrim's Progress: Jewish Immigrants from Eastern Europe in the United States, 1890–1914," *Journal of Economic History* (March 1978), pp. 235–251.

CHAPTER 2: ARRIVAL AND RECEPTION

1. André Billy and Moïse Twersky, *L'épopée de Ménaché Foïgel*, 3 vols. (Paris: Plon, 1927–28), 1:175.

2. The eastern European emigrants were not alone in choosing a route through France. In the period 1885–87, for example, 126,704 foreigners (including 554 Russians and Rumanians) emigrated *from* France. Italians, Swiss, Spaniards, and Germans left France for the United States (the choice of 42 percent of them) or Argentina (32 percent). These two destinations were the most popular for French emigrants as well (50 percent heading for Argentina; 32 percent for the United States). Prince de Cassano, *Procès-verbaux sommaires du Congrès international de l'inter-*

vention des pouvoirs publics dans l'émigration et l'immigration, tenu à Paris du 12 au 14 août 1889 (Exposition universelle internationale de 1889) (Paris: Imprimerie nationale for the Ministère du commerce, de l'industrie et des colonies, 1890), pp. 37–38.

3. See Paris, Bibliothèque de l'histoire de la ville de Paris, Ochs (newspaper clippings) Collection, D1218–D1234 (1892–1900). To see how *Le Petit Journal* evolved later, see Janine Ponty, "'Le Petit Journal' et l'affaire Dreyfus (1897–1899): Analyse de contenu," *Revue d'histoire moderne et contemporaine* 24 (October–December 1977): 641–56.

4. Paris, Alliance israélite universelle (hereafter cited as AIU) Archives, France IXD51: Emigration—Divers, France IXD52: Russie—Emigration, 1881–91, France IH1: Sociétés. See also *L'Univers Israélite* (Paris, hereafter cited as *UI*), January 27, 1911.

5. Roger Ikor, *Les fils d'Avrom: Les eaux mêlées* (Paris: Albin Michel, 1955), p. 299.

6. 45% = 35,000 immigrants (see Appendix A) ÷ 75,000 Jews in Paris. Jacob Lestchinsky estimate in *Dos yidishe folk in tsifern* (Berlin: Klal-Verlag, 1922), p. 152. Cf. Ben-Simon Donath's study of consistorial marriage registers (which generally underestimate eastern European immigrants) in Doris Ben-Simon Donath, *Sociodémographie des Juifs de France et d'Algérie, 1867–1907*, P.O.F.-Etudes (Paris: Presses orientalistes de France, 1976), pp. 108–10; and Szajkowski, who, on the other hand claims that at the time of the Dreyfus affair the eastern European Jews in Paris already outnumbered the French Jews. Zosa Szajkowski, *Di profesyonele bavegung tsvishn di yidishe arbeter in Frankraykh biz 1914* (Paris: Fridman, 1937), p. 32.

7. J. Tchernoff, *Dans le creuset des civilisations*, 4 vols. (Paris: Editions Rieder, 1937), 2:97; Szajkowski, "The European Attitude to Eastern European Jewish Immigration (1881–1893)," *Publications of the American Jewish Historical Society* 41 (December 1951): 149.

8. *Bulletin de l'Alliance israélite universelle*, 2e sér., no. 4 (1881–82): 22, and ibid, no. 28 (1903): 33–38; Jean Jaurès, "L'autocratie, voilà l'ennemi," *Les nouveaux cahiers* 11 (Autumn 1967): 35–39; Madeleine Rebérioux, "Jean Jaurès et Kichinev," ibid, pp. 29–34.

9. *Le Paris*, August 23, 1892; *Le Figaro* (Paris), August 24, 1892.

10. Compare the *Le Paris* articles of August 23 and August 25, 1892.

11. *L'Intransigeant* (Paris), August 28, 1892; *La Libre Parole* (Paris), August 23 and August 24, 1892.

12. *La Libre Parole* (Paris), August 5, 1892, and *Le Jour* (Paris), December 18, 1892.

13. *La Libre Parole* (Paris), August 5, 1892; see also idem., August 23, 1892, and *Le Jour* (Paris), December 18, 1892. A petition against the immigrants was signed by a group of small shopkeepers in the Pletzl area in 1910 or 1911. Maurice Lauzel, *Ouvriers juifs de Paris: Les casquettiers* (Paris: Edouard Cornély et Cie., 1912), p. 8; cf. Szajkowski, p. 37.

14. *La Libre Parole* (Paris), August 23, 1892; *L'Intransigeant* (Paris), August 27, 1892.

15. Charles Fegdal, "Le Ghetto parisien contemporain," *La Cité* (Paris), 14 (1915): 230. The Left Bank Russian colony was also described as follows: "High school boys and virgins; students, engineers, workers of all communist tendencies; libertarian Bakuninites and Kropotkinites; serene sociologists; ideological poets, wild dreamers, propagandists of the word or of the deed, those threatened with prison or escaped from it." *Action* (Paris), December 3, 1911.

16. Police report entitled "Les réfugiés révolutionnaires russes à Paris," p. 16, File F⁷ 12894, Archives nationales, Paris; see also Paris, Ministère des affaires étrangères Archives, Dossier NS Russie, vol. 12: Agitation, révolution et anarchie, 1880–1904.

17. "Les réfugiés révolutionnaires russes," p. 26. See Appendix A concerning the total number of Russian refugees estimated by the police.

18. Léonty Soloweitschik, *Un prolétariat méconnu* (Brussels: Henri Lamertin, 1898).

19. Paul Pottier, "Essai sur le prolétariat juif en France," *Revue des Revues*, 3d ser., 28 (March 1899): 490.

20. Nancy L. Green, "Socialist Anti-Semitism, Defense of a Bourgeois Jew and Discovery of the Jewish Proletariat" (forthcoming, 1985, *International Review of Social History*).

21. *UI*, November 1, 1880. Note the early date (pre-massive immigration) of this remark.

22. *Archives Israélites* (Paris, hereafter cited as *AI*), May 1, 1913; see also ibid., November 21, 1889.

23. Phyllis Cohen Albert, *The Modernization of French Jewry: Consistory and Community in the Nineteenth Century* (Hanover, New Hampshire: Brandeis University Press, 1977); cf. Patrick Girard, *Les Juifs de France de 1789 à 1860: De l'émancipation à l'égalité* (Paris: Calmann-Lévy, 1976). Michael Marrus, *The Politics of Assimilation: A Study of the French Jewish Community at the Time of the Dreyfus Affair* (Oxford: Oxford University Press, 1971).

24. Paula Hyman, *From Dreyfus to Vichy: The Remaking of French Jewry* (New York: Columbia University Press, 1979); David H. Weinberg, *A Community on Trial: The Jews of Paris in the 1930s* (Chicago: University of Chicago Press, 1977).

25. Zadoc Kahn, *Sermons et allocations*, 3d series, 3 vols. (Paris: A. Durlacher, 1894), 2:227.

26. "Les Juifs roumains à Paris," *Le Figaro* (Paris), August 25, 1892.

27. According to Doris Ben-Simon Donath, if the agricultural sector is discounted, the stratification of the Parisian Jewish community in 1872 corresponded precisely to that of the Parisian population in general. Ben-Simon Donath, pp. 164, 170. See also David Cohen's recent study of the social mobility of the Jews during the Second Empire: *La Promotion des Juifs en France à l'époque du Second Empire (1852–1870)* (Aix-en-Provence: Publications de l'Université de Provence, 1980).

28. Bernard-Lazare, *Le Nationalisme juif* (Paris: Kadimah, 1898), p. 5.

29. Bernhard Blumenkranz, ed., *Histoire des Juifs en France* (Paris: Privat, 1972), p. 325.

30. See an alternative interpretation of native Jewish response to Jewish immigrants set in the context of German administrative policy by Jack Wertheimer, " 'The Unwanted Element': East European Jews in Imperial Germany," *Leo Baeck Institute Yearbook* 26 (1981): 23–46.

31. Dissenting voices were heard, especially in *L'Univers Israélite*, which criticized the French Jews for "hav[ing] sacrificed on the altar of patriotism their religious sympathies and fraternal pity." November 1, 1893. In 1909 the paper spoke out against the French loan to Russia both because of the situation of the Jews in that country and because the Russians were stealing away French savings! *UI*, February 5, 1909.

The most virulent criticism against the Russian loan came from a Russian Jew (under the name Xhaïm) who published two pamphlets, *Aux Français* (Paris: Imprimerie Xhaïm, n.d. [post-1910]) and *Aux banquiers juifs* (Paris: Imprimerie Goupy, n.d.). To the former he cried: "It is Jewish blood which has paid for your alliance [with Russia]" (p. 13). To the latter he made the same accusation, but it was more poignant in the fratricide implied: "You adore neither the God of Israel . . . [nor any other] but the golden calf" (p. 3). "This people that you bend under the yoke, this people is your brethren by origin. Centuries ago, when all of Israel was bent under the yoke, the Jews at least felt it. But since, having won French naturalization, you believe yourselves liberated from any moral bond, and under the cover of French nationality, you commit your crimes" (p. 6).

32. See Theodor Herzl's conclusions from the Dreyfus affair in *The Jewish State*, in Arthur Hertzberg, ed., *The Zionist Idea* (New York: Atheneum, 1975), p. 209; see also Nancy L. Green, "The Dreyfus Affair and Ruling Class Cohesion," *Science and Society* 43 (Spring 1979): 29–50.

33. In Hertzberg, p. 209.

34. Michel Rudnianski and Patrick Girard, "Les relations entre Israélites français et Juifs russes," 2 vols. (maîtrise, U.E.R. d'Histoire, Université de Paris I, 1971–72), 1:69; cf. Hyman on immigrant-native relations in this period, pp. 115–27.

35. On the history of the Alliance, see André Chouraqui, *Cent ans d'histoire—L'Alliance israélite universelle et la renaissance juive contemporaine (1860–1960)* (Paris: Presses universitaires de France, 1965); and Mika'el Graetz, *Ha-periferiyah hayetah le-merkaz* (Jerusalem: Mossad Bialik, 1982) on the origins of the Alliance.

36. Letter from Veneziani, June 29, 1882, Eisenberg-Borenstein Collection, Microfilm Roll 1, YIVO Archives, New York.

37. E.g., Schafier to Loeb, September 2, 1881, France IXD52: Russie—Emigration 1881–91, File "Juifs de Brody, 1881–82," AIU Archives.

38. Veneziani to AIU, July 28, 1882, France IXD52, File "Affaires de Russie, Emigration de 1882—Brody," AIU Archives; idem, September 29, 1882.

39. As Zosa Szajkowski noted, "The principle of every European committee was to facilitate the migration of refugees, but not to their own country." Szajkowski, "European Attitude," p. 137.

40. *AI*, November 29, 1906.

41. AIU Archives, France IXD51, IXD52 and VID22. Organized emigration to Palestine was out of the question as far as most French philanthropists were concerned, not only because Zionism was incompatible with patriotism to France, but also because of the poor economic opportunities then existing in Palestine. Only Edmond de Rothschild in France, who became known as *HaNadiv Hayadua*, the well-known benefactor, envisaged colonization of Palestine in the early 1890s as an answer to the problem of Russian Jewry. However, his efforts met with little success. See David Druck, *Baron Edmond de Rothschild, The Story of a Practical Idealist* (New York: Hebrew Monotype Press, 1928).

42. See *Bulletin de l'Alliance israélite universelle*, 2e sem. no. 25 (1900), p. 28, and letter from AIU, March 24, 1882, Eisenberg-Borenstein Collection, Microfilm Roll 1, YIVO.

43. Comité de bienfaisance to AIU, August 8, 1894, France IH1: Sociétés, File "Comité de bienfaisance," AIU Archives.

44. Veneziani to AIU, July 26, 1882, France IXD52, File "Affaires de Russie, Emigration de 1882—Brody," AIU Archives; cf. *UI*, November 1, 1880.

45. Excerpt from minutes of May 4, 1893, meeting of the Marseilles Alliance, France IXD52, File "Emigration: Paris, Russie 1891," AIU Archives.

46. Comité de bienfaisance to AIU, July 1905 and May 1906, France IH1: Sociétés, File "Comité de bienfaisance," AIU Archives.

47. *UI*, April 6, 1906; cf. Hirsch to AIU, August 7, 1891, France IXD51: Emigration—Divers, AIU Archives.

48. *AI*, December 1, 1904.

49. *AI*, January 26, 1905.

50. *AI*, November 2, 1882. See also June 14, 1894. For efforts to disperse the ghetto of immigrants from the center of Paris to the outlying districts, see *AI*, February 29, 1912, and March 7, 1912.

51. The correspondence between Marseilles and Paris is especially revealing. In 1892 the Paris office requested that no more immigrants coming via Turkey be sent to Paris via Marseilles. The Marseilles correspondent agreed but complained: It was unfair that Marseilles, which represented only one-twentieth of the French Jewish community, should have to bear the expense of the Russian immigrants as well as the refugees from North African anti-Semitism who had arrived at the port the previous year. The Alliance responded with money to reimburse repatriation funds only. Later the Marseilles correspondent felt compelled to apologize about some immigrants sent from Marseilles who had apparently gone to the Jewish agencies in Paris for help. He assured the Paris office that the Marseilles authorities had allowed the immigrants to continue to Paris only under the express condition that they go neither to the Alliance nor to the Comité de bienfaisance once there. Aristide Vidal-Naquet (in Marseilles) to AIU (Paris), September 21 and October 21, 1892, December 18, 1905; AIU to Vidal-Naquet, September 1892; excerpt from minutes of May 4, 1893 meeting of the Marseilles Alliance, France IXD52, File "Emigration: Paris, Russie 1891," AIU Archives.

52. For Sarrebourg, Saverne, and Nancy: France IXD52, File "Juifs de Brody, 1881–82"; for the rest: France VID22: Russie Emigration, 1882–92, AIU Archives. Sarrebourg revoked its decision in September, writing that the Russian situation seemed to be improving and therefore most of the immigrants could be repatriated.

53. Letter, December 22, 1882, France IXD52, File "Affaires de Russie, Emigration de 1882—Brody," AIU Archives.

54. Confidential Minutes of June 17, 1901, Meeting of Central Alliance Committee Regarding the Situation of the Jews in Rumania, France VD19: Israélites roumains, File "Politique extérieure, Situation des Juifs en Roumanie, 1872–1935," AIU Archives.

55. Ibid.

56. See, e.g., Arcadius Kahan, "The Early Modern Period," in Nachum Gross, ed., *Economic History of the Jews* (New York: Schocken Paperback, 1976), pp. 74–75; and Albert Blanc, *L'Immigration en France et le travail national* (Lyons: A. Rey, 1901), pp. 1–31.

57. *AI*, July 5, 1900; see also *UI*, July 20, 1900.

58. *AI*, "Quelques remarques sur la population juive en France," December 8, 1904. *AI* articles pointing to Jewish workers with no mention of those in Paris: petroleum workers in Galicia—February 19, 1885; in Amsterdam and London—July 17, 1890; in Russia, Poland, the Near East—August 20, 1891; in the United States and England—September 17, 1891, and July 28, 1892; review of Soloweitschik's book—July 21, 1898; "La misère prolétarienne juive" in Galicia (the first time the term "proletarian" is used; this article is explicitly addressed to all anti-Semites who think that all Jews are rich exploiters)—March 23, 1899; Jewish proletariat in Russia and Algeria—June 22, 1899; Russian-Jewish proletariat in England—January 11, 1900; proletarian Jews in London and New York—July 24, 1902; Jewish proletariat in Rumania—January 29, 1903; Jewish proletariat in Russia—February 11, 1904; Jewish

artisans in Russia—January 23, 1913; Jewish poor in Russia, Rumania, Galicia, and North Africa—July 2, 1913.

59. Alfred M. Naquet, "Discussions d'interpellations sur la question juive," *Journal officiel de la Chambre des députés* (Paris), May 27, 1895.

60. Lazare, "La Solidarité juive," *Entretiens politiques et littéraires*, October 1, 1890, pp. 230, 231, 232; see Nelly Jussem-Wilson, "Bernard Lazare's Jewish Journey," *Jewish Social Studies* 26 (July 1964): 146–68; idem, *Bernard-Lazare* (Cambridge: Cambridge University Press, 1978); W. Rabi's portrait of Lazare in Lazare's pamphlet *Antisémitisme et révolution* reprinted by the Cercle Bernard Lazare (Paris: n.d.), pp. 17–40, in which he cites Herzl's description of Lazare as a "spécimen du Juif français subtil" (p. 36); and Marrus, chapter 7. For a modern version of the distinction between *juif* and *israélite* see Dominique Schnapper, *Juifs et Israélites* (Paris: Gallimard, 1980).

61. Tchernoff, 4:281; "Bernard Lazare," *La Presse Nouvelle Hebdomadaire* (Paris), September 22, 1978; and report, February 14, 1897, BA958: Bernard Lazare, Préfecture de Police Archives, Paris. Maxime Rodinson tells the story of how his father led a group of immigrant workers at the turn of the century to see Bernard Lazare in order to engage his help. Lazare was reportedly moved to tears upon meeting them, for although he was very interested in the Jewish proletariat he had never really met one before! Even if Lazare's tears are apocryphal, the story is an important indication of how relative ignorance of the immigrants in Paris could affect even leftist Jewish intellectuals. Interview, Maxime Rodinson, Paris, October 8, 1976.

After a trip to Rumania in 1900 Lazare wrote a particularly scathing letter to the Alliance criticizing its policy with regard to the immigrants: "The Alliance is powerless to procure for them shelter, bread, and the means to earn a living. This is a shame and an intolerable scandal. . . . [The unfortunate are] brutally sent away from the Alliance offices, poorly received on rue Rodier, at the welfare bureau; many of them wander the streets of Paris. . . . If this situation continues, the rest of us, who unfortunately can only defend our persecuted brothers through word and text, will be obliged to denounce the persecution of Jews against Jews alongside the Rumanian persecutions. You allow these unfortunates who knock at your door to be sent back to Rumania where you know that misery and death by starvation—I exaggerate not—await them." Bernard Lazare to President of the Alliance israélite universelle, August 1, [illeg., ca. 1900–1901], Bernard-Lazare manuscripts, Box 12, AIU Archives.

62. André Spire, *Quelques Juifs et demi-Juifs*, 2 vols. (Paris: Grasset, 1928), 1:20.

63. In Hertzberg, p. 209.

64. Ikor, p. 119; cf. Pierre Aubéry, *Milieux juifs de la France contemporaine à travers leurs écrivains* (Paris: Plon, 1962), p. 162.

65. E.g., *AI*, October 18, 1900; *UI*, January 18, 1901.

66. See the distinction between *juif* and *israélite* on the basis of *enracinement* (rootedness) made by Anatole Leroy-Beaulieu, *Les Juifs et l'antisémitisme, Israël chez les nations*, 5th ed. (Paris: Calmann-Lévy, 1893), p. 385.

67. José Jehouda, *De père en fils* (Paris: Grasset, 1927), p. 26.

68. *AI*, January 26, 1905.

69. And contrasting with the bourgeois ideal of small families. The French Jewish community's demographic pattern had followed that of French society as a whole in slowing down after 1850. As one character in *L'épopée de Ménaché Foïgel* explained it from the perspective of Russia: " 'In a little while, Paris will cease to exist! . . . The Parisians don't want to have any more children; when those people who now live in Paris die, there will be no one to replace them.' 'There will always be the Jews,' said Ménaché. 'But no, not even the Jews! Because they've begun to imitate

the goïm.' " Billy and Twersky, 1:163–64. The *UI* asked worriedly with regard to the immigrants: "Does a social body which does not have enough vital energy to reproduce itself have enough to adopt and assimilate others?" *UI*, February 7, 1913; see also *UI*, November 26, 1909, and March 1, 1912; and *AI*, April 9, 1891.

70. *AI*, July 13, 1893. On Moses as a socialist see October 14, 1886.

71. *AI*, October 1, 1885. It may be noted that the *AI* took twenty-seven lines to criticize the nine-line insert in the *Cri du Peuple*.

72. Paris Committee minutes, May 7 and December 7, 1882, cited in Szajkowski, "European Attitude," p. 153.

73. *AI*, November 8, 1894.

74. See Marrus's discussion of Kahn's concept of the "community of suffering" in Marrus, chapter 3.

75. Université populaire juive, *Compte rendu et statuts, 1902–3* (Paris: Imprimerie N.L. Danzig, 1904); on these organizations cf. Hyman, pp. 81, 120–27, 135, 138; and chapter 5 ("The Philanthropic Intersection") in my dissertation, "Class Struggle in the Pletzl," University of Chicago, 1980.

76. *AI*, November 27, 1902.

77. *UI*, March 15, 1912.

78. Tchernoff, 4:281; see also *AI*, March 5, 1902, and January 21, 1904: "un foyer d'instruction et de solidarité juive."

79. *UI*, March 13, 1908.

80. Rudnianski and Girard, pp. 206–7; *AI*, December 13, 1888.

81. *UI*, October 26, 1906. See also *UI*, January 26, 1906, and December 17, 1909, and Association consistoriale israélite de Paris Archives (hereafter cited as ACIP), B91, File "L'Atelier."

82. Soutien aux émigrants to AIU, February 1907 and 1914, France IXD51: Emigration—Divers, AIU Archives.

83. ACIP, B95 (1913), File "Fondation de Rothschild."

84. Léon Kahn, *Les sociétés de secours mutuels* (Paris: A. Durlacher, 1887), pp. 150–51; Szajkowski, "Yidishe fakhshuln in Frankraykh in 19tn yorhundert," *YIVO-Bleter* 42 (1962): 120.

85. AIU Archives, France IH1, File "Le Toit familial."

86. AIU Archives IH1, File "Refuge du Plessis-Piquet."

87. Now known as CASIP, the Comité d'action sociale israélite de Paris. For the following, see Comité de bienfaisance israélite de Paris, *Assemblées générales, 1888–1920* (Paris: Alcan-Lévy, 1888–99, Imprimerie Simon Franck, 1902–20).

88. Outgoing letter, December 4, 1884, Register BB52, p. 12074, ACIP.

89. Zosa Szajkowski stated that the sales contract of the rue Eugène Sue and cité Jeanne d'Arc buildings expelled French workers from their apartments. Szajkowski, "European Attitude," pp. 151–52. However, an article in *Le Temps* (Paris), September 23, 1882, and one in the *AI* of May 15, 1894, said that the immigrants had been placed in newly constructed housing. For 1892, see *UI*, September 1, 1892, and Rudnianski and Girard, p. 216.

90. *AI*, December 23, 1909.

91. *AI*, May 26, 1887.

92. *AI*, April 18, 1889.

93. *AI*, October 18, 1900, and September 24, 1903.

94. *AI*, December 23, 1909.

95. AIU to Comité de bienfaisance, September 28, 1906, and January 6, 1899, France IH1: Sociétés, File "Comité de bienfaisance," AIU Archives.

96. Comité de bienfaisance to AIU, January 5, 1894, see also ibid.; and January

22, 1895, France IH1, File "Comité de bienfaisance," AIU Archives; *UI*, September 26, 1913.

97. *AI*, May 30, 1895.

98. Cf. *Le Matin* (Paris), July 28, 1893, in which the AIU emphasized that it had had no warning of the immigrants' arrival.

99. And he responded vehemently: "Either the Alliance accept the situation [expulsions] and in that case take control of the [aid] movement, or else not accept it, and in that case take a backseat and leave it to those who have taken an energetic lead [in this matter] . . ." Hirsch to AIU, August 7, 1891, France IXD51: Emigration— Divers, AIU Archives.

100. Wolf Speiser, *Kalendar* (Paris: n.p., 1910).

CHAPTER 3: LEBN VI GOT IN FRANKRAYKH?

1. The name was changed in 1900 upon the request of the inhabitants.

2. Cited in Robert Anchel, "The Early History of the Jewish Quarter in Paris," *Jewish Social Studies* 2 (1940): 54.

3. Ibid, pp. 59–60.

4. Léon Kahn, *Les Professions manuelles et les institutions de patronage* (Paris: A. Durlacher, 1885), pp. 21, 64.

5. Cf. Kahn, p. 75, and Doris Ben-Simon Donath, *Socio-démographie des Juifs de France et d'Algérie, 1867–1907*, P.O.F.-Etudes (Paris: Publications orientalistes de France, 1976), p. 77.

6. Cf. Ben-Simon Donath, p. 146 (for all of Paris); and Paris, Association consistoriale israélite de Paris Archives (hereafter cited as ACIP), MM6: Recensement de 1872—Population juive du 4ème arrondissement.

7. By contrast, the Jews who lived in the 9th, 10th, and 11th arrondissements were mostly larger-scale merchants, white collar employees, or professionals. Ben-Simon Donath, pp. 158, 160, 162.

8. Seventeen percent figure derived from ACIP, MM6. For information on the origins of the Parisian Jewish community in 1809 see Kahn, *Les Juifs à Paris depuis le VIe siècle* (Paris: A. Durlacher, 1889), p. 100; for 1872 see Ben-Simon Donath, pp. 94, 104, 109–10; Zosa Szajkowski, *Poverty and Social Welfare among French Jews, 1800–1880* (New York: Editions historiques franco-juives, 1954), p. 87; and Michel Roblin, *Les Juifs de Paris: Démographie, économie, culture* (Paris: A. et J. Picard et Cie., 1952), p. 54.

9. Ben-Simon Donath, p. 114.

10. Ibid., p. 115, derived from marriage registers. Cf. Table 5b, based on the 1872 census.

11. The breakdown between Russians and Rumanians in the 1901 census bears this out: 12.1 percent of the Russians in Paris but 22.6 percent of the Rumanians chose Montmartre. In the 4th arrondissement, the proportions were pretty much the same: 20.6 percent of the Russians, 19.5 percent of the Rumanians in Paris. *Annuaire statistique de la ville de Paris, Année 1901* (Paris: Imprimerie municipale, 1903), p. 201.

12. Audré Billy and Moïse Twersky. *L'épopée de Ménaché Foigel*, 3 vols. (Paris: Plon, 1927–28), 2:96–97.

13. Roger Ikor, *Les fils d'Avrom: Les eaux mêlées* (Paris: Albin Michel, 1955), pp. 210–12.

14. In the 5th: 9 percent of the Rumanians in Paris, 6.1 percent of the Russians;

in the 13th: 3.1 percent of the Russians, 0.6 percent of the Rumanians. *Annuaire statistique,* p. 201.

15. George Weisz, *The Emergence of Modern Universities in France, 1863–1914* (Princeton: Princeton University Press, 1983), chapter 7. See also my article in *Pluriel,* no. 27 (1981), pp. 51–59 "L'émigration comme émancipation" on Russian Jewish women attending the Université de Paris in this period.

16. *Archives Israélites* (Paris, hereafter cited as AI), December 13, 1888; *L'Eclair,* September 28, 1896; Michel Rudnianski and Patrick Girard, "Les relations entre Israélites français et Juifs russes," 2 vols. (maîtrise, U.E.R. d'Histoire, Université de Paris I, 1971–72), p. 212; Police report entitled "Les réfugiés révolutionnaires russes à Paris," p. 17, F⁷ 12894, Archives nationales, Paris.

17. J. Tchernoff, *Dans le creuset des civilisations,* 4 vols. (Paris: Editions Rieder, 1937) 2:88.

18. Ibid, 4:142, 3:15. For a compelling plea in favor of the poor foreign students and an excellent description of their difficulties (adaptation of language, education, and even thought process that was necessary), see *L'Univers Israélite* (Paris, hereafter cited as UI), December 20, 1912.

19. Maxime Rodinson, interview in Paris, October 8, 1976.

20. The mistrust of Yiddish had its forebears in the late eighteenth century when Turgot wrote (with regard to Jewish business dealings): "All of their signatures are in a corrupted Hebrew which gives them a marvelous aid in preserving their secret." In 1806 an anti-Semitic lawyer, Poujol, stated that the Jews use their language to carry on espionage. Szajkowski, "Der kamf kegn yidish in Frankraykh," *YIVO-Bleter* 14 (1939): 50, 57. In the period under study, a police report sent from La Rochelle to Paris speculated on a Yiddish tract that had been confiscated, that it was "composed in characters which are special and unknown for whomever does not possess the key to them. It is probable that the confidential orders of the C.G.T., from which this document emanates, are all composed in such characters." Report, August 4, 1911, F⁷ 13740: Habillement, File "Habillement," Archives nationales.

21. *UI,* July 25, 1913. See also *UI,* January 16, 1889, September 8, 1911, and July 25, 1913, and *AI,* February 9, 1905. During World War I the Consistoire requested that Yiddish not be used for religious services for fear of bringing suspicion on the community. On the wartime language dispute see Minutes, January and February 1916, AA20: Procès-verbaux, ACIP; *AI,* June 28, 1917; and Paula Hyman, *From Dreyfus to Vichy: The Remaking of French Jewry, 1906–1939* (New York: Columbia University Press, 1979), pp. 118–19, 127.

22. *UI,* February 16, 1892. Cf. Szajkowski, *Etyudn tsu der geshikhte fun ayngevandertn yidishn yishev in Frankraykh* (Paris: Fridman, 1936), pp. 137–51. On Yiddish theater and other immigrant organizations cf. Hyman, pp. 77–83.

23. *Der idisher arbayter* (Paris), January 3, 1914. For many of the cultural events of the 1911–14 period, see the advertisements and announcements that appeared in *Der idisher arbayter* as well as the leaflets in New York, Bund Archives, Pariz: Bundisher fareyn "Kemfer" afishn.

24. Szajkowski, *Etyudn,* p. 147; B. Vinogura, "Materialn tsu der geshikhte fun ayngevandertn yidishn yishev in Frankraykh," *Naye prese* (Paris), February 1, 1936.

25. Szajkowski, *Etyudn,* pp. 117–19; *Le Jour* (Paris), December 18, 1982.

26. See especially: David Diamant, "Les Juifs immigrés en France et le mouvement progressiste, 1900–1934" (unpublished), pp. 24–25; Szajkowski, "150 yor yidishe prese in Frankraykh," *Yidn in Frankraykh,* ed. E. Tcherikower, 2 vols. (New York: YIVO, 1942), 1:236–302; idem, *Etyudn,* pp. 46, 112; idem, *Di profesyonele*

bavegung tsvishn di yidishe arbeter in Frankraykh biz 1914 (Paris: Fridman, 1937), p. 70; and *Der idisher arbayter* (Paris), July 4, 1914.

27. *L'Univers Israélite* noted that the proportion of immigrants among religious Jews had risen from 25 percent in 1896 to 60 percent in 1908. *UI*, February 5, 1909. This is not only a considerable increase but is significant compared to the 45 percent of the Jewish population that the immigrants represented. See also *AI*, June 28, 1883.

28. *AI*, June 11, 1914; cf. *UI*, October 26, 1900, and November 9, 1900.

29. Billy and Twersky, 1:167.

30. "Les réfugiés révolutionnaires russes," p. 5; Tchernoff, 4:279; *UI*, October 19, 1900; *AI*, September 12, 1901. See "Les réfugiés révolutionnaires russes," pp. 4–5, for the police department's evaluation that the Russian Jews were more outwardly religious than really believers in order to receive philanthropic aid from the rich Parisian Israélites. Or, as Harry Golden put it, an eastern European "freethinker" and Socialist may still have gone to *shul* (temple) regularly because: "These people are my brethren, they are the people among whom I was raised, I love them. Dudja Silverberg goes to *shul* to speak with God, I go to *shul* to speak with Dudja." Isaac Metzger, ed., *Bintel Brief* (New York: Ballantine, 1971), p. 70.

31. Tchernoff, 3:14–15.

32. For the following discussion of immigrant religious life see Paris, ACIP, AA19: Procès-verbaux, 1906–15; BB50–59: Lettres envoyées, 1882–91; and the B series (*Lettres reçues*), from 1888 to 1917, particularly the files labeled "Sociétés," "Oratoires," "Commission du 4ème Arrondissement," etc. See also Paris, Consistoire central Archives, I^cc 77: Lettres du Ministère de l'intérieur et des cultes, 1899–1905; and Roger Kohn, "L'organisation de l'éducation juive chez les immigrés d'Europe orientale à Paris," *YOD*, vol. 3, fascicule 2 (n.d.), pp. 87–90.

33. The Consistoire could be useful in this regard to both parties. It gave information to the Ministère des cultes, for example, with regard to Rabbi Lubetzki's character (favorable) when the latter applied for naturalization. Ministère des cultes to Consistoire central, June 22, 1899, I^cc 77, Consistoire central Archives. With regard to Rabbi Kahn's support of immigrant talmud-torahs, see ACIP, K17: Imprimés, File "1901."

34. ACIP, B60.

35. *AI*, March 31, 1904, and *UI*, June 28, 1907. Kohn had also previously come into conflict with the Consistoire over *mariages à domicile* (home ceremonies) which the Consistoire opposed. Kohn argued that some families were too poor to pay for an official Consistorial wedding (although this was not the problem in the Gunzberg case). On the marriage problem of eastern European immigrants in France due to conflicting Russian and French legislation, further complicated by the separation of church and state in France in 1905, see *AI*, July 11, 1912, and January 30, 1913; *UI*, June 28, 1907, January 31, March 27, and April 3, 1908, January 3 and 10, 1913; and ACIP, AA19.

36. See Hyman's discussion of "Who Shall Rule?", pp. 139–43.

37. ACIP, B78, "Associations cultuelles."

38. ACIP, B95, "Oratoire Ste. Isaure."

39. ACIP, B95, "Commission du 4ème arrondissement."

40. Ibid.

41. ACIP, B95, "Oratoire Ste. Isaure."

42. ACIP, B90, "Union des Communautés." This file, along with ACIP, B95, "Commission du 4ème arrondissement" and ACIP, AA19, pp. 190–93, 212–17, are those that deal with the Agoudath controversy.

43. "Orthodoxy is only a pretext for justifying enrollment under the banner of a

foreign, fanatical rabbi, maintaining among his followers the ideas and prejudices of another civilization." ACIP, B95, "Commission du 4ème arrondissement." After World War I, with the ever-increasing immigration of eastern European Jews, the rue des Tournelles temple did eventually become the religious center of eastern European Jewry in the Pletzl.

44. *AI*, June 18, 1914.

45. William H. Sewell, Jr., *Work and Revolution in France: The Language of Labor from the Old Regime to 1848* (New York: Cambridge University Press, 1980), p. 231; see also pp. 163–66, 184–85, 256–57.

46. Abraham Uhafti, interview in Fontenay-sous-Bois, October 27, 1978.

47. Szajkowski, *Etyudn*, pp. 33–41.

48. ACIP, B60, B65. The bylaws of the Chevré Kadischa de Varsovie are almost identical to those of the Ahavath Reim, both being modeled after the standard French mutual aid society bylaw form. Political discussions were forbidden according to such bylaws, although there is some question as to whether this prohibition was actually complied with. See Szajkowski, "Dos yidishe gezelshaftlekhe lebn in Pariz tsum yor 1939," *Yidn in Frankraykh*, ed. E. Tcherikower, 2 vols. (New York: YIVO, 1942), 2:226–27; Tchernoff, 4:278; and Paris, Préfecture de Police Archives (hereafter cited as APP), BA157: Chapeliers.

49. Szajkowski, "Yidishe gezelshaftlekhe lebn," p. 220.

50. APP, BA1708: Russo-juifs à Paris, Files "Bureau russe du travail," "Pièces communes," and "La Table d'hôte des emigrés."

51. See Fernand Pelloutier, *Histoire des Bourses du travail* (Paris: Gordon et Breach, 1971), esp. pp. 111–14, 127, 135–41, where he lists the various functions of the Bourses as: placement offices, libraries, places where professional training and economic, scientific, and technical talks could be held, refuges for traveling workers, and coordination centers for workers' demands.

52. APP, BA1708, "La Table d'hôte des émigrés."

53. Speiser counted approximately two hundred members in 1910. Wolf Speiser, *Kalendar* (Paris: n.p., 1910), pp. 58–60; *AI*, February 23, 1893, cf. May 10, 1894; *UI*, March 16, 1893; Paris, Alliance israélite universelle (hereafter cited as AIU) Archives, France IH1: Sociétés, File "Association des étudiants russes"; Rudnianski and Girard, p. 227.

54. Report, November 21, 1913, BA1709: Russo-juifs à Paris, File "Société philanthropique et de fraternité des ouvriers russes de Paris," APP.

55. When a similar initiative to organize immigrant societies by French Jews was announced several months later in *L'Univers Israélite*, H. Cherchevsky, President of the Commission d'initiative pour l'organisation d'une fédération des sociétés juives de Paris, wrote a letter to the editor commenting: "Without insisting on the coincidence of these two initiatives, I must express my surprise that we [the immigrants] only heard of this [French] initiative through your paper." *UI*, February 28, 1913.

56. On the role of the Fédération between the wars see David Weinberg, *A Community on Trial: The Jews of Paris in the 1930s* (Chicago: University of Chicago Press, 1977); and Hyman, pp. 80–81, 85–87, 150–51, and 207–16. For earlier (unsuccessful) attempts at immigrant society consolidation, see Szajkowski, *Profesyonele bavegung*, pp. 80–81.

57. Novochelski to AIU, January 23, 1888, France IX D51: Emigration—Divers, AIU Archives; a Société russe de bienfaisance de Paris of 1895 is probably but another name for Novochelski's organization. See Comité de bienfaisance to AIU, June 23, 1895, France IH1, "Comité de bienfaisance," AIU Archives; and Rudnianski and Girard, p. 219.

58. Statuts de la Prévoyante israélite (Paris: Imprimerie Cemenoff, 1893); ACIP, B60, B65.

59. By 1913 the school had sixty-five students. *UI*, September 12, 1913; APP, BA1708, "Pièces communes."

60. Société philanthropique de l'Asile israélite de Paris (hereafter cited as Asile), *Rapport de l'exercice 1905–6* (Paris: Imprimerie N. L. Danzig, n.d.), pp. 13–14.

61. *UI*, November 26, 1909.

62. Asile, *Rapport de l'exercice 1912*, p. 24.

63. Asile, *Rapport de l'exercice 1905–6*, p. 19; ibid., *1909*, p. 11; Asile to AIU, June 1907, France IH1, File "Asile de jour israélite," AIU Archives; ACIP, B78, "Associations cultuelles."

64. See especially APP, BA1708–9: Russo-juifs à Paris, BA1507–8: Anarchistes, BA1324: Russie, and BA1144: Pierre Lawroff; Paris, Archives nationales, F⁷ 12519–21: Anti-tsariste, F⁷ 12894: Réfugiés et révolutionnaires russes en France, 1907–12, and F⁷ 13065: Anarchistes et révolutionnaires étrangers en France, 1912.

65. "Les réfugiés révolutionnaires russes," p. 36.

66. APP, BA1098.

67. "Les réfugiés révolutionnaires russes," p. 5.

68. Report, February 23, 1912, BA1708, "Bureau russe du travail," APP.

69. In addition to APP, BA1144, and BA1709 see E. Tcherikower, "Peter Lavrov and the Jewish Socialist Emigrés," *YIVO Annual of Jewish Social Science* 7 (1952): 132–45; Charles Rappoport, "The Life of a Revolutionary Emigré (Reminiscences)," *YIVO Annual of Jewish Social Science* 6 (1951): 206–36; *AI*, October 11, 1883, and October 1, 1885.

70. Report, December 19, 1891, BA1709, File "Société de Juifs russes dite 'Bene Sion,'" APP; A. Frumkin, *In friling fun idishn sotsializm* (New York: Yubiley Komitet, 1940), p. 213. Ossip Zetkin, later Clara Zetkin's husband, was for a time the secretary of the Russian Workers' Society. Rappoport, p. 219.

71. APP, BA1709, File "Narodnia Volia."

72. Approximately 250 people attended. APP, BA1709, File "Le Collège Russe"; Szajkowski, *Profesyonele bavegung*, p. 63; Tchernoff, 4:54.

73. APP, BA1709, File "La Russie Révolutionnaire."

74. "Les réfugiés révolutionnaires russes," p. 26.

75. Tchernoff, 4:147–48. See also Szajkowski, *Profesyonele bavegung*, pp. 61, 63, and Marc Jarblum, "Deux rencontres avec Lénine," *Les nouveaux cahiers* 20 (Spring 1970): 8–16.

76. Szajkowski, *Profesyonele bavegung*, pp. 60–63, 69–71. See also *Der idisher arbayter*, May 1, 1912, and August 3, 1912.

77. APP, BA1708, File "Cercle ouvrier russe de Paris"; Reports, April 12, June 9, June 22, August 6, and November 13, 1912, F⁷ 12894, File "Notes," Archives nationales.

78. "Les réfugiés révolutionnaires russes," p. 26; APP, BA1709, File "La Bounda" and BA1708, File "Bibliothèque russo-juive-ouvrière"; *Der idisher arbayter*, February 7, 1914; Speiser, p. 31. There is some question as to the origins of the Bund in Paris. Franz Kurski, long time archivist for the Bund, gave the earliest date of 1898 in an article in *Unzer shtime* (Paris), February 4, 1939, explicitly correcting Szajkowski, who in an earlier article and in *Etyudn*, pp. 115–17, dated the founding of the Kemfer to 1904. A leaflet announcing the ten-year jubilee of the Parisian Kemfer group was dated January 13, 1912. New York, Bund Archives, Pariz: Bundisher fareyn "Kemfer" afishn. On the history of the Bund see Henry J. Tobias, *The Jewish Bund in Russia from its Origins to 1905* (Stanford: Stanford University Press, 1970); Jonathan

Frankel, *Prophecy and Politics: Socialism, Nationalism and the Russian Jews, 1862–1917* (Cambridge: Cambridge University Press, 1981); and Robert Brym, *The Jewish Intelligentsia and Russian Marxism* (New York: Schocken Books, 1978).

79. "Les réfugiés révolutionnaires russes," p. 26.

80. APP, BA1709, File "Société philanthropique et de fraternité des ouvriers juifs russes à Paris dit 'Groupe montmartrois' " and BA1709, File "Anarchistes russes à Paris"; "Les réfugiés révolutionnaires russes," pp. 5, 30, 33, and 39; Rudolf Rocker, *In shturem*, trans. J. Birnbaum (from German) (Argentina: London 'Fraye Arbetershtime' Grupe, 1952), pp. 35–47, 424–26; Szajkowski, *Etyudn*, pp. 110–13; and idem, *Profesyonele bavegung*, pp. 57–59, 66–70, 78.

81. Reports, May 31, June 3, June 10, July 17, September 29, and October 13, 1909, BA1709, File "Groupe des émigrés juifs de Paris," APP.

82. Pierre Aubéry, "Mécislas Golberg, anarchiste," *Le Mouvement Social*, no. 52 (July–September 1965), pp. 97–109; *Le Figaro* (Paris), May 2 and 4, 1907; Szajkowski, *Profesyonele bavegung*, pp. 58–59.

83. Report, April 28, 1910, F⁷ 12894, File "1910," Archives nationales.

84. Anonymous letter to police, February 1, 1905, and report, April 16, 1909, BA1708, File "Société des étudiants russes," APP.

85. Another example would be the Zionist groups that made an appearance in Paris before World War I. A group Bene Sion met in the 3rd and 11th arrondissements from the late 1880s until 1893; another group called Palestinak appeared in late 1891 to 1892 (in the 18th) with the purpose of founding communist colonies in Palestine; and still another group called Mevassereth Zion existed in 1895. The Labor Zionists (Poalei-Zion) and Socialist Zionists (interested in a Jewish homeland anywhere, not necessarily in Palestine) also appeared in Paris from the early 1900s on. In general, however, the Zionist movement was not important among the eastern European Jews in Paris before World War I. The movement itself was just beginning to gather strength and often found political or economic conditions in Palestine unfavorable to it. More likely, those who had emigrated to the West had already made their choice. APP, BA 1709, "Société de Juifs russes dite 'Bene Sion' "; Szajkowski, *Profesyonele bavegung*, pp. 62–63; idem, *Etyudn*, p. 119; *Der idisher arbayter*, July 4, 1914; Rudnianski and Girard, pp. 218, 227; and correspondence from Paris in *Der nayer veg* (Vilna), April 28, May 5, and May 26, 1906; *Unzer veg* (Vilna), September 1, 1907; *Dos vort* (Vilna), May 25 and June 25, 1907; and *Yidisher arbayter pinkes* (Warsaw: n.p., 1927), p. 59 (with many thanks to the late Hillel Kempinski for these sources). Cf. Hyman, chapter 6; and Catherine Levigne, "Le Mouvement sioniste en France des environs de 1880 à 1921." *Le Monde Juif*, no. 88 (October–December 1977), pp. 137–53.

86. For more information on these political groups and their contacts with French Socialists, see especially, APP, BA1324 and BA1709; and Nancy L. Green, "Eléments pour une étude du mouvement ouvrier juif à Paris au début du siècle," *Le Mouvement Social* no. 110 (January–March 1980) pp. 51–73; and idem, "Socialist Anti-Semitism, Defense of a Bourgeois Jew and Discovery of the Jewish Proletariat" (forthcoming, 1985, *International Review of Social History*).

87. Estimated at one-third of the Russian immigrants according to Jacques Lederman, interview in Paris, October 12, 1977.

88. Rappoport, pp. 236–37; Szajkowski, *Etyudn*, pp. 117–19, 145.

89. See, e.g., the description of Chinese, Lebanese, and other immigrant religious and mutual aid societies in L. A. Fallers, ed., *Immigrants and Associations* (The Hague, Paris: Mouton, 1967).

CHAPTER IV: OCCUPATIONAL STRUCTURE

.1. Henri Dagan, "Le prolétariat juif mondial," *La Revue blanche*, October 15, 1901, p. 268.

2. Karpel and Dinner for the Groupe des ouvriers juifs socialistes de Paris, *Le prolétariat juif: Lettre des ouvriers juifs de Paris au Parti socialiste français* (Paris: Imprimerie Typographique J. Allemane, 1898), p. 8.

3. Paul Pottier, "Essai sur le prolétariat juif en France," *Revue des Revues*, 3d sér., 28 (March 1899): 482. Cf. Dagan, pp. 264–65; Alfred H. Fried, "Das jüdische Proletariat in Frankreich," *Jüdische Statistik*, ed. Alfred Nossig (Berlin: Pass und Garleb, 1903), p. 386; and Michael Marrus, *The Politics of Assimilation* (Oxford: Oxford University Press, 1971), p. 45.

4. *Archives Israélites* (Paris), August 30, 1900, and January 24, 1907.

5. The Comité de bienfaisance estimated in 1904 that (only) 40 percent of the Jewish indigent population was comprised of Russian Jews, while Rudnianski and Girard estimate the proportion of immigrant Jews among the Jewish poor at that time at over 65 percent. Comité de bienfaisance to Alliance israélite universelle, July 1904, France IH1: Sociétés, File "Comité de bienfaisance," Alliance israélite universelle Archives, Paris; Michel Rudnianski and Patrick Girard, "Les relations entre Israélites français et Juifs russes," 2 vols. (maîtrise, U.E.R. d'Histoire, Université de Paris I, 1971–72), p. 218. It must be noted that both of these estimates have to do with the period *before* the 1905 immigratiion.

6. Pottier, pp. 485 and 488.

7. Zosa Szajkowski, "The European Attitude to Eastern European Jewish Immigration (1881–93)," *Publications of the American Jewish Historical Society* 41 (December 1951): 151.

8. Derived from *Annuaire statistique de la ville de Paris, Année 1909* (Paris: Imprimerie municipale, 1911), p. 678. According to an 1889 report the imbalance in favor of Russian males was even greater—1.32:1. Prince de Cassano, *Procès-verbaux sommaires du Congrès international de l'intervention des pouvoirs publics dans l'émigration et l'immigration, tenu à Paris du 12 au 14 août 1889 (Exposition universelle internationale de 1889)* (Paris: Imprimerie nationale for the Ministère du commerce, de l'industrie et des colonies, 1890), p. 10.

9. Société philanthropique de l'Asile israélite de Paris (hereafter cited as Asile), *Rapports des exercices 1910–12* (Paris: Imprimerie N. L. Danzig, n.d.).

10. Report, February 23, 1912, BA1708: Russo-juifs à Paris, File "Bureau russe du Travail," Préfecture de police Archives, Paris; *L'Univers Israélite* (Paris), March 1, 1912, and November 26, 1909.

11. A higher male-female ratio among the Italian community—1.6:1—is one indication of a less familial and more purely economic immigration in France. The higher percentage of economically active persons among the German immigrants (61 percent as compared to 46 percent for the Russian immigrants) is another. De Cassano, p. 10; Georges Mauco, *Les étrangers en France* (Paris: Armand Colin, 1932), p. 45.

12. *Archives Israélites*, February 29, 1912.

13. Pottier, p. 486; cf. Fried, p. 387.

14. Pottier, p. 486; cf. Fried, p. 388. See also *L'Univers Israélite*, November 11, 1910, in which the "ingenuity . . . and surprising sobriety" of the immigrant workers were praised for reducing "the causes of destruction and death"; the anti-Semitic stereotypes of the "dirty Jew" were thereby also implicitly refuted.

15. Doris Ben-Simon Donath, *Socio-démographie des Juifs de France et d'Algérie, 1867–1907*, P.O.F.-Etudes (Paris: Publications orientalistes de France, 1976), p. 307.

16. *Der idisher arbayter* (Paris), July 4, 1914.

17. Szajkowski, *Etyudn tsu der geshikhte fun ayngevandertn yidishn yishev in Frankraykh* (Paris: Fridman, 1936), pp. 129–30.

18. Dagan, p. 267.

19. Szajkowski, "European Attitude," p. 151; Léon Kahn, *Le Comité de bienfaisance* (Paris: A. Durlacher, 1886), p. 25; and Report, November 3, 1912, BA1708, "Bureau russe du travail," Préfecture de police Archives.

20. Asile, *Rapports des exercices, 1906–12*; Wolf Speiser, *Kalendar* (Paris: n.p., 1910).

21. It must also be taken into consideration that immigrant responses upon arrival may have been colored by expectations with regard to job availability. There is no way of knowing the number of cap sellers who became cap makers, a more productive, i.e., useful, trade upon crossing the frontier, or the number of simple ironers who listed themselves as tailors for immigration purposes. Word traveled fast about the necessity of exaggerating, if not lying, about qualifications, and such hints were part of the passwords sent along in letters from the New World back to the Old.

22. In the peak years, 1906–9, the eastern Europeans accounted for 72.3 percent of the Asile's visitors.

23. As quoted by Judith Friedlander (anthropologist, working on eastern European Jewish immigrants in Paris) from one of her informants. Letter to the author, November 15, 1979.

24. Mlle. Schirmacher, *La spécialisation du travail—Par nationalités, à Paris* (Paris: Arthur Rousseau, 1908), p. 36.

25. Report, November 3, 1912, BA1708, "Bureau russe du travail," Préfecture de police Archives.

26. Ibid., July 19, 1918, BA1709: Russo-juifs à Paris, File "Liste des révolutionnaires russes soumis à examen."

27. Arthur Ruppin, *Les Juifs dans le monde moderne*, trans. M. Chevalley (Paris: Payot, 1934), p. 188.

28. For example, Léonty Soloweitschik on London, *Un prolétariat méconnu* (Brussels: Henri Lamertin, 1898), pp. 47–48; and G.M. Preiss on Manhattan in *Nedel'naia Khronika Voskhoda* 17 (Odessa, 1891), cited by Arcadius Kahan in "Economic Opportunities and Some Pilgrims' Progress: Jewish Immigrants from Eastern Europe in the United States, 1890–1914," *The Journal of Economic History* 38 (March 1978): 247. See also A. Menes's critique of the Jewish Colonization Association report in Jacob Lestschinsky, ed., *Shriftn far ekonomik un statistik* 1 (Berlin: YIVO, 1928), pp. 255–56.

It may be added that a disdain for commercial activity was not the province of statisticians alone. Yankel Mykhanowitzki's comment, when his son expressed the desire to open a store, was: "Le commerce, pfeh! Un métier de feignants, ca!" His son understood: "Pour papa, un commerçant, c'était un simple parasite." Roger Ikor, *Les fils d'Avrom: Les eaux mêlées* (Paris: Albin Michel, 1955), pp. 344, 348.

29. Furthermore, there is a problem of interpretation of occupational data. A *fourreur* or furrier, for example, may be a fur-worker or a fur dealer; a *diamantaire* may be a diamond-cutter or a diamond merchant. (This problem seems to occur more often in French than in English.) In the manuscript census data of 1872, for example, occupations were often qualified by *ouvrier en* (worker in) or *marchand de* (merchant of), but this was seldom the case in the processed Asile or Speiser data. At the risk of being overly productive-determinist, which I criticize above, I have, in general,

classified job categories as productive unless they were specifically indicated to be otherwise. This corresponds to the descriptive accounts of the Jewish working population found elsewhere, and, in any case, still leaves room for those who identified themselves as merchants.

30. Cf. the occupational statistics for 1907–9 calculated by Paula Hyman, *From Dreyfus to Vichy: The Remaking of French Jewry, 1906–39* (New York: Columbia University Press, 1979), pp. 73–74, Appendix A and footnote 56, p. 264.

31. Confetti, at only 50 to 60 centimes a kilogram was not a bad item, selling better than ties or shoes; apparently, confetti fanatics would even buy it in order to stock up! *Archives Israélites*, February 26, 1903.

32. See Thomas Kessner, *The Golden Door: Italian and Jewish Immigrant Mobility in New York City, 1880–1915* (New York: Oxford University Press, 1977).

33. Cf. Michel Roblin, *Les Juifs de Paris: Démographie, économie, culture* (Paris: A. et J. Picard et Cie., 1952), who emphasizes the petit-bourgeois aspect of the incipient merchant; and Kessner, esp. pp. 19, 51 (note), 55, 60–61, 88, and 108 on the relation of peddling to social mobility; with Pottier, pp. 482–92, whose analysis is evident in the title of his article: "Essai sur le prolétariat juif en France." See also Szajkowski, *Poverty and Social Welfare Among French Jews, 1800–1880* (New York: Editions historiques Franco-juives, 1954), pp. 38, 40, where he explicitly refutes Roblin's characterization of the Jewish community.

34. The *Archives Israélites*, noting this factory in the 19th arrondissement, lauded it as both charitable and productive, November 8, 1883.

35. Eighteen seventy-two figure derived from Paris, Association consistoriale israélite de Paris Archives, MM6: Recensement de 1872—Population juive du 4ème arrondissement; 1912 figure cited by Losovsky in Fédération des syndicats ouvriers de la chapellerie française, *15e Congrès national (Bort, 1912)* (Paris: Imprimerie La Productrice, 1913), p. 61.

36. Speiser, p. 47.

37. Paris, Association consistoriale israélite de Paris Archives, AA9, 19–20: Procès-verbaux, and BB50–59: Lettres envoyées.

38. Police report entitled "Les réfugiés révolutionnaires russes à Paris," p. 8 F⁷ 12894, Archives nationales, Paris.

39. Ibid., p. 12; *La Vérité*, March 23, 1894, wrote about the "faussaires habiles" who lived off of falsifying documents; see also Charles Lopata, *J'ai survécu* (Paris: Editions Droit et Liberté, 1977), p. 51.

40. André Billy and Moïse Twersky, *L'épopée de Ménaché Foïgel*, 3 vols. (Paris: Plon, 1927–28), 2:28.

41. J. Tchernoff, *Dans le creuset des civilisations*, 4 vols. (Paris: Editions Rieder, 1937), 2:110.

CHAPTER V: AT WORK, ON STRIKE

1. Alfred H. Fried, "Das jüdische Proletariat in Frankreich," *Jüdische Statistik*, ed. Alfred Nossig (Berlin: Pass und Garleb, 1903), p. 387.

2. The major sources used for the description of workshop conditions here and below are: Paris, Préfecture de police Archives (hereafter cited as APP), BA157 (Chapeliers), BA182 (Casquettiers), BA1356 and 1410 (Boulangers), BA1372 and 1422 (Ebénistes), BA1393–94 (Tailleurs), BA1423 and BA1444 (Habillement); *Der idisher arbayter* (Paris, hereafter cited as YA), 1911–1914; *L'Ouvrier chapelier* (Paris), 1896–1914; Pierre du Maroussem, *La petite industrie (salaires et durée du travail)* (Paris: Office du travail, 1896); Office du travail, *Associations professionnelles ouvrières* (Paris:

Imprimerie nationale, 1901); Alfred Picard, general editor, *Exposition universelle internationale de 1889 à Paris: Rapports du jury international*, Classe 36: *Habillement des deux sexes*, by Albert Leduc (Paris: Ministère du commerce, de l'industrie et des colonies, 1891); *Exposition universelle internationale de 1900 à Paris: Rapports du jury international*, Groupe XIII: *Fils, tissus, vêtements*, 2ème partie—Classes 85 et 86, by Léon Storch, Julien Hayem, and A. Mortier (Paris: Ministère du commerce, de l'industrie, des postes et des télégraphes, 1902); François Fagnot, *Réglementation du travail en chambre (rapport des séances du 18 mars et 27 avril 1904)* (Paris: Félix Alcan, n.d.); and Joseph Klatzmann, *Le travail à domicile dans l'industrie parisienne du vêtement* (Paris: Armand Colin, 1957).

3. Wolf Speiser, *Kalendar* (Paris: n.p., 1910), p. 48.

4. Mlle. Schirmacher, *La spécialisation du travail—Par nationalités, à Paris* (Paris: Arthur Rousseau, 1908), p. 71.

5. Ibid., p. 92.

6. The most extensive account of this strike is found in APP, BA1394, File "Grève des tailleurs pour dames chez Paquin, Doucet, King, Doeuillet, Raudnitz, Bechoff et Berr, février 1901." See also Office du travail, *Bulletin de l'Office du travail (1901)*, pp. 174–75, which reported the number of strikers at two thousand.

7. *Archives Israélites* (Paris), February 14, 1901.

8. *La Libre Parole* (Paris), February 5, 7, and 11, 1901. As has already been seen in chapter 1, approximately 85 percent of the womenswear tailors were foreigners (as compared to 35 percent in menswear), most of whom were Jewish.

9. Storch, Hayem, and Mortier, p. 42.

10. Information on strikes has been compiled largely from the police reports and *Der idisher arbayter* listed in footnote 2 above, along with Zosa Szajkowski, *Di profesyonele bavegung tsvishn di yidishe arbeter in Frankraykh biz 1914* (Paris: Fridman, 1937), and Office du travail, *Statistiques des grèves et des recours à la conciliation et à l'arbitrage, 1891–1920* (Paris: Imprimerie nationale).

11. APP, BA1394, File "Grève . . . Ribby, novembre 1911."

12. On the 1911 tailors' strike, ibid. On the leatherworkers' strike see YA, August 3, 1912. See also YA, October 9, 1911, and September 7, 1912, on the hours issue.

13. YA, September 7, 1912.

14. APP, BA1393, File "Grève . . . Braunstein, septembre 1904."

15. APP, BA1394, File "Grève . . . Bernard, septembre 1910."

16. Michelle Perrot, *Les ouvriers en grève, France 1871–1890*, 2 vols. (Paris: Mouton and Ecole Pratique des Hautes Etudes, 1974), See especially I:seconde partie, ch. II, "Revendications et griefs."

17. Ezra Mendelsohn, *Class Struggle in the Pale: The Formative Years of the Jewish Workers' Movement in Tsarist Russia* (Cambridge: Cambridge University Press, 1970), p. 87.

18. See especially Maurice Lauzel's interesting monograph, *Ouvriers juifs de Paris: Les casquettiers* (Paris: Edouard Cornély et Cie., 1912); and Maurice et Léon Bonneff, *La vie tragique des travailleurs* (Paris: Jules Rouff & Cie., 1908), pp. 317–38 on "Les ouvriers juifs de Paris." Capmaking in London in the 1890s was also in predominantly Jewish hands. Jerry White, *Rothschild Buildings* (London: Routledge & Kegan Paul, 1980), p. 222.

19. Fédération des syndicats ouvriers de la chapellerie française, 15ᵉ Congrès national (Bort, 1912) (Paris: Imprimerie La Productrice, 1913), p. 61.

20. Roger Ikor, *Les fils d'Avrom: Les eaux mêlées* (Paris: Albin Michel, 1955), pp. 159, 161.

21. APP, BA182, File "Février 1886—Grève, Herse et Weidenbach."

22. On the 1901 strike see Office du travail, *Bulletin (1901)*, pp. 696–97; idem, *Statistiques des grèves . . . 1901*, strike no. 229; Henri Dagan, *De la condition du peuple au XXe siècle* (Paris: V. Giard et E. Brière, 1904), pp. 364–66; and Szajkowski, *Etyudn tsu der geshikhte fun ayngevandertn yidishn yishev in Frankraykh* (Paris: Fridman, 1936), pp. 92–100. On the 1906 strike see Office du travail, *Statistiques des grèves . . . 1906*, strike no. 598; and Szajkowski, *Profesyonele bavegung*, pp. 101–2.

23. Losovsky's reports on the 1912 strike are found in Fédération des syndicats ouvriers de la chapellerie française, pp. 13–18, 60–64, and *L'Ouvrier chapelier* (Paris), April to November 1912. See also Office du travail, *Statistiques des grèves . . . 1912*, strikes nos. 370, 371, and 506; *YA*, May 1 and August 3, 1912; New York, Bund Archives, Yidn in Frankraykh and Pariz: Bundisher fareyn "Kemfer" afishn files; Albert Matline, Secretary of the Syndicat des chapeliers, modistes et casquettiers, "Le syndicat des casquettiers à 70 ans," unpublished memoir; and Szajkowski, *Profesyonele bavegung*, pp. 141–47.

24. Two known waiters' strikes occurred: in 1913 at Lander's restaurant and in 1914 at Kowarsky's restaurant. *YA*, March 7 and April 11, 1914; Szajkowski, *Profesyonele bavegung*, p. 261.

25. *YA*, May 1, 1912.

26. On the 1908 strike see report, January 28, 1908, BA1708: Russo-juifs à Paris, File "Restaurants et coopératives russes à Paris," APP; Office du travail, *Statistiques des grèves . . . 1908*, strike no. 104; idem, *Bulletin (1908)*, pp. 232–33. On the 1909 strike see idem, *Statistiques des grèves . . . 1909*, strike no. 98.

27. New York, Bund Archives, Kemfer file, in which one leaflet lists five struck bakeries but seventy strikers; Office du travail, *Statistiques des grèves . . . 1913*, strike no. 128; and APP, BA1394, File "Grève . . . Galeries Lafayette, février 1913."

28. New York, Bund Archives, Kemfer file.

29. *YA*, June 29, 1912; see also issues dated August 3, September 7, and October 5, 1912.

30. *YA*, April 11, 1914.

31. See, e.g., Fédération des syndicats ouvriers de la chapellerie française, *XIIIe Congrès national (Chazelles-sur-Lyon, 1906)* (Paris: Maison des fédérations, 1906), pp. 50–51; Fédération nationale des cuirs et peaux, *7e Congrès national (Graulhaut, 1911)* (Paris: Maison des fédérations, n.d.), p. 45.

32. New York, Bund Archives, Kemfer file.

33. APP, BA1393, File "Grève . . . K(r)emler, février 1905."

34. Frederick Engels, *The Condition of the Working Class in England* (London: Panther Books Ltd., 1969), p. 108.

35. Paul Gemähling, *Travailleurs au rabais, La lutte syndicale contre les sous-concurrences ouvrières* (Paris: Bloud et Cie., 1910), p. 253.

36. Pierre du Maroussem, *La question ouvrière*, vol. 2: *Ebénistes du faubourg St. Antoine* (Paris: Arthur Rousseau, 1892), p. 228.

37. *YA*, September 7, 1912.

38. APP, BA1394, File "Grève . . . Galeries Lafayette, septembre 1916."

39. APP, BA1394, File "Grève . . . Printemps, mars 1916."

40. E.g., APP, BA1394, File "Grève . . . Galeries Lafayette, février 1913"; *YA*, January 4 and February 8, 1913; cf. Szajkowski, *Profesyonele bavegung*, pp. 191–96.

41. APP, BA1394, File "Grève . . . Galeries Lafayette, février 1913."

42. APP, BA1394, File "Grève . . . Maurice, février 1916."

43. APP, BA1394, File "Grève . . . Wormser et Boulanger, février 1916" and File "Grève . . . Galeries Lafayette, avril 1915."

44. Szajkowski, *Profesyonele bavegung*, pp. 93–94. See also *L'Ouvrier chapelier* (Paris), May 1, 1912.

45. New York, Bund Archives, Kemfer file.

46. YA, August 3, 1912.

47. On the problem of defining façonniers see George Mény, *La lutte contre le sweating-system* (Paris: Librairie des Sciences politiques et sociales and Marcel Rivière et Cie., 1910), p. 16; Fagnot, p. 3. Cf. Szajkowski, *Profesyonele bavegung*, pp. 252, 256, on the union sections' difficulties in defining homeworkers and façonniers for membership purposes, and Paula Hyman, *From Dreyfus to Vichy* (New York: Columbia University Press, 1979), pp. 106–7 on later Jewish labor movement policies toward the façonnier question.

48. Lauzel, p. 20.

49. YA, October 9, 1911. A leatherworker also criticized the façonniers for writing home about how one could make a living in Paris, thereby bringing more "sheep" to Paris. YA, June 7, 1913.

50. YA, August 3, 1912.

51. New York, Bund Archives, Kemfer file. In the same leaflet the bakery workers complained of other tactics used by their bosses such as hiring "apaches" to beat up the strikers and trying to bribe a striker in order to weaken workers' unity.

52. Michelle Perrot, talk given at Jacques Droz's seminar, Université de Paris, Spring 1976. See also idem, *Les ouvriers en grève*, 2: chapter VIII.

53. YA, November 17, 1911, June 29 and August 3, 1912.

54. New York, Bund Archives, Yidn in Frankraykh file; YA, January 3, 1914.

55. New York, Bund Archives, Yidn in Frankraykh file; YA, September 7 and October 5, 1912.

56. An interesting attempt to frighten actual or potential strikebreakers from committing such a deed took the form of a short story that appeared in *Der idisher arbayter* on March 7, 1914. The story recounted how a strikebreaker, glad to have the opportunity to earn some money, nevertheless became fearful at what he was doing; he dreamt that the strikers would dynamite the factory. When he told the foreman of his dream the next day, the foreman reassured him that the factory was being watched by the police. He returned to work but was still fearful of every noise. "Then all of a sudden all went black, there was an explosion . . . an explosion in his heart. He had suffered a heart attack."

57. YA, March 7, 1914.

58. APP, BA1394, File "Grève . . . Rosenthal, février 1912."

59. On the 1905 strike see APP, BA1393, File "Grève . . . Braunstein, août 1905." On the 1909 strike see APP, BA1394, File "Grève générale d'ouvriers tailleurs-pompiers, avril 1909."

60. Office du travail, *Statistiques des grèves . . . 1911*, strike no. 505; APP, BA1394, File "Grève . . . Galeries Lafayette, septembre 1916."

CHAPTER VI: IMMIGRANT UNIONIZATION IN PROCESS

1. Peter Stearns, *Revolutionary Syndicalism and French Labor: A Cause Without Rebels* (New Brunswick, N.J.: Rutgers University Press, 1971).

2. Edward Shorter and Charles Tilly, *Strikes in France, 1830–1968* (Cambridge: Cambridge University Press, 1974), p. 192.

3. Michelle Perrot, talk given at Jacques Droz's seminar, Université de Paris, Spring 1976. See idem, *Les ouvriers en grève, France 1871–90*, 2 vols. (Paris: Mouton et Cie. and Ecole Pratique des Hautes Etudes, 1974), 2:troisième partie, chapter VIII.

4. E.g., Paris, Préfecture de police Archives (hereafter cited as APP), BA157: Chapeliers.

5. Ministère de l'intérieur to Ministère des affaires étrangères, July 4, 1898, NS Russie, vol. 80: Russes en France 1895–1918, pp. 59–63, Ministère des affaires étrangères Archives, Paris. On the other mutual aid societies see Zosa Szajkowski, *Di profesyonele bavegung tsvishn di yidishe arbeter in Frankraykh biz 1914* (Paris: Fridman, 1937), pp. 24–27; idem, *Etyudn tsu der geshikhte fun ayngevandertn yidishn yishev in Frankaykh* (Paris: Fridman, 1936), pp. 54–60; idem, "Dos yidishe gezelshaftlekhe lebn in Pariz tsum yor 1939," *Yidn in Frankraykh*, ed. E. Tcherikower, 2 vols. (New York: YIVO, 1942), 2:234. Nancy L. Green, "Class Struggle in the Pletzl: Jewish Immigrant Workers in Paris, 1881–1914." Ph.D., University of Chicago, 1980, Appendix F.

6. The formation of union sections as opposed to separate unions was undoubtedly partly due to legal restrictions. The law of March 21, 1884, legalizing unions, prohibited foreigners from being members of a union's central committee. Therefore, immigrant unions could not exist unless the son (or daughter) of an immigrant (automatically French according to a law of 1889), a naturalized immigrant, or even a "front" was to comply with the regulation. A. Roux, head of the hatmakers' union, filled this function for the capmakers. Much easier, however, was the formation of union sections within the French union, which is what most of the Jewish immigrants did. See Maurice Didion, *Les salariés étrangers en France* (Paris: V. Giard et E. Brière, 1911), p. 97; Albert Matline, secretary of the Syndicat des chapeliers, modistes et casquettiers, interview in Paris, May 12, 1977; Szajkowski, *Profesyonele bavegung*, p. 123. (Mutual aid societies, it may be noted, were allowed to have foreign officials, although they could be dissolved at any time by ministerial decree, as some were. See Green, Appendix F.)

7. Report, May 9, 1906, BA1372: Ebénistes, APP.

8. On the beginnings of the Russian woodworkers' section see report, December 21, 1900, BA1422: Ebénistes, APP; *Unzer shtime* (Paris), February 4, 1939; and Szajkowski, "Yidishe gezelshaftlekhe lebn," p. 234. More generally see Léon and Maurice Bonneff, *La vie tragique des travailleurs*, 3d ed. (Paris: Jules Rouff et Cie., 1908), pp. 335–38; and Szajkowski, *Profesyonele bavegung*, pp. 26–27, 201–11. On the Jewish labor movement in this period in general, see Paula Hyman, *From Dreyfus to Vichy: The Remaking of French Jewry* (New York: Columbia University Press, 1979), pp. 92–99. For the interwar period, see Hyman, chapter 4, and David Weinberg, *Les Juifs à Paris de 1933 à 1939* (Paris: Calmann-Lévy, 1974), chapter 6.

9. On the furworkers' section see Szajkowski, *Profesyonele bavegung*, pp. 27, 153–58, 165–76; idem, "Yidishe gezelshaftlekhe lebn," p. 234; and *Der idisher arbayter* (Paris, hereafter cited as YA), June 7, 1913.

10. On the bakers' section see YA, January 4, 1913; Szajkowski, *Profesyonele bavegung*, pp. 27, 216–17, 220–21; and idem, "Yidishe gezelshaftlekhe lebn," p. 234.

11. *La Presse nouvelle hebdomadaire* (Paris), November 18, 1977; more generally on the leatherworkers' section see Szajkowski, *Profesyonele bavegung*, pp. 240–43; idem, "Yidishe gezelshaftlekhe lebn," p. 234; and YA, October 9, 1911.

12. APP, BA1393, File "Février 1900—Grève, Doucet."

13. YA, June 29, 1912. On the organizing of the tailors see APP, BA1393, File "Grève . . . Braunstein, septembre 1904"; YA, August 3, 1912, and July 4, 1914; Szajkowski, *Profesyonele bavegung*, pp. 185–86; idem, "Yidishe gezelshaftlekhe lebn," p. 234.

14. On the organizing of the tinsmiths, see YA, October 5, 1912 and July 4, 1914; and Szajkowski, *Profesyonele bavegung*, p. 257. On the metalworkers' section see *Unzer veg* (Vilna), October 10, 1907, and talk of another one in a police report,

October 28, 1913, BA1708: Russo-juifs à Paris, File "Bibliothèque russe," APP. For the typographers see *YA*, October 5, 1912, February 8, 1913, July 4, 1914, and report, December 27, 1912, BA1708, File "Bureau russe du travail," APP.

15. *YA*, February 7 and March 7, 1914; Szajkowski, *Profesyonele bavegung*, pp. 255–61; idem, "Yidishe gezelshaftlekhe lebn," p. 234; and *La Presse nouvelle hebdomadaire* (Paris), November 18, 1977.

16. For the interwar history of the Intersyndical Commission, see Hyman, pp. 103–8, and Weinberg, pp. 159–60.

17. An earlier attempt in April 1909 had been unsuccessful. See Szajkowski, *Profesyonele bavegung*, pp. 30–31. The similar German organization, the Deutsche Gewerkschaftskartel, founded in Paris in 1908, was referred to as a model in *YA*, October 5, 1912 and May 1, 1913.

18. New York, Bund Archives, Kemfer file.

19. *YA*, May 1, 1912.

20. *YA*, June 29, 1912; cf. Szajkowski, *Profesyonele bavegung*, p. 187.

21. *YA*, January 4, 1913.

22. *YA*, September 13 and October 18, 1913.

23. *YA*, April 5, 1913.

24. Henri Dagan, *De la condition du peuple au XXe siècle* (Paris: V. Giard et E. Brière, 1904), pp. 368–69.

25. Jean Vial, in *La Coutume chapelière: Histoire du mouvement ouvrier dans la chapellerie* (Paris: Editions Domat-Montchrestien, 1941), p. 373, only counted 567 members in 1912. Cf. Paul Pottier, "Essai sur le prolétariat juif en France," *Revue des revues*, 3d ser., 28 (March 1899): 485; Bonneffs, p. 332; Ministère du travail et de la prévoyance sociale, *Elections en 1909 des responsables des syndicats ouvriers* (n.p., Imprimerie nationale, 1909), p. 61; and Fédération des syndicats ouvriers de la chapellerie française, *15e Congrès national (Bort), 1912* (Paris: Imprimerie La Productrice, 1913), p. 61.

26. The bylaws are found in Szajkowski, *Etyudn*, pp. 74–76. On ibid., p. 61, is reproduced a strident declaration of the mutual aid society as it strove toward workers-only membership.

27. Ibid., pp. 64–70.

28. Matline, "Le syndicat des casquettiers à 70 ans," unpublished memoirs.

29. *Forverts* (New York), October 21, 1941, and Matline, "Syndicat des casquettiers," n.p. Cf. *Morgn-Frayhayt* (New York), July 3, 1968, which gives as 1910 the year in which the capmakers turned to Losovsky. Losovsky remained the secretary of the capmakers' union until 1913, when he resigned for personal reasons. See also *Unzer Vort* (Paris), January 1 and 2, 1957, and Szajkowski, *Profesyonele bavegung*, pp. 122–24.

30. On Losovsky, see Georges Haupt and Jean-Jacques Marie, *Les Bolsheviks par eux-mêmes* (Paris: Maspero, 1969), p. 280, and *Great Soviet Encyclopedia*, trans. of 3rd ed., "A. Lozovskii," 14:657–58. For later accounts of his activities in Paris see especially reports, April 27, 1917, BA1709: Russo-juifs à Paris, File "Comité de l'émigration russe," and April 28, 1918, BA1708, File "Pièces communes," APP.

31. Losovsky's writings on this subject have been reprinted: Dridzo Losovsky, *L'internationale syndicale rouge* (Paris: Maspero, 1976).

32. New York, Bund Archives, Yidn in Frankraykh file.

33. Szajkowski, *Etyudn*, pp. 78–79.

34. The stipulations of these agreements along with the minutes of the capmakers' union are found among Losovsky's papers in New York, Columbia University, Russian and Eastern European History and Culture Archives (hereafter cited as

REEHC), 1.1.3.2: Lozovskii, File "Manuscripts," pp. 6–7. See also *L'Ouvrier chapelier* (Paris, hereafter cited as O Ch), November 1, 1912. The complete records of the capmakers' union are now also available at the Central Archives for the History of the Jewish People in Jerusalem.

35. The provisions of the Convention collective have been found in Matline, "Syndicat des casquettiers," n.p. It may be noted that the hatters in general, with their long history of organization, had had continuous bargaining relations with their employers throughout the nineteenth century. The first formal collective bargaining agreement took place in mining, however, in 1889, and such agreements were rare before 1914. It was not until 1919 that a law was passed that gave collective bargaining agreements legal standing and enforceability; thus a flurry of agreements were passed that year. See Val Lorwin, *French Labor Movement* (Cambridge: Harvard University Press, 1954), pp. 25–26; and Stearns, pp. 88–92.

36. Szajkowski, *Profesyonele bavegung*, pp. 151–52.

37. YA, June 7, 1913.

38. Its bylaws are found in REEHC, 1.1.3.2., "Manuscripts," pp. 38–40. See also Szajkowski, *Profesyonele bavegung*, pp. 124–26.

39. YA, December 7, 1912, September 13, October 18, and November 29, 1913.

40. L'Union's bylaws are found in New York, Bund Archives, Kemfer file. A very complete account of the workings of the cooperative is found in O Ch, October 1 and December 1, 1912, and April 1, 1914. See also Matline, "Syndicat des casquettiers," n.p. For an interesting photograph of the cooperatives' members, in which one member is pointedly reading *La Bataille syndicaliste*, see Hyman, photo facing p. 178.

41. On all of these cooperatives see YA, issues 17 through 23 (August 9, 1913 through March 7, 1914). The Jewish capmakers and bakers in Paris were looked to as an example for the Jewish bakers in London who wrote to *Der idisher arbayter* in September 1913 for help to start their own cooperative. YA, September 13, 1913.

42. YA, January 3, 1914.

43. See Georges Hoog, *La coopération de production, Origines et institutions* (Paris: Presses universitaires de France, 1942), pp. 151–55; and the discussion of the Hatmakers' Federation with regard to aiding cooperatives in Fédération des syndicats ouvriers de la chapellerie française, *XIIIe Congrès National (Chazelles-sur-Lyon), 1906,* pp. 45–56.

44. YA, November 2, 1912.

45. YA, March 8 and April 5, 1913.

46. For the statistics of the Caisse d'assurance contre le chômage see REEHC, 1.1.3.2. "Manuscripts," pp. 1–3. See also O Ch, August 1, 1912, and Szajkowski, *Profesyonele bavegung*, p. 120.

47. YA, April 5, May 1, June 7, and July 5, 1913.

48. YA, March 8, 1913. In the next issue (April 5) it was further specified that such an unemployment fund could only be used for exceptional periods of unemployment and not for the morte-saison itself, which would be financially impossible. The workers, knowing the regularity of the morte-saison, were expected to save ahead, and the unemployment fund would only be called upon if the normal morte-saison for a particular trade were extended, or if a worker was ill and could not work during the full season.

49. On the Arbeter ring see especially YA, February 8, July 5, and October 18, 1913. For its activities in the United States and England see Melech Epstein, *Jewish Labor in the U.S.A.* (New York: Trade Union Sponsoring Committee, 1950), chapter 17; Irving Howe, *World of Our Fathers* (New York: Simon and Schuster, 1976),

pp. 357–59; William Fishman, *East End Jewish Radicals, 1875–1914* (London: Duckworth, 1975), p. 273; and Jerry White, *Rothschild Buildings: Life in an East End Tenement Block, 1887–1920* (London: Routledge & Kegan Paul, 1980), pp. 253–55.

50. See YA, June 7, 1913, and January 3 and February 7, 1914. On this mutual aid benefits controversy see also Szajkowski, *Profesyonele bavegung*, pp. 81–83, 244–49; and idem, *Etyudn*, pp. 73–74.

51. YA, October 9, 1911.

52. YA, February 8, 1913; see also his article in the April 5, 1913, issue.

53. Cf. Fédération des syndicats ouvriers de la chapellerie française, *15e Congrès National (Bort), 1912*, p. 61; and Maurice Lauzel, *Ouvriers juifs de Paris: Les casquettiers* (Paris: Edouard Cornély et Cie., 1912), p. 41.

54. YA, October 9, 1911; REEHC, 1.1.3.2., "Manuscripts," pp. 16–17.

55. REEHC, 1.1.3.2, "Manuscripts," 4th subfolder, pp. 10–11.

56. See Szajkowski, *Profesyonele bavegung*, pp. 109–21.

57. For the bichonneurs' section's bylaws see REEHC, 1.1.3.2., "Manuscripts," pp. 8–9. On the cutters and pressers see Szajkowski, *Profesyonele bavegung*, pp. 109–22, 129–32.

58. Report, September 6, 1913, BA1708: Russo-juifs à Paris, File "Pièces communes," APP; on political influence in the trade union movement see Szajkowski, *Profesyonele bavegung*, pp. 57–74 and Hyman, pp. 91–96.

59. See chapter 3 above.

60. Report, April 23, 1917, BA1708, File "Le Comité exécutif des représentants des organisations politiques en France," APP.

61. YA, February 7, 1914.

62. YA, October 5 and December 7, 1912.

63. YA, November 2, 1912.

64. See YA, November 17, 1911, June 29, 1912, January 3, and July 4, 1914; and Szajkowski, *Profesyonele bavegung*, pp. 57–59, 66–69, 78, 187.

65. J. Tchernoff, *Dans le creuset des civilisations*, 4 vols. (Paris: Editions Rieder, 1937), 2:65–66; and Ronald Sanders, *The Downtown Jews* (New York: Signet, New American Library, 1976), pp. 194, 345–46. Emigration was sometimes castigated on these grounds. See H. J. Tobias and C. E. Woodhouse, "Political Reaction and Revolutionary Careers: The Jewish Bundists in Defeat, 1907–10," *Comparative Studies in Society and History* 19 (July 1977): 367–96.

66. YA, September 7, 1912, and June 29, 1912.

67. Szajkowski, *Profesyonele bavegung*, p. 51; YA, September 7, 1912; and Wolf Speiser, *Kalendar* (Paris: n.p., 1910), p. 45.

68. Ezra Mendelsohn, *Class Struggle in the Pale: The Formative Years of the Jewish Workers' Movement in Tsarist Russia* (Cambridge: Cambridge University Press, 1970).

69. Ibid., p. 42.

70. Ibid., p. 85. See also Jewish Colonization Association, *Recueil de matériaux sur la situation économique des israélites de Russie*, 2 vols. (Paris: Félix Alcan, 1906, 1908), 1:319, 2:165, 183, on the propensity of the Jewish workers to strike.

71. Described as such by A. Liesen, quoted in Mendelsohn, p. 116.

72. Ibid., p. 10.

73. Interviews with Albert Matline, January to May 1977, and Jacques Lederman, October 12, 1977.

74. See Henry J. Tobias, *The Jewish Bund from its Origins to 1905* (Stanford: Stanford University Press, 1970); Jonathan Frankel, *Prophecy and Politics: Socialism, Nationalism, and the Russian Jews, 1862–1917* (Cambridge: Cambridge University Press, 1981); and Robert Brym, *The Jewish Intelligentsia and Russian Marxism* (New York: Schocken Books, 1978).

CHAPTER VII: CLASS AND COMMUNITY

1. Reports of this and the September 16 meeting are found in *L'Univers israélite* (Paris), September 8, 1899; *Journal du peuple* (Paris), September 18, 1899; *L'Aurore* (Paris), September 18, 1899; *Les Droits de l'homme* (Paris), September 17 and 19, 1899; and *L'Echo sioniste* (Paris), September 16, 1899.

2. The usage of French Revolutionary language should be noted.

3. Ibid.

4. The resolution as cited in the *Journal du peuple* read "inculcated prejudice" (*préjugé inculqué*) instead of "disgraceful trap" (*piège infâme*) in describing anti-Semitism.

5. Karpel and Dinner for the Groupe des ouvriers juifs socialistes de Paris, *Le prolétariat juif: Lettre des ouvriers juifs de Paris au Parti socialiste français* (Paris: Imprimerie typographique J. Allemane, 1898), p. 15.

6. Val Lorwin, *French Labor Movement* (Cambridge: Harvard University Press, 1954), pp. 11–12.

7. Ibid., pp. 21–24; see also Jacques Julliard, *Fernand Pelloutier et les origines du syndicalisme d'action directe* (Paris: Seuil, 1971). Karpel was treasurer of the capmakers' union. Bernard-Lazare and the anarchist Mécislas Golberg may also have had a hand in the writing of this letter. See *La Presse nouvelle hebdomadaire* (Paris), September 22, 1978, although Henry Bulawko believes that Bernard-Lezare's role was rather that of financing the letter's publication, "Les Socialistes et 'l'Affaire,'" *Les nouveaux cahiers* 27 (Winter 1971–72): 26.

8. Lorwin, p. 24.

9. *XIXe Siècle* (Paris), July 21, 1899.

10. See report, July 2, 1914, BA1423: Syndicat général, Travailleurs de l'habillement, 1909–18, Préfecture de police Archives (hereafter cited as APP), Paris; and Paris, Archives nationales, F^7 13740: Habillement, File "Presse 1914."

11. E.g., the Hatters' Federation's 1,000 franc grant and 4,000 franc loan at the time of the 1912 strikes. Fédération des syndicats ouvriers de la chapellerie française, *15e Congrès national (Bort), 1912* (Paris: Imprimerie La Productrice, 1913), p. 63; cf. Jean Vial, *La Coutume chapelière, Histoire du mouvement ouvrier dans la chapellerie* (Paris: Editions Domat-Montchrestien, 1941), p. 343. Michelle Perrot notes that the hatters' union (one of the earliest constituted) had one of the largest strike funds and was the union best able to subsidize its trade's strikes (71 percent of them). Perrot, *Les ouvriers en grève, France 1871–90*, 2 vols. (Paris: Mouton and Ecole Pratique des Hautes Etudes, 1974), 2:523, 525. In other instances the French woodworkers' union voted five francs per month in support of the Jewish workers and the French bakers' cooperative aided the Jewish one financially. Zosa Szajkowski, *Di profesyonele bavegung tsvishn di yidishe arbeter in Frankraykh biz 1914* (Paris: Fridman, 1937), pp. 212, 230.

12. APP, BA1393: Tailleurs, File "Grève . . . Braunstein, août 1905"; BA1394: Tailleurs, Files "Grève des tailleurs pour dames chez Paquin, Doucet, King, Doeuillet, Raudnitz, Bechoff et Berr, février 1901" and "Grève . . . Galeries Lafayette, septembre 1916."

13. See *L'Humanité* (Paris), October 4, 1913.

14. See report, March 19, 1916, BA1423, APP, where Dumas interrupted a meeting of the garment workers' union (concerning ways of ending the war) to complain that the mostly foreign audience was not qualified to discuss the issue.

15. See Robert F. Byrnes, *Anti-Semitism in Modern France* (New York: Howard

Fertig, 1969); and the recent book by Stephen Wilson, *Ideology and Experience: Antisemitism in France at the Time of the Dreyfus Affair* (Rutherford and London: Fairleigh Dickinson University Press and Associated University Presses, 1982).

16. Stephen Wilson, "Le Monument Henry: La structure de l'antisémitisme en France, 1898–99," *Annales E.S.C.* 32 (March–April 1977): 265–91. However, as I point out in my article on "The Dreyfus Affair and Ruling Class Cohesion," *Science and Society* 43 (Spring 1979): 43, even though Wilson found a significant 39 percent of the subscribers to be workers or artisans, this figure represented only 1.9 times their proportion of the active population of France, whereas the clergy, student, and military subscribers overrepresented their occupational categories by as much as 15.5, 14.3, and 9.5 times respectively.

17. *XIXe Siècle* (Paris), July 21, 1899.

18. See Nancy L. Green, "Socialist Anti-Semitism: Defense of a Bourgeois Jew and Discovery of the Jewish Proletariat" (forthcoming, *International Review of Social History*, 1985); and Victor M. Glasberg, "Intent and Consequences: the 'Jewish Question' in the French Socialist Movement of the Late Nineteenth Century," *Jewish Social Studies* 36 (January 1974): 61–71.

19. Karpel and Dinner, pp. 9, 17–18.

20. Ibid., p. 20.

21. Harvey Goldberg, "Jean Jaurès and the Jewish Question: The Evolution of a Position," *Jewish Social Studies* 20 (April 1958): 70–93.

22. *Forverts* (New York), May 5, 1911; see also *Archives israélites* (Paris), April 20, 1911, and Szajkowski, pp. 37–44, for the most extensive account of this affair.

23. *Der idisher arbayter* (Paris, hereafter cited as YA), August 9, 1913; report, April 26, 1911, BA1423, APP.

24. *La Guerre sociale* (Paris), December 20–26, 1911.

25. Bernard-Lazare, *Antisémitisme, son histoire et ses causes* (Paris: Léon Chailley, 1894), pp. 384–86; see also his comment in *Tribune libre* (Paris), May 24, 1896.

26. *Rapports sur l'application pendant l'année 1907 des lois réglementant le travail* (Paris: Imprimerie nationale for the Ministère du commerce, de l'industrie, des postes et des télégraphes, 1908), p. 2 (emphasis added).

27. Cited in Maurice Hollande, *La défense ouvrière contre le travail étranger* (Paris: Bloud et Cie., 1913), p. 200.

28. *La Guerre sociale* (Paris), December 20-26, 1911.

29. Ibid., January 3–9, 1912. The equivocal nature of Pouget's remarks is similar to the weak resolution voted in September 1891 at the Brussels Congress of the Second International condemning both anti-Semitic and philo-Semitic "excitations." See Léon Seilhac, *Les Congrès ouvriers en France de 1876 à 1897* (Paris: A. Colin et Cie., 1899), pp. 222–23.

30. On the hatters see Fédération des syndicats ouvriers de la chapellerie française, p. 107, as well as *L'Ouvrier chapelier* (Paris), December 12, 1910, and Szajkowski, pp. 83–84. On the woodworkers see Paul Gemähling, *Travailleurs au rabais, La lutte syndicale contre les sous-concurrences ouvrières* (Paris: Bloud et Cie., 1910), p. 232, and YA, July 4, 1914.

31. "An old worker" replied in the next issue of *Der idisher arbayter* (August 9, 1913) that this suggestion was "not only reactionary but also utopist" because any action on the part of the International would only (maybe) discourage unionized workers from coming to Paris, while nonunion workers would continue to immigrate, which would be even worse.

32. Paul Pottier, "Essai sur le prolétariat juif en France," *Revue des revues*, 3d ser., 28 (March 1899): 485.

33. ". . . considering that the workshops and worksites of France are increasingly invaded by foreigners working cheaply and causing the lowering of French salaries . . . [it was] decided to safeguard the right to life by work [*le droit à la vie par le travail*] of the French proletariat, but rejecting as contrary to the indispensable union of all workers the expulsion or limitation of foreign labor. . . ." Gemähling, p. 220.

34. See Yves Le Febvre, *L'ouvrier étranger et la protection du travail national* (Paris: C. Jacques et Cie., 1901), pp. 133–34.

35. Gamähling, p. 222.

36. YA, October 9, 1911.

37. See, e.g., YA, May 1, August 3, and November 2, 1912, February 8, March 8, May 1, and June 7, 1913, and April 11, 1914.

38. See YA, November 17, 1911, and October 5, 1912.

39. YA, November 17, 1911.

40. YA, June 29, 1912.

41. Regarding French funds sent to *Der idisher arbayter*, see, e.g., APP, BA1423, report, January 7, 1912; and YA, August 9, 1913.

42. The Jewish immigrants had been marching in May Day celebrations ever since 1906 but generally joined other immigrants—Germans, Poles, Czechs—to do so. New York, Bund Archives, Kemfer file; Szajkowski, pp. 27, 74, 102. Jean Vial, in his work on the hatters, complained more generally of immigrant workers' separate unionism: "We thought they were assimilable; but they unite among themselves, never with us." Vial, p. 315.

43. On the tailors see report, October 3, 1904, BA1393: Tailleurs, File "Grève . . . Braunstein, septembre 1904" APP. On the furworkers see YA, June 7, 1913. On the leatherworkers and bakers see YA, October 9, 1911.

44. YA, October 5, 1912.

45. Examples where the "specific exploitation" of the Jewish workers was mentioned but not defined are: YA, May 1, 1912, and July 4, 1914. For its definition see YA, October 5, 1912.

46. See chapter 5 above.

47. Pottier, p. 486. See also ibid., pp. 491–92. Cf. Mlle. Schirmacher, *La spécialisation du travail—Par nationalités à Paris* (Paris: Arthur Rousseau, 1908), p. 98.

48. Léon and Maurice Bonneff, *La vie tragique des travailleurs*, 3d ed. (Paris: Jules Rouff et Cie., 1908), p. 329.

49. Roger Ikor, *Les fils d'Avrom: Les eaux mêlées* (Paris: Albin Michel, 1955), pp. 154, 139.

50. YA, July 5, 1913.

51. Henri Dagan, *De la condition du peuple au XXe siècle* (Paris: V. Giard et E. Brière, 1904), p. 366.

52. New York, Bund Archives, Kemfer file.

53. Perrot, 2:3ème partie, chapters VII and VIII; see especially pp. 547–52, 595 and 605.

54. Michael P. Hanagan, *The Logic of Solidarity: Artisans and Industrial Workers in Three French Towns, 1871–1914* (Urbana: University of Illinois Press, 1980); on women's networks, see, e.g., Temma Kaplan, "Female Consciousness and Collective Action: The Case of Barcelona, 1910–1918," *Signs* 7 (Spring 1982): 545–66; and Meredith Tax, *The Rising of the Women: Feminist Solidarity and Class Conflict, 1880–1917* (New York: Monthly Review Press, 1980). On this issue see also Gareth Stedman Jones, "Working-Class Culture and Working-Class Politics in London, 1870–1900," Journal of Social History, VII (1974): 460–508; Herbert Gutman, *Work, Culture and Society in Industrializing America, 1815–1919* (New York: Alfred A. Knopf, 1976); Alan Dawley, *Class and Community: The Industrial Revolution in Lynn* (Cam-

bridge: Harvard University Press, 1976); David Montgomery, *Workers' Control in America* (Cambridge: Cambridge University Press, 1979): and Ira Katznelson, *City Trenches* (Chicago: University of Chicago Press, 1981).

55. E.g., APP, BA1393, 1394.
56. Szajkowski, pp. 99–100.
57. Ibid., p. 28.
58. Ibid., p. 261.
59. Ibid., p. 229.
60. YA, May 1, 1913.
61. APP, BA1394: Tailleurs, File "Grève . . . Ribby, mai 1913". On the bakers see *L'Humanité* (Paris), April 10, 1913. On the waiters see YA, April 11 and May 7, 1914.
62. YA, May 1 and November 29, 1913.
63. E.g., YA, October 5, 1912; see also ibid., October 9, 1911 and Szajkowski, p. 107. On the social ostracism of strikebreakers, cf. Perrot, 2:515–19.
64. Both in YA, December 7, 1912.
65. Ezra Mendelsohn, *Class Struggle in the Pale: The Formative Years of the Jewish Workers' Movement in Russia* (Cambridge: Cambridge University Press, 1970), p. 155. See also ibid., p. 125.
66. See e.g., YA, February 7 and July 4, 1914.
67. YA, May 1, 1912, April 5, 1913, January 3, and April 11, 1914; and Szajkowski, p. 209.
68. YA, September 13, 1913.
69. Perrot, 2:607–610.

CONCLUSION

1. *La Presse nouvelle hebdomadaire* (Paris), November 18, 1977, on the 1,500 unionized workers. (This article also estimates *Der idisher arbayter*'s printing at only 800.) Cf. Appendix A on the number of Jewish immigrants in Paris.
2. See especially *Der idisher arbayter*, January 3, 1914.
3. To the call of posters such as that reproduced in Paula Hyman, *From Dreyfus to Vichy: The Remaking of French Jewry* (New York: Columbia University Press, 1979), between pp. 178 and 179. See also idem, pp. 54–59; Maurice Vanikoff, *La commémoration des engagements volontaires des juifs d'origine étrangère 1914–1918* (Paris: Le Volontaire Juif, 1932); Sholem Shvartzbard, *In krig—Mit zikh aleyn* (Chicago: Arbayters-Verlag, 1933); André Spire, *Les Juifs et la guerre* (Paris: Payot, 1917), particularly chapter 1 on "Jewish loyalty"; and the brochure entitled "France et Russie," describing the activities of the Société de secours aux russes combattants sous les drapeaux français, in the Archives of the Association consistoriale israélite de Paris, B105.
4. Roger Ikor, *Les Fils d'Avrom: Les eaux mêlées* (Paris: Albin Michel, 1955), p. 146.
5. As Yankel Mykhanowitzki explained the origins of such a fear: "You, foreigner, what are you doing mixing in French politics? Show me that paper! . . . Anarchist, naturally! Okay, go to prison! You're expelled! Go back to where you came from! . . . Politics, that doesn't concern foreigners . . . a foreigner must not make any noise." Ibid., pp. 156, 305. See also *Der idisher arbayter* (Paris), July 4, 1914.
6. Cf. Jerry White, *Rothschild Buildings: Life in an East End Tenement Block, 1887–1920* (London: Routledge & Kegan Paul, 1980), pp. 255–61, on individualism as impeding class consciousness.
7. *Daily News Record* (New York City, professional organ of the garment indus-

try), February 22, 1977. (I would like to thank Robert H. Green for bringing this to my attention.)

8. *The Paris Metro,* March 30, 1977.

9. Ibid.

10. *Le Monde* (Paris), March 26, 1980.

11. See "Les immigrés victimes de la crise," *Le Monde* (Paris), June 17, 18, 19–20, 1977.

SELECTED BIBLIOGRAPHY

ARCHIVAL MATERIAL

Alliance israélite universelle (AIU) Archives, Paris.
 France IH1: Sociétés.
 France IIA6: Charles Netter—Mission à Brody.
 France VD9: Israélites roumains.
 France VID22: Russie—Emigration, 1882–92.
 France IXD51: Emigration—Divers.
 France IXD52: Russie—Emigration, 1881–91.
 Russie IC1: Persécution et pogrommes.
 Russie IC2: Emigration.
 Russie IC3: Révolution 1917.
 Russie IC4: St. Petersbourg/Sokolow.
 MS 587:   Isidore Loeb: Professions des Juifs de France: 1840–90.
 Bernard-Lazare manuscripts.
Archives nationales, Paris.
 F⁷12894-96: Réfugiés et révolutionnaires russes en France, 1907–12.
 F⁷13740: Habillement.
 F¹⁹11158: Associations cultuelles, déclarations et statuts, 1906–23.
Bund Archives, New York.
 Yidn in Frankraykh file.

Kemfer file.
Pariz: Bundisher fareyn "Kemfer" afishn file.
Association consistoriale israélite de Paris Archives (ACIP).
AA9:   Registre des délibérations du Conseil d'administration, procès-verbaux (1901–5).
AA19-20: Procès-verbaux (1906–19).
B47-105: Lettres reçues (1882–1918, selected dossiers).
BB50-59: Lettres envoyées (1882–91).
MM6:   Recensement de 1872—Population juive du 4ème arrondissement.
I^{cc}77:   Lettres du Ministère de l'intérieur et des cultes (1899–1905).
Ministère des affaires étrangères Archives, Paris.
Europe 1918–29, File "Russie 128: Religion israélite."
Europe 1918–29, File "Pologne 60: Israélites 1918–19."
NS Russie, vol. 12: Agitation, révolution et anarchie, 1880–1904.
NS Russie, vol. 13: Agitation, révolution et anarchie, 1880–1904.
NS Russie, vol. 80: Russes en France 1895–1918.
Ochs Collection (newspaper clippings), Bibliothèque de l'histoire de la ville de Paris.
D1218–D1234 (1892–1900)
Préfecture de police Archives, Paris (APP).
BA157:   Chapeliers, Chambre syndicale et société de secours mutuels des ouvriers
BA182:   Casquettiers, Grèves des ouvriers
BA958:   Bernard-Lazare.
BA1144:   Pierre Lawroff.
BA1324:   Affaires concernant la Russie.
BA1355:   Boulangers, Grèves des
BA1372:   Ebénistes, Grèves des ouvriers
BA1393-94: Tailleurs, Grèves des ouvriers
BA1410:   Boulangerie, Chambre syndicale de la
BA1422:   Ebénistes, Chambre syndicale des
BA1423:   Habillement, Chambre syndicale de l'
BA1444:   Tailleurs, Chambre syndicale des
BA1507-8: Anarchistes, L'Internationale du 3e arrt.; Groupes du 18e arrdt.
BA1671:   Roumains à Paris (various files on Rumanian organizations).
BA1708-9: Russo-juifs à Paris (various reports on Russian and Jewish refugee organizations in Paris).
Russian and East European History and Culture Archives, Columbia University, New York (REEHC).
1.1.3.2.: Alexander Lozovskii.
YIVO Archives, New York.
France boxes.
Leah M. Eisenberg–Julius Borenstein Collection, Microfilm Roll 1.

NEWSPAPERS AND PERIODICALS

Alliance israélite universelle. *Bulletin semestriel*, 1881–1913.
Archives israélites (Paris), 1880–1920 (AI).

Annuaire statistique de la ville de Paris, 1880–1920.

Comité de bienfaisance israélite de Paris. *Assemblées générales*, 1888–1920.

Ecole du travail. *Comptes rendus*, 1880–1918.

Der idisher arbayter (Paris), 1911–14 *(YA)*.

Di idishe tribune (Paris), October 1915.

Di naye prese (Paris), 1934–37 (retrospective articles).

Office du travail. *Bulletins*, 1900–12.

———. *Statistiques des grèves et des recours à la conciliation et à l'arbitrage*, 1891–1920.

L'Ouvrier chapelier (Paris), 1896, 1899–1903, 1907–14 *(O Ch)*.

Société philanthropique de l'Asile israélite de Paris. *Rapports des exercices*, 1905–20.

La Tribune russe (Paris), 1904–13.

L'Univers israélite (Paris), 1880–1920 *(UI)*.

Université populaire juive. *Compte rendu et statuts*, 1902–3.

PRINTED PRIMARY AND SECONDARY SOURCES

Jews in Eastern Europe

Baron, Salo W. *The Russian Jew under Tsars and Soviets*. New York: The Macmillan Co., 1964.

Brym, Robert. *The Jewish Intelligentsia and Russian Marxism*. New York: Schocken Books, 1978.

Chmerkine, N. *Les conséquences de l'antisémitisme en Russie*. Paris: Guillaumin et Cie., 1897.

Dawidowicz, Lucy S., ed. *The Golden Tradition: Jewish Life and Thought in Eastern Europe*. Boston: Beacon, 1967.

Dubnow, S. M. *History of the Jews in Russia and Poland*. Trans. I. Friedlaender. 3 vols. New York: KTAV, 1975.

Frankel, Jonathan. *Prophecy and Politics: Socialism, Nationalism and the Russian Jews, 1862–1917*. Cambridge: Cambridge University Press, 1981.

Gille, Bertrand. *Histoire économique et sociale de la Russie: Du moyen-âge au vingtième siècle*. Paris: Payot, 1949.

Gliksman, Georges. *L'aspect économique de la question juive en Pologne*. Paris: Editions Rieder, 1929.

Greenberg, Louis. *The Jews in Russia—The Struggle for Emancipation*. New Haven: Yale University Press, 1944, 1951.

Iancu, Carol. *Les Juifs en Roumanie (1866–1919): De l'exclusion à l'émancipation*. Etudes historiques 4. Aix-en-Provence: Editions de l'Université de Provence, 1978.

Jewish Colonization Association. *Rapport de l'Administration centrale au Conseil d'administration pour l'année 1900*. Paris: Imprimerie R. Veneziani, 1901.

———. *Recueil de matériaux sur la situation économique des Israélites de Russie*. 2 vols. Paris: Félix Alcan, 1906, 1908.

Les Juifs de Roumanie. Paris: Ligue des droits de l'homme et du citoyen, 1917.

Les Juifs de Russie. Recueil d'articles et d'études sur leur situation légale, sociale et économique. Paris: Léopold Cerf, 1891.

Kissman, Joseph. "Di idishe emigratsie fun Rumanye biz der ershter velt-milkhome." *YIVO-Bleter* 19 (March–April 1942): 157–91.

Kuznets, Simon. "Immigration of Russian Jews to the United States: Background and Structure." *Perspectives in American History* 10 (1976): 35–124.

Lazare, Bernard-. "Les Juifs en Roumanie," *Cahiers de la quinzaine*, 3ème sér., 8ème cahier (1902).

Lestschinsky, Jacob. *Der idisher arbayter (in Rusland)*. Vilna: Vilna-Tsukunft, 1906.

Levin, Nora. *While Messiah Tarried: Jewish Socialist Movements, 1871–1917*. New York: Schocken Books, 1977.

Mahler, Raphael. "The Economic Background of Jewish Emigration from Galicia to the United States." *YIVO Annual of Jewish Social Science* 7 (1952): 255–67.

Mendelsohn, Ezra. *Class Struggle in the Pale: The Formative Years of the Jewish Workers' Movement in Tsarist Russia*. Cambridge: Cambridge University Press, 1970.

Menes, A. "Di idishe industrye-bafelkerung in Rusland 1897." *Shriftn far ekonomik un statistik*. Ed. Jacob Lestschinsky. Vol. 1. Berlin: YIVO, 1928.

Petresco-Comnène, N. *Etude sur la condition des Israélites en Roumanie*. Paris: Pédone, 1905.

Phalippou, H. J. "Juifs en Russie." *La Revue socialiste* 29 (1899): 188–98.

Rouanet, Gustave. "Les Juifs en Roumanie." *La Revue socialiste* 36 (1902): 82–106.

Rubinow, Isaac M. *Economic Condition of the Jews in Russia*. New York: Arno Press, 1975.

Sincerus, Edmond. *Les Juifs en Roumanie, Depuis le Traité de Berlin (1878) jusqu'à ce jour*. London: Macmillan and Co., Ltd., 1901.

Stanislawski, Michael. *Tsar Nicholas I and the Jews*. Philadelphia: Jewish Publication Society, 1983.

Szajkowski, Zosa. "How the Mass Migration to America Began." *Jewish Social Studies* 4 (October 1942): 291–310.

Tobias, Henry J. *The Jewish Bund in Russia from its Origins to 1905*. Stanford, California: Stanford University Press, 1972.

French Jewish Community

Albert, Phyllis Cohen. *The Modernization of French Jewry: Consistory and Community in the Nineteenth Century*. Hanover, N. H.: Brandeis University Press, 1977.

Anchel, Robert. "The Early History of the Jewish Quarters in Paris." *Jewish Social Studies* 2 (1940): 45–60.

———. *Les Juifs de France*. Paris: J. B. Janin, 1946.

———. *Napoléon et les Juifs*. Paris: Presses universitaires de France, 1928.

Aubéry, Pierre. *Milieux juifs de la France contemporaine à travers leurs écrivains*. Paris: Librairie Plon, 1962.

Baron, Salo W. "The Impact of the Revolution of 1848 on Jewish Emancipation." *Jewish Social Studies* 11 (1949): 195–248.

Ben-Said, Laurent. "Cent ans de fidelité à la république." *Histoire*, no. 3 (November 1979), pp. 41–62.

Ben-Simon Donath, Doris. *Socio-démographie des Juifs de France et d'Algérie, 1867–1907*. P.O.F.-Etudes. Paris: Publications orientalistes de France, 1976.

Birnbaum, Pierre. *Le Peuple et les gros*. Paris: Grasset, 1979.

Bloch, Jean-Richard. . . . *et compagnie*. Paris: Nouvelle revue française, 1918.

Blumenkranz, Bernhard, ed. *Histoire des Juifs en France*. Paris: Privat, 1972.

Bourdrel, Philippe. *Histoire des Juifs de France*. Paris: Albin Michel, 1974.

Byrnes, Robert F. *Anti-Semitism in Modern France*. New York: Howard Fertig, 1969.

Cahen, Edmond. *Juifs, non! . . . Israélite*. Paris: Librairie de France, 1930.

Chouraqui, André. *Cent ans d'histoire—L'Alliance israélite universelle et la renaissance juive contemporaine (1860–1960)*. Paris: Presses universitaires de France, 1965.

Cohen, David. *La Promotion des Juifs en France à l'époque du Second empire (1852–1870)*. 2 vols. Aix-en-Provence: Publications de l'Université de Provence, 1980.

Debré, Moses. *The Image of the Jew in French Literature from 1800–1908*. New York: KTAV, 1970.

Delahache, Georges. "Juifs." *Cahiers de la quinzaine* 3ème sér., 5ème cahier (1905), pp. 1–45.

Drumont, Edouard. *La France juive, Essai d'histoire contemporaine*. 2 vols. Paris: C. Marpon and E. Flammarion, 1886.

Du Camp, Maxime. *Paris bienfaisant*. Paris: Hachette, 1888.

Eberlin, E. *La Double tare*. Paris: Editions SNIE, 1935.

Eisenmann, Jacques. "Zadoc Kahn: Le pasteur et la communauté." *Les nouveaux cahiers* 41 (Summer 1975): 20–40.

Girard, Patrick. *Les Juifs de France de 1789 à 1860: De l'émancipation à l'égalité*. Paris: Calmann-Lévy, 1976.

Graetz, Mika'el. *Ha-periferiyah hayetah le-merkaz*. Jerusalem: Mossad Bialik, 1982.

Green, Nancy L. "The Dreyfus Affair and Ruling Class Cohesion." *Science and Society* 43 (Spring 1979): 29–50.

Gygès. *Les Israélites dans la société française*. Paris: Imprimerie Gouin, 1956.

Hertzberg, Arthur. *The French Enlightenment and the Jews: The Origins of Modern Anti-Semitism*. New York: Schocken Books, 1968.

Jussem-Wilson, Nelly. "Bernard-Lazare's Jewish Journey: From Being an Israelite to Being a Jew." *Jewish Social Studies* 26 (July 1964): 146–68.

———. *Bernard-Lazare*. Cambridge: Cambridge University Press, 1978.

Kahn, Léon. *Le Comité de bienfaisance*. Paris: A. Durlacher, 1886.

———. *Les Juifs à Paris depuis le VIe siècle*. Paris: A. Durlacher, 1889.

———. *Histoire des écoles communales et consistoriales israélites de Paris (1809–84)*. Paris: A. Durlacher, 1884.

———. *Les professions manuelles et les institutions de patronage*. Paris: A. Durlacher, 1885.

———. *Les sociétés de secours mutuels*. Paris: A. Durlacher, 1887.

Kahn, Zadoc. *Sermons et allocutions*. 3d ser. 3 vols. Paris: A. Durlacher, 1894.

Lazare, Bernard-. *Antisémitisme et révolution*. Paris: Cercle Bernard-Lazare, n.d.

———. *L'antisémitisme, son histoire et ses causes*. Paris: Léon Chailley, 1894.

———. "La conception sociale du Judaïsme." *La Grande revue* (Paris), September 1, 1899.

———. *Contre l'antisémitisme (histoire d'une polémique)*. Paris: Stock, 1897.

———. "L'esprit révolutionnaire dans le judaïsme." *Revue bleue* (Paris), May 20, 1893.

———. *Le fumier de Job*. Paris: Editions Rieder, 1928.

———. *Le nationalisme juif*. Paris: Kadimah, 1898.

———. *Les porteurs de torches*. Paris: Armand Colin, 1897.

Leroy-Beaulieu, Anatole. *L'antisémitisme.* Paris: Calmann-Lévy, 1897.

———. *Les Juifs et l'antisémitisme, Israël chez les nations.* 5th ed. Paris: Calmann-Lévy, 1893. Reprinted by Calmann-Lévy, 1983.

Leven, N. *Cinquante ans d'histoire—L'Alliance israélite universelle.* 2 vols. Paris: Félix Alcan, 1920.

Marrus, Michael R. *The Politics of Assimilation: A Study of the French Jewish Community at the Time of the Dreyfus Affair.* Oxford: Oxford University Press, 1971.

Naquet, Alfred. "Discussions d'interpellations sur la question juive." *Journal officiel de la Chambre des députés* (Paris), May 27, 1895.

Posener, S. "The Immediate Economic and Social Effects of the Emancipation of the Jews in France." *Jewish Social Studies* 1 (1939): 271–326.

Rabi. *Anatomie du Judaïsme français.* Paris: Les Editions de Minuit, 1962.

Roblin, Michel. *Les Juifs de Paris: Démographie, économie, culture.* Paris: A. et J. Picard et Cie., 1952.

Schnapper, Dominique. *Jewish Identities in France: An Analysis of Contemporary French Jewry.* Chicago: University of Chicago Press, 1983.

Spire, André. *Les Juifs et la guerre.* Paris: Payot, 1917.

———. *Quelques Juifs et demi-Juifs.* 2 vols. Paris: Grasset, 1928.

———. *Souvenirs à bâtons rompus.* Paris: Albin Michel, 1962.

Szajkowski, Zosa. "The Alliance Israélite Universelle and East European Jewry in the 1860s." *Jewish Social Studies* 4 (April 1942): 139–60.

———. "Conflicts in the Alliance Israélite Universelle and the Founding of the Anglo-Jewish Association, the Vienna Allianz and the Hilfsverein." *Jewish Social Studies* 19 (1950): 29–50.

———. "Emigration to America or Reconstruction in Europe." *American Jewish Historical Quarterly* 42 (September 1952): 157–216.

———. "The European Attitude to Eastern European Jewish Immigration (1881–93)." *Publications of the American Jewish Historical Society* 41 (December 1951): 127–62.

———. "The Growth of the Jewish Population of France." *Jewish Social Studies* 8 (1946): 179–96, 297–315.

———. "Jewish Emigration Policy in the Period of the Rumanian 'Exodus' 1899–1903." *Jewish Social Studies* 13 (1951): 47–70.

———. *Poverty and Social Welfare Among French Jews, 1800–80.* New York: Editions historiques franco-juives, 1954.

———. "Yidishe fakhshuln in Frankraykh in 19tn orhundert." *YIVO-Bleter* 42 (1962): 81–120.

Weill, Julien. *Zadoc Kahn (1839–1905).* Paris: Félix Alcan, 1912.

Wilson, Stephen. *Ideology and Experience: Antisemitism in France at the Time of the Dreyfus Affair.* London and Toronto: Farleigh Dickinson University Press and Associated University Presses, 1982.

Jewish Immigrants in France

Aubéry, Pierre. "Mécislas Golberg, anarchiste." *Le Mouvement Social,* no. 52 (July–September 1965), pp. 97–109.

Billy, André and Twersky, Moïse. *L'épopée de Ménaché Foïgel.* 3 vols. Paris: Plon, 1927–28.

Bonneff, Léon et Maurice. *La vie tragique des travailleurs.* 3d ed. Paris: Jules Rouff et Cie., 1908.

Dagan, Henri. "Le prolétariat juif mondial." *La Revue blanche* 26 (October 15, 1901): 241–70.

De Rochegude, Marquis, *Promenades dans toutes les rues de Paris, IVe arrondissement.* Paris: Hachette, 1910.

Diamant, David. "Les juifs immigrés en France et le mouvement progressiste, 1900–34." (unpublished)

Dridzo-Losovsky. *L'internationale syndicale rouge.* Paris: Maspero, 1976.

Eberlin, Elie and Delahache, Georges. "Juifs russes." *Cahiers de la quinzaine.* 6ème sér., 6ème cahier (December 1904).

Etudiants socialistes russes israélites de Paris. "Antisémitisme et sionisme." *Les Temps nouveaux* (Paris), September 1900.

Fegdal, Charles. "Le ghetto parisien contemporain." *La Cité* 14 (1915): 221–36.

Frid, Sh. "Lozovski—Der nomen vert oft dermont in di depeshn, vos kumen fun Moskve." *Forverts* (New York), October 21, 1941.

Fried, Alfred H. "Das jüdische Proletariat in Frankreich." *Jüdische Statistik.* Ed. Alfred Nossig. Berlin: Pass und Garleb, 1903.

Frumkin, A. "Der Parizer 'Pletzl.'" *Forverts* (New York), August 31, 1912.

"Fun unzer post." *Forverts* (New York), May 5, 1911.

Green, Nancy L. "Eléments pour une étude du mouvement ouvrier juif à Paris au début du siècle." *Le Mouvement Social,* no. 110 (January–March 1980), pp. 51–73.

———. "L'Emigration comme émancipation: Les femmes juives d'Europe de l'Est à Paris, 1881–1914." *Pluriel,* no. 27 (1981), pp. 51–59.

Haupt, Georges and Marie, Jean-Jacques. *Les Bolcheviks par eux-mêmes.* Paris: Maspero, 1969.

Hillairet, Jacques. *Dictionnaire historique des rues de Paris.* 5th ed. Paris: Editions de Minuit, 1963.

Hyman, Paula E. *From Dreyfus to Vichy: The Remaking of French Jewry.* New York: Columbia University Press, 1979.

———. "From Paternalism to Cooptation: The French Jewish Consistory and the Immigrants, 1906–39." *YIVO Annual of Jewish Social Sciences* 17 (1978): 217–37.

Ikor, Roger. *Les fils d'Avrom: Les eaux mêlées.* Paris: Albin Michel, 1955.

Jacques, Maître. "Prolétariat juif." *Les Droits de l'homme* (Paris), September 17, 1899.

Jarblum, Marc. "Deux rencontres avec Lénine." *Les nouveaux cahiers* 20 (Spring 1970): 8–16.

Karpel and Dinner for the Groupe des ouvriers juifs socialistes de Paris. *Le prolétariat juif: Lettre des ouvriers juifs de Paris au Parti socialiste français.* Paris: Imprimerie typographique J. Allemane, 1898.

Kurski, Franz. "Der Bund in Pariz." *Unzer shtime* (Paris), February 4, 1939.

Lauzel, Maurice. *Ouvriers juifs de Paris: Les casquettiers.* Paris: Edouard Cornély et Cie., 1912.

Lévy, Jacob. *Juifs d'aujourd'hui: Les Pollaks.* Paris: Ferenczi et Fils, 1925.

Lopata, Charles. *J'ai survécu.* Paris: Editions droit et liberté, 1977.

Mendl, Hersh. *Mémoires d'un révolutionnaire juif.* Trans. Bernard Suchecky (from Yiddish). Grenoble: Presses universitaires de Grenoble, 1982.

Menes, A. "Yidn in Frankraykh (An ekonomish-statistishe studye)." *YIVO-Bleter* 11 (May 1937): 329–55.

"La Misère en Israël." *Le Figaro* (Paris), July 1, 1892.

"Paris vu par une émigrée de l'Est." *Le Monde* (Paris), May 7–8, 1978.

Pottier, Paul. "Essai sur le prolétariat juif en France." *Revue des revues*, 3d ser., 28 (March 1899): 482–92.

Rappoport, Charles. "The Life of a Revolutionary Emigré (Reminiscences)." *YIVO Annual of Jewish Social Sciences* 6 (1951): 206–36.

Rocheman, Lionel. *Devenir Cécile.* Paris: Editions Ramsay, 1977.

Rocker, Rudolf. *In shturem.* Trans. J. Birnbaum (from German). Buenos Aires: London "Fraye Arbaytershtime" Grupe, 1952.

Roland, Charlotte. *Du ghetto à l'occident, Deux générations yiddiches en France.* Paris: Editions de Minuit, 1962.

Rozenberg, Nathan. "Solomon Lozovski—Vi ikh gedenk im." *Morgn-Frayhayt* (New York), July 3, 1968.

Rudnianski, Michel and Girard, Patrick. "Les relations entre Israélites français et Juifs russes." 2 vols. Maîtrise, U.E.R. d'Histoire, Université de Paris I, 1971–72.

Ryba, Raphael. "Der antviklungs-veg fun Parizer Bund." *Unzer shtime* (Paris), December 7, 1947.

———. "Yidishe sotsialistisher farband 'Bund' in Frankraykh." *Unzer tsayt*, no. 3–4 (November–December 1947), pp. 159–62.

Schneeberg, Edouard. *Calendrier 5672* [September 1911–September 1912]. Paris: n.p., n.d.

Section française de l'Internationale ouvrière, 4e section. *Les écoles juives de la ville de Paris.* Paris: n.p., n.d. [ca. 1907; see UI, February 22, 1907]

Shvartzbard, Sholem. *In krig—Mit zikh aleyn.* Chicago: Arbayters-Verlag, 1933.

Speiser, Wolf. *Kalendar.* Paris: n.p., 1910.

Steingart, Tsirl. "Der Bund in Frankraykh." *Unzer tsayt*, no. 10–12 (October–December 1972), pp. 105–9.

Sylvère, Jacques. "Albert Matline: Dirigeant du syndicat des casquettiers." *La Presse nouvelle hebdomadaire* (Paris), November 4, 1977.

Szajkowski, Zosa. *Etyudn tsu der geshikhte fun ayngevandertn yidishn yishev in Frankraykh.* Paris: Fridman, 1936.

———. "150 yor yidishe prese in Frankraykh." *Yidn in Frankraykh.* Ed. E. Tcherikower, 2 vols. New York: YIVO, 1942.

———. "Der kamf kegn yidish in Frankraykh." *YIVO-Bleter* 14 (1939): 46–77.

———. *Di profesyonele bavegung tsvishn di yidishe arbeter in Frankraykh biz 1914.* Paris: Fridman, 1937.

———. "Dos yidishe gezelshaftlekhe lebn in Pariz tsum yor 1939." *Yidn in Frankraykh.* Ed. E. Tcherikower. 2 vols. New York: YIVO, 1942.

Tcherikower, Elias. "Peter Lavrov and the Jewish Socialist Emigrés." *YIVO Annual of Jewish Social Science* 7 (1952): 132–45.

Tchernoff, J. *Dans le creuset des civilisations.* 4 vols. Paris: Editions Rieder, 1936–38.

Tsher-Ski, A. [Szajkowski] "Di Drayfus-afere, di arbeter-emigrantn un di Frantseyzish-yidishe firers." *Yidn in Frankraykh.* Ed. E. Tcherikower. 2 vols. New York: YIVO, 1942.

Vanikoff, Maurice. *La commémoration des engagements volontaires des juifs d'origine étrangère 1914–18.* Paris: n.p., 1932.

Weinberg, David H. *A Community on Trial: The Jews of Paris in the 1930s.* Chicago: University of Chicago Press, 1977.

Yidishe intersindikale komitye bay der C.G.T. [Commission intersyndicale juive auprès de la C.G.T.]. *In kamf far frayhayt* [*Combattants de la liberté*]. Paris: Farlag Oyfsnay, 1948. (half in Yiddish, half in French)

Xhaïm. *Aux Français.* Paris: Imprimerie Xhaïm, n.d. [post-1910].

———. *Aux banquiers juifs.* Paris: Imprimerie Goupy, n.d.

Yakubovitsh, Y. "Interesante zikhroynes vegn Lozovski." *Unzer vort* (Paris), January 1–2, 1957.

Social and Economic Conditions in France, the Labor Movement and the Jewish Question

Bulawko, Henry. "Les Socialistes et 'l'Affaire.'" *Les nouveaux cahiers* 27 (Winter 1971–72): 26–30.

Chevalier, Louis. *La formation de la population parisienne au XIXe siècle.* Institut national d'études démographiques—Travaux et documents 10. Paris: Presses universitaires de France, 1950.

Girardet, Raoul. *Le nationalisme français 1871–1914.* Paris: Armand Colin, 1966.

Goldberg, Harvey. "Jean Jaurès and the Jewish Question: The Evolution of a Position." *Jewish Social Studies* 20 (April 1958): 70–93.

Green, Nancy L. "Socialist Anti-Semitism, Defense of a Bourgeois Jew and Discovery of the Jewish Proletariat." Forthcoming, *International Review of Social History,* 1985.

Haupt, Georges, Lowy, Michael, and Weill, Claudie. *Les Marxistes et la question nationale, 1848–1914.* Paris: Maspero, 1974.

Jaurès, Jean. "L'autocratie, voilà l'ennemi!" *Les nouveaux cahiers,* no. 11 (Autumn 1967), pp. 35–39.

Julliard, Jacques. *Fernand Pelloutier et les origines du syndicalisme d'action directe.* Paris: Seuil, 1971.

Landes, David S. *The Unbound Prometheus: Technological Change and Industrial Development in Western Europe from 1750 to the Present.* Cambridge: Cambridge University Press, 1969.

Lefranc, Georges. *Le mouvement syndical sous la Troisième république.* Paris: Payot, 1967.

Levasseur, E. *Questions ouvrières et industrielles en France sous la Troisième république.* Paris: Arthur Rousseau, 1907.

Lichtheim, George. "Socialism and the Jews." *Dissent* 15 (1968): 314–32.

Lorwin, Val. *French Labor Movement.* Cambridge: Harvard University Press, 1954.

Ministère du travail et de la prévoyance sociale. *Elections en 1909 des représentants des syndicats ouvriers.* n.p.: Imprimerie nationale, 1909.

———. *Sociétés de secours mutuels du département de la Seine, 1907, 1908.* Melun: Imprimerie administrative, 1907, 1908.

———. *Statuts-modèles pour sociétés de secours mutuels.* Melun: Imprimerie administrative, 1913.

Moss, Bernard. *The Origins of the French Labor Movement, 1830–1914: The Socialism of Skilled Workers.* Berkeley: University of California Press, 1976.

Péguy, Charles. "Notre Jeunesse." *Cahiers de la quinzaine.* 11ème sér., 12ème cahier (1910).

Perrot, Michelle. *Les ouvriers en grève, France 1871–90.* 2 vols. Paris: Mouton and Ecole Pratique des Hautes Etudes, 1974.

Pouget, Emile. "La question des étrangers—L'invasion." *La Guerre sociale* (Paris), December 20–26, 1911.

————. "La question des étrangers—Le péril antisémite." *La Guerre sociale* (Paris), January 3–9, 1912.

Rebérioux, Madeleine. "Jean Jaurès et Kichinev." *Les nouveaux cahiers*, no. 11 (Autumn 1967), pp. 29–34.

Résultats statistiques du recensement général de la population (1901), vol. 1: *Régions de Paris, du Nord et de l'Est.* Paris: Imprimerie nationale, 1904.

Résultats statistiques du recensement des industries et professions (1896), vol. 1: *Région de Paris au Nord et à l'Est.* Paris: Imprimerie nationale for the Office du travail, 1899.

Shorter, Edward and Tilly, Charles. *Strikes in France, 1830–1968.* Cambridge: Cambridge University Press, 1974.

Silberner, Edmund. "Anti-Jewish Trends in French Revolutionary Syndicalism." *Jewish Social Studies* 15 (July–October 1953): 195–202.

————. "French Socialism and the Jewish Question, 1865–1914." *Historia Judaica* 16 (April 1954): 4–37.

Stearns, Peter. *Revolutionary Syndicalism and French Labor: A Cause without Rebels.* New Brunswick, New Jersey: Rutgers University Press, 1971.

Szajkowski, Zosa. *Antisemitizm in der Frantseyzisher arbeter-bavegung.* New York: Zosa Szajkowski, 1948.

Tabarant. *Socialisme et antisémitisme.* Paris: Imprimerie Kugelman, 1898.

Parisian Light Industry

Aftalion, Albert. *Le développement de la fabrique et le travail à domicile dans les industries de l'habillement.* Paris: J-B Sirey and Journal du Palais, 1906.

Aine. *Les patronnes, employées et ouvrières de l'habillement à Paris, leur situation morale et matérielle.* Paris: Société d'économie sociale, 1897.

Benoist, Charles. *Les ouvrières de l'aiguille à Paris.* Paris: L. Chailley, 1895.

La chapellerie ouvrière française—Le 8ème congrès national d'Aix (1892), Résumé historique de la société générale des ouvriers chapeliers et des syndicats ou sociétés corporatives de France 1880–90. Paris: Imprimerie J. Allemane, 1892.

Commission déléguée de la Société des chapeliers détaillants de Paris. *Rapport sur les produits de l'industrie de la chapellerie, le 8 juillet 1889 (Exposition universelle de 1889).* Paris: Michels et Fils, n.d.

De Vissec, L. Delpon. "De la distribution du travail à domicile dans l'industrie de la confection parisienne." *Mémoires et documents du Musée social* 5 (March 1908): 81–95.

Du Maroussem, Pierre. *La petite industrie (salaires et durée du travail)*, vol. 2: *Le vêtement à Paris*. Paris: Imprimerie nationale for the Office du travail, 1896.
————. *La question ouvrière*, vol. 2: *Ebénistes du faubourg St.-Antoine*. Paris: Arthur Rousseau, 1892.

Exposition universelle internationale de 1900 à Paris: Rapports du jury international, Groupe XIII: *Fils, tissus, vêtements, 2ème partie—Classes 85 et 86*, by Léon Storch (Classe 85), Julien Hayem, and A. Mortier (Classe 86). Paris: Imprimerie nationale for the Ministère du commerce, de l'industrie, des postes et des télégraphes, 1902.

Fagnot, François. *Réglementation du travail en chambre (rapport des séances du 18 mars et 27 avril 1904)*. Association nationale française pour la protection légale des travailleurs 7. Paris: Félix Alcan, n. d.

Fédération d'industries des travailleurs de l'habillement. *Comptes rendus des 6e (1906), 7e (1908), 8e (1910) et 9e (1912) Congrès nationaux*.

Fédération des syndicats ouvriers de la chapellerie française. *Comptes rendus des 13e (1906), 14e (1909), et 15e (1912) Congrès nationaux*.

Fédération des travailleurs des cuirs et peaux et similaires. *Comptes rendus des 3e (1903), 4e (1905), 5e (1907), 6e (1909), et 7e (1911) Congrès nationaux*.

Grandgeorge, Gaston and Guérin, Louis. *L'industrie textile en France, Rapports 1904–7*. Paris: Imprimerie nationale for the Ministère du commerce, de l'industrie et des colonies, 1905–8.

Grumberg, Jean-Claude. *L'Atelier*. Paris: Stock, Théâtre Ouvert, 1979.

Miller, Michael B. *The Bon Marché: Bourgeois Culture and the Department Store, 1869–1920*. Princeton: Princeton University Press, 1981.

Klatzmann, Joseph. *Le travail à domicile dans l'industrie parisienne du vêtement*. Paris: Armand Colin, 1957.

Mény, Georges. *La lutte contre le sweating-system*. Paris: Librairie des sciences politiques et sociales and Marcel Rivière et Cie., 1910.

Office du travail. *Associations professionelles ouvrières*, vol. 2: *Cuirs et peaux, industries textiles, habillement, ameublement, travail du bois*. Paris: Imprimerie nationale, 1901.

Picard, Alfred, general ed. *Exposition universelle internationale de 1889 à Paris: Rapports du jury international*, Classe 36: *Habillement des deux sexes*, by Albert Leduc. Paris: Imprimerie nationale for the Ministère du commerce, de l'industrie et des colonies, 1891.

Rapports sur l'application pendant l'année [1894–1913] des lois réglementant le travail. Paris: Imprimerie nationale for the Ministère du commerce, de l'industrie, des postes et des télégraphes, 1895–1914.

Sylvère, Jacques. "Le 'Sweating System,' Naissance de la machine à coudre." *La Presse nouvelle hebdomadaire* (Paris), June 16, 1978.

Vanier, Henriette. *La mode et ses métiers: Frivolités et luttes des classes, 1830–1870*. Paris: Armand Colin, 1960.

Vial, Jean. *La coutume chapelière, Histoire du mouvement ouvrier dans la chapellerie*. Paris: Domat-Montchrestien, 1941.

Worth, Gaston. *La couture et la confection des vêtements de femme*. Paris: Imprimerie Chaix, 1895.

Migrant Labor

Bonnet, Jean-Charles. *Les pouvoirs publics et l'immigration dans l'entre-deux guerres.* Centre d'histoire économique et sociale de la région lyonnaise 7. Lyon: Université de Lyon II, 1976.

Burawoy, Michael. "The Function and Reproduction of Migrant Labor: Comparative Material from South Africa and the United States." *American Journal of Sociology* 81 (March 1976): 1050–86.

Castells, Manuel. "Migrant Workers and Class Struggle in Advanced Capitalism: The Western European Experience." *Politics and Society* 5 (1975): 33–66.

Castles, Stephen and Kosack, Godula. *Immigrant Workers and Class Struggle in Western Europe.* London: Oxford University Press, 1973.

Cedetim. *Les immigrés.* Paris: Stock, 1975.

Cross, Gary. *Immigrant Workers in Industrial France: The Making of a New Labor Class.* Philadelphia: Temple University Press, 1983.

De Cassano, Prince. *Procès-verbaux sommaires du Congrès international de l'intervention des pouvoirs publics dans l'émigration et l'immigration, tenu à Paris du 12 au 14 août 1889 (Exposition universelle internationale de 1889).* Paris: Imprimerie nationale for the Ministère du commerce, de l'industrie et des colonies, 1890.

Didion, Maurice. *Les salariés étrangers en France.* Paris: V. Giard et E. Brière, 1911.

Eveille. *L'assistance aux étrangers en France.* Paris: Jouve et Boyer, 1899.

Freeman, Gary P. *Immigrant Labor and Racial Conflict in Industrial Societies: The French and British Experience 1945–1975.* Princeton: Princeton University Press, 1979.

Gemähling, Paul. *Travailleurs au rabais, La lutte syndicale contre les sous-concurrences ouvrières.* Paris: Bloud et Cie., 1910.

Girard, Alain and Stoetzel, Jean. *Français et Immigrés.* Institut national d'études démographiques—Travaux et documents 19. Paris: Presses universitaires de France, 1953.

Granotier, Bernard. *Les travailleurs immigrés en France.* Paris: Maspero, 1976.

Gutman, Herbert. *Work, Culture and Society in Industrializing America, 1815–1919.* New York: Alfred A. Knopf, 1976.

Hollande, Maurice. *La défense ouvrière contre le travail étranger.* Paris: Bloud et Cie., 1913.

Jackson, J. A., ed. *Migration.* Sociological Series 2. Cambridge: Cambridge University Press, 1969.

Koeppel, Barbara. "The New Sweatshops." *The Progressive* (Madison), November 1978.

Le Febvre, Yves. *L'ouvrier étranger et la protection du travail national.* Paris: C. Jacques et Cie, 1901.

Luce, Charles Louis. *La situation des travailleurs étrangers en France (En ce qui concerne les lois et règlements de police).* Paris: Imprimerie Paul Dupont, 1924.

McNeill, William H. and Adams, Ruth S., eds. *Human Migration.* Bloomington: Indiana University Press, 1978.

Mauco, Georges. *Les étrangers en France.* Paris: Armand Colin, 1932.

Paon, Marcel. *L'immigration en France.* Paris: Payot, 1926.

Piore, Michael J. *Birds of Passage: Migrant Labor and Industrial Societies.* Cambridge: Cambridge University Press, 1979.

Prato, Giuseppe. *Le protectionnisme ouvrier.* Trans. with an introduction, Georges Bourgin. Paris: Marcel Rivière et Cie., 1912.

Safa, Helen I. and Du Toit, Brian M., eds. *Migration and Development: Implications for Ethnic Identity and Political Conflict.* The Hague: Mouton and Co., 1975.

Schirmacher, Mlle. [Kathie]. *La spécialisation du travail—Par nationalités, à Paris.* Paris: Arthur Rousseau, 1908.

Shaw, R. Paul. *Migration Theory and Fact: A Review and Bibliography of Current Literature.* Bibliographic Series 5. Philadelphia: Regional Science Research Institute, 1975.

Tapinos, Georges P. *L'économie des migrations internationales.* Paris: Armand Colin and Fondation nationale des sciences politiques, 1974.

Ward, Antony. "European Capitalism's Reserve Army." *Monthly Review* 25 (November 1975): 17–38.

Weill, Claudie. "Le débat sur les migrations ouvrières dans la Deuxième internationale." *Pluriel,* no. 13 (1978), pp. 55–73.

Zolberg, Aristide R. "International Migration Policies in a Changing World System." *Human Migration.* Eds. William H. McNeill and Ruth S. Adams. Bloomington: Indiana University Press, 1978.

Methodology and Comparative Studies in Jewish History

Baron, Salo W. *History and Jewish Historians.* Philadelphia: Jewish Publication Society of America, 1964.

———. *A Social and Religious History of the Jews.* 3 vols. 2nd ed. New York: Columbia University Press, 1957.

Baron, Salo W., Kahan, Arcadius and others. Ed. Nachum Gross. *Economic History of the Jews.* New York: Schocken Paperback, 1976.

Dubnow, Simon. *History of the Jews.* trans. from the 4th Russian ed. 5 vols. South Brunswick, N.J.: A. S. Barnes and Co., Inc., 1973.

———. *Nationalism and History, Essays on Old and New Jerusalem.* Ed. Koppel S. Pinson. New York: Atheneum, 1970.

Endelman, Todd. *The Jews of Georgian England, 1714–1830.* Philadelphia: Jewish Publication Society of America, 1979.

Hertzberg, Arthur, ed. *The Zionist Idea.* New York: Atheneum, 1975.

Katz, Jacob. *Out of the Ghetto: The Social Background of Jewish Emancipation, 1770–1870.* Cambridge: Harvard University Press, 1973.

Kriegel, Annie. *Les Juifs et le monde moderne.* Paris: Seuil, 1977.

Léon, Abraham. *La conception matérialiste de la question juive.* Intro. Maxime Rodinson. Paris: Etudes et Documentation Internationales, 1968.

Mahler, Raphael. *A History of Modern Jewry 1780–1815.* New York: Schocken Books, 1971.

Marienstras, Richard. *Etre un peuple en diaspora.* Paris: Maspero, 1975.

Poliakov, Léon. *Histoire de l'antisémitisme.* 4 vols. Paris: Calmann-Lévy, 1955–77.

Ruppin, Arthur. *The Jews in the Modern World.* London: Macmillan and Co., Ltd., 1934.

Sachar, Howard Morley. *The Course of Modern Jewish History.* New York: Delta-Dell, 1958.

Sartre, Jean-Paul. *Réflexions sur la question juive.* Paris: NRF-Gallimard, 1954.
Zborowski, Mark and Herzog, Elizabeth. *Life is with People.* New York: International Universities Press, Inc., 1952.

Jewish Immigrants and Jewish Migrations

Aschheim, Steven. *Brothers and Strangers: The Eastern European Jew in Germany and German Jewish Consciousness, 1800–1923.* Madison: University of Wisconsin Press, 1983.
Gartner, Lloyd P. *The Jewish Immigrant in England 1870–1914.* 2nd ed. London: Simon Publications, 1973.
Hersch, Liebman. "Jewish Migrations During the Last 100 Years." *The Jewish People, Past and Present.* 3 vols. New York: Jewish Encyclopedic Handbooks, Inc., 1955. 1:407–30.
———. *Le Juif errant d'aujourd'hui.* Paris: M. Giard et E. Brière, 1913.
Howe, Irving. *World of Our Fathers.* New York: Touchstone, Simon and Schuster, 1976.
Kessner, Thomas. *The Golden Door: Italian and Jewish Immigrant Mobility in New York City, 1880–1915.* New York: Oxford University Press, 1977.
Kulischer, Eugene. *Jewish Migrations: Past Experiences and Post-War Prospects.* New York: The American Jewish Committee, 1943.
Lestschinsky, Jacob. *Dos idishe folk in tsifern.* Berlin: Klal-Verlag, 1922.
———. *Di yidishe vanderung far di letste 25 yor.* Berlin: HIAS-Emigdirekt, 1927.
———. "Jewish Migrations, 1840–1946." *The Jews.* Ed. Louis Finkelstein. 2 vols. New York: Harper and Row, 1955.
———, ed. *Shriftn far ekonomik un statistik.* Vol. 1. Berlin: YIVO, 1928.
Sanders, Ronald. *The Downtown Jews.* New York: Signet, New American Library, 1976.
Wertheimer, Jack. " 'The Unwanted Element': East European Jews in Imperial Germany." *Leo Baeck Institute Yearbook* 26 (1981): 23–46.
Wischnitzer, Mark. *To Dwell in Safety: The Story of Jewish Migrations Since 1800.* Philadelphia: Jewish Publication Society of America, 1948.
Yod (Paris). Volume 5, fascicule 2. "Migrations."

Jewish Labor and Jewish Labor Movements

Abramsky, Chimen. "The Jewish Labour Movement: Some Historiographical Problems." *Soviet Jewish Affairs,* no. 1 (June 1971), pp. 45–51.
"American Jewish Labor Movement." *American Jewish Historical Quarterly* 65 (March 1976).
Berman, Hyman. "A Cursory View of the Jewish Labor Movement: An Historiographical Survey." *American Jewish Historical Quarterly* 52 (December 1962): 79–97.
Bloom, Bernard. "Yiddish-Speaking Socialists in America 1892–1905." *The American Jewish Archives* 12 (April 1960): 34–70.
Borochov, Ber. *Nationalism and Class Struggle.* New York: Socialist Zionist Union, n.d.

Cahnman, Werner J. "Role and Significance of the Jewish Artisan Class." *The Jewish Journal of Sociology* 7 (December 1965): 210–19.

Cerf, Marcel. "Le syndicalisme juif." *La Presse nouvelle hebdomadaire*, November 18, December 2, December 16, December 30, 1977, and January 13, 1978.

Fishman, William J. *East End Radicals 1875–1914*. London: Duckworth, 1975.

Frumkin, A. *In friling fun idishn sotsializm*. New York: Yubiley komitet, 1940.

Hourwich, Isaac. *Immigration and Labor*. New York: G. P. Putnam's Sons, 1912.

Kahan, Arcadius. "Economic Opportunities and Some Pilgrims' Progress: Jewish Immigrants from Eastern Europe in the U.S., 1890–1914." *The Journal of Economic History* 38 (March 1978): 235–51.

Levin, Nora. *While Messiah Tarried—Jewish Socialist Movements 1871–1917*. New York: Schocken, 1977.

Mendelsohn, Ezra., general ed. "Essays on the American Jewish Labor Movement." *YIVO Annual of Jewish Social Sciences* 16 (1976).

Mishkinsky, Moshe. "The Jewish Labor Movement and European Socialism." *Jewish Society Through the Ages*. Ed. H. H. Ben-Sasson and S. Ettinger. New York: Schocken, 1969.

———. *Sotsyalizm Yehudi u-tenu'at ha-po'alim ha-yehudit ba-me'ah ha-19* (Jewish Socialism and the Jewish Labor Movement in the 19th Century) Jerusalem: The Historical Society of Israel, 1975.

Soloweitschik, Léonty. *Un prolétariat méconnu*. Brussels: Henri Lamertin, 1898.

White, Jerry. *Rothschild Buildings: Life in an East End Tenement Block, 1887–1920*. London: Routledge and Kegan Paul, 1980.

Wischnitzer, Mark. *A History of Jewish Crafts and Guilds*. New York: Jonathan David, Publishers, 1965.

INTERVIEWS

Diamant, David. Former director of the Institut historique Maurice Thorez. Paris, September 6, 1976.

Gronovski, Ludwik. Jewish immigrant labor leader. Paris, September 19, 1977.

Heilbronn, Max. Former *directeur-général* of Galeries Lafayette. Paris, November 22, 1976.

Klatzmann, Joseph. Son of a Jewish immigrant pieceworker and author of *Le travail à domicile*. Paris, May 25 and June 22, 1979.

Lederman, Jacques. Secretary of the Syndicat des maroquiniers. Paris, October 12, 1977.

Matline, Albert. Secretary of the Syndicat des chapeliers, modistes et casquettiers. January 28, February 4, February 11, 1976, and May 12, 1977.

Paillet-Petit, Mme. Former *petite-main* at the Société parisienne de confection (S.P.C.). Paris, November 24, 1976.

Rodinson, Maxime. Rodinson's father was an immigrant labor leader. Paris, October 8, 1976.

Spire, Mme. André. Paris, March 11, 1977.

Uhafti, Abraham and Sarah. Early Pletzl residents. Fontenay-sous-Bois, October 27, 1978.

INDEX

Italicized page numbers refer to illustrations and tables.